T0408049

Obstacles to Environmental Progress

Obstacles to Environmental Progress

A U.S. perspective

Peter C. Schulze

To our sons, Ben and Matt, the other members of their generation and future generations.

praemonitus, praemunitus
(forewarned is forearmed)

First published in 2022 by
UCL Press
University College London
Gower Street
London WC1E 6BT

Available to download free: www.uclpress.co.uk

Text © Author, 2022
Images © copyright holders named in captions, 2022

The author has asserted his rights under the Copyright, Designs and Patents Act 1988 to be identified as the author of this work.

A CIP catalogue record for this book is available from The British Library.

Any third-party material in this book is not covered by the book's Creative Commons licence. Details of the copyright ownership and permitted use of third-party material is given in the image (or extract) credit lines. If you would like to reuse any third-party material not covered by the book's Creative Commons licence, you will need to obtain permission directly from the copyright owner.

This book is published under a Creative Commons Attribution-Non-Commercial 4.0 International licence (CC BY-NC 4.0), https://creativecommons.org/licenses/by-nc/4.0/. This licence allows you to share and adapt the work for non-commercial use providing attribution is made to the author and publisher (but not in any way that suggests that they endorse you or your use of the work) and any changes are indicated. Attribution should include the following information:

Schulze, P. C. 2022. *Obstacles to Environmental Progress: A U.S. perspective*. London: UCL Press. https://doi.org/10.14324/111.9781800082076

Further details about Creative Commons licences are available at https://creativecommons.org/licenses/

ISBN: 978-1-80008-209-0 (Hbk)
ISBN: 978-1-80008-208-3 (Pbk)
ISBN: 978-1-80008-207-6 (PDF)
ISBN: 978-1-80008-210-6 (epub)
DOI: https://doi.org/10.14324/111.9781800082076

Contents

List of figures

Endangered Species Preservation Act, 1968 Wild and Scenic Rivers Act, 1969 National Environmental Policy Act, 1970 Clean Air Act amendments, 1972 Federal Water Pollution Control Amendments, Federal Insecticide, Fungicide, and Rodenticide Act, Marine Mammal Protection Act, Coastal Zone Management Act, Marine Protection, Research, and Sanctuaries Act, 1973 Endangered Species Act, 1974 Safe Drinking Water Act, Forest and Rangelands Renewable Resources Planning Act, 1975 Eastern Wilderness Areas Act, Hazardous Materials Transportation Act, 1976 Resource Conservation and Recovery Act, Toxic Substances Control Act, 1977 Clean Water Act amendments, 1980 Comprehensive Environmental Response, Compensation, and Liability Act, 1986 Emergency Planning and Community Right to Know Act, 1988 Ocean Dumping Ban Act, 1990 Clean Air Act amendments, Oil Pollution Act, 1996 Food Quality Protection Act, Safe Drinking Water Act amendments, 2006 Magnuson-Stevens Fishery Conservation and Management Reauthorization Act, 2016 Frank R. Lautenberg Chemical Safety for the 21st Century Act.

photo is from a location near the Red River inflow while the bottom photo is from the opposite end of the lake near the dam. Except during floods, as water moves downstream through the reservoir, suspended material responsible for the turbidity in the upper image sinks to the lake bottom, thereby displacing water storage capacity. Photographer: Peter C. Schulze.

revolution, higher rates of damage than repair as of the early-twenty-first century, but future reduction in damage rate and increase in repair rate until repair exceeds damage and society learns to avoid new damage (damage rate becomes zero). As that situation continues, the cumulative impact approaches zero but remains negative because some damage is never successfully repaired. Figure by the author.

List of tables and boxes

List of abbreviations

CFC   chlorofluorocarbon
EPA   United States Environmental Protection Agency
EU   European Union
GDP   gross domestic product
GMO   genetically modified organism
GNP   gross national product
NASA   United States National Aeronautics and Space Administration
PAC   political action committee
UN   United Nations
US   United States
WTO   World Trade Organization

Preface

Achieving real environmental sustainability will require bringing present environmental impacts within sustainable limits and preventing creation of new problems. Neither would be sufficient alone; both are necessary. This book is limited to one aspect of the challenge of bringing impacts within sustainable limits – better understanding of immediate obstacles that impede progress on existing problems. As we shall see, the same obstacles apply to both modest and momentous problems. I focus on the United States (US) because that is the country I know best. Most of the obstacles are applicable in similar cultural and political settings elsewhere, but additional obstacles are important in other circumstances, and some discussed here, such as resistance to perceived infringements on individual liberties, would be less important in other cultural settings.

I hope a compendium of obstacles to progress on existing environmental problems will be useful for three purposes. First, I hope to help readers better anticipate, and thus more readily overcome, obstacles they may encounter as they strive for environmental progress. Second, I hope to attract scholarly attention to the set of obstacles as related, mutually reinforcing phenomena that need to be better understood. Finally, I hope to help expand awareness of how opponents of environmental protection distort and exaggerate obstacles in efforts to manipulate public opinion.

All obstacles discussed here receive attention separately in the diverse literature of various academic disciplines, but I have not seen them considered together. Various books and articles by authors, from philosophers to statisticians to historians of science, address obstacles to detecting and understanding problems. Multiple exposés use narrative accounts to illuminate how opponents of environmental protection exaggerate scientific uncertainty to quell demands for action – prominent examples include the Ehrlichs' *Betrayal of Science and Reason* (1996), Beder's *Global Spin* (2002), Oreskes and Conway's *Merchants of Doubt* (2010), Layzer's *Open for Business* (2012), Jamieson's *Reason in a Dark*

Time (2014) and Mayer's *Dark Money* (2016). Some of these, as well as environmental law and policy textbooks, address political obstacles to action. In advance of the 2020 US presidential election and 2022 congressional elections, the media gave much attention to efforts to suppress voting and otherwise stymie the will of the US majority. The adaptive management and socioecological resilience literature of C. S. Holling and his successors considers aspects of why responses to problems sometimes fail. I intend to add to these contributions by succinctly synthesizing all major immediate, practical obstacles to progress on existing environmental problems.

I focus on obstacles to progress on specific, individual problems. I do not address the reasons we cause environmental problems or propose any sort of theory of comprehensive solutions. This limited objective of addressing particular problems can be criticized as naïve because our environmental predicament cannot be overcome by attacking problems piecemeal, and many problems are interrelated.[1] Moreover, efforts to alleviate one problem may cause or exacerbate others, and addressing existing problems may have no bearing on creation of new problems. However, the track record of environmental protection demonstrates problems can often be productively addressed one by one. Such piecemeal efforts cannot be sufficient but are necessary.

Even though attacking problems individually risks unintended consequences and, by itself, cannot achieve sustainability, we nevertheless must become better at overcoming obstacles to progress on existing problems because many problems exist. Moreover, when ignored, processes such as climate change, soil degradation, overharvesting and biodiversity loss not only persist but worsen. If we are to achieve real sustainability, rather than just win battles here and there yet lose the war, we must get systematically better at both preventing new environmental problems *and* bringing existing impacts within sustainable limits.

I perceive three broad categories of obstacles to environmental progress. Limits on our ability to understand the world around us and value systems that deprioritize environmental concerns comprise two deep, conceptual categories. Practical factors that repeatedly and predictably cause failure of environmental initiatives make up the third. The latter include obstacles to detecting and understanding environmental problems, deciding to respond, and responding effectively.

For five reasons explained in the Introduction, this book focuses on the third category of practical obstacles to overcoming existing environmental problems, but the deeper, conceptual obstacles are ultimately at least as important. I find compelling the arguments of Aldo

Leopold, Jared Diamond and others that achieving real sustainability will require expansion of the range of questions considered matters of ethics and concomitant shrinkage of those considered merely on the basis of self-interest, or in other words, changes in value systems such that environmental sustainability enjoys priority. Meanwhile, I take solace in Martin Luther King Jr.'s paraphrasing of nineteenth-century Unitarian Theodore Parker, that 'the arc of the moral universe is long, but bends toward justice', and Aldo Leopold's similar conclusion when he observed that in the three thousand years since Odysseus's Greece, 'ethical criteria have been extended to many fields of conduct, with corresponding shrinkages in those judged by expediency only'.[2] I hope Leopold's and King's expectations for the future will be borne out, but I do not aspire to assess that question. In other words, though I believe real sustainability will require shifts in conceptual obstacles rooted in value systems and world views, not merely overcoming immediate, practical obstacles to individual problems as they occur, I neither attempt to advance broader discussions of what would be required to achieve justice, nor do I seek to provide a thorough road map to sustainability. This book's objective is much more modest.

The goal of sustainability places an emphasis on future generations, but environmental problems and injustices also harm people alive today. Those suffering from injustice or other hardships cannot reasonably be expected to focus their concern on the distant future. Therefore, justice and quality of life for present generations is not only an eminently worthy goal in and of itself, it is almost certainly a necessity for generating deep, broad support for viewing sustainability as an ethical matter. This subject is also, however, generally beyond the present scope, though some chapters necessarily touch on it.

Society will hopefully come to view harm to the environment as a matter of right and wrong, as Aldo Leopold admonished in his Land Ethic.[3] If so, fewer rules and policies will be necessary. But that may take a while. I assume that for the time being, many environmental problems will continue to be addressed as policy matters. In other words, though few of us like to be told what to do, environmental protection will continue to do just that; policies will continue to seek to limit environmentally harmful activities and promote improved practice. I take it for granted that such policies are often necessary and desirable because, on balance, they do more good than harm. Thus, I concur with Gretchen Daily and Paul Ehrlich that in the near term it is most reasonable to expect people to behave more or less as they do now, rather than assuming everyone will become saints, and with David Orr that finding our way out of this predicament will depend on informed, engaged citizens working through a democratically controlled government.[4]

Our environmental predicament can be addressed from various perspectives. Mine is rooted in a background in the natural sciences. My professional interests in obstacles to environmental progress first developed during college and graduate school, notably including when I had opportunities to teach ecology courses for Dartmouth College students in Costa Rica, where contrasts between environmental damage and protection are starkly visible across barbed wire fences. My interests expanded when I worked on industrial ecology with engineers at the National Academy of Engineering and have grown ever since while teaching environmental studies, environmental policy, ecology, ecosystem restoration and directing the Austin College environmental studies programme and Sneed Prairie restoration.

Notes

1   Lazarus, 'Environmental law after Katrina: reforming environmental law by reforming environmental lawmaking', 2007.
2   Diamond, *Collapse*, 2005, 432–4, 523–4; King, 'How long?', 1965; Leopold, *A Sand County Almanac*, 1949, 202; Parker, *Ten Sermons of Religion*, 1853, 84–5.
3   Leopold, 'The land ethic', in *A Sand County Almanac*, 1949, 201–26.
4   Daily and Ehrlich, 'Population, sustainability, and Earth's carrying capacity', 1992; Orr, 'Four challenges of sustainability', 2002.

Acknowledgements

My interests in the environment began as a child growing up in Rhode Island, Michigan and Colorado. I had an exceptional high school biology teacher, the author Paul Richard, and many other fine teachers during my undergraduate and grad school years, including Sumner Richman at Lawrence University, and Carol Folt, John Gilbert, Dick Holmes, David Peart and Christopher Reed at Dartmouth College, and learned much from fellow graduate students, including Michelle Dionne, Hugh MacIsaac, Marianne Moore, Nick Rodenhouse, Doug Schaefer and Chris Whelan.

Later, working at the National Academy of Engineering and teaching at a liberal arts college have given me opportunities to learn from experts in related fields such as conservation biology and ecosystem restoration, and more distant fields such as environmental policy and the intersections of ecology with economics, engineering and political science. I have also benefited from interactions with local, state and federal officials, environmental attorneys and environmental activists. These various experiences have led me to directly encounter or otherwise learn of all the obstacles discussed here.

Many people have helped directly with this project. In addition to the many fine students with whom I have discussed these issues, I have benefited from conversations with my graduate school cohort, former professors, engineers and others at the National Academy of Engineering, colleagues at Austin College and any number of other environmental advocates and officials. In addition to those mentioned above, I am particularly thankful for conversations with Mark Leighton of Harvard University, Brad Allenby, Jesse Ausubel and Bob Frosch at the National Academy of Engineering, my Austin College colleagues George Diggs, Mari Elise Ewing and Keith Kisselle, and John Ockels, founder and Director of the Texas Illegal Dumping Resource Center. The last-named four also provided helpful comments on various drafts.

Several other individuals also helped with earlier drafts. Jim Yarbrough offered suggestions based on his decades of experience as an

EPA administrator. My current and former Austin College colleagues Nate Bigelow, Kerry Brock, Bob Cape, Karánn Durland, Mike Imhoff, Rebecca Jones, Jackie Moore, Danny Nuckols, Brian Watkins, and especially Dave Baker all made valuable suggestions or assisted with references. Lehigh University political scientist Al Wurth and retired Austin College sociologist Bart Dredge provided multiple insightful suggestions on every chapter. I doubt that I would have taken on this project if not for everything I learned from Al while I was a postdoc at Lehigh University, and from John Ockels since joining Austin College. (I had not yet included the story about Ockels in Chapter 20 when he read a draft. He is charmingly modest and would have objected.)

Many others also helped. Austin College present and former librarians Shannon Fox, Pat Means, John West and especially Andrew Smith located numerous references, as did my son Ben. Fred Block helped with the chapter on market fundamentalism. Halil Cakir explained changes in EPA procedures for monitoring atmospheric lead concentrations. Cathy Darnell provided the 1994 Chagnon and Harper reference. David Kinkela provided information on the history of DDT. Ya-Wei Li shared his extensive understanding of the Endangered Species Act. Carrie Page explained the complicated history of Dallas-Fort Worth Clean Air Act state implementation plans. Justin Pidot helped with Wyoming bill SF0012. Henry Singer relayed obscure references regarding opposition to highway expansion in northern Michigan. Brian Czech, Drew Jenkins, Julie Smartz and Daniel Wendt assisted with obtaining necessary permissions for using images. Anne Fleming, Tammy Kimbler and Hugh MacIsaac confirmed the correctness of various descriptions. Four anonymous reviewers provided valuable critiques and suggestions.

The Austin College Cullen and Richardson Fund and Austin College alumnus and trustee Joe Sanders enabled this book to be published Open Access. Austin College deans Beth Gill, Steve Goldsmith, and Mike Imhoff provided time during two sabbaticals.

From the initial proposal stage to the book's final production, the staff of University College London Press and their professional affiliates have done a wonderful job. Most notably, Commissioning Editor Chris Penfold seamlessly evaluated my proposal and administered the review and revision process. Jonathan Dore oversaw the various stages of production, superbly copy-edited the final draft, and also provided extensive advice and guidance through the latter editing stages. I am also grateful for the assistance of Grace Patmore and others at UCL Press and their contractors with whom I did not work directly. I really cannot imagine a more excellent or satisfying process from proposal submission to publication.

My wife Helen and sons Ben and Matt patiently put up with this project for years. All three also offered helpful suggestions here and there, as did my mother, Suzanne Schulze. My father died before I began this project, but I think I inherited much of my love for the outdoors from him. We walked the woods and canoed the streams of northern Michigan almost every summer, and my parents let me have a tiny rowboat on Rhode Island's Woonasquatucket Reservoir when I was quite young.

I have enjoyed working on this project and cannot adequately thank these people, nor can I appreciate all the ways they and others have helped me better understand our environmental predicament and the possibilities for escaping it. Of course, remaining limitations on my understanding and errors or shortcomings in the following are my responsibility alone.

1
Introduction

We have a serious problem. We are beyond the carrying capacity of the planet. Carrying capacity is the population an environment can support. When a population is degrading its environment's support potential, then, by definition, it is beyond carrying capacity and present practices cannot continue – they are not sustainable.[1]

We are altering the composition of the atmosphere and the oceans, eroding soil, overharvesting fish and trees, depleting aquifers and non-renewable resources, releasing persistent toxins, mixing up natural assemblages of species, all but eliminating some ecosystems, and driving species to extinction. All of these reduce the planet's potential to support life. The longer this situation persists, the poorer an inheritance we will bequeath to our descendants.

The scale of our enterprise is the root cause of our predicament because environmental problems result from too much or too little of something. If there were just a few of us, we would not have an appreciable impact. But there are nearly eight billion of us – nearly three times as many as when I was born – and many of us, myself included, consume a tremendous quantity of resources and produce a great deal of waste. The planet cannot continue to provide what we are asking of it, even though about half of humanity is presently unable to consume enough for a decent life.

Our descendants' and other species' well-being depends upon a successful shift to environmental sustainability – by which I mean acting in a manner that does not degrade the planet's life-support potential. We have a great responsibility and a great challenge, but we also have the luxury of historical perspective, and the fortunate among us have access to resources not previously dreamt of even by royalty. We owe it to future generations to use our awareness, ingenuity and access to resources to shift our trajectory.

To achieve sustainability of an agricultural society is perhaps one of the most challenging problems humans have ever faced, perhaps the greatest problem given its implications for all future generations. The works of George Perkins Marsh, Tom Dale, Vernon Gill Carter, Clive Ponting, Jared Diamond and others suggest no agricultural civilization has achieved true sustainability.[2] And our society is not merely agricultural, but industrial.

The challenges are not only complex, but from the perspective of our evolutionary history they are also brand new. To quote E. O. Wilson, 'The real problem of humanity is the following: we have paleolithic emotions; medieval institutions; and god-like technology.'[3]

Whether our present systems of government are up to the task remains to be seen.[4] Only time will tell. But progress is not only possible, it has happened before. A mere half a century ago the air and water in North America and Western Europe were much more polluted than today. The rivers in Buffalo, Chicago, Cleveland and Detroit were so contaminated with oil they often caught fire.[5] Residents of Los Angeles teared up on bad-air days; wastes were disposed of in unregulated 'dumps' or even into waterways (Figure 1.1).

Thanks to the nation's major environmental laws, such as the Clean Air Act and Clean Water Act, and thanks to the preceding public demand for those laws, US air and water pollution have declined dramatically. Today, Los Angelenos can see clearly across their streets (though often not to the horizon). The last US river fire was in 1969. Dozens of fish species have returned to once flammable, fishless rivers. Following the directions in the photo at the top of Figure 1.1 could now land you in jail, and concentrations of major toxic air pollutants have plummeted (Figure 1.2).

The size of the annual Antarctic stratospheric ozone hole has been declining;[6] many pesticides are less toxic than their predecessors; and many endangered species are recovering.[7] Ecosystem restoration has become an academic subdiscipline and a growing industry. Colleges and universities were just beginning to teach these subjects when I was an undergraduate, but environmental studies and science programmes are now almost ubiquitous.

A longer view leaves an even greater impression of progress. One hundred years ago, smokestacks were a symbol of prosperity. Much city water was not fit to drink. Gaining title to a homestead required

Figure 1.1: *Top:* Municipal sign instructing residents to dump garbage at the edge of a waterway. Source: unattributed, *Reclamation Era,* 'Pollution Control Agency Welcomed to Interior', 61. *Bottom:* Air pollution in Los Angeles, March 1960. Source: Charles E. Young Research Library, '*Los Angeles Times* Photographs Collection'.

'improving' property by clearing trees. As Aldo Leopold lamented, 'A stump was our symbol of progress.'[8]

Historical treatment of wildlife was shocking. During the sixteenth century, the English Parliament directed churchwardens to pay bounties for dead foxes, hawks, hedgehogs, jays, kingfishers, ospreys, otters, polecats, stoats, and weasels. Sixteen centuries earlier the Romans killed

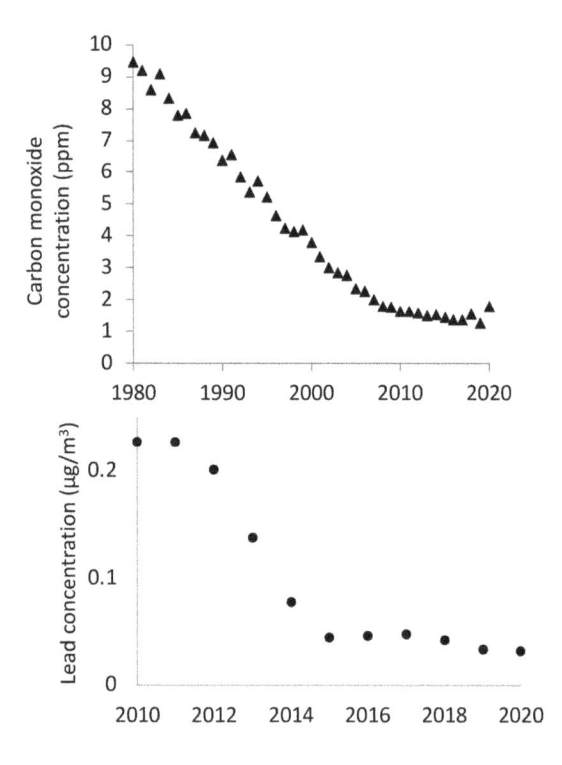

Figure 1.2: Declines in US atmospheric concentrations of the toxic air pollutants carbon monoxide (1980 to 2020) and lead (2010 to 2020). Carbon monoxide declined 81% from 1980 to 2020 while lead declined 86% from 2010 to 2020. Data source: EPA, 'National air quality: status and trends of key air pollutants', n.d. The concentration of lead had already declined some 70 per cent from 2001 to 2010 (EPA, 'Our nation's air: status and trends through 2010', 2012, 16). Pre-2010 lead data are not displayed here because the EPA changed protocols during 2009, so pre-2010 data are not directly comparable to later data (EPA, 'AQS memos – technical note – lead data reporting to AQS', n.d.).

9,000 animals to celebrate the dedication of the Colosseum, apparently just to thrill the crowds.[9] Environmental progress is not merely possible; it has been achieved.

But all is by no means well. Since the 1990s, US federal laws passed earlier have been incrementally implemented, some states have made policy progress,[10] and some renewable energy technologies, such as wind and solar power, have become more widely adopted. But there have been no new major, nationwide, successful environmental initiatives in the United States for twenty-five years; only a few modest laws have passed.[11]

Worldwide, air and water quality have improved in many places, but even in wealthy countries air quality suffers and many rivers are not fit for swimming, let alone drinking. Pollution is downright ghastly in some parts of the world. We continue to erode soil and deplete aquifers, fisheries and forests. I can walk into a big box store, buy neurotoxic pesticides, take them home and sprinkle them all over the yard or even inside my home if I so choose. Concentrations of greenhouse gases keep setting records.[12] Our combination of habitat destruction, overharvesting, pollution, and transport of non-native species is responsible for the sixth mass extinction in the history of the Earth and tremendous damage to the planet's life-support capacity.[13]

Meanwhile, new problems continue to arise, including pollutants that mimic natural hormones, earthquakes caused by oil and gas operations, possible health hazards due to nanoparticles, striking declines in butterflies, other pollinators and perhaps insects generally, uranium in water supplies, releases of methane and other materials from below melting permafrost, and perhaps declines in human fertility.

These problems persist despite centuries of warnings. Rachel Carson's *Silent Spring* warned about toxins in 1962. Thirteen years earlier, Aldo Leopold's essay 'The land ethic', in his *Sand County Almanac*, explained why a new ethical relationship with nature was an ecological necessity. At the beginning of the twentieth century, Gifford Pinchot warned of the folly of destroying forests. During the middle of the nineteenth century, Henry David Thoreau advised that 'in Wildness is the preservation of the World', John Muir suggested we see ourselves as 'a small part of the one great unit of creation', and George Perkins Marsh tallied our impacts in *Man and Nature*, warning that we were 'breaking up the floor and wainscoting and doors and window frames of our dwelling, for fuel to warm our bodies and seethe our pottage'.[14] Thomas Malthus warned in 1798 that population growth would exceed agricultural capacity.[15] Patrick Henry not only exclaimed, 'Give me liberty or give me death', but, speaking to the Virginia Assembly, apparently also stated, 'since the achievement of our independence, he is the greatest patriot who stops the most gullies'.[16] Perhaps Henry had not only seen the sorry condition of Virginia, but had also read Plato's 2,400-year-old description of the consequences of overgrazing in his *Critias*:

> What actually remains is like our small and barren islands, and, compared to the land it once was, Attica of today is like the skeleton

revealed by a wasting disease, once all the rich topsoil has been eroded and only the thin body of the land remains ... what we now call the Rocky Barrens were covered with deep rich soil. And in the mountains there were dense forests of which there still survives clear evidence. Some of our mountains can now grow just barely enough for bees, but it was not so long ago that [lofty trees grew there]. There can still be found intact rafters cut from trees that were felled and brought down to be used for the greatest building projects. And there were many trees that were cultivated for their fruit and they provided limitless fodder for flocks of sheep and goats.

Every year there was a harvest of Zeus-sent rain. It was not lost, as it is now, as it flows off the hard surface of the ground into the sea, but the deep soil absorbed the rain and it stored it away as it created a reservoir with a covering of clay soil above it; and, as it distributed the water it had absorbed from the high places into its hollows, it produced an abundant flow of water to feed springs and rivers throughout every region of the country. There are even today some sacred monuments at these ancient springs that are evidence of the truth of what we are now saying about our country.[17]

Despite Plato's warning, Aldo Leopold was still alerting readers to the consequences of soil erosion 2,400 years later, explaining that muddy rivers were '...washing the future into the sea'.[18] They still are, and Wendell Berry can still sum up our track record of care for the earth as like the three-legged pig – 'too well loved to be eaten all at once'.[19]

Millions of people have heard and heeded these and other warnings, thousands of organizations are working on solutions and support for policy change is widespread,[20] but sustainability remains a distant goal. With so much warning, awareness, concern and effort, why do problems persist? What obstacles prevent faster progress?

You can probably quickly think of several. I perceive three fundamental categories of obstacles. All three can block progress and are therefore critical. Deep, conceptual obstacles comprise two categories; the third is a set of more immediate, more practical obstacles. I hope better understanding of the various obstacles will foster acceleration in environmental progress.

Limits on our potential to understand and control the world around us comprise one category. These include constraints on our cognitive and perceptive faculties, mathematical limits on certainty, and factors that restrict our ability to direct global and smaller-scale physical, chemical, biological, and social phenomena. Together, these render us unable to fully direct or even predict the future. When I teach introductory environmental studies, I use a simple exercise to introduce this topic.

I ask students to identify likely consequences of a fee intended to reduce vehicle fuel consumption. We quickly develop a cluttered diagram of one thing leading to another. I hope the exercise provides four insights. First, many changes will occur. Second, some of those changes would come as a surprise in the absence of intentional foresight. Third, though we may be able to anticipate that if A goes up B will go down (such as if gasoline prices go up substantially, discretionary driving will decline somewhat, at least initially), it would be much harder to determine the quantitative relationship between A and B. (How much will driving distances decline? Will the relationship between A and B be linear or nonlinear?) Fourth, we will fail to identify some consequences; unanticipated changes are almost certain despite our best attempts at anticipation.

Furthermore, even if we could anticipate every change, many relationships among variables cause changes so precisely dependent upon starting conditions that we cannot predict future details. The simplest such example I know is the behaviour of a double pendulum (a pendulum with a second pendulum attached to its lower end). If you spin a double pendulum, you can confidently predict that it will eventually come to rest, but no one can precisely predict how it will spin in the meantime.[21] If we cannot predict the details of a simple device's swing, we certainly will not be able to predict everything about the future, and if we cannot predict everything, some things, indeed many things, will happen that we did not anticipate. Some of those things will cause environmental problems.

Meanwhile, even when we can anticipate a consequence, we may lack the means to affect its trajectory. To take a trivial example, I would like to cause native species, such as a grass called big bluestem, to thrive where students, colleagues and I are trying to restore grassland to a former farm, but after twenty years its establishment has been spotty. We can easily disperse seeds, but we do not control the rain or numerous other variables important to the species establishment.

More momentously, climate change sets in motion positive feedbacks (such as when floating ocean ice melts, leaving the ocean surface darker and thus causing it to absorb more heat that accelerates further melting). No matter how hard we try, we may not be able to precisely control such large-scale processes any more than we can precisely control the weather. Thus, factors that limit our capacity to predict, understand, and direct the future comprise a set of conceptual obstacles to environmental progress.

World views, value systems, and perspectives that deprioritize protection of the planet's life-support capacity comprise a second set of conceptual obstacles. I suspect our evolutionary roots bear much responsibility here. Social scientists could provide more nuance, but as a biologist, I perceive the situation as follows. We are descended from inconceivably long sequences of ancestors. During that time, natural selection favoured traits that fostered survival and reproduction. Every one of your ancestors – for billions of years[22] – managed to survive until they reproduced, otherwise you would not be here. That means natural selection prioritized overcoming short-term problems, such as starvation and predator evasion. Once those ancestors evolved into hunting and gathering humans, they were critically dependent upon not only immediate surroundings but also the other members of their small group, and all of our ancestors were hunting and gathering humans for about 99 per cent of human history. Thus, natural selection must have sculpted our brains to prioritize the near term, form close relationships with small groups of people, and be wary of those we do not know. But now we need to make good decisions about the long term for the sake of billions of people, including distant generations.

The socio-cultural developments of the last ten or twenty thousand years have resulted in a current (and still rising) population of almost eight billion people with remarkably diverse and wonderful cultures, value systems, perspectives, and world views, but the legacy of natural selection that prioritized dependence on a small group for solving short-term problems is not ideally suited to prioritizing the large-scale, long-term life-support capacity of the entire planet. Consequently, some evolutionary tendencies that were well suited to prior circumstances are not necessarily helpful for enabling billions of people to collaborate on protecting that life-support capacity. Indeed, our values and perspectives, and therefore our actions (mine included), often damage rather than foster that capacity. (In contrast, many other cultural tendencies of hunting and gathering groups were and are conducive to sustainability, as discussed in Chapter 9. Those too were surely selected for.)

Those two types of conceptual obstacles – limited ability to predict and direct the future, and perspectives that prioritize the short term and nearby – are daunting, but they are subjects of other books, not this one. This book focuses on the third type: immediate, practical obstacles to progress on specific, existing environmental problems, such as scientific uncertainty about the existence of a problem or its causes, political controversy regarding expenditure or priority, and inadequacies in the design or implementation of responses.

The practical obstacles I focus upon are rooted in the conceptual obstacles. For instance, whether one would support a land-use restriction or budget for protection of an obscure insect species is likely to depend on one's views of the relationship of humans to other species and the ethics of anthropogenically driven extinction. Other practical obstacles are rooted in the conceptual challenges of complexity and limits to our intellectual faculties, such as when our inability to disentangle and meaningfully interpret some numerical results constrains the design of experiments and thus the hypotheses we can test.

Though the obstacles are interrelated and all three types are critical, this book focuses on the immediate, practical obstacles for five reasons. First, others have extensively discussed the importance of conceptual obstacles,[23] but I have never seen the practical or immediate obstacles considered as a set of related phenomena to be systematically understood. Second, I suspect most people striving for environmental progress devote much of their time to overcoming these more immediate, practical obstacles. In other words, most of us have limited opportunity or potential to advance the boundary of predictive abilities or influence societal norms, but we do have opportunities to improve a recycling system, restore some ecosystem damage, increase the efficiency of a green technology, or help meet demands for contraception. Third, both novices and the larger society often fail to anticipate these practical obstacles, resulting in ad hoc, reactive responses where systematic anticipation and preparation might be more effective. Fourth, opponents of environmental efforts routinely cite one or more of the practical obstacles as the basis of their opposition. Such arguments lose impact if a compelling case can be made that the concerns are illusory, have been exaggerated, or otherwise can be overcome. Fifth and finally, I hope articulation of a set of practical obstacles and some suggestions for overcoming them will inspire others to refine the following descriptions; identify any omissions; advance understanding of each one; and further develop ideas about how these stumbling blocks may be dismantled or avoided, all so that environmental progress can accelerate.

Chapters 2–19 each focus on one practical obstacle. Those chapters fall into three subsets: obstacles to detecting and understanding problems and their causes, obstacles to responding, and obstacles to effective responses. I identify eighteen obstacles across the three groups. Often, practical and conceptual barriers are so intertwined that practical obstacles cannot meaningfully be considered in isolation. Thus, the following chapters note connections when necessary. The final chapter offers some recommendations for tackling these obstacles, and describes contemporary examples of progress where obstacles have been creatively overcome.

The same obstacles apply to both modest and momentous challenges, from increasing recycling on a small college campus to preventing climate change. They apply both in cases when conceptual obstacles are also important and when conceptual obstacles either do not pertain or are of negligible consequence. For the sake of future generations – of our species and others – we must become better at overcoming all of them.

To those familiar with US history, political roadblocks may immediately seem, and often probably are, most important, but various other hurdles occur even in the absence of political opposition. For example, if you have ever wondered about the risk of exposure to some potentially toxic chemical, you can probably think of several scientific challenges to determining whether a hazard exists, and if so, which compound or compounds are responsible. To take a simpler example, for years we have tried to produce an uncontaminated stream of recyclables on the Austin College campus, but contamination persists. There is no serious opposition to recycling, but we still have not achieved this goal. Indeed, this is a simple but common problem, as became apparent when China raised its purity standards for imported recyclables, leading to the breakdown of many municipal US recycling operations.[24] Even though it is easy to specify materials a recycler will accept, it is difficult to prevent contamination.

At the federal level as well as in many states, proposed increases in environmental protection are often politically controversial. There are many reasons for controversy, including wariness about the potential of the federal government to effectively address problems and reluctance to allow increases in federal power. Today, Republicans often oppose government intervention in the market, or question the severity of environmental problems or the potential of the government to alleviate them, while Democrats generally hold the opposite views.[25] Under such a circumstance, with a large group routinely opposed to further environmental protection, federal stalemate often ensues because the framers of the US Constitution, fearful of tyranny, designed a system intended to prevent increases in federal government power except when demanded by large majorities.

Circumstances differed during the heyday of US environmental progress, from the passage of the Clean Air Act in 1963 through the Clean

Air Act amendments of 1990. Opponents of environmental protection were not yet organized; acrid smog, oily beaches and burning rivers inspired demand for action; and environmental protection enjoyed bipartisan support. Indeed, Republican presidents signed most of the nation's major environmental laws (Figure 1.3). Since the 1980s, however, the political climate has polarized and opponents of further environmental protection have organized.[26]

Consequently, federal stalemate has ensued. Old laws remain on the books, but few new federal laws have been passed. The lack of climate change legislation is the most obvious example. Bipartisan consensus was forthcoming when environmental problems were plainly visible to casual observers and opponents were not yet organized. Today, the parties are polarized and many problems, such as climate change, depletion of renewable resources, and spread of invasive species are neither as apparent nor as obviously undesirable to casual observers. Resumption of environmental progress will almost certainly require both widespread understanding of and support for action on these less apparent problems.

For me, it is helpful to keep in mind that people can learn, and political parties are malleable. It may seem the US is stuck in permanent partisan stalemate, and reports of irrational responses to evidence make for depressing reading, but party stances and cultures shift. Viewed from an ecological time scale, the partisan divide regarding environmental protection is a recent phenomenon. No law of nature dictates that political groups cannot evolve and cooperation cannot recover.

Indeed, party stances have recently shifted in other ways. For example, during the late twentieth century and early 2000s, presidential nominees from both parties were free trade enthusiasts, but during the 2016 election the three leading presidential candidates, Hillary Clinton, Donald Trump and Bernie Sanders, all opposed a free trade agreement then under negotiation. That change, however, is almost trivial compared to the long-term shifts in the two dominant parties.[27]

The partisan divide in the US is wide today, but preference for environmental protection seems to be growing again.[28] Passive preferences will not suffice, however. Barriers to progress must be overcome.

I hope the following elucidation of predictable obstacles will not overwhelm but will forewarn and thus forearm. Articulation of obstacles risks causing despondency because we are never going to have complete predictive ability, deeply rooted values resist change, and many practical obstacles exist. I recommend keeping in mind that every case of environmental progress represents an instance of overcoming every

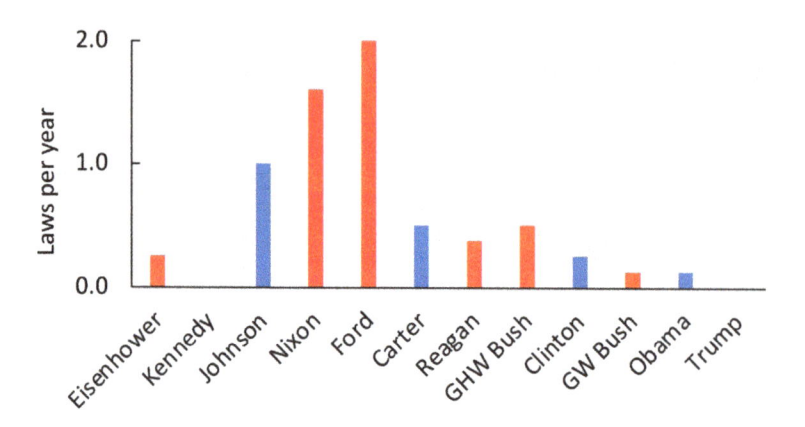

Figure 1.3: Major environmental laws passed per year during each presidential administration since the 1950s. Republican presidencies in red, Democratic presidencies in blue. Neither 'environmental' nor 'major' law is precisely definable. This graph includes the following laws: 1955 National Air Pollution Control Act, 1956 amendments to the Federal Water Pollution Control Act of 1948, 1963 Clean Air Act, 1964 Wilderness Act, 1965 Motor Vehicle Air Pollution Control Act, Water Quality Act, 1966 Endangered Species Preservation Act, 1968 Wild and Scenic Rivers Act, 1969 National Environmental Policy Act, 1970 Clean Air Act amendments, 1972 Federal Water Pollution Control Amendments, Federal Insecticide, Fungicide, and Rodenticide Act, Marine Mammal Protection Act, Coastal Zone Management Act, Marine Protection, Research, and Sanctuaries Act, 1973 Endangered Species Act, 1974 Safe Drinking Water Act, Forest and Rangelands Renewable Resources Planning Act, 1975 Eastern Wilderness Areas Act, Hazardous Materials Transportation Act, 1976 Resource Conservation and Recovery Act, Toxic Substances Control Act, 1977 Clean Water Act amendments, 1980 Comprehensive Environmental Response, Compensation, and Liability Act, 1986 Emergency Planning and Community Right to Know Act, 1988 Ocean Dumping Ban Act, 1990 Clean Air Act amendments, Oil Pollution Act, 1996 Food Quality Protection Act, Safe Drinking Water Act amendments, 2006 Magnuson-Stevens Fishery Conservation and Management Reauthorization Act, 2016 Frank R. Lautenberg Chemical Safety for the 21st Century Act.

encountered obstacle. Forewarning of obstacles in other circumstances often enables preparation and fosters success. In that spirit, I hope this book will cultivate faster environmental progress by helping readers anticipate, understand and overcome obstacles, and by fostering scholarly interest in the obstacles as phenomena to be better understood.

If progress does not accelerate, we will repeat a pattern of responding too slowly as problems worsen. We need to learn the lessons of tobacco and lead. Cigarettes were nicknamed 'coffin nails' seventy years before the US Surgeon General declared them harmful.[29] Ben Franklin described lead hazards two hundred years before the US restricted its use in gasoline.[30] Our track record on climate change is similar. Elisha Foote described the warming effect of carbon dioxide and other greenhouse gases in 1856. Forty years later, Svante Arrhenius predicted climate change. More than a century after Foote's discovery, President Johnson's Science Advisory Committee warned him about global warming.[31] Yet, another half century later, the US still lacks a sustained national response. Indeed, during 2021, more than 160 years after Foote's discovery of the greenhouse effect, and despite at least 55 Gulf of Mexico oil spills in the wake of Hurricane Ida, a Biden Administration agency, the Bureau of Ocean Energy Management, sought to lease 30 million more hectares of the Gulf for new oil and gas production.[32] We have been taking too long to overcome obstacles to environmental progress.

Such examples can make prospects seem bleak, but these are not the first daunting problems. People have made great progress in other realms. Some 120 years ago, nearly one third of infants in Washington, DC died before their first birthday. Infant mortality is still too high, but is down 95 per cent since. Over the same period, workplace fatalities declined 95 per cent and tuberculosis, diphtheria, pertussis, polio, typhoid and dysentery were virtually eliminated.[33] The oldest generation among us did all that while surviving the Depression and the Dust Bowl, outlawing child labour, winning World War II and making gains in civil rights. Perhaps present generations can make similar progress this century in preventing overharvesting, soil erosion, aquifer depletion, the spread of invasive species and emissions of toxins and greenhouse gases.[34] Maybe a grand challenge is just what the US needs.[35] Got anything better to do?

> *The future depends on what we do in the present.*
> – widely attributed to Mahatma Gandhi

Notes

1 Dasgupta, 'Foreword', 2018, xi. People define 'sustainable' variously. I contend sustainability can only be confirmed in retrospect and provisionally to the date of confirmation. Non-sustainability is easier to define and recognize. I consider a process non-sustainable if it degrades any condition or process it depends upon.

2 Dale and Carter, *Topsoil and Civilization*, 1955; Diamond, *Collapse*, 2005; Marsh, *Man and Nature*, 1965; Ponting, *A New Green History of the World*, 2007.

3 *Harvard Magazine*, 'An intellectual entente', 2009.

4 Lazarus, 'Environmental law after Katrina: reforming environmental law by reforming environmental lawmaking', 2007.

5 Hartig, *Burning Rivers*, 2010, 8; EPA, 'National air quality', n.d.

6 Cereceda, 'The Antarctic ozone hole is among the largest on record, how does it affect me?', 2021; Kuttippurath and Nair, 'The signs of Antarctic ozone hole recovery', 2017; Kuttippurath et al., 'Exceptional loss in ozone in the Arctic winter/spring of 2019/2020', 2021, 14019–20.

7 M. W. Schwartz, 'The performance of the Endangered Species Act', 2008.

8 Leopold, 'The population wilderness fallacy', 1918, 43.

9 Ponting, *A New Green History of the World*, 2007, 137–41.

10 Dennis and Eilperin, 'States aren't waiting for the Trump Administration on environmental protections', 2019.

11 A law was passed outlawing 'microbeads' in liquid hand soap and other consumer products, but that hardly constitutes a major federal initiative. Likewise, the Toxic Substances Control Act was reformed, but environmental experts disagree about whether the reform's implementation represents an improvement or a lost opportunity. A third example is the 2002 Pipeline Safety Improvement Act. Davenport and Huetteman, 'Lawmakers reach deal to expand regulation of toxic chemicals', 2016; Lipton, 'The chemical industry scores a big win at the EPA', 2018; Parker, 'The pipeline industry meets grief unimaginable, 2004; Schwartz, J., 'Ban on microbeads proves easy to pass through pipeline', 2015.

12 US greenhouse gas emissions declined about 11 per cent from 2007 to 2019, largely as a result of shifts in electricity generation, with perhaps some decline due to economic recession following 2008 stock market declines. Emissions from electricity generation declined as utilities shifted from burning coal to natural gas and building wind turbines. The shift from coal to natural gas has been attributed partly to declines in natural gas prices as a result of developments in fracking and horizontal drilling technology. Meanwhile, wind-generated electricity became more economical. The official greenhouse gas emissions records may, however, underestimate fugitive methane emissions for oil and gas operations and therefore underestimate US greenhouse gas emissions. If the US declines are real, they have occurred despite a lack of successful federal government leadership. During the early 2010s, the Obama Administration signed the Paris Climate Agreement and began development of federal climate change policy, but the Trump Administration reversed course, withdrew from the Paris Agreement's international effort and championed coal mining and consumption. The Biden Administration has re-engaged with the Paris Climate Agreement but has been in office less than one year as of this writing. Meanwhile, the US Congress has repeatedly failed to pass climate change legislation, though some states have passed their own statutes. See Alvarez et al., 'Assessment of methane emissions from the US oil and gas supply chain', 2018; Hmiel et al., 'Preindustrial $^{14}CH_4$ indicates greater anthropogenic fossil CH_4 emissions', 2020; Kusnetz, 'US emissions dropped in 2019', 2020; EPA, 'Greenhouse gas inventory data explorer', n.d.; US National Oceanic and Atmospheric Administration, 'The NOAA annual greenhouse gas index (AGGI)', 2021.

13 Amundson et al., 'Soil and human security in the 21st century', 2015; Crutzen and Stoermer, 'The Anthropocene', 2000; Díaz et al., *The Global Assessment Report on Biodiversity and Ecosystem Services: Summary for policymakers,* 2019; Millennium Ecosystem Assessment, *Ecosystems and Human Well-being: Synthesis,* 2005; Pimm et al., 'The biodiversity of species and their rate of extinction, distribution, and protection', 2014; Rockström et al., 'Planetary boundaries', 2009.

14 Carson, *Silent Spring,* 1962; Leopold, *A Sand County Almanac,* 1949, 201–26; Marsh, *Man and Nature,* 1965, 52 (originally published 1864); Muir, *A Thousand-Mile Walk to the Gulf,* 2008, 88; Pinchot, 'Prosperity', 2008, 177; Thoreau, *The Portable Thoreau,* 1977, 609.

15 Malthus, *An Essay on the Principle of Population*, 1986, 8. Much of the remainder of Malthus's book is an exposition of this position. Some argue that his basic thesis was wrong. At the risk of being simplistic, it is worth noting that the number of hungry people today is almost equal to the entire population of the planet during Malthus's lifetime.

16 This quote is widely referenced as having been made to the Virginia Assembly sometime during the late eighteenth century, but most quotations give no specific source. One early reference is available online at the website of the Biodiversity Heritage Library. See M. N., 'On improvement of lands in the central region of Virginia', 1834, 586.

17 Cooper, *Plato Complete Works*, 1997, 1297.

18 Leopold, *A Sand County Almanac*, 1949, 132.

19 Berry, *The Way of Ignorance and Other Essays*, 2005, 25.

20 Hawken, *Blessed Unrest*, 2007, 11–12; Popovich, 'Where Americans (mostly) agree on climate change policies, in five maps', 2018; Yale Program on Climate Change Communication, 'Yale climate opinion maps 2020'.

21 Video of computer simulation of a double pendulum on the YouTube channel Think Twice (https://www.youtube.com/watch?v=d0Z8wLLPNE0, accessed 3 January 2021).

22 I can easily type 'billions of years' but I am sure I cannot really comprehend a billion years. This is, I think, a consequence of that natural selection acting upon my ancestors and favouring good comprehension of time frames from seconds or fractions of sections to a few years or so.

23 For instance Cohen, *Understanding Environmental Policy*, 2006, 3–4, 131–4; Daly, *Beyond Growth*, 1996, 1–23; Daly and Cobb, *For the Common Good*, 1989, 121–206; Jamieson, *Reason in a Dark Time*, 2014, 72–8; Kampourakis and McCain, *Uncertainty*, 2020; Layzer, *Open for Business*, 2012, 11–30; Morgan et al., *Uncertainty*, 1990; Rovelli, 'Science is not about certainty', 2014; Quinn, *Ishmael*, 1992; Salzman and Thompson, *Environmental Law and Policy*, 2014, 31–49; Z. Smith, *The Environmental Policy Paradox*, 2004, 7–28. Readers who have not previously encountered the literature on the limits to understanding might start with an online recording of a World Science Festival discussion titled The Limits to Understanding (https://www.youtube.com/watch?v=DfY-DRsE86s, accessed 17 December 2021).

24 Corkery, 'As costs skyrocket, more US cities stop recycling', 2019.

25 For instance Gallup, 'Economy tops voters list of key election issues', 2020; League of Conservation Voters, '2020 national environmental LCV scorecard'.

26 Beder, *Global Spin*, 2002, 15–25; Jamieson, *Reason in a Dark Time*, 2014, 81–96; Layzer, *Open for Business*, 2012; Z. Smith, *The Environmental Policy Paradox*, 2004, 17.

27 Cobb, 'What is happening to the Republicans?', 2021, 28–9.

28 Saad, 'Americans as concerned as ever about global warming', 2019.

29 No-To-Bac advertisement, 'Coffin Nails', 1896.

30 Morgan, *Not Your Usual Founding Father*, 2006, 75–8; Rosner and Markowitz, 'Why it took decades of blaming parents before we banned lead paint', 2013.

31 Arrhenius, 'On the influence of carbonic acid in the air upon the temperature of the ground', 1896; Foote, 'On the heat in the sun's rays', 1856; Foote, 'Circumstances affecting the heat of the sun's rays', 1856; US President's Science Advisory Committee, Environmental Pollution Panel, *Restoring the Quality of Our Environment*, 1965, 9, 112–31.

32 Migliozzi and Tabuchi, 'After Hurricane Ida, oil infrastructure springs dozens of leaks', 2021; US Department of the Interior Bureau of Ocean Energy Management, 'Lease Sale 257', 2021.

33 Armstrong et al., 'Trends in infectious disease mortality in the US during the 20th century', 1999; Hibbs, 'The present position of infant mortality', 1915; MacDorman and Mathews, 'Recent trends in infant mortality in the United States', 2008; US Department of Health and Human Services, 'Achievements in public health, 1990–1999: improvements in workplace safety – US, 1900–1999', 1999.

34 Díaz et al., *The Global Assessment Report on Biodiversity and Ecosystem Services*, 2019.

35 Gallup, 'Confidence in institutions', n.d.

Part I

Obstacles to detecting and understanding environmental problems

Problems cannot be prevented until they have been detected and their causes identified. Burning rivers are easy. When a river is on fire, both the problem and basic cause are obvious – flammable material on the water. Unlike a burning river, many present environmental problems are obscure, as are their causes. Challenges of detecting problems and understanding causes create the first seven obstacles to progress. Problems may go undetected either because no one is on the lookout or because evidence of the problem is hard to detect. Once problems are detected, four types of obstacles create barriers to understanding causes. Many potentially instructive experiments cannot be performed. Problems can hide in false negatives of statistical tests. Later, when cause-and-effect relationships have been documented with experiments, it can remain difficult to interpret the relevance of experimental data for more general circumstances. Finally, unreliable results of occasional shoddy or fraudulent science complicate understanding. Collectively, these obstacles often cause decades to pass between when a problem first occurs and when its cause or causes are understood.

2
No one on watch

Cleveland's burning river and Los Angeles's horrid air were plainly apparent to casual observers, and their causes were relatively straightforward. A few more recent environmental catastrophes, such as the 2010 BP Deepwater Horizon oil platform explosion in the Gulf of Mexico, the 2011 Fukushima nuclear reactor meltdown and the 2013 Lac-Mégantic, Quebec explosion of a train carrying Bakken shale oil, have been similarly dramatic, but many present problems are obscure. Casual observers could detect a burning river, but cannot detect stratospheric ozone depletion, climate change, spread of non-native species or uranium in drinking water. Such inconspicuous problems can grow unnoticed for decades in the absence of intentional effort at anticipation or detection. Unfortunately, despite a history of unpleasant surprises, we lack a system to look out for new, obscure problems.[1]

New environmental problems frequently result from widespread adoption of technological innovations. The latest devices are often useful, profitable, enjoyable or even life-saving. Moreover, many provide environmental benefits, such as energy savings. However, many have undesirable, unintended consequences.[2] Children play with a screen rather than outdoors. Parents check their phones rather than interacting with infants. Corporations seek to track our every move. Some experts fear artificial intelligence could turn against us. And where the environment is concerned, the manufacture, use and disposal of our vast array of products releases millions of chemicals of unknown toxicity and is changing the composition of the atmosphere and oceans.

This chapter uses historical examples to illustrate the potential of new technologies to cause unintended environmental consequences and argues for learning to anticipate, and when possible, prevent such unpleasant surprises. Until we get better at doing so, obliviousness to new hazards will serve as an obstacle to environmental progress because we do not devote effort to unrecognized problems.

Legacy of unintended consequences

Stratospheric ozone depletion due to chlorofluorocarbons (CFCs) and related chemicals provides one of the most profound cases of an unintended environmental consequence of a new technology.[3] CFCs and related compounds make excellent refrigerants, propellants and fire retardants, benefits recognized shortly after their invention. Not until fifty years later, however, did anyone realize they also destroy stratospheric ozone.

CFCs were first synthesized in the 1920s. They replaced ammonia in refrigeration. An alternative refrigerant was desirable because ammonia can explode, spewing toxic fumes. In contrast, CFCs are nontoxic and relatively inert. In a 1930 article describing one of the first CFCs, Thomas Midgley and Albert Henne wrote, 'Dichlorodifluoromethane is less toxic than carbon dioxide, as non-inflammable as carbon tetrachloride, and very satisfactory from every other standpoint.'[4]

Not until half a century later, during the 1970s, did scientists begin to wonder whether escaped CFCs might affect the atmosphere. They knew relative inertness allowed CFCs to persist in the air, but the same low reactivity suggested the compounds were benign. Then, in 1974, Sherwood F. Rowland and Mario Molina discovered that CFCs destroy ozone (O_3) in the stratosphere, the layer of atmosphere from about 10 to 50 km above sea level.[5] Once mixed to that elevation, the intense ultraviolet light at those high altitudes breaks CFCs into reactive, ozone-destroying components. Bill McKibben, in his book *The End of Nature*, relates Rowland's recollection of the day he realized this. 'The work is going very well', he told his wife, 'but it looks like the end of the world'.[6] End of the world was an exaggeration, but by destroying stratospheric ozone, CFCs destroy one of the conditions necessary for life on land. Before the ozone layer developed, only aquatic creatures had evolved. Water blocks ultraviolet light, so marine organisms could survive before the ozone layer formed, but terrestrial creatures could not.

Chemical reactions in the stratosphere produce ozone (O_3) from oxygen gas (O_2), the form of oxygen we breathe. For its first few billion years, Earth's atmosphere contained little breathable oxygen. Then, roughly two billion years ago, the ancestors of today's cyanobacteria evolved the ability to photosynthesize. They gave off oxygen gas as a by-product. The stratospheric ozone layer eventually formed from atmospheric reactions of O_2 produced by those early photosynthesizers and their descendants, algae and plants.

The stratosphere blocked most ultraviolet light ever since. Once protected from ultraviolet radiation, life could spread onto land. Today's cyanobacteria are most often visible as pond scum. Thus, we should give thanks to the ancestors of pond scum not only for the oxygen we breathe, but also for protection from carcinogenic ultraviolet radiation.

Once the hazard of ozone depletion was widely appreciated, nations ratified the Montreal Protocol, a 1987 agreement to phase out ozone-depleting chemicals. The agreement is widely considered the greatest example of international environmental cooperation. If countries comply with the Protocol, the ozone layer may recover as soon as 2050.[7] We all owe a great debt to Drs Rowland, Molina and their colleagues.

CFCs are just one innovation whose undesirable consequences became clear only decades after their widespread adoption. Paul Müller was awarded the Nobel Prize in Physiology and Medicine in 1948 'for his discovery of the high efficiency of DDT as a contact poison against several arthropods [insects and their relatives]'.[8] DDT saved many people from malaria, but is not as safe as initially thought and some used it indiscriminately. Fish died in lakes sprayed for mosquitoes; bald eagles and other raptors failed to reproduce when DDT damaged their eggs; and there is reason for concern about long-term human exposure.[9] Like CFCs, DDT seemed like a wonder chemical, but it too had undesirable consequences that went unrecognized for a long time – until after wallpaper laced with DDT was installed in babies' nurseries (Figure 2.1) and children ran behind spray trucks, enjoying the cooling effect of the damp insecticidal mist on hot summer days.[10]

CFCs and DDT are just two of many compounds once thought safe but now recognized as having undesirable side effects. Some other examples are remarkable. A 1930s soil erosion textbook instructs schoolchildren to kill gophers with strychnine. 'To 1 gallon of sweet potatoes … add ¼ ounce of strychnine alkaloid, dusting it on the bait from a pepper box while the potato strips are being stirred.' There is no mention of taking any precaution.[11] Strychnine, which is sometimes called strychnine alkaloid, was until recently sold as Wilco Gopher Getter Ag Bait, but unlike the pure formulation recommended in the textbook, the Wilco product was only 0.5 per cent strychnine, merely 1/200th as strong as what the textbook recommended. Nevertheless, the product label read, 'Product is a highly toxic poison. It should not be inhaled, ingested, or allowed to come into contact with open cuts. Convulsive

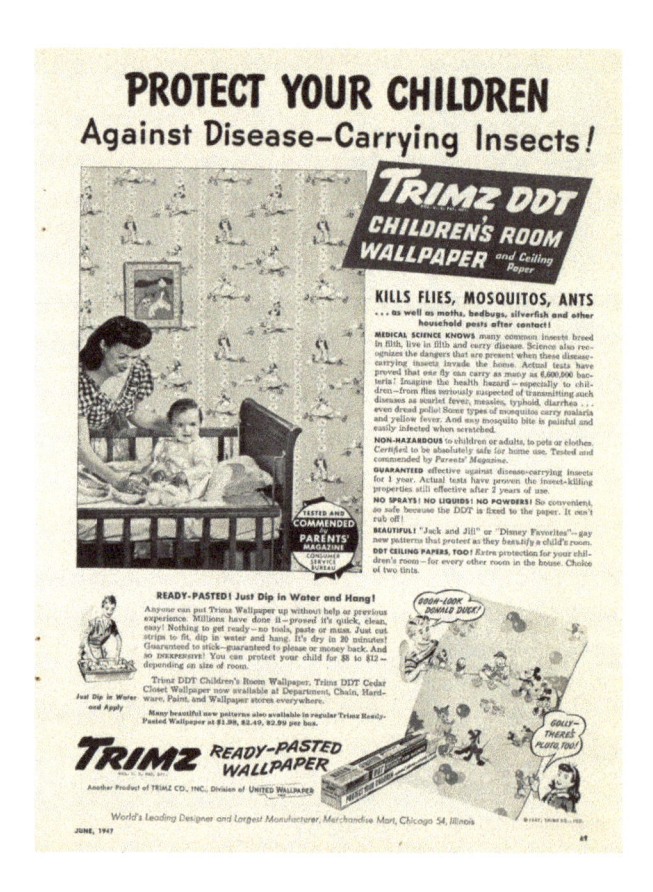

Figure 2.1: June 1947 *Women's Day* magazine advertisement for DDT-containing wallpaper for babies' nurseries. Source: Science History Institute, 'Digital Collections', n.d.

poison, fatal if swallowed.' The instructions for physicians read, 'Administer 100% oxygen by positive pressure to provide as much pulmonary gas exchange as possible, despite seizures. Administer anticonvulsant drugs intravenously to control convulsions ... Be prepared to maintain pulmonary ventilation mechanically. Tracheotomy may be necessary if seizures are prolonged.' As of late 2021, the product is no longer available on the Wilco website, but only two years earlier the US Environmental Protection Agency (EPA) mandated the wearing of technically sophisticated respirators when working with the material.[12]

Older readers will remember pumping leaded gasoline. Tetraethyl lead boosted octane, but polluted air with a neurotoxin. Air-lead concentrations plummeted after elimination of leaded gasoline. Dr Midgley of chlorofluorocarbon fame has the dubious distinction of being responsible for the widespread use of both chlorofluorocarbons and tetraethyl lead, but in his day august organizations celebrated his innovations. He was elected president of the American Chemical Society and to membership in the National Academy of Sciences.

Some abandoned technologies are so bizarre they sound like spoofs. During the early twentieth century, one could buy radioactive radium face creams, tonics, toothpaste, bread, chocolate and even suppositories. According to the manufacturer, the suppositories were 'perfectly harmless' and caused, 'weak discouraged men' to 'bubble over with joyous vitality'.[13] Later, during the middle of the twentieth century, shoe stores measured feet with the X Ray Pedoscope, which avoided the need to remove one's old shoes (Figure 2.2). The Pedoscope was really nutty, since old shoes needed to come off anyway to try on the new ones the stores sought to sell.[14]

Figure 2.2: X-ray shoe-fitting device. The customer stood holding the bar while placing their feet in the dark opening. An X-ray source below the feet enabled the customer, salesperson, and a third person to view the foot bones from above. This particular machine was manufactured by the Pedoscope Company of London and is housed at the museum of the University Hospital of Lyon, France. Photographers: Roxanne Poudenas and Léo Lespets. https://commons.wikimedia.org/wiki/File:Podoscope_par_The_Pedoscope_Compagny_01.jpg. CC BY-SA 4.0.

In 1964 the US Congress requisitioned $17.5 million to study the potential of Operation Plowshares, which would have used 'nuclear excavation' to dig a second canal through Central America. The task would have required 20,000 times the energy of the Hiroshima bomb.

> Be it enacted by the Senate and House of Representatives of the US of America in Congress assembled, that the President is authorized to appoint a Commission … for the purpose of determining the feasibility of, and the most suitable site for, the construction of a sea level canal connecting the Atlantic and Pacific Oceans: the best means of constructing such a canal, whether by conventional or nuclear excavation, and the estimated cost thereof … There are hereby authorized to be appropriated such amounts as may be necessary to carry out the provisions of this Act, not to exceed $17,500,000.[15]

Thankfully, the commission decided Operation Plowshares was not a good idea. Virtually every environmental problem is an unintended consequence of a technological innovation. Tractors cause soil erosion. High-tech fishing boats deplete fisheries. Drills and pumps deplete groundwater. Fertilizer pollutes rivers, lakes and the ocean. Submarine-detection sonar kills whales. Fossil-fuel combustion changes the climate. The technologies all have great value, but their side-effects are considerable. Indeed, Lehigh University political scientist Al Wurth notes that 'side effect' is a euphemism: given their importance, some side effects should be considered main effects.[16]

These examples illustrate how widely adopted innovations sometimes have profound, unanticipated, undesirable consequences. By failing to systematically guard against such consequences, we proceed as if undesirable side-effects will not occur despite a track record to the contrary.[17] We tend to ignore the precautionary principle.

Lack of precaution

The precautionary principle counsels caution in the face of uncertainty, especially when catastrophic or irreversible consequences might occur. It captures the wisdom of old aphorisms such as 'look before you leap', 'an ounce of prevention is worth a pound of cure', 'better safe than sorry' and 'it's hard to put the genie back in the bottle'. Critics argue the precautionary principle would stifle innovation, but precaution need not mean inaction, be expensive or even interfere with action.

We routinely take precautions against familiar hazards. Moreover, such efforts are often effective and not burdensome. I have involved students in various activities that college administrators now classify as 'inherently hazardous', such as working from small boats on large lakes or the ocean, scuba diving, hiking in rainforests at night and burning fields to restore grassland. Simple precautions dramatically reduce risks of these activities. We wear life jackets, obtain scuba certification and take numerous measures to ensure fires burn only where intended.[18]

More generally, when we recognize a legacy of hazards, we eventually devise precautions. Neither bicyclists, ice hockey players, nor skiers wore helmets when I was young, but they do now. Few people need reminders to wear seatbelts. My sons cannot believe their grandmother sold a 1965 Ford Mustang for $250, but if she still had it, we would rarely drive it because today's cars are much safer – the subsequent designs having incorporated numerous precautions. All of these precautions are effective but none of them are burdensome.

The cumulative effect of precautions in ship safety are especially impressive. Old shipwrecks litter coasts, but shipwrecks rarely occur today thanks to safety innovations that have neither prevented shipping nor rendered it unprofitable. Whereas past sailors died awful deaths and cargoes were lost, today lighthouses and buoys mark shallow water, ships are far more seaworthy, captains use multiple sensors to avoid groundings and collisions, and the Coast Guard stands ready. Commercial vessel fatalities are so rare they often make international news.

Meanwhile, we carry insurance against other familiar hazards, such as car accidents, house fires and (in some countries) medical expenses. Indeed, many consider gaps in US medical insurance coverage a national tragedy. Organizations take precautions too. Businesses analyse risks and make contingency plans. Intelligence agencies spy. Militaries play war games.

Many laws and regulations even require precautions. For example, the US Food and Drug Administration evaluates side effects before approving medicines (hence the ubiquitous advertisement disclaimers). Laws, regulations and agencies address the safety of aircraft, cars and electronic devices. The precautions are not perfect, but are effective. Flying is remarkably safe. Home appliances rarely electrocute users.

As these examples illustrate, we expect precautions against familiar hazards. This is because, though not perfect and occasionally excessive, precautions often provide great benefits at modest cost. Indeed, controversy abounds when the public perceives inadequate precaution, whether to prevent concussions, epidemics or climate change.

Existing environmental protections serve as precautions against some well-known environmental harms. The Federal Insecticide, Fungicide, and Rodenticide Act regulates sale and use of chemical compounds designed to kill. As the strychnine example illustrates, many herbicides and pesticides used prior to that law's passage were exceedingly toxic. Today's biocides are far from harmless, but their toxicities to some non-target organisms have been determined and container labels include warnings. Other laws, such as the Clean Air and Water Acts, regulate pollutant emissions from industrial facilities, motor vehicles, and other sources. Air and water remain polluted, but much less than before passage of these laws, as the photos in the introduction attest.

In all these cases, precautions taken sooner would have reduced damages and suffering. Fewer sailors would have drowned. Fewer lives would have been lost in road or workplace accidents. Fewer athletes would have suffered concussions. Fewer people would have been harmed by pollution. Earlier precaution would have provided earlier benefits.

Imagine if we became proficient at anticipating and avoiding potential harms. What if we acted upon the hazard of climate change when it was first widely recognized during the 1970s, or even when the greenhouse effect was first detected by Elisha Foote in 1856 or global warming was predicted by Svante Arrhenius in 1896? Surely, we would still have used fossil fuels, but we might not by now depend on them so heavily or waste them so often. Imagine how much easier the challenge of climate change would be if serious international action had begun in the 1970s.

Faster detection and response would reduce suffering and environmental damage, but despite the legacy of unintended consequences, we generally do not take precautions, environmental or otherwise, until harms become broadly recognized. Widespread anxieties over location tracking, facial recognition and vulnerabilities of critical computer systems indicate contemporary concern over inadequate precaution. Perhaps these technologies could have provided the same benefits with less hazard if systematic precautionary efforts went hand in hand with technology development. Neither ships nor cars have become less useful as a consequence of innovative precautions.

It took decades for society to appreciate the hazards of CFCs and DDT because there was no concerted effort to do so. Even today, with the benefit of hindsight, we do not systematically guard against the next undesirable unintended consequence. Do you know anyone employed to anticipate future environmental problems? I do not, and I know many environmental professionals. Such flying blind is the environmental equivalent of operating sensitive computer systems while assuming no one will attempt to hack them, or conducting foreign affairs while assuming other nations do not spy and would never seek advantage.

Back in 1972, the US created the Office of Technology Assessment and charged it with anticipating unintended consequences of new technologies. Its staff produced hundreds of studies before being defunded in 1995, including a 700-page 1993 report warning of climate change. In theory, the Government Accountability Office took over responsibility for this work, but whereas the Office of Technology Assessment produced hundreds of reports during its brief tenure, the Government Accountability Office produced only about one technology assessment per year between 2000 and 2020.[19]

Thirty years ago, as a Fellow of the National Academy of Engineering, I heard early 'industrial ecologists' discuss questions such as whether steel or aluminium car parts would be better for biodiversity and which type of solder would best reduce the environmental impact of telephones. Today, a small cadre of analysts toil away making such evaluations. They publish articles in the *Journal of Industrial Ecology* and support each other's efforts through the Society for Environmental Toxicology and Chemistry, but a few scientists and engineers at universities and progressive corporations cannot handle the magnitude of the challenge on their own.

Many new technologies and their associated products will presumably have no serious undesirable consequences, but given the historical record, it seems safe to assume others will, at least as long as we make no concerted effort to anticipate and prevent them. Consider one relatively recent development.

Until the late-twentieth century, no one wore stain-resistant fabrics because such fabrics did not exist. Now millions of people wear them. Could the stain resistance have any consequences beyond aesthetics? For years, I purchased the same cotton trousers from a mail-order company; then they stopped selling untreated ones. Like so many others, I now frequently wear permanent-press, stain-resistant trousers.

I found myself wondering about the chemicals and processes that impart stain resistance. Early non-stick cookware and furniture fabrics were widely treated with polyfluoroalkyl substances (PFAS), compounds now understood to be toxic and persistent in the environment.[20] Since concerns about those materials have arisen, consortia with industry connections have begun testing fabrics for hazardous chemicals and labelling products that pass their tests,[21] but as far as I can tell, the only

US regulations regarding clothing fabrics are summarized in a National Institute of Standards and Technology guide.[22] That document describes a variety of regulations involving fire resistance and strangulation and choking hazards, but makes no reference to the materials used to impart stain or wrinkle resistance. Though millions of people have routinely worn these compounds for years, only since the early 2000s have researchers begun to investigate whether the treated clothing might be unhealthy.[23] With any luck, modern clothing fabrics are safe, but what about other poorly understood chemical exposures, such as the cocktails of synthetic chemicals routinely detected in drinking water and blood tests?[24]

Even anticipated hazards, such as spills from offshore oil drilling, sometimes receive minimal precaution. Commenting on the 2010 Gulf of Mexico Deepwater-Horizon oil platform disaster, former EPA Administrator William Reilly called clean-up technology 'primitive' and '…wholly disproportionate to the tremendous technological advances that have allowed deep-water drilling to go forward'.[25] That the drillers harboured a cavalier attitude to potential problems was obvious in BP's memorable announcement that they would use a 'junk shot' to try to stop the Deepwater Horizon spill. The 'junk shot' was an attempt to clog the spewing pipe with plastic waste, knotted rope and golf balls.[26] Predictably, it did not work. The situation may not have improved much since then. During 2021, aerial images detected at least 55 oil spills off the Louisiana coast in the wake of Hurricane Ida.[27]

Systems perspective

All these cases of unintended consequences are examples of 'system' problems. We take action A because we desire result B, but we often overlook that A will have consequences besides B, and B will have its own consequences. We fail to ask: '*Then* what happens?' To ponder what else will happen is to engage in systems thinking – trying to anticipate how one change in a 'system' (a set of interacting components) will cause other changes.[28]

Horizontal drilling and hydraulic fracturing for oil and natural gas ('fracking') provide an opportunity to illustrate the insights of systems thinking. These technologies made accessible previously uneconomic oil and gas deposits, increased the amount of oil and gas 'production', and reduced prices and imports. A few years ago, this development was widely supported with a bumper sticker that read, 'Drill baby, drill'.

Unfortunately, however, the techniques risk contaminating groundwater, disposal of their wastewater causes earthquakes, burning the fuel pollutes air and causes climate change, and the apparent abundance of supply fosters complacency about the necessity of developing alternative energy sources. The bumper sticker was evidently inspired by the intended benefit but ignored the many unintended consequences.

A systems perspective is particularly useful in positive feedback situations. Here positive feedback refers not to encouraging critiques such as 'good dog', but to relationships where an increase in A causes an increase in B, which in turn causes another increase in A and so on. Positive feedbacks lead to runaway circumstances. A familiar example occurs when a microphone gets too close to a loudspeaker. The noise from the speaker reaches the microphone, is boosted by the amplifier and then the speaker emits a yet louder sound, at which point the cycle repeats uncomfortably until the holder of the microphone realizes what is happening and moves away from the loudspeaker.

Similarly, traffic jams and road building often interact in positive feedback. Traffic jams lead to demands for larger roads, which attract more development to their immediate vicinity and thus attract more traffic, eventually causing larger traffic jams that lead to renewed calls for larger roads and so on. Houston now has 20-lane highways but terrible traffic jams. More lanes will temporarily help, but over time will only worsen the problem. This example of positive feedback is almost trivial, however, compared to the tragic positive feedback of population growth and increased agricultural production.

Unfortunately, the long-term historical relationship between agricultural production and population growth has also represented positive feedback. As conservationist Peter Farb explained, 'Intensification of production to feed an increased population leads to a still greater increase in population.'[29] Despite agricultural innovations and international efforts to feed the hungry, the Food and Agricultural Organization of the United Nations estimated that the number of hungry people reached one billion for the first time in 2009. One billion people was the approximate population of the entire world when Malthus first raised concerns about whether agricultural productivity could keep pace with population growth.[30] Viewed from a systems perspective, any real solution to hunger must break the cycle Farb described by alleviating present hunger *without* fostering an increase in future hunger. Fortunately, both the number of hungry people and the average global fertility rate have both fallen since 2009. (The average global fertility rate has been falling since the 1960s.)[31]

Relying on economic growth to overcome economic problems suffers the same positive feedback pitfall. Governments encourage increased economic production as a means of lifting the poor out of poverty and satisfying the demands of the rich, but the appeal of the resulting new products create new wants that get satisfied with new income generated from yet more production. In other words, people work to earn money to satisfy wants (and of course needs), but their effort results in production of goods, including new innovations, that, when marketed, increase others' desires. Those others then work to satisfy their new wants, producing yet more goods marketed to others, and so on in a positive feedback that grinds away at the planet's stock of resources and generates more waste and new types of wastes whose consequences we only partially understand. Reflecting on this circumstance, the wise gorilla Ishmael in Daniel Quinn's novel of the same name describes modern humans as prisoners of a mother culture, employed in a prison industry – consuming the world.[32]

> As society becomes increasingly affluent, wants are increasingly created by the process by which they are satisfied.[33]

Systems thinking is no magic bullet; just as engineers cannot precisely predict the failure of a spacecraft and physicians cannot precisely predict a patient's future health, a systems perspective will not enable anticipation of all consequences of an action. But physicians and engineers enjoy valuable predictive abilities despite incomplete understanding. Likewise, we can predict some system consequences if we try, as the traffic and food production examples illustrate. In other words, even limited analysis frequently provides critical insights, thereby enabling alteration of plans and avoidance of some undesirable consequences.

Rather than closing the Office of Technology Assessment, we could develop our abilities to anticipate 'side effects'. We could expand precaution from familiar to unfamiliar circumstances. Rather than funding a few industrial ecologists and a few theoreticians at a non-profit institute in Santa Fe, New Mexico,[34] we could employ a cadre of professional practitioners to apply systems perspectives broadly. Colleges and universities could create departments dedicated to prediction of unintended consequences. We could take Kurt Vonnegut's suggestion to appoint a Secretary of the Future.[35] Such efforts would avoid at least *some* otherwise unpleasant surprises. Until we become adept at doing so, our failure to anticipate and prevent surprises will impede environmental progress because we do not address problems we have not perceived.

Notes

1   Weale (*The New Politics of Pollution*, 1992, 93–118), Carter (*The Politics of the Environment*, 2001, 167–9) and Rosenbaum (*Environmental Politics and Policy*, 2002, 64–75) describe the piecemeal, retroactive and remedial approaches typical of federal environmental ministries and agencies. Such approaches have been unavoidable because the relevant authorizing statues have been reactive, not proactive, each addressing only a subset of issues.
2   Undesirable side-effects of technological innovation are not limited to environmental problems. Gray, 'The paradox of technological development', 1989, 192–8.
3   The stratosphere begins about 10 km above the surface of the earth. Ozone in the stratosphere occurs naturally and blocks most ultraviolet light from reaching creatures at the planet's surface. This stratospheric ozone is sometimes referred to as 'good ozone' for that reason. Ozone in the troposphere (below the stratosphere, including at ground level) is largely a byproduct of air pollution, causes respiratory and other problems, and causes 'ozone alert days' in many major metropolitan areas. This tropospheric ozone is the same molecule as stratospheric ozone, but, as a result of its altitude, is harmful to life and is therefore sometimes called 'bad' ozone.
4   Midgley and Henne, 'Organic fluorides as refrigerants', 1930, 542.
5   Molina and Rowland, 'Stratospheric sink for chlorofluoromethanes', 1974; Newbold, *Life Stories*, 2000, 134–40.
6   McKibben, *The End of Nature*, 1989, 41.
7   Rigby et al., 'Increase in CFC-11 emissions from eastern China based on atmospheric observations', 2019; Strahan and Douglass, 'Decline in Antarctic ozone depletion and lower stratospheric chlorine determined from aura microwave limb sounder observations', 2018. Unfortunately, Rigby et al. suggests China may have recently been out of compliance with the Montreal Protocol.
8   Nobel Prize, 'Paul Müller – Facts'.
9   Bowerman et al., 'A review of factors affecting productivity of bald eagles in the Great Lakes Region', 1995; Carson, *Silent Spring*, 1962, 120–2; Chen et al., 'Residential exposure to pesticide during childhood and childhood cancers', 2015; National Pesticide Information Center, 'DDT fact sheet', 1999. For a broader discussion regarding DDT see Kinkela, *DDT and the American Century*, 2011.
10 Austin College Emeritus Professor Kerry Brock's experience as a child in Texas (personal communication, 10 November 2021). Many images of such spraying are available on the internet, but I have not found any that reference an original source.
11 Burges, *Soil Erosion Control*, 1938, 166–7.
12 Arrington, 'Addition of PF10 respirator to strychnine labels as required by the EPA letter dated July 19, 2019'; Wilco Distributors Inc., 'Rodent baits, rodent traps, rodent solutions'.
13 Herzig, 'Removing roots', 1999; Oak Ridge Associated Universities Museum of Radiation and Radioactivity, 'Vita Radium Suppositories', n.d.
14 Duffin and Hayter, 'Baring the sole', 2000.
15 The quotation is from US Congress Public Law 88-609, 88th Congress, S. 2701, 22 September 1964; the project is the subject of Kirsch, *Proving Grounds*, 2005.
16 Personal communication, 3 October 2015.
17 Wurth notes that some consequences generally considered unanticipated and unintentional may actually have been anticipated by a few specialists but were unpublicized. Personal communication, 3 October 2015. See also Price, 'Cambridge, cabs and Copenhagen', 2013.
18 Archer, 'Sneed prairie prescribed fire', 2019. (This is a three-minute video of two prescribed fires that I directed during January 2019 at the Austin College Sneed Prairie. Despite the scene at about 2:15 on the video, precautions made the fires quite safe. Those precautions did not reduce the fire's effectiveness for prairie restoration.)
19 Princeton University, 'The OTA legacy'; US Government Accountability Office, 'Technology Assessments', n.d.; US Congress, Office of Technology Assessment, *Preparing for an Uncertain Climate*, 1993.

20 Renfrew and Pearson, 'The social life of the "forever chemical"', 2021.
21 BLUESIGN, https://www.bluesign.com/en; OEKO-TEX; https://www.oeko-tex.com/en/ (both accessed 2 January 2021).
22 Benson and Reczek, *A Guide to US Apparel and Household Textiles Compliance Requirements*, 2016. Of course, innovations may also have unintended benefits, environmental or otherwise. Stain-resistant fabrics could hypothetically result in less frequent washing, and therefore less detergent use and attendant water pollution. More significantly, more than a century ago internal combustion engines solved the problem of urban manure from horse-drawn vehicles.
23 Bernard, 'When wrinkle-free clothing also means formaldehyde fumes', 2010; Deardorff, 'Scientists', 2012; Stuart, 'Are nanotextiles making fabric laws wear thin?', 2011; Yetisen et al., 'Nanotechnology in textiles', 2016.
24 Conney and Burns, 'Metabolic interactions among environmental chemicals and drugs', 1972; Duncan, 'The pollution within', 2006; Evans, S., et al., 'PFAS contamination of drinking water far more prevalent than previously reported', 2020; Kristof, 'Contaminating our bodies with everyday products', 2015.
25 *Dallas Morning News*, 'BP spill, other disasters expose technological limits', 2010.
26 Fountain, '"Junk shot" is next step for leaking Gulf of Mexico well', 2010.
27 Migliozzi and Tabuchi, 'After Hurricane Ida, oil infrastructure springs dozens of leaks', 2021.
28 A system is simply any set of interacting components. You are a system; my laptop is a system; a society is a system; the biosphere is a system. Aside from the universe, any given system is a subsystem of some larger system.
29 Quinn, *Ishmael*, 1992, 111.
30 FAO, '1.02 billion hungry people', 2009.
31 World Bank, 'Arable land (hectares per person)', n.d.
32 Quinn, *Ishmael*, 254.
33 Galbraith, *The Affluent Society*, 1998, 129.
34 Santa Fe Institute, 'About', n.d.
35 Brancaccio and Long, 'What if we had a Secretary of the Future', 2016.

3
Detection challenges

The previous chapter discussed unanticipated environmental problems. Once a problem is anticipated or imagined, the next step is to determine whether it is real. This is not always easy.

Consider a newly manufactured chemical released into the environment. What health problems or ecosystem impacts might result? Might it compromise immune functioning, cause cancer, interfere with cardiovascular fitness or cause some other human ailment? If so, whose health should be monitored? What features of their health should be monitored? What if symptoms do not appear for years?

If there is a concern regarding other species or ecosystem processes, what species or ecosystem processes should be monitored? Might some species be more sensitive than others? If so, which ones? What variables would you measure? How, where and for how long would you make those measurements? How would you determine whether measured variables had changed since before you started measuring? When would you have enough data to draw conclusions? Perhaps the new chemical is harmless. If so, how would one know?

Confirmation of new environmental hazards to human health face two routine challenges: determining whether an ailment has really become more common, as opposed to simply being detected more often, and detecting hazards that do not produce symptoms until many years after exposure. These same two challenges complicate detection of ecosystem problems, but in that arena they are joined by four others. First, unlike humans, other species do not self-report problems. Second, there are many fewer ecosystem experts than human health experts. Third, normal ecosystem functioning is not as well understood as normal human health. And fourth, ecosystem monitoring involves more theoretical, logistical and financial constraints than human health monitoring.

Shrouded signals

Suppose there is concern that an ailment has become more common, such as an apparent cluster of cancer cases. Is there some new hazard in the environment? Just because some people have become sick does not mean there is a new problem. Most illnesses are not novel. People have always become sick. There may be little available data for comparing past and present prevalence of an illness, and even if such data are available, an apparent increase could be an artefact of better detection, or due to random variation or some non-environmental cause, not a result of a new environmental contaminant.

The challenge of distinguishing increased frequency from increased detection is responsible for debates regarding whether important ailments, such as autism or low sperm counts, have become more common. Few health problems could have more implications for humans than infertility and yet, despite decades of reported sperm counts, there is still no consensus whether a real decline has occurred or only an apparent decline that is an artefact of changes in data-collection methods.[1]

When a problem becomes more common, evidence of its rise may be hidden in background variation from time to time, place to place or other 'noise' in the data. Analysts use statistical procedures to identify a signal amid a noisy background. The calculations depend on comparison of the frequencies of actual observations to random variation that might otherwise occur. Such techniques merely test whether an apparent pattern would be a likely result of chance. They cannot determine whether a pattern is actually due to chance in a particular case. Thus, they cannot determine with certainty whether an apparent cluster of cases is a mere coincidence. (Chapter 5 further considers the potential and limits of such analyses.)

Detecting a problem amid natural background variation is even more challenging in ecosystem research than human health research. Imagine a decline in a fish harvest. Is the fish population declining? Did bad weather interfere with the year's catch? Was the fleet simply unlucky? If a beetle outbreak kills some trees, is there a new problem? There have always been beetles in the woods and trees are not immortal. A few dead trees would not be noteworthy. Is an observed dieback merely a case of random variation or an indication of something more serious?

Herpetologists documented widespread amphibian declines during the late-twentieth century, with many species endangered and others apparently already extinct. But a worldwide decline had been occurring for decades before experts realized the magnitude of the problem.[2] With no one expecting a global decline, there was no system in place to detect a pattern across different ecosystems or continents. No one was responsible for monitoring the big picture. Likewise, around the end of the 2000s, biologists raised concerns about widespread insect declines, but again, limited historical data and few systematic measurements render the evidence ambiguous.[3]

Another challenge occurs when many years pass between exposure and the onset of symptoms. In such cases, a cause may have come and gone long before the signal appears. For example, the horrible symptoms of mad-cow disease (bovine spongiform encephalopathy or BSE) take years to manifest, as do many cancers. Some nutrition specialists think sugar and grain consumption, especially wheat, may foster dementia, but dementia rarely strikes before old age. That hypothesis is controversial, and I am not qualified to offer diet advice, but if the hypothesis is correct, it will be too late for those who have consumed large quantities of conventional bread – 'the staff of life'.

Many ecosystem problems are so incremental they progress for decades or centuries before consequences become apparent. Erosion is a classic example. Anyone who sees farm soil blowing in the wind or watches the flow of a muddy stream can detect evidence of erosion, but it is more difficult to detect a resulting decline in crop production. Many crops are annuals – plants that complete their life cycle in one year. The roots of annuals typically reach only a fraction of a metre below the soil surface. Therefore, erosion of deep, fertile soil may not affect crop production until so much soil has been lost that the remaining, limited soil depth begins to constrain root growth, especially if fertilizers supplement soil fertility. Likewise, aquifers decline incrementally, deforestation advances incrementally and greenhouse gases accumulate incrementally. Critical consequences, such as wells running dry, lack of trees to harvest or obvious climate changes, may not become apparent until the responsible actions have occurred for hundreds of years or more. (The incremental nature of environmental problems also creates a different obstacle – lack of political urgency – the subject of Chapter 12.)

Climate change provides a familiar example of the challenge of detecting incremental change amid a noisy background. Multiple types of observations provide evidence of contemporary, rapid, anthropogenic climate change, including rising air temperatures and sea levels, melting glaciers, loss of polar ice, increases in ice-free seasons of northern lakes, and perhaps most significantly, shifts in the ranges of species and the seasonal timing of their behaviours and life cycles. The preponderance of evidence has led most experts to conclude that human activities are altering the climate. But imagine this was a new question and you were tasked with determining whether climates are changing.

How much data would you require? From how many locations would you require temperature measurements, with what frequency of measurement? How long a record would you require before you would be confident that present temperatures differ from past temperatures, and those differences are not just part of some natural cycle? What else would you want to know to determine whether a change is 'natural' or a result of human activity? How could you obtain these data?

Even simpler concerns face substantial detection challenges. Detection of a familiar problem in a new location, such as pollution of a stream, is often fairly simple, but not always. I occasionally receive requests from local residents to 'test a water sample'. For what would I test?

Imagine a river covered with dead fish. Is the water polluted or was the die-off natural? How would you determine whether water is polluted? Keep in mind that seriously polluted water may look crystal clear. The obvious option is to monitor for the pollutant, but which of thousands of potential pollutants would you seek? Would you test for all of them? Tests typically cost $20 to $500 per pollutant.[4] Professor Hugh MacIsaac of the University of Windsor dreams of sticking a finger in water and being able to know everything about it,[5] but he is unlikely to see his dream fulfilled.

Rather than seeking a particular pollutant, one can monitor for more generic evidence of ecosystem damage – some change that many pollutants could cause – such as a change in the acidity (pH) or oxygen content of water. Such measures are akin to human vital signs. Unusual values provide evidence of a problem, but it is possible to be gravely ill despite normal vital signs, and even when an abnormal vital sign occurs, the culprit remains to be determined. Dead fish, for example, could result from a pathogen, insufficient oxygen, one of many toxins or some combination of causes. The task is simpler if a pollutant is directly observable, such as oil on water, but what if the pollutant is released only intermittently? It may be far downstream before dead fish float to the surface.

Determination of which species are present and which are absent can provide evidence of pollution because some species are more pollution-tolerant than others.[6] Pollution episodes often eliminate pollution-intolerant species, in which cases collections turn up only pollution-tolerant species. But compared to chemical measurements, biological analyses are generally more time consuming and harmful to ecosystems (because specimens die in the process), sample analysis requires experienced biologists who can identify a wide variety of species, and interpretation of results requires detailed information on the pollution tolerance of dozens of species.

Lack of reference ecosystems

Complicating matters further, in many cases few or no examples of healthy ecosystems remain. It is as if doctors sought to determine whether a patient was healthy but had never seen a healthy person. Austin College students and faculty are working to restore native prairie to Clinton and Edith Sneed's former farm. How will we know if we are successful? We need intact, healthy prairies for comparison. Fortunately, there is one three-hectare example of such a prairie a few kilometres away. That small remnant of the once vast Blackland Prairie of Texas persists because former Professor of Economics and tallgrass prairie expert Hugh Garnett recognized its unusual condition and purchased it for the sole purpose of its conservation. Dr Garnett had both the rare knowledge to recognize its stellar condition and the wherewithal to buy it with no expectation of financial return. If not for both of those circumstances and his interest and generosity, the last local example of intact prairie would almost certainly have been developed by now. The next closest example is about an hour's drive away. In other words, over thousands of square kilometres, only a few tiny patches of healthy prairie remain.

In other cases, there are no local examples of intact ecosystems. For example, as a result of damaged watershed vegetation, all streams in Grayson County, Texas, where Austin College is located, suffer from an unnatural combination of extreme runoff after rain followed by low or no flow between rains. Many streams that historically flowed during all but the most severe droughts now only flow after rains. Indeed, my students and I have observed that the greatest biological diversity in local streams is immediately downstream from wastewater treatment plants. Those are the only creeks in the area with a reliable volume of water flow every day.

Shortage of specialists

Lack of healthy ecosystems for comparison is only one obstacle to detecting and understanding ecosystem damage. Another obstacle that may surprise non-biologists is lack of experts capable of identifying relevant species. As a graduate student, I had opportunities to work as a teaching assistant in Costa Rica. One evening while eating dinner at Monteverde Cloud Forest Reserve, one of the world's most famous and heavily visited tropical preserves, I found myself talking with a young Costa Rican biologist. I no longer recall his name, but I remember the conversation. He was exceptionally modest, but knew all the tree species in the forest. Such ability is not unusual in a northern forest with a few dozen species, but a tropical forest can have hundreds of species in a few hectares, many with similar leaves and bark. I suspected few people could identify all of the Monteverde trees, but he claimed otherwise. When I pressed, he conceded that only three other people could identify the trees – his brother and two others. These are the trees of one of the most famous rainforest reserves in the world and only a few people could identify all of the trees, let alone know anything about the biology of the rarer ones.

Unfortunately, it is not unusual for only a small handful of people to have expertise in a given group of species. Like the trees of Monteverde, only a few specialists in North America and Europe can confidently identify tiny planktonic animals called rotifers – even though rotifers constitute an entire phylum, occur in virtually all fresh water and are an important food for young fish. Because almost no one knows what they are looking at, few would be capable of detecting a change in an ecosystem's rotifers, even if the necessary water samples were available. I knew there were few rotifer experts, but I was not sure how few, so I checked with one of them, Ripon College Emeritus Professor of Biology Robert Wallace. He knew of just four people in all of the United States and Canada, including himself, the same number as those who could identify the trees of Monteverde.

Perhaps you have seen a guide to the birds or trees of your area. Such guides include all local bird and tree species, but insect guides include only some species. Insect guides are not complete because for most places no one knows all the insects. For some ecosystems, even qualified ornithologists are rare. While surveying an Ecuadorian rainforest in 1993, the ornithologist Theodore Parker tragically died in a small plane crash. He could identify some four thousand tropical birds by song. Vegetation hides birds, but not their songs. No one else in the world could so readily identify the most diverse forests. The tragic death of just one biologist seriously complicated efforts to assess tropical rainforest biodiversity.[7]

> Except for the vertebrates (consisting of 63,000 described species of birds, mammals, reptiles, amphibians and fishes) and the flowering plants (with approximately 270,000 species), relatively little is collectively known about millions of kinds of fungi, algae and most diverse of all, the insects and other invertebrate animals. And that matters, a lot: These least understood minions are the foundation of the living world. They are the little things that run the Earth.[8]

Imagine if a patient was suspected of having liver disease but only a few pathologists in the entire world had the expertise to analyse a biopsy. If a tree species at Monteverde suffers from a disease, it may be difficult to find someone capable of even identifying the tree species, let alone diagnosing the disease or determining its cause. If a toxin decimates a lake's rotifers few will be able to tell, even though rotifers are critical prey of the youngest fish. That so few people have these abilities is a tragic failure of societal investment.[9]

Minimal monitoring

Even with qualified professionals available, a change in a lake's rotifers would go undetected unless someone had been monitoring their populations. Society has so far not chosen to fund much ecosystem monitoring. The consequence is a relative paucity of information on the condition of ecosystems and their species. Declines in the extent of native ecosystems, well-known species, and some taxa are obvious or becoming apparent, but the condition of individual locations and their species are often poorly known.[10] For example, as of 2021, the EPA reports that states and tribes (the entities primarily responsible for water-quality monitoring under the US Clean Water Act) have assessed only about 20 per cent of streams and rivers, 40 per cent of lakes and 30 per cent of bays.[11] Even more remarkably, many states rely upon volunteer-based water monitoring programmes that make only the simplest measurements of water temperature, turbidity, oxygen concentration and pH.[12] Many pollutants have no effect on such variables, and if they do, the effect may be transitory and thus go undetected if sampling does not coincide with a spill or other pollutant discharge. Who would propose a similar medical system? Individual and public health would depend upon a few widely scattered volunteers with stethoscopes and thermometers doing all they could, but reaching only a tiny fraction of the population. (Whether medical systems are adequate is obviously beyond our scope, but even the existing US system is far more intensive and extensive than ecosystem monitoring.)

At least monitoring is legal in most places. Incredibly, during 2015 Wyoming passed a law that made it illegal to collect evidence of pollution, apparently even on public land and even by photograph. University of Denver law professor Justin Pidot noted that the law, 'turns a good Samaritan who volunteers her time to monitor our shared environment into a criminal', and correctly predicted the law would be found unconstitutional, but the statute demonstrated the extent to which some elected officials are willing to go to prevent detection of environmental problems.[13]

Systems for tracking pollutant releases from industry provide further evidence of underinvestment in monitoring. Rather than hiring qualified, independent technicians to collect such data, industries are routinely allowed to report their own releases. The Toxic Release Inventory of the Emergency Planning and Community Right-to-Know Act requires annual reports to the EPA from states and industrial facilities that release any of 600 chemicals.

Toxic Release Inventory reports are accessible online. One facility in my area reported releasing 1,954 kg of N-methyl-2-pyrrolidone during 2019, another reported releasing 3,660 kg of styrene.[14] Such data are not independently confirmed, even by spot checking, and provide no information on whether releases happened continually at low quantities or intermittently at higher quantities and therefore higher concentrations. Presumably due to staffing limitations, the EPA has only a rudimentary system for checking the data quality based on mechanisms like looking for large changes from one year to another and suspiciously low numbers for a given type of facility. Furthermore, Toxic Release Inventory regulations do not require reporting on toxins in products themselves and exempt many toxins and toxin sources, including agriculture.[15] Though much better than nothing, the Toxic Release Inventory reflects minimal societal investment in rigorous pollution monitoring.

Effective monitoring is yet more difficult when problems cross administrative boundaries or institutional responsibilities overlap or leave gaps. The implications of such mismatches are considered more thoroughly in Chapter 17. For now, consider how they complicate detection of hazards, such as whether water quality is suitable for swimming.

Lake Texoma, a large reservoir on the Red River along the border of Oklahoma and Texas, receives treated wastewater from several towns and small cities, is surrounded by thousands of homes with septic tanks and is in a watershed with extensive livestock pastures, all potential sources of contamination. Strong thunderstorms cause tremendous runoff into the reservoir's tributaries. According to the US Army Corps of Engineers, Lake Texoma hosts no fewer than six million visits by swimmers, water skiers and others annually.[16]

At least five state and federal agencies have some responsibility for Lake Texoma and three do some water-quality sampling, but no single agency is responsible for the safety of swimmers everywhere on the lake and all are distracted by other higher priorities. As a result, there is no monitoring system capable of detecting short-term water pollution events associated with heavy rains – the sort of events that cause beach closures elsewhere.[17] The US Geological Survey has measured water quality at 11 sites in the lake, but has not tested for bacterial contamination; it is not responsible for visitor safety.[18] The Red River Authority measures the bacterium *Escherichia coli* (*E. coli*) and other indicators of sewage contamination quarterly at four sites, but not in response to rainfall events. They sample easily accessible and thus inexpensive locations, which is understandable since their mission focuses on water supply, not water safety.[19] The US Army Corps of Engineers follows standard EPA protocols and federal regulations for detecting chronic contamination at the beaches they manage and requires some other beach operators to do the same, but does not have the funding to monitor all possible recreational sites or collect measurements in response to runoff events when significant contamination would be most likely.

It is not difficult to detect this type of pollution. An Austin College undergraduate, Nichole Knesek, quickly confirmed *E. coli* contamination in Lake Texoma because she collected samples following storms in locations where pollution seemed most likely. She singlehandedly detected evidence of an improperly operated municipal wastewater treatment plant. The state and federal agencies had not discovered the problem because they had not sampled where or when problems were most likely.[20] In other words, a lone undergraduate looking where and when problems might be expected rapidly found problems undetected by three government agencies that had collected samples for years. This example demonstrates how even extensive monitoring can fail to detect important problems if those responsible for the monitoring are focused on other concerns.

A worse situation results if those responsible for monitoring have an incentive not to find problems – like the mayor in the movie *Jaws* (1975) who does not want to close the beach after a shark sighting. Local politicians were dismayed when the Army Corps of Engineers closed Lake Texoma to recreation in 2011 during a bloom of cyanobacteria. In response, some officeholders undertook unprecedented monitoring efforts and argued that the Corps of Engineers had used excessively strict criteria for closing the lake.[21] The same officials had previously displayed no apparent interest in water-quality monitoring.

More recently, when Hurricane Harvey dumped 1,270 mm of rain on the Houston area during August 2017, damaged industrial facilities released some 18,260 tons of harmful chemicals. The US National Aeronautics and Space Administration (NASA) offered to fly a pollution-monitoring airplane above Houston, but EPA and Texas officials declined the offer, supposedly because they were concerned the additional data might cause 'confusion'. Michael Honeycutt, the director of toxicology for the State of Texas told NASA officials, '… we don't think your data would be useful'. According to the same *Los Angeles Times* report, Honeycutt had previously speculated that air pollution is good for human health.[22] Meanwhile, Texas officials had removed 75 per cent of ground-based monitoring stations in advance of the hurricane, ostensibly to protect the units from damage. (Many of the industrial facilities are located in low-income neighbourhoods with populations dominated by people of colour, an issue addressed in Chapter 13.)[23]

A similar resistance to finding problems seems to occur in Canada, downstream from the tar sands mines in the Athabasca River watershed of Alberta. According to independent scientific reviews, the system for monitoring for water pollution there is woefully inadequate. A 'community group', the Regional Aquatics Monitoring Program, largely funded by energy companies, has repeatedly reported satisfactory water quality in the river, but independent reviews found those conclusions unwarranted and considered sampling deficiencies so severe that the programme has little hope of detecting water quality problems. Some reviewers have suggested that monitoring system is intended to fail to detect problems.[24]

Whereas it sounds straightforward to go out and check for a problem, problems can be difficult to detect because of uncertainty about what to look for, where to look, when to look, signals hidden in noise, a shortage of experts or a shortage of reference ecosystems to serve as models of health. The challenge is made vastly harder by society's reluctance to invest in ecosystem monitoring, relying instead largely upon volunteers, self-reporting by industry and other minimal approaches, including some with in-built conflicts of interest. Despite these challenges, many problems have been detected. The task then shifts to understanding their causes.

Notes

1   Levine et al., 'Temporal trend in sperm count', 2017; Myers et al., 'Autism spectrum disorder', 2019.
2   Green et al., 'Amphibian population declines', 2020.
3   Didham et al., 'Interpreting insect declines', 2020, 103–8.
4   Jacob Lowe, SteriCycle, personal communication, 14 October 2021.
5   Personal communication, 28 February 2022.
6   See for instance Weigel and Dimick, 'Development, validation, and application of a macroinvertebrate-based Index of Biotic Integrity for nonwadeable rivers of Wisconsin', 2011.
7   Schulenberg, 'Obituary: Theodore Parker III', 1993.
8   Wilson, 'The global solution to extinction', 2016.
9   One manifestation of poor ability to distinguish species is the remarkable tendency of so many people to kill any 'bug' they encounter indoors or even to prophylactically poison their homes on the outside chance that some dangerous arthropod may crawl or fly in. Many species are beneficial, all have ecological roles and most are harmless to humans, but overreaction is common. One of my colleagues interviewed a pest control contractor who claimed that when his work was done nothing would live in the house. That contractor did not get the job.
10 Sánchez-Bayo and Wyckhuys, 'Worldwide decline of the entomofauna', 2019; Wagner et al., 'Insect decline in the Anthropocene', 2021.
11 EPA, 'Supplemental module', 2021.
12 Overdevest et al., 'Volunteer stream monitoring and local participation in natural resource issues', 2004.
13 Gruver, 'Wyoming laws aimed at trespassing activists struck down', 2018; Pidot, 'Forbidden data', 2015; Wyoming Senate, 'Enrolled act no. 61, Senate', 2015.
14 Figures come from the EPA Toxic Release Inventory Explorer 2019 report for zip codes 75020 and 75090 (EPA, 'TRI explorer release reports', 2019). The World Health Organization and International Labour Organization's Chemical Safety Card for styrene reads, 'Do NOT let this chemical enter the environment.' The N-methyl-2-pyrrolidone card says, 'Animal tests show that this substance possibly causes toxic effects upon human reproduction.' International Labour Organization, 'International chemical safety cards (ICSCs)', n.d.; EPA, 'Toxic release inventory program', n.d.
15 Salzman and Thompson, *Environmental Law and Policy*, 2014, 225.
16 US Army Corps of Engineers, 'Welcome to Lake Texoma', n.d.
17 Kistemann et al., 'Microbial load of drinking water reservoir tributaries during extreme rainfall and runoff', 2002.
18 US Geological Survey, 'National Water Information System', n.d.
19 Red River Authority of Texas, 'Water quality monitoring programs' (at Water Quality & Planning > Clean Rivers Program > Regional Monitoring).
20 Knesek, '*Escherichia coli* concentrations in Lake Texoma', 2000; Richardson, 'Pottsboro is fined by TCEQ', 2007, A1 and A3.
21 Cannon, 'Blue-green algae health hazard in Lake Texoma', 2011, A8; Lillis et al., 'Grayson County, Texas Health Department blue-green algae response strategy', 2012.
22 Rust and Sahagún, 'Must reads: post-Hurricane Harvey, NASA tried to fly a pollution-spotting plane over Houston', 2019.
23 Phillips, 'Preparing for the next storm', 2018.
24 Nikiforuk, *Tar Sands*, 2010, 77.

4
Limits on experiments

Once detected, the next step is to understand a problem's cause or causes. As we have seen, many problems are unintended consequences of new technologies, but most products are launched without evaluation of potential side effects. Consequently, causes of new problems are often unknown. Their determination requires scientific research.

The record of science and technology in leading to flashy new products, from Mars rovers to smartphones and self-driving cars, may give the impression that scientists can quickly figure out anything. On the contrary, however, progress is often slow. If this were not the case, there would be little uncertainty regarding questions scientists have studied for years, such as the causes of honeybee colony failures or the risks of exposure to oestrogen-mimicking chemicals or solvent vapours. Perhaps most obviously, reporters would no longer ask which human diet is healthiest.[1]

If science was easy, there would be no debate about ideal diets. But diet advice varies both over time and wildly at any given time. My mother notes that when she was young eggs were considered health food; later they were considered unhealthy; now a nutrition researcher I know considers eggs a 'perfect' food. Few scientific questions are more basic than which foods promote health, and yet eggs were good, then they were bad, and now are good again. The eggs themselves have not changed, but the evidence and its interpretation have.

If science were easy, we would know whether we should eat eggs, grains, butter or beef. Much diversity of opinion regarding these and similar issues is rooted in hucksterism or ulterior motives. But disagreement and controversy would fade more quickly if scientific conclusions were comprehensive and indisputable. Science provides a powerful route to understanding natural phenomena, but it is not automatic, takes time, sometimes errs and cannot eliminate uncertainty.

Imagine the challenge of disentangling cause-and-effect relationships in a cluster of cancer cases where, as usual, dozens of contaminants occur in low concentrations in patients' blood samples. The toxicity of most contaminants has never been studied. Moreover, analysts typically have limited information regarding patients' exposures to sources of contaminants and little if any knowledge of the interactive effects of multiple contaminants.[2] Furthermore, those contaminants may have had nothing to do with the cancers. Under such circumstances, how would you determine whether the cluster is a mere coincidence or evidence of a local cause?

As every schoolchild learns, science is based upon testing hypotheses – conjectures – about relationships among variables. For example, a medical experiment might compare the effects of a new drug and a placebo on blood pressure. This is a powerful approach. If it did not work, bridges would collapse, spacecraft would miss targets and seeing a physician would be as likely to make you worse as better, maybe more so.

Science textbooks routinely illustrate the scientific method with some version of Figure 4.1, often in their first chapter. Though fundamentally correct, the diagram gives a false impression that the process of creating new scientific understanding is so straightforward that it is almost automatic. Reality is not so simple. If it were, eggs would

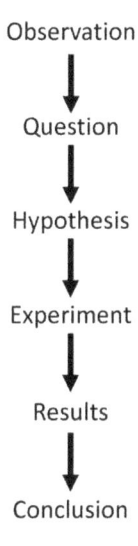

Figure 4.1: A typical textbook diagram illustrating the steps of the scientific method. Figure by the author.

not go from being good for us to bad for us to good again. Each step in the diagram presents challenges.

Sometimes it is easy to test a hypothesis and draw firm conclusions. For example, my first college chemistry course included a test of the hypothesis that salt reduces the freezing point of water. We prepared mixtures of water with different concentrations of salt and then viewed droplets of each mixture with a microscope while reducing the temperature. We noted the temperatures when ice crystals became visible. The higher the salt concentration, the lower the temperature required to freeze water. The effect is easy to observe and highly reproducible.

Unfortunately, however, environmental problems do not typically lend themselves to such simple experiments. Determination of the freezing point of a water droplet is simple; determination of whether a newly manufactured compound may harm human health, other species or ecosystem processes is not. Consequently, decades, or in the case of climate change even a century may pass between when a problem is first suspected and when experts confirm its existence and cause or causes.

This chapter and the next three describe several obstacles to determining the cause or causes of problems, such as cancer clusters. This chapter reviews ethical, financial, analytical, temporal and technological constraints upon formal experiments. By formal experiment I mean a study in which one or more variables of interest are manipulated in an attempt to test for an effect on one or more other variables of interest. For example, medical researchers might give one group of subjects a new drug formulation and another group a placebo to test the hypothesis that the new drug reduces blood pressure. Such experiments, if otherwise well designed, can detect evidence of cause-and-effect relationships. Many other useful studies, such as epidemiological studies that check for associations among variables but do not manipulate any variables, or studies that confirm a change over time in the environment, are tremendously valuable but are not formal experiments. Because no variable has been intentionally manipulated, such studies can only test for associations (correlations) among variables.

This chapter describes limitations on the types and scale of formal experiments (henceforth experiments) that scientists can perform. The next three chapters describe uncertainties associated with the use of statistical procedures to detect patterns in data, hazards of extrapolating from study results to more general circumstances, and confusion due to scientific errors. Collectively, these obstacles slow scientific progress and foster controversy by making science more challenging than implied by Figure 4.1.

Ethics

Ethical constraints preclude many potentially instructive experiments. The most obvious constraints are ethical restrictions against studies that might harm human subjects. Ethical scientists do not perform experiments that intentionally expose humans to suspected harms, such as potentially harmful chemicals. Therefore, researchers concerned about harm to humans can only run experiments on other species and extrapolate results to humans.[3] Many people consider this a sensible compromise, but humans may be more or less sensitive than other species to any given toxin. Unfortunately, there is no accepted theory regarding how to extrapolate health consequences from other species to humans (an example of the challenges of extrapolation discussed in Chapter 6).

When many people or individuals of other species already suffer from an ailment, epidemiological studies provide an alternative to experiments. Epidemiological studies retrospectively test for associations between environmental factors and one or more ailments. For example, studies have documented correlations between asthma attacks and atmospheric ozone concentration, between autism and air pollution, and between leukaemia and benzene exposure.[4] Epidemiological studies often provide the best available evidence, but uncertainties regarding individual exposures and undocumented differences among subjects complicate the interpretation of results. Furthermore, epidemiological studies are possible only after many people have been exposed to a potential hazard. The challenges of epidemiological studies are one reason for seesawing dietary recommendations. Analysts search for patterns of health or illness in groups with different dietary histories, but dietary histories are typically only one of many differences between study subjects, so effects of diets are difficult to disentangle from other factors.

Ecosystem studies face fewer ethical restrictions, but ethical considerations nevertheless constrain potential experiments. For example, some of the most instructive data on the effect of acid precipitation have come from experiments that acidified entire lakes, but the decision to acidify an entire lake cannot be taken lightly because of the tremendous consequences for the lake and all of the creatures in it. Experiments of this sort have been considered acceptable because the insights have potential to inform management and protection of thousands of similar lakes, but few such experiments have been performed because of the financial constraints discussed in the next section of this chapter.

When Austin College began to restore prairie to an old farm, I proposed using a neighbour's cattle as an analogue for the bison that historically grazed the area, but some colleagues were concerned that even carefully managed cattle would cause damage. They had observed many cases of damage due to poorly managed cattle. My colleagues eventually consented, but their reservations were reasonable and ethically based. Fortunately, the carefully managed cattle seem to be assisting the restoration.

Budgets

Experiments require expertise and equipment, but budgets are limited. Limited funding precludes innumerable potential studies. For example, the entire proposed 2018 US federal budget for basic research in natural sciences and the environment was $255 million, less than the cost of three F35 fighter airplanes and much less than one per cent of ExxonMobil's 2012 profit.[5] Larger budgets for equipment, staff and other expenses would allow more experiments, and those experiments could involve more replicates (subjects of study, such as patients in a clinical trial). More replicates generally make results more reliable.

Funding limitations are apparent from the small scale of experiments that test major human health questions. For instance, a widely reported 2014 human diet study found people lost more weight after one year on a high fat diet than a high carbohydrate diet. The results suggested that people should eat more fat and fewer carbohydrates, but the study involved only 120 people. Should millions of people consider altering their diets on the basis of one year of data for 120 others? The experiment may have had an otherwise impeccable design, but the authors would almost certainly have preferred a budget that allowed a larger, longer-term study.[6]

As noted, society has not required toxicity testing before marketing millions of manufactured chemicals.[7] In other words, no one has been willing to fund the necessary experiments. During the early 1990s, toxicologists estimated proper experiments would cost about $2 million per chemical tested. That sounds like a lot, but at that rate, after adjusting for subsequent inflation, the toxicity of all 85,000 chemicals inventoried for the Toxic Substances Control Act could be tested for about one fifth of the trillion dollar estimated lifetime cost of the F35 fighter jet programme. We have evidently been more interested in funding fighter planes than toxicity tests.[8]

Ecosystem experiments receive far less funding than human health experiments, and there are more possible cause-and-effect pathways in ecosystems than individual humans.[9] The diet study scale with 120 subjects may sound small for an important study of human health, but 120 replicates would be unprecedented for an ecological experiment. My most recent papers on zooplankton had 12 and 18 replicates respectively.[10] Neither has been criticized for inadequate replication because these are substantial numbers of replicates for ecological research.

Other evidence of financial limitations is apparent in the modest scale of ecological experiments. The largest field experiments have acidified an entire small lake or contaminated a small lake with the active ingredient in human birth control pills, but these studies manipulated only one lake in each case. They did not manipulate multiple replicate lakes as one would test a new drug on multiple people, rather than just one person.[11] Moreover, only a few research teams worldwide have sufficient budgets to perform such 'whole ecosystem' studies on even one lake, and even those have struggled to maintain funding.[12]

Most researchers are relegated instead to studying small segments of ecosystems, or facsimiles of ecosystems. For example, the Austin College's tallgrass prairie restoration experiment I manage occupies 40 hectares, about 100 acres. We would run a larger study if we could have bought the adjacent property when it was for sale, but we lacked the $300,000 purchase price.

The US National Science Foundation's Cedar Creek Ecosystem Long Term Research Station provides a much more prominent example. Cedar Creek scientists use replicate 'fields' of about 100 square metres to test fundamental hypotheses about the relationship between species diversity and ecosystem functioning (Figure 4.2).[13] This is one of the longest-running, largest-scale and most respected ecosystem experiments in the world, yet the experiments are limited to replicates the size of a small yard for attempting to understand the most fundamental questions of ecosystem ecology.

Further sense of the dearth of funding is apparent from the poor compensation of many ecological internships. For example, a state-sponsored internship on Kure Atoll in Hawaii, advertised under the heading 'Chance of a Lifetime', requested the following experience, skills and abilities: native plant propagation; shorebird and seabird monitoring and identification; data management; carpentry; solar equipment maintenance; small boat experience; and knowledge of Hawaiian plants. Interns were expected to carry 20 kg equipment loads for 16 km per day, work long hours in hot and sunny or cold and rainy conditions, be able to swim, have perfect or perfectly corrected eyesight and be able to 'bend or stoop for long periods of time'. Moreover, to avoid introducing invasive species, any shoes or other clothing brought to the site had to be purchased

Figure 4.2: Some of the small plots that serve as replicates for ecosystem experiments at the US National Science Foundation's Cedar Creek Long Term Ecological Research station. Source: US National Science Foundation Long Term Ecological Network, 'Cedar Creek Ecosystem Science Reserve', n.d.

new in Hawaii and frozen for 48 hours beforehand. Interns with these qualifications were expected to volunteer for this work, without pay. Announcements of other internship positions on the main email list for ecologists, ECOLOG-L, regularly seek similarly long lists of qualifications for unpaid work under challenging conditions.[14]

Indeed, such circumstances have raised the question whether conservation is becoming a privileged, rich-person's career because of the lack of early-career funding and expectations that applicants for paid positions have a track record of unpaid internships.[15] By comparison, during 2015 one of my eldest son's undergraduate friends held an investment banking summer internship that required no heavy lifting and paid $25,000, while the Mars Curiosity Rover mission involved 500 people in 12 countries supported by 7,000 others, all of whom were presumably working for pay, not merely volunteering.[16] Excluding those who cannot afford to accept unpaid internships and expecting financial sacrifices of others who can is yet one more way that funding limitations hamper understanding of environmental problems and therefore serve as an obstacle to environmental progress.

Analytical constraints

Experiments test hypotheses, but just because a hypothesis can be posed does not mean a suitable experiment can be designed and executed. Many hypothetical experiments cannot be run because the complexity of their designs would render the results uninterpretable.

A few terms will be useful for understanding the analytical limits on designs of formal experiments. An *independent variable* might affect another variable but could not be affected by it. Conversely, a *dependent variable* is one that might be affected by an independent variable but cannot affect an independent variable.[17] For example, salt can affect the freezing point of water but the freezing point of water cannot alter salt concentration, so salt is an independent variable and freezing point is a dependent variable. (Curiously, variables are deemed 'dependent' when an experiment tests *whether* they are affected by an independent variable, not *because* they are affected by an independent variable. Thus, dependent variables do not necessarily depend on tested independent variables.)

A *hypothesis* is a conjecture about a relationship between two or more variables. A *null hypothesis* posits that an independent variable has no effect upon a dependent variable. An *alternative hypothesis* posits that an independent variable affects a dependent variable. In the case of the salt and freezing point experiment, the alternative hypothesis was supported – that salt affects the freezing point of water.

Experiments are performed on individual *subjects*, or more formally, *experimental units*. A *factor* is an independent variable, such as salt concentration, whose quantity or condition is manipulated. Experiments test for effects of one or more factors on one or more dependent variables. A *treatment* is a particular level or condition of a factor. If an experiment involves more than one factor, a treatment may be a particular combination of levels of two or more factors. An unmanipulated treatment, in which all factors occur at natural levels, is a *control*. *Replicates* are experimental units to which the same treatment is applied. When individual humans serve as replicates, they are often called subjects.

Consider an example. If an experiment tests the effect of water pH (acidity vs. alkalinity) on the growth of individual fish in aquaria, pH is the manipulated factor. Each container of water whose pH is manipulated or left at the natural, control, value, is a replicate of a particular treatment (pH level).

Such a study could also include other factors. For example, it could include multiple species of fish or manipulate other aspects of water chemistry besides pH. The simplest experiments test only two levels of one factor. Complex experiments typically manipulate more than two levels of two or more factors.

One dependent variable in the pH experiment could be the growth rate of individual fish. Researchers could also measure other dependent variables, such as survival, fat content or some other measure of fish health. Experiments often measure multiple dependent variables after manipulating one or more independent variables.

Manipulated factors are not the only independent variables. Any variable whose state or magnitude cannot be affected by the manipulation of other independent variables is itself an independent variable. For example, in the pH experiment, the temperature and oxygen concentration of the water would be additional independent variables.

While manipulating one or more independent variables, researchers typically hold others constant to avoid unwanted sources of variation in results. For example, a simple study of pH on fish growth would place individual fish in separate aquaria and expose each to a particular pH. To maximize the chance of detecting any effect of pH, some other variables held constant could include aquarium size, water source, water temperature and water oxygen concentration. Furthermore, the researchers might use a single size, sex and species of fish. Holding these other variables constant increases the chance of detecting any effect of pH on growth rate because these other variables might have their own effects. (Holding other independent variables constant is often referred to as 'controlling' those variables, but that use of the term 'control' should not be confused with a 'control' treatment in which no variables are manipulated.)

But what if the effect of pH depends on the level of some other independent variable that has been held constant? For example, perhaps the effect of pH depends on the temperature of the water. In this case, if the experiment is performed at only one water temperature, the results could be misleading if applied to circumstances with other water temperatures.

Data analysts use the term 'interaction' for the situation where the effect of one independent variable depends on the level of another independent variable. You are probably familiar with some such interactions. For example, my mother was prescribed a statin drug to reduce cholesterol. Her doctor instructed her to avoid grapefruit because compounds in grapefruit increase the effective dose of statins and therefore increase the chance of undesirable side effects. In the terminology of data analysis, something in grapefruit interacts with the effect of statins. Interactions are common. You have probably seen or heard warnings against consuming alcohol when taking certain medications or seen advertisements that list various contraindications for prescribing advertised drugs.

Interactions also affect ecosystems. For example, acid rain falling on a lake underlain by limestone bedrock has little effect, but the same acid rain can kill fish and other creatures in a lake underlain by granite. Limestone dissolves in and neutralizes acid but granite does not. One can observe this effect in cemeteries. Acid rain dissolves limestone tombstones, eventually rendering their inscriptions illegible, but granite tombstones resist the acid and thus still look new after a century or more.

Multiple, independent environmental hazards often have additive effects that are worse in combination than individual threats alone. For example, salmon simultaneously face threats from fishing, diversion of water from rivers, migration barriers (dams), muddy logging runoff, pollution, and genetic contamination and parasites from aquaculture.[18] Amphibians suffer from non-native fungi, non-native predators, ultraviolet radiation, habitat loss, acidification and pollution.[19] The decline in pollinating insects is apparently a result of the combined effects of multiple pesticides, parasites inadvertently brought from overseas, loss of native food plants and habitat loss.[20]

The potential for complex interactive effects is even greater in ecosystems than in individual humans because ecosystems have so many more components. Multitudes of species interacting in countless ways create circumstances where a single factor, such as a change in temperature or increase in ultraviolet radiation, can potentially affect hundreds of processes.[21] For example, when acid deposition reduces the pH of lake water, effects could impact each individual of hundreds of species. Meanwhile, the acid will also alter the solubility of chemicals in the water. Those chemical changes may subsequently harm some species but not others. Imagine a predator and prey species in an ecosystem, such as a fish and a small aquatic insect. As Schindler and his colleagues found, a reduction in pH could be toxic to the insect, driving it extinct from the system, while the fish is not obviously directly harmed by the pH change. But the loss of the insect could doom the fish population through elimination of an important food source. Ecologists call the pH effect on the insect a *direct* effect and the effect of the pH change on the fish (by way of the insect) an *indirect* effect. Indirect effects are ubiquitous.[22]

Given the possibility of interactive, additive and even potentially synergistic or multiplicative effects of multiple hazards, it might seem logical to run experiments with every plausible combination of potential hazards. However, such massive experiments would face insurmountable logistical barriers and require unheard-of budgets. Even if the logistics were manageable and budgets were adequate, statistical complexities beyond our scope would render the results uninterpretable because a vast number of interactions that cannot be disentangled could account for any given measurement of a dependent variable.[23] Thus, it is not feasible to run experiments to test cause-and-effect relationships of combinations of multiple pesticides in a beehive or dozens of low-concentration, man-made chemicals in your bloodstream or mine. An exasperated doctor once told me of a patient – anonymously of course – who came to her after having been prescribed six different psychoactive medicines. The doctor exclaimed: 'No one in the world knows the effect of combining these drugs.' No one knows because the necessary experiments are effectively impossible to perform.

Because experiments with multiple factors are uninterpretable, expensive, and logistical nightmares, researchers rarely attempt experiments with more than a few treatments. For example, the US Centers for Disease Control Agency for Toxic Substances and Disease Registry reported only fourteen analyses of chemical mixtures as of October 2021, two more than it reported in 2013.[24] That is 12 mixtures, not 12 per cent of all possible mixtures, and this is the case even though interactions between medications and environmental contaminants were first detected decades ago.[25] With thousands of chemicals in use, the number of possible mixtures is astronomical. Consequently, we not only lack information on the toxicity of most chemicals acting alone, we have little information on their interactive effects. What is in your processed food, shampoo, body wash, deodorant, sunscreen or makeup? I hope it all is harmless, individually and in combination, but the fact is, in the vast majority of cases no one knows.

Complex interactions create another barrier to experimentation. Experiments are designed to test particular hypotheses. Thus, hypotheses must be imagined before experiments are executed. When cause-and-effect pathways are complex, the explanatory hypotheses may not have been imagined, just as chlorofluorocarbons were used for decades before anyone imagined a risk to stratospheric ozone.

Consider an example. Several years ago, rare birds started washing up dead along the shores of the Great Lakes. Researchers eventually identified a complex cause-and-effect pathway that began with the introduction of small Eurasian molluscs called zebra and quagga mussels (*Dreissena polymorpha* and *Dreissena bugensis*). Biologists had raised concerns about these and other non-native species introductions, but the pathway to the bird deaths is so complex and circuitous that even experienced invasive-species biologists could not have been expected to imagine it.

The mussels were inadvertently spread during the late 1980s from ships that had taken on mussel larvae in ballast water at Eurasian ports. Mussels feed by filtering planktonic algae from water. After multiplying in the Great Lakes, they filtered so much algae that the lakes' waters became clearer. Thanks to clearer water, more light reached the lake bottoms, which enabled the filamentous alga *Cladophora* to thrive attached to rocks. Sand stirred up by waves scrapes *Cladophora* off the rocks, after which it accumulates on beaches and in deeper water during calmer weather. Decomposition of accumulated *Cladophora* in deep water creates anaerobic conditions that foster growth of *Clostridium botulinum*, which produces a neurotoxin responsible for botulism. The *Clostridium* and its toxin disperse in the water.

Mussels filter the *Clostridium* from the water and then are eaten by small (also non-native) fish called gobies. The gobies become paralyzed by the botulism toxin, rise towards the surface, and thus become easy prey for birds and larger fish. Both the larger fish and birds die and wash up on beaches, where yet other birds are poisoned by scavenging the dead fish. As of 2011, more than 90,000 loons, grebes and other waterfowl had died.[26] One might have anticipated increased growth of attached algae on rocks due to water made clearer by mussels' filtering, but I am unaware of anyone anticipating botulism outbreaks or bird deaths, and botulism outbreaks are only one of several food web changes associated with the mussel invasion.

Unfortunately, surprise shifts in food webs like the effect of these mussels on Great Lakes waterfowl are not unusual. The multitude of indirect effects in ecosystems has resulted in a track record of surprising ecological changes in response to human impacts and natural variation.[27] Experienced ecologists can predict that complex consequences will occur, but cannot reliably predict which complex consequences will occur or even imagine all of the reasonable possibilities, and therefore cannot be expected to run tests of unimagined processes. Rather, they are often limited to piecing together complex cause-and-effect pathways from disparate evidence, more like a detective solving a crime than a chemist synthesizing new compounds in a lab.

> … no matter how intently one studies the hundred little dramas of the woods and meadows, one can never learn all of the salient facts about any one of them.[28]

Urgency

Time creates another constraint. Policymakers need information sooner rather than later. Even if one had replicate Earths with which to run climate-change experiments, a 100-year experiment would be little help for informing policy now. The difficulty of studying slow processes, such as the growth of trees or whales, changes in soil or how childhood exposure to a potential carcinogen might cause cancer in the elderly, forces scientists to seek understanding from short-term experiments on related phenomena. One might, for example, fertilize a forest with carbon dioxide for a few years and measure tree rings to try to understand the consequences of higher atmospheric carbon dioxide concentrations, but it would be difficult to predict long-term consequences for an entire forest from such short-term experiments. Indirect effects might need more time to manifest and might be reflected in something other than tree-growth rates. Faster immediate growth might, for instance, deplete a soil nutrient, resulting in slower future growth. Or faster growth might reduce protein content of leaves, thereby reducing their nutritional value for caterpillar larvae. Fewer, smaller larvae could then impact birds, which could then affect dispersal of tree seeds, which could then affect the future composition of the forest, and so on. But these effects could require many years to manifest – time frames too long to inform policy now.

Technological and logistical constraints

Finally, lack of measurement technology or suitable systems to study preclude otherwise potentially instructive experiments. Some experiments are infeasible because necessary technology does not exist. Others are infeasible because the systems of interest cannot be studied as intact wholes.

Even if a biologist had proposed, in the Great Lakes example, that non-native mussels might lead to bird deaths from botulism poisoning, they would not have been able to test the complete cause-and-effect pathway in grand experiments because such experiments would be unethical, unaffordable and in any case infeasible because suitable study subjects do not exist. Scientists can manipulate a small lake, but not an entire Great Lake, and if they could, they would not. Rather, scientists are often limited to reductionist experiments that divide a system into components and test the effects of manipulations on those isolated components. For example, one could test whether zebra mussels clarify aquarium water, whether accumulations of *Cladophora* foster growth of *Clostridium* and whether fish poisoned by *Clostridium* are especially vulnerable to birds. But it would require a leap of faith to believe that the results of a suite of such reductionist experiments could suffice for predicting the actual effects of zebra mussel invasions, and even if they did, they would only support predictions regarding one effect of the mussels. Such experiments would be like trying to anticipate the effects of a drug on a patient after only administering the drug to separate organs in isolation. The experiments would provide useful information and some resulting predictions may turn out correct, but any experienced analyst would be wary of undetected consequences not apparent from such short-term reductionist experiments.

In other cases, scientists do not have the measurement technology to track variables of interest and must settle for measuring other, less instructive variables. As noted, my friend Professor Hugh MacIsaac dreams of sticking his finger in a lake and knowing everything about it, like the *Star Trek* doctor who scans patients with what looks like a cell phone and provides an immediate diagnosis, but neither technology exists. (Moreover, modest budgets often prevent ecologists from using the most powerful technology that does exist.) Useful probes and sensors of various sorts are available, but they are expensive and cannot measure everything of interest.

Any experienced scientist could describe constraints posed by technological limitations. For example, it would be easier to track the progress of the Austin College prairie restoration if we could take aerial photographs and use computer software to automatically tally the abundance and locations of every plant, but aerial photographs do not have adequate resolution to identify all species, and image analysis software cannot make sufficiently subtle distinctions. Therefore, people capable of identifying plants must walk through fields and record observations. This produces data for dozens of locations in each field, but it takes days each year and only accounts for a fraction of plant species in a fraction of each field.

To summarize this and the previous chapter, consider how monitoring challenges and constraints on experiments would collectively hinder diagnosis of a fish population crash in, for example, the Baltic Sea. The Baltic has been fished for hundreds of years and receives pollution from several nations. Since fish are unevenly distributed, mobile and not visible from the surface, a population crash will only be detectable if it is so pronounced that it appears in catch records or if researchers happen to have collected detailed, long-term measurements of fish abundance.

If a decline is detected, many causes could be responsible, including overfishing, climate change, pollution, interactions among species (including newly arrived, non-native species) or a combination of these or other factors. Because researchers cannot set up replicate Baltics, and it would be unethical to intentionally manipulate the entire sea, experiments must investigate the problem indirectly, such as with laboratory experiments on the effect of temperature or pollutants on species of concern. If researchers confirm a decline in abundance and narrow the cause down to, for instance, reduced reproduction because of pollution, they still must determine which of thousands of contaminants is responsible. Clearly, understanding the cause of such a fishery crash could be much more complicated than implied by simple diagrams like Figure 4.1. The diagram portrays the essence of science, but scientific progress is not as simple, fast or certain as the diagram suggests.

Problems cannot be prevented until their causes are understood. Determination of causes often requires experiments, but many potentially instructive experiments would be unethical, prohibitively expensive, analytically intractable, too slow to produce results or precluded by logistical or technological limitations. Thus, scientists often cannot test the hypotheses of greatest interest because they cannot perform the necessary experiments. They are therefore limited to testing related hypotheses with the best feasible experiments. Once results are available, appropriate conclusions often remain uncertain because of limitations of statistical analyses and the challenge of extrapolating from experimental conditions to general circumstances, the topics of the next two chapters.

Notes

1   Bushnell, 'Solvents, ethanol, car crashes and tolerance', 2013; Goulson, 'An overview of the environmental risks posed by neonicotinoid insecticides', 2013; Hristov et al., 'Factors associated with honey bee colony losses', 2020; Kidd et al., 'Collapse of a fish population after exposure to a synthetic estrogen', 2007; O'Connor, 'Is there an optimal diet for humans?', 2018; Patel et al., 'Pharmaceuticals of emerging concern in aquatic systems', 2019, 3561–7; Siviter et al., 'Agrochemicals interact synergistically to increase bee mortality', 2021.
2   Duncan, 'The pollution within', 2006.
3   Of course, there are also ethical concerns associated with running experiments on other species but so far society has generally considered the value of many such studies worth the harm imposed on the subjects. This is a contentious issue, with strong resistance, for example, to testing cosmetics on animals or using primates in medical or toxicological research.
4   Bushnell, 'Solvents, ethanol, car crashes and tolerance', 2013; Laumbach, 'Outdoor air pollutants and patient health', 2010; Roberts et al., 'Perinatal air pollutant exposures and autism spectrum disorder in the children of Nurses' Health Study II participants', 2013.
5   Insinna, 'Inside America's dysfunctional trillion-dollar fighter-jet program', 2019; Isidore, 'Exxon Mobil profit is just short of record', 2013; US National Science Foundation, 'Federal R&D funding, by budget function', 2019 (see table 4 at 'Data tables: Federal budget authority for R&D and R&D plant').
6   Bazzano et al., 'Effects of low-carbohydrate and low-fat diets', 2014.
7   Salzman and Thompson, *Environmental Law and Policy*, 2014, 210–12.
8   Erickson, 'How many chemicals are in use today?', 2017; Insinna, 'Inside America's dysfunctional trillion-dollar fighter-jet program', 2019; Yang, 'Introduction to the toxicology of chemical mixtures', 1994, 3.

9   It is difficult to tally the total amount of money spent on research on a given subject from all government and private sources, but the relative scales of the budgets for the US National Institutes of Health and the National Science Foundation give some sense of the difference in funding for health versus environmental research. As of 2019, the National Institutes of Health budget was $38 billion per year, some five times the 7.8 billion dollar National Science Foundation budget. Moreover, only a small fraction of the National Science Foundation budget is invested in environmental research. National Institutes of Health funding for diabetes alone was $1.1 billion, more than ten times the entire National Science Foundation budget for biological sciences (and only about 20 per cent of the biological sciences budget is allocated for environmental research), so the National Institutes of Health diabetes research budget is some fifty times the National Science Foundation environmental biology budget. See US National Science Foundation, 'NSF & Congress', n.d.; US National Science Foundation, 'FY 2022 budget request to Congress', n.d.; US National Institutes of Health, 'Total NIH budget authority', n.d.; US National Institutes of Health, 'Estimates of funding for various research, condition, and disease categories (RCDC)', 2021.

10 Schulze et al., 'The effect of suspended sediments on Lake Texoma *Daphnia*', 2006; Schulze, 'Evidence that fish structure the zooplankton communities of turbid lakes and reservoirs', 2011.

11 Kidd et al., 'Collapse of a fish population after exposure to a synthetic estrogen', 2007; Schindler et al., 'Long-term ecosystem stress', 1985.

12 *CBC News*, 'Funding for experimental lakes area brings stability, opportunity for research', 2016; McDiarmid, 'Budget cuts claim famed freshwater research facility', 2012.

13 Tilman et al., 'Biodiversity and ecosystem stability in a decade-long grassland experiment', 2006.

14 State of Hawai'i Department of Land and Natural Resources, Division of Forestry and Wildlife, Kura Atoll internship, announced by email 5 January 2015.

15 Hance, 'A rich person's profession?', 2017.

16 Lakdawalla, 'Drilling with Curiosity', 2018.

17 Some statistical analyses treat particular variables as 'independent' and others as 'dependent' even when no variables have been manipulated (studies that do not involve formal experiments). This often occurs when it is not feasible to manipulate the variables of interest, such as in epidemiological studies. In such cases, 'dependent' variables may affect 'independent' variables. For example, a study might treat age, height, weight and blood pressure as independent variables and test for an association of one or more of those with annual income, which would thus be treated as a dependent variable. However, annual income might affect (even if indirectly) weight or blood pressure, in which case an 'independent' variable would depend on a 'dependent' variable. The latter is not possible in formal (manipulative) experiments.

18 Miller, 'In central California, coho salmon are on the brink', 2010; Tian et al., 'A ubiquitous tire rubber-derived chemical induces acute mortality in coho salmon', 2020.

19 Blaustein et al., 'The complexity of amphibian population declines', 2011; James Collins, 'Amphibian decline and extinction', 2010.

20 Hristov et al., 'Factors associated with honey bee colony losses', 2020.

21 Blaustein et al., 'The complexity of amphibian population declines', 2011; Hristov et al., 'Factors associated with honey bee colony losses', 2020.

22 Schindler et al., 'Long-term ecosystem stress', 1985.

23 Cox, 'Interaction', 1984, 18–19.

24 US Centers for Disease Control, Agency for Toxic Substances and Disease Registry, 'Interaction Profiles for Toxic Substances', n.d.

25 Conney and Burns, 'Metabolic interactions among environmental chemicals and drugs', 1972; Todd et al., 'Toxicological Profile for Diazinon', 2008; Wu et al., 'Influence of cimetidine on the toxicity and toxicokinetics of Diazinon in the rat', 1996.

26 Ricciardi and MacIsaac, 'Impacts of biological invasions on freshwater ecosystems', 2011, 217.

27 Blaustein et al., 'The complexity of amphibian population declines', 2011; Doak et al., 'Understanding and predicting ecological dynamics', 2008; Hristov et al., 'Factors associated with honey bee colony losses', 2020; Ricciardi and MacIsaac, 'Impacts of biological invasions on freshwater ecosystems', 2011; Sinclair and Byrom, 'Understanding ecosystem dynamics for conservation of biota', 2006, 65–71 and 74–5; Yeakel and Dunne, 'Modern lessons from ancient food webs', 2015.

28 Leopold, *A Sand County Almanac*, 1949, 32–3.

5
Probabilistic reasoning

While the adage that 'statistics don't lie but liars use statistics' draws attention to liars, it belies a misunderstanding of statistics. Statistics can lie – or at least fool. Statisticians understand this, but statistical novices often do not.

If statistics do not lie and scientists move methodically from observations to conclusions, then competent, honest, objective scientists employing statistical tests will quickly answer scientific questions. But, as we have seen, the scientific process is more complicated than simple diagrams imply. In practice, it is often difficult to detect problems (Chapters 2 and 3), identify causes (Chapter 4 and this chapter) and know what to infer from scientific results (Chapter 6). As we shall see in this chapter, statistical tests are useful for characterizing uncertainty, but they cannot eliminate uncertainty.

Data complexity

Some processes are simple and their understanding straightforward, such as the effect of salt on the freezing point of water. One can easily obtain highly reproducible results demonstrating that effect. The resulting data would look like the left graph in Figure 5.1, with a lower freezing temperature as salt concentration increases. Simple cause-and-effect processes combined with precisely reproducible measurements from simple experiments often result in this sort of obvious relationship. Reasonable people agree about the correct descriptions of such patterns. For example, reasonable people would agree that the graph on the left shows that freezing temperature declines as salt concentration increases.

But the correct interpretation may be unclear when data result from more complex processes. Data for tests on the effect of water pH (acidity or

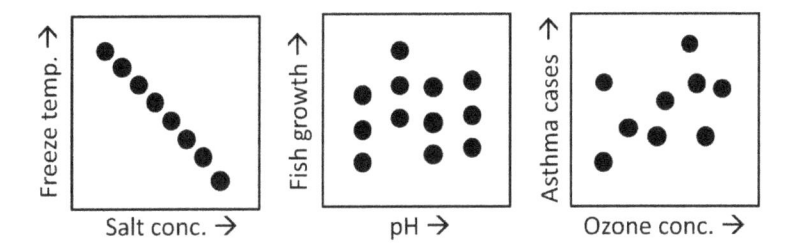

Figure 5.1: Variation in clarity of patterns in hypothetical data. Figure by the author.

alkalinity) on the growth rate of fish might produce the middle graph. Repeated tests at a given pH would not give precisely the same results because different fish are not identical, genetically or otherwise, and therefore may respond differently to pH. Does the middle graph suggest an intermediate pH is optimal? That growth increases as pH increases? Or that there is no clear relationship between pH and growth rate? Reasonable people might disagree about how to interpret the middle graph.

Consider the messier situation that would result from testing for a relationship between ozone concentrations and incidence of asthma attacks. Such data would not be based on a highly controlled experiment like a test of the effect of salt concentration on freezing point, or water pH on fish growth, but rather on ozone measurements in various locations combined with reports of asthma attacks from similar locations. Meanwhile individual asthmatics, like fish, are not identical. Data from such a study might look something like the graph on the right. Do you perceive evidence of a relationship between those variables? Here again, reasonable people might disagree.

Statistical tests are useful when reasonable people would disagree about whether data show a pattern or about how a pattern should be described, because statistical tests provide an objective means of testing for evidence of a pattern and describing pattern features.

Coincidence versus cause and effect

Statistical tests use probability theory to calculate the likelihood that a random process would produce a pattern at least as pronounced as an observed result. Statistical tests cannot distinguish random apparent patterns from actual relationships among variables, and they certainly cannot determine why variables may be related. Rather, *they merely calculate how frequently a random process would produce at least as pronounced a pattern in data.*

Statistical tests are useful, but they cannot avoid two hazards. First, sometimes they fail to detect a relationship among variables. Second, at other times they suggest variables are related when an apparent pattern is actually coincidental. These hazards are intrinsic to statistical tests. No one has devised a means to prevent them.[1]

Consider another hypothetical example. Imagine that five people who work in the same building develop frequent headaches. Assume these people have nothing in common except working in the same building. Does something about working in the building cause headaches or is the situation a mere coincidence? Without more information, you cannot be sure. Neither can a statistical test. After all, statistical tests merely apply calculations to numbers, producing other numbers.

Consider a simpler, less fraught example. Imagine you saw two dice lying on a table as in Figure 5.2. Would you conclude that they landed that way randomly or that someone intentionally set them that way? You might be willing to bet whether the dice had been rolled or placed, but if the only available information is what you see in the photo, you simply could not *know* how the dice got that way. The best data analyst in the world has no way to overcome the same predicament. Without more evidence, there is no way to know for certain how the dice got that way or whether five cases of illness in one building are merely a coincidence.

Figure 5.2: Did these dice land this way after being rolled, or were they set this way? Photographer: Peter C. Schulze.

So what good are statistical tests? Would they be helpful for determining whether a building is carcinogenic? Recall that statistical tests do one thing: calculate the probability that random variation would lead to a pattern in data at least as pronounced as an observed pattern. If the calculated chance is high, analysts conclude they have insufficient evidence that the variables are related. In the headache example, they would conclude that the headaches could easily co-occur merely by coincidence[2] – in other words, the data are not sufficient for rejecting the null hypothesis that there is no relationship among the tested variables (headache occurrence and work location). On the other hand, if the calculated chance is low, analysts conclude the data are consistent with an alternative hypothesis – such as that the measured variables are related, or more precisely, the data are consistent with the hypothesis that the headaches result from something about the common experience of the patients.

How much chance is there of rolling two ones as in the photo? Each die has a one sixth chance of showing one dot. The probability of two independent events both happening is the product of their individual probabilities, so the likelihood of rolling two ones at once is one sixth multiplied by one sixth. Thus, we can expect a pair of ones in 1 of 36 rolls of two dice, or roughly three times in 100 rolls. Of course, because this is a chance process, it may happen more or less often if you test it by rolling dice. But if you roll a pair of dice thousands of times, you will get two ones about 3 per cent of the time.

How statistics work

The procedure for calculating the chance of rolling two ones is a simple case of the same procedure used in statistical tests. Statistical tests calculate how often chance alone would produce a pattern at least as strong as an observed pattern.

Such an after-the-fact calculation cannot enable one to determine whether dice in a photograph were intentionally placed or randomly rolled. For the same reason, a statistical calculation alone cannot enable determination of whether several cases of an illness are a coincidence or not. Such calculations merely estimate the frequency with which chance alone would produce as notable an observation.

The end-product of such statistical tests is a *p-value*, the probability that a random process, such as rolling dice, would be expected to generate a pattern as strong as an observed pattern. Thus, the p-value for rolling two ones is one thirty-sixth, or about 0.03. Statistical tests such as regression and analysis of variance require more complicated calculations, but they ultimately produce p-values ranging between zero and one. A p-value of 0.001 means there is one chance in a thousand of a random process producing as strong a pattern. A p-value of 0.50 means a random process would produce as pronounced a pattern one half of the time.

Such calculations are so often misunderstood and misused that in 2016 the American Statistical Association published a statement on proper uses of p-values, which was followed by an entire 2019 issue of *American Statistician* with further guidance.[3] Interested readers should consult those sources. Here, I merely seek to explain how limitations of statistical procedures serve as an obstacle to understanding environmental phenomena and therefore an obstacle to environmental progress.

Calculating a p-value for a group of people experiencing headaches is more complicated than for a roll of two dice. In the headache case, the calculation would need to consider factors such as the frequency of headaches in the larger population and the number of people in the building who do not get headaches. However, the basic result would be the same, a calculation of the likelihood that a random process would result in at least as strong a pattern as that observed. (In this case, 'at least as strong a pattern' would mean the chance of five or more people in the building experiencing frequent headaches.)

After collecting data and making statistical calculations, researchers have three things on which to base conclusions. They have prior understanding of the general subject,[4] the data for the case in question and a calculation of the likelihood that a random process would produce a pattern as strong as whatever they observed (a p-value). Analysts then use p-value calculations to determine whether a result is 'statistically significant'. Statistical significance is shorthand for calling a pattern in data strong enough to consider it consistent with a hypothesis that the variables in question are related. For example, a statistically significant result regarding the headache cases would be consistent with the hypothesis that something the employees have in common is responsible for the headaches. Note that 'consistent with' by no means equals 'is proof of', as we shall see.

How strong a pattern should analysts require before attributing statistical significance? In other words, how small a p-value is sufficient to conclude data are consistent with a hypothesis of a relationship among the variables? Unfortunately, there is no theoretical basis for determining a correct answer to this critical question. Instead, merely by *convention* analysts have generally considered p-values of 0.05 and lower statistically significant. In other words, most analysts have considered results statistically significant if random processes would produce as pronounced a pattern in no more than five per cent of cases. Of course, there is really little difference between a p-value of 0.04 and 0.08, let alone between 0.049 and 0.051, but 0.05 has often been treated as a categorical threshold despite its definition and its basis only in convention. The American Statistical Association warns against such simplistic usage, with some authors advocating abandonment of the term 'statistically significant' because it has so often been interpreted to indicate so much more than it does.

Without getting into the nuances of p-value interpretation or whether to use the term statistically significant, the lower the p-value, the more reason to suspect the headaches have resulted from something patients have in common. On the other hand, the higher the p-value, the more reason to conclude present evidence is compatible with the hypothesis that the cluster of headache cases is mere coincidence.

There are only two possibilities, either the patients have all been exposed to the same causative agent or the cases are coincidental. Without additional evidence, even the most expert analysts cannot draw certain conclusions about whether something about the building causes headaches. They cannot determine *whether* chance processes caused the observed pattern. They can merely conclude how likely such a pattern would be on the basis of chance alone.

False negatives

Perhaps you have recognized the two errors possible in every analysis based on a p-value calculation. Analysts can conclude a pattern is consistent with the hypothesis of some relationship among variables when there is no such relationship – the apparent pattern in data is mere coincidence – and analysts can fail to detect evidence of a relationship that *does* exist.[5] Statisticians call these 'type I' and 'type II' errors respectively, presumably so the rest of us will have difficulty remembering which is which. Table 5.1 shows the four possible combinations of the real state of the world (top row) and analysts' conclusions (left column) for any given hypothesis test.

A type I error occurs when analysts conclude data support a hypothesis of a relationship among variables when, in fact, the variables are unrelated (the apparent relationship is coincidental). A type II error occurs when researchers fail to detect evidence of a relationship, but the variables are indeed related, as when for months during early 2020, the World Health Organization held that masks were not helpful for deterring the spread of COVID-19 because they erroneously concluded fine aerosols

Table 5.1: Possible outcomes of statistical analyses

	Variables unrelated	Variables related
Results consistent with alternative hypothesis of relationship among variables	**Statistical result misleading: type I error**	Statistical result matches the true state of the world
Results consistent with null hypothesis of no relationship among variables	Statistical result matches the true state of the world	**Statistical result misleading: type II error**

The two possible circumstances regarding whether variables are related (top row) and the two possible results of a statistical test for evidence of a relationship (left column), giving four possible combinations of circumstances and statistical results, only two of which are correct.

did not transmit the virus.[6] False positives result from type I errors. False negatives result from type II errors. In the absence of other evidence, analysts cannot know whether a p-value has led them to a correct conclusion or to type I or II error.

Others have distinguished type I and II errors with the story of the boy who cried wolf. The boy first cries wolf when there is no wolf. The villagers believe him – committing a type I error. Later, when there really is a wolf, he cries wolf again, but they no longer believe him – committing a type II error. Type I errors conclude nothing is something. Type II errors conclude something is nothing. Type I and II errors are technical examples of a common, familiar phenomenon: false impressions.[7]

Risks of type I and II errors are a major reason why careful analysts qualify their conclusions. Returning to the headache cluster example, careful analysts would either state that data *are consistent with the hypothesis that there is a common causative agent responsible for the headaches* or that *they have inadequate evidence that any apparent pattern is more than mere coincidence*. Careful analysts will not write 'We have proven there is a relationship between the variables', or 'There is no relationship between the variables.' If the boy who cried wolf had been a good statistician, he would have run to the village screaming, 'My observations are consistent with the hypothesis of a wolf.' (If he had been a good biologist, he would not have been scared of a healthy wolf.)

The high bar of a low p-value. Type I errors (false positives) are a problem for the progress of science in general, but type II errors (false negatives) are particularly relevant for our purposes because they cause hazards to go undetected. What is more, type II errors are common. To understand why this is so, first consider the choice of a p-value of 0.05 as the threshold for concluding data are consistent with an alternative (rather than null) hypothesis.

Why choose 0.05 as the p-value threshold? Why not use a higher p-value, such 0.1, 0.2 or even 0.5? The convention of requiring a low p-value before concluding data provide evidence of a relationship exists for a good reason – to avoid jumping to conclusions. Researchers agree not to conclude that data support a hypothesis of a relationship among variables until evidence is compelling. They set this high bar of a low p-value because research builds on prior research. One errant conclusion that a relationship exists could lead much subsequent research astray.

When results are not 'statistically significant', researchers conclude they lack adequate evidence to support the hypothesis that the variables in question are related, which is correctly interpreted as, 'We do not know whether the variables are related.' Such a conclusion is unlikely to lead careful researchers astray because experienced researchers realize type II errors (false negatives) are common and thus the variables may indeed be related even though, by the criterion of a p-value, insufficient evidence supports that conclusion. If they are deeply interested in the question, they can study it further.

In contrast, type I errors (false positives) can lead researchers seriously astray. Subsequent studies may accept such a conclusion and attempt to build upon it. In theory, someone else will test whether they can reproduce the same result – whether the result is reproducible – but in practice this may not occur. It is more fun to find something new than confirm something old; there may be no funding available to repeat someone else's study; and new discoveries advance careers more than confirmation of others' prior discoveries.[8]

Consider one small example of how research relies on the correctness of prior conclusions. My master's degree research analysed distributions of zooplankton in Lake Michigan.[9] I drew conclusions about which zooplankton occur at which depths and proposed an explanation. Like practically any explanation, mine hinged not only on my data, but also on extensive prior understanding of a set of cause-and-effect processes established by others. Thus, my explanation required not only that I interpreted my data correctly, but also that several prior studies had all reached correct conclusions about relationships among variables. I found the equivalent of evidence of an association between A and H, but that conclusion hinged upon A causing B, B causing C, and so on to H. However, I only measured A and H. I did not study the six steps between. I had read published evidence consistent with the conclusions that A caused B, B caused C and so on, so I concluded the complete set of results were consistent with the hypothesis that A caused H by way of the intervening steps.

My conclusion was reasonable – if all the prior authors drew correct conclusions. But if any of them had made a type I error, my explanation would have been wrong. Thus, I benefited from my predecessors guarding against premature conclusions. In other words, I benefited from my predecessors using a low p-value as a threshold for concluding they had evidence of a relationship among variables. (As far as I know, my chain of conclusions is still sound, but future research may reveal a type I error somewhere in the chain.)

Since new studies routinely depend on previous studies in this manner, careful researchers place a premium on avoiding hasty conclusions that variables are related. In other words, we wish to avoid type I errors. Thus, we agree to require a low p-value threshold for concluding data are consistent with a hypothesis of a relationship among variables. This makes sense for basic research, *but it creates an obstacle to detecting hazards – an obstacle that might be called 'the high bar of a low p-value'.*

A low p-value threshold creates a low risk of type I error, *but at the cost of increasing the risk of type II error* (Figure 5.3). In much basic research this is not a tremendous problem. If I had failed to detect some influence on the depths of Lake Michigan zooplankton (that is, if I had made a type II error) no tremendous harm would have resulted. Someone else would eventually have collected more compelling evidence, and no great hazard would have existed in the meantime. No one would have died.

But what if I had been studying a new industrial procedure that harms workers, a newly manufactured chemical that damages

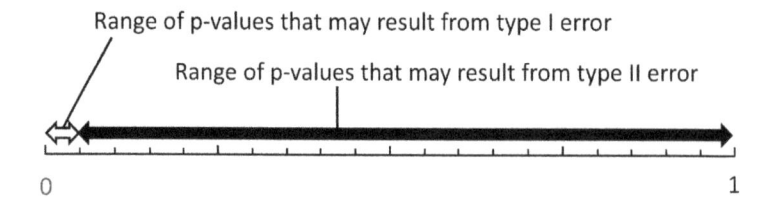

Figure 5.3: Range of possible p-values. Note how much larger a range of p-values may result in a type II error (false negative) than a type I error (false positive). Figure by the author.

stratospheric ozone or a new pesticide that inadvertently kills harmless endangered species? In these cases, if a hazard went undetected due to a type II error, serious harm could have occurred before some other study reached the correct conclusion. Moreover, if an initial study finds no evidence of a hazard, others might not bother to look harder, especially if they misinterpreted 'no evidence of a relationship' as meaning 'no relationship'.[10]

Every conclusion that evidence is insufficient to support a hypothesis of a relationship among variables risks a type II error. Thus, all analyses that fail to detect evidence of a hazard risk type II errors because data analyses underlie such decisions (unless the decisions have even less basis), and practically any analysis of complex data will involve p-value calculations. In other words, decisions that processes are sufficiently safe rely upon an absence of type II errors, but type II errors are common and – without doing further research – analysts have no way to know when they have occurred.

Whereas we expect type I errors in roughly one in twenty statistical tests, type II errors are more likely. Their precise probability depends on four factors, the p-value threshold (which as we have seen is typically set at 0.05), the strength of the association between the variables, the amount of variation in measurements of the variables, and the number of replicates in each treatment or the number of samples in a correlational study. When strongly related variables are studied with methods that produce highly reproducible measurements in experiments with many replicates, the chance of type II error is low, but when weakly related variables are studied with imprecise measurements or in experiments with few replicates, the chance of type II error is high. For example, if an air pollutant causes a modest but relevant increase in asthma attacks, but the frequency of attacks is imprecisely measured and the study includes only a small number of patients, a type II error is likely – the study is unlikely to detect the effect of the air pollutant on asthma.[11] On the other hand, if a drug has a dramatic effect on blood pressure, the study measures blood pressures precisely and the study involves many patients, the probability of type II error is low – the study will almost certainly detect the effect of the drug.

Various analyses suggest studies with few replicates or other design problems often produce type II errors.[12] Indeed, the chance of a type II error is typically several times larger than the five per cent chance of a type I error.[13] Thus, the conventional choice of a low p-value as a guard against type I error causes a high probability of type II error. Those type II errors can cause environmental and health hazards to go undetected.[14]

The possibility of type II errors is why careful researchers describe results based on p-values greater than 0.05 as providing insufficient evidence to determine whether variables are related. Unfortunately, the substantial possibility of false negatives may be overlooked when, as often happens, careful, nuanced conclusions are misreported as 'no effect …', as in these typical newspaper headlines 'No toxic effect from controversial food packet chemical, say experts', '[US Department of Energy] study: fracking chemicals didn't taint water', and 'Regulators say injection wells did not cause earthquakes'.[15] 'No evidence of an effect' should not be distorted into 'no effect' because a false negative may have occurred. In other words, absence of evidence is not evidence of absence. Evidence may be absent because the relationship in question does not exist or because the study failed to detect the relationship. If multiple, well-designed studies fail to detect a relationship, lack of a relationship may eventually be concluded with some confidence, but even then, the possibility of a false negative exists.

Because type II errors are especially likely in poorly designed studies with few replicates and imprecise measurements, a biased researcher who wishes to conclude that variables are unrelated need merely design a sloppy, inadequately replicated study that would enable detection of only the most massive effect.[16] My father smoked for decades but did not get lung cancer. Imagine he was the focus of a study of the effect of smoking on cancer, but he was the only subject of the study. Such a study would have found no evidence that smoking causes lung cancer, but smoking does cause lung cancer. It is preposterous to think one would attempt to understand such an association from the study of one patient, but there are many insidious ways a biased researcher can design an experiment so that it is unlikely to detect an effect. As you read news reports, note how often there is no basis for assessing the actual design of an experiment and therefore no basis for determining whether the study had much chance of detecting an effect. And realize that if one does not want to find an effect, one can increase the likelihood of a type II error by running a poorly designed study with an inadequate number of replicates or other design flaws.

The US Department of Energy fracking study mentioned above focused on a single well. Duke University biologist Rob Jackson, interviewed for the news report but not involved in the study, called the study useful and important but 'wondered whether the unidentified drilling company might have consciously or unconsciously taken extra care with the research site, since it was being watched'.[17] A study of one well would be a more ambitious undertaking than a study of one smoker, but it is still a study of only one subject. A study of one smoker would not be reported, but this study of one well received a great deal of attention. There is no way to know whether false negatives occurred in this fracking study, but false negatives would have been of less concern in a study of 100 wells.

The significance of the high bar of a low p-value may be easier to appreciate if we imagine applying similar logic in other potentially hazardous circumstances. Imagine, for example, if investors bought stocks only when they were highly confident of price increases, if military leaders defended only against threats that they were highly confident would come to pass or if people bought insurance only against risks that impact 95 per cent of the population. Stock prices would plummet; military planning would be ineffective; and few would buy homeowners' insurance.

We routinely guard against familiar hazards, but not against unfamiliar hazards. Type II errors occur in studies of new questions – such as new and thus unfamiliar potential hazards. When problems are hidden behind type II errors, people will often worry about other things, with the consequence that undetected problems persist.

Scientists will continue to insist upon a low p-value threshold to guard against premature conclusions in basic research. Therefore, those who seek to protect against environmental harms must understand the certainty of frequent false negatives and thus not equate *absence of evidence* of a harm with *evidence of absence* of a harm.

> The prevailing regulatory approach in the US is reactionary rather than precautionary. That is, instead of taking preventive action when uncertainty exists about the potential harm a chemical or other environmental contaminant may cause, a hazard must be incontrovertibly demonstrated before action to ameliorate it is initiated. Moreover, instead of requiring industry or other proponents of specific chemicals, devices, or activities to prove their safety, the public bears the burden of proving that a given environmental exposure is harmful.[18]

Notes

1   I am using so-called 'frequentist' statistical procedures for my examples. Some prefer 'Bayesian' statistical procedures, but these suffer from the same fundamental dependence on expected probabilities. Others prefer confidence intervals over p-values, but they suffer from the same fundamental problem, as explained by Van der Linden and Chryst, 'Why the "new statistics" isn't new', 2015.

2   Chance or randomness is actually a subtle concept. Here, I am equating *random* with *stochastic*, which means apparently random, that is to say lacking a detectable pattern. The two are

difficult to distinguish in practice. We think of coin flips as random, but the way a coin lands is determined from how it was initially held, precisely how fast and high it was flipped, the resistance of the air, the force of gravity, the stiffness of the surface on which it lands, etc. So, coin flips are not actually random, but stochastic. A sequence of coin flips will not be distinguishable from a truly random sequence, and therefore a coin flip is a fair way to determine which team starts with the ball even if the coin flip is not, strictly speaking, random. Likewise, when cards are shuffled the final order is strictly determined by the initial order and all of the steps that happened in the flipping process – how the deck was divided before shuffling, the sequence with which cards were released from the left and right hands, how many times that procedure was repeated, how the final deck was cut, and so on. As with a coin flip, the process is not truly random, but its products would be indistinguishable from stacks of cards whose orders were generated randomly. We use coin flips and shuffling to simulate randomness because true randomness is not feasible to generate in those circumstances.

3   *American Statistician*, 'Statistical Inference in the 21st Century', 2019; Colquhoun, 'The reproducibility of research and the misinterpretation of p-values', 2017; Wasserstein and Lazar, 'The ASA's statement on p-values', 2016.

4   Bayesian statistical procedures use prior understanding to estimate probabilities of various results. Interested readers are encouraged to read about the differences between Bayesian and frequentist statistical procedures. Those details are beyond our scope.

5   Lemons et al., 'The precautionary principle', 1997.

6   Mandavilli, '239 experts with one big claim', 2020.

7   Phaedrus understood impressions could be mistaken long ago, when he wrote 'Things are not always what they seem …' The rapper, songwriter, and music producer T-Pain noted the same more recently when he observed, 'people don't think it be like it be, but it do.' Plato, *The Fables of Phaedrus*, Book IV, Fable II, 'The Weasel and the Mice', 1887; T-Pain (musician Faheem Rashad Najm) 15 December 2016, Twitter, also attributed to baseball player Oscar Gamble.

8   M. Baker, '1,500 scientists lift the lid on reproducibility', 2016, 452–4.

9   Schulze and Brooks, 'The possibility of predator avoidance by Lake Michigan zooplankton', 1987.

10 Some courts have found that regulators can act when some studies suggest harm but others do not. However, that situation cannot occur until multiple research teams study the same potential hazard, which is unlikely unless initial studies provide reason for concern. Furthermore, other courts have concluded that conflicting scientific results are not sufficient basis for action. Jasanoff, 'Science, politics, and the renegotiation of expertise at the EPA', 1992, 198; Salzman and Thompson, *Environmental Law and Policy*, 2014, 214-15.

11 Meanwhile, when studies with few replicates and imprecise measurements produce low p-values, in addition to a possible type I error, the magnitude of influence of an independent variable may be overestimated (as explained by Loken and Gelman, 'Measurement error and the replication crisis', 2017).

12 Reinhart, *Statistics Done Wrong*, 2015, 18–22; Tsang et al., 'Inadequate statistical power to detect clinically significant differences in adverse event rates in randomized controlled trials', 2009.

13 Unfortunately, the probabilities of type I and II errors are inversely related. Reducing one – by shifting the p-value threshold – increases the other. A low p-value threshold reduces the chance of type I error but increases the chance of type II error, and vice versa.

14 Dayton, 'Reversal of the burden of proof in fisheries management', 1998; Hoenig and Heisey, 'The abuse of power', 2001, 19; Lemons et al., 'The precautionary principle', 1997; Oreskes, 'Playing dumb on climate change', 2015; Reinhart, *Statistics Done Wrong*, 2015, 21–2.

15 Begos, 'DOE study', 2013; Jka, 'No toxic effects from controversial food packet chemical, say experts', 2013; Mills, 'Regulators say injection wells did not cause earthquakes', 2015; Suryanarayanan and Kleinman, 'Be(e)coming experts', 2013, 3–4.

16 Bailar, 'How to distort the scientific record without actually lying', 2006, 219.

17 Begos, 'DOE study', 2013.

18 President's Cancer Panel 2008–9 Annual Report, quoted in Reuben, 'Reducing environmental cancer risk', 2010, ii.

6
Inference and extrapolation

Constraints on the designs of experiments, together with possibilities of type I and II errors, cause careful scientists to draw only provisional, not certain, conclusions. These are not the only reasons scientists draw provisional conclusions. Two other factors increase uncertainty. Research results may be mistaken (the topic of the next chapter), and it is never precisely clear how results of experiments apply more generally.

Inductive reasoning

Some hypotheses can be tested by simply observing naturally occurring circumstances. In other cases, formal experiments are necessary. Either way, effective hypothesis tests result either in evidence consistent with a null hypothesis (such as variable X does not affect variable Y) or evidence consistent with an alternative hypothesis (such as variable X does affect variable Y).

The value of hypothesis tests depends upon inductive reasoning, which is inference from cases analysed to more general circumstances. For example, that one can observe the effect of salt on the freezing point of water is, in and of itself, trivial, but the inference that a bit of salt on icy roadways can prevent deadly accidents is not. Likewise, the results of a test of a promising drug that appears to lower blood pressure are interesting, not primarily because of effects on a small group of test subjects who took the drug, but because those results suggest the drug might help a multitude of others. But there is no guarantee results of a particular study will apply to broader circumstances.

Philosopher of science Hans Reichenbach and others use the colour of crows to illustrate why inference based upon hypothesis tests cannot demonstrate with certainty that a circumstance always occurs.[1]

Consider the hypothesis that 'all crows are black'. Even if one has seen a million black crows and never seen a crow of another colour, there is no guarantee that the next crow will be black. Even if one thinks one has seen every crow, one may be mistaken. Furthermore, one cannot see every future or past crow. Thus, no matter how many crows have been studied, even if all of them have been consistent with the hypothesis that all crows are black, there is no way to be certain, to prove, that all crows are black.[2] Given the many crows I have seen and heard about, I am confident the great majority of crows are black, but I do not know for a fact that all crows are black. This is the inherent limitation of inductive reasoning. Even if all observed cases are consistent with a hypothesis, another case may differ.

This limitation of inductive reasoning is not restricted to purely observational studies, such as analyses of the colour of crows. It also applies to results of experiments. Just because salt reduced the freezing point of water in one circumstance does not guarantee salt reduces the freezing point of water in all other circumstances. It is possible that some difference in circumstances could interfere with the effect of salt on freezing temperature. Just because a drug lowers the blood pressure of patients in a study does not mean it will lower the blood pressure of all future patients. Future patients may differ in some manner from studied patients. They may be older, younger, healthier or sicker, or carry genetic variants not present in the studied patients. One or more of these differences might alter the effect of the drug on blood pressure.

Consider an actual case of inference. Several years ago, my students and I were studying the zooplankton genus *Daphnia* (Figure 6.1) in the large reservoir mentioned earlier, Lake Texoma. *Daphnia* are tiny crustaceans, relatives of shrimp, about a millimetre long – roughly the size of the head of a pin. They are widespread in the world's lakes, where they eat algae and are eaten by small fish.[3]

We found only small or spiny *Daphnia* species in the turbid regions of the lake. This was surprising because small size and spines protect zooplankton from predation by fish that use vision to detect prey, but turbid water was thought to protect zooplankton from visually foraging fish. If so, smallness and spines would confer no advantage in muddy water.

On the basis of those observations, I suspected the fish could see the plankton despite the turbidity, and posed the hypothesis that only small or spiny *Daphnia* species would be found with fish in other turbid sites. Other students and I tested that hypothesis by sampling other turbid reservoirs. After we searched twelve sites and found no exceptions to the pattern, we gave up. We had seen twelve black crows and decided we had

Figure 6.1: *Daphnia* giving birth to several young (one emerging from mother's carapace). Photographer: Marek Miś. Accessed 11 November 2021. https://commons.wikimedia.org/wiki/File:Rodz%C4%85ca_dafnia.jpg#file. CC BY 4.0.

invested enough time and gasoline dragging small boats to turbid lakes. I published a report on the observations and predicted only small and spiny *Daphnia* would be found with fish in typical turbid locations elsewhere.[4]

I wonder whether that prediction is correct. Some turbid lake that has never been studied might harbour large, non-spiny *Daphnia* coexisting with fish, just as the next crow you see might be white. But like people who would not spend their time searching for a non-black crow, I concluded there were better uses for our time than trying to find a large, non-spiny *Daphnia* with fish in yet another turbid lake. But I did not prove that never occurs. Inductive reasoning cannot do that.

Because inductive reasoning, from specific cases to generalities, cannot guarantee all future cases will be like those so far observed, careful scientists draw only tentative conclusions. They do not conclude all crows are black or only small and spiny *Daphnia* occur in turbid reservoirs. Rather, depending on the evidence they conclude either, 'The evidence is consistent with the hypothesis that all crows are black', or 'Available evidence is consistent with the hypothesis that only small and spiny *Daphnia* occur in turbid lakes with fish.'

> No matter how many times the results of experiments agree with some theory, you can never be sure that the next time the result will not contradict the theory ... Each time new experiments are observed to agree with the predictions the theory survives, and our confidence in it is increased; but if ever a new observation is found to disagree, we have to abandon or modify the theory.[5]

The notion of only provisionally accepting a hypothesis may seem weak, but compared to arguments one hears on a daily basis, it is quite rigorous.[6] Compare the basis for and cautious wording of such conclusions to the claims of salespeople, prosecutors and politicians. They generally mention only the positive features of their cars, reasons to find the defendant guilty and reasons to vote for them. Imagine how helpful it would be if car salespeople and politicians explained the reasons to consider a different car or candidate.

As we saw in the discussion of experiments, controlling variables not intended for study makes it easier to detect the effects of factors of interest, but also limits the relevance of results. If one studies the effect of pH on only one fish species, then one does not know whether pH has the same effect on other species. Studies of multiple species would be more informative, but one cannot study everything. Thus, every experiment involves trade-offs between controlling variables to maximize the chance of detecting an effect of a factor and controlling so many variables that the relevance of the results to other circumstances is suspect.

Fortunately, even though the logic of inference precludes concluding that all future cases will match those already studied, as a subject receives further attention, evidence accumulates. When corroborating evidence from different studies accumulates, experts gain confidence in whatever hypothesis the evidence supports. Thus, it is possible to imagine a continuum of certainty regarding whether – and if so, how – two variables are related. Before any theoretical analysis, observation or intentional study, a rational person would be entirely uncertain about whether two unfamiliar variables are related. Later, upon investigation, researchers may obtain evidence consistent with a relationship among variables or they may fail to find any evidence of a relationship. If scientists deem a potential relationship important enough to attract numerous studies, but no study detects evidence of a relationship, eventually most scientists will provisionally accept the null hypothesis that the variables are not related and move on to other questions. Conversely, if multiple, unrelated studies consistently find evidence of a relationship among variables, most scientists will provisionally accept the hypothesis that the variables are related and may even make predictions on the basis of that relationship.

When a hypothesis of a relationship among variables is repeatedly supported by evidence and the hypothesis has great explanatory power, it may eventually garner the status of a theory,[7] or perhaps even a scientific law, as in the theory of evolution or the law of gravity. The theory of evolution and the law of gravity have so much empirical support that most scientists would consider it a waste of time to question whether their basic features are correct. That does not mean understanding cannot improve, but general predictions based on the theory can be made with great confidence. For example, I have no way to be absolutely certain that the effect of gravity will occur in every instance on the surface of this planet, but I have enough confidence in that prediction that a few years ago, while hiking with my family, I insisted we turn back rather than cross a steep snowfield for which we lacked proper equipment and where a slip and fall would have resulted in almost certain death – due to the effect of gravity.

Likewise, when pest resistance genes were incorporated into widely planted crops, I was confident (as practically any biologist would have been) that more news reports of pesticide-resistant insects would soon follow, as they did. These predictions, based on the force of gravity and power of selection (natural or artificial) to drive evolution, represent instances of confident understanding that allows confident predictions, but in many other areas understanding is often much less robust, especially when a subject has only begun to be investigated.

Excessive extrapolation

The logic of inferential reasoning necessitates extrapolation when interpreting the implications of results. Experiments test particular conditions intended to approximate more general circumstances. Clinical trials test drugs on a few people to assess efficacy and safety for a larger population. Lab experiments expose a few fish to toxins to assess likely impacts on other fish, even other fish species. But one can extrapolate too far, as occurred when researchers concluded that DDT and chlorofluorocarbons were completely safe to use.[8]

Excessive extrapolation is apparent when the US Food and Drug Administration approves a medicine on the basis of clinical trials but subsequently withdraws that approval after the drug has been in widespread use. Problems that do not appear during trials sometimes become apparent later when a drug is given to patients who are younger, older, sicker or otherwise different from clinical trial participants, or when interactions between a drug and other factors are not detected in trials but become apparent when vastly more people take the drug.

From 1980 to 2009 the Food and Drug Administration approved 740 new pharmaceuticals and related products but withdrew approval for 118 others.[9] That some prior approvals are eventually reversed is understandable and to be expected. If the agency is too reluctant to approve new, safe medicines, patients who could have benefited suffer, but if they approve drugs too rapidly, patients may suffer from side effects hidden by type II errors or side effects that affect members of the population not represented among trial participants. In other words, the Food and Drug Administration must make decisions despite constraints on the designs of experiments, risks of type I and II errors and extrapolation from clinical trials to the larger population. This is a fate they share with all policymakers – having to make decisions based on imperfect information.

In retrospect, however, some withdrawals are consequences of experiment designs that controlled too many independent variables. Recall that it is easiest to detect effects of experimental factors if other independent variables are held constant. Doing so maximizes the chance of detecting the 'signal' (such as the effect of a drug) of the manipulated variable from the 'noise' of variation due to other factors (such as patient age) that might affect a dependent variable (such as blood pressure).

Though it seems incredible in retrospect, until the 1990s drug tests routinely excluded women as test subjects. In other words, sex of the study subjects was held constant just as one might hold constant the temperature of aquarium water in studies of fish. The usual stated rationale for excluding females was concern that women's greater short-term hormonal variation would complicate results. You may be wondering, 'Then how did anyone know whether the drugs were safe for women?' The answer is that they did not know. They merely extrapolated from the data for men when approving the prescribing of the drugs to women. In other words, they assumed that if the drugs were safe for men, they would also be safe for women.

Retrospective analyses of female patients have detected many drugs with different effects on women than men. For example, according to a *Scientific American* review, women have more difficulty quitting opioid painkillers, are more sensitive to some sleeping pills and react differently than men to antidepressants and anti-anxiety medications.[10]

Extrapolation pitfalls also plague efforts to understand chemical hazards. Because it is unethical to test suspected hazards on humans, experiments use mice or other species. Humans and other species sometimes respond similarly to toxins, but not always. For example, physiological differences make chocolate toxic to dogs but not humans.[11] What conclusions about hazards to humans would you draw from studies of mice? The relevant physiology for newly suspected toxins is generally unknown, and no accepted theory exists for extrapolating toxicity estimates across species.

Recognizing the uncertainty associated with extrapolation from one species to another, regulators employ safety factors so as to err on the side of caution. For example, if consumption of 1 milligram of a substance per kilogram of body weight is toxic to mice, human ingestion limits might be set to 0.01 or 0.001 milligram per kilogram. Imagine the controversy this creates. Some will consider such safety factors inadequate while others consider them excessive.

The problem of how to extrapolate from other species to humans is just one hurdle to interpreting results of experiments on other species. People are exposed to low toxin concentrations for decades, but it is not feasible to run experiments so long. The public and policymakers desire answers promptly, and test animals are short-lived. Therefore, rather than exposing test animals to low doses for decades, researchers run shorter experiments with higher doses. Here again, there is no accepted theory for extrapolating from short-term, high-dose exposure to long-term, low-dose exposure. Thus, assessing the implications for humans from toxicity experiment data for other species requires two types of extrapolation, from one species to another and from high-dose, short-term experiments to low-dose, long-term exposure.

Extrapolation is as uncertain and unavoidable in ecosystem research. For example, sewage treatment plants must periodically pass 'bioassay' tests of whether the zooplankton *Ceriodaphnia dubia* survive for a standard period when grown in treatment plant effluent. If enough *Ceriodaphnia* survive, effluent is deemed acceptable. Bioassays are useful because any number of contaminants can kill *Ceriodaphnia*, alerting plant managers to a problem, but bioassays require substantial extrapolation when used as a tool for assessing the effectiveness of wastewater treatment.

Effluent bioassays require an organism that is easy to transport and grow in laboratories (so test procedures can be standardized).

Ceriodaphnia are so tough that newborns can be sent through the mail in little vials of water and populations readily thrive in laboratory cultures. Other zooplankton species are much more sensitive. Perhaps the durability that enables *Ceriodaphnia* to survive transport and laboratory conditions also makes them relatively insensitive to some contaminants. If so, approving wastewater on the basis of *Ceriodaphnia* bioassays may doom more sensitive species downstream.[12] But extrapolation of bioassay results is unavoidable because it would be infeasible to run tests on all potentially affected species. Bioassays are useful – they detect many circumstances of unsatisfactory water quality – but they do not ensure effluent water is harmless.

Inductive reasoning requires extrapolation, but one never knows precisely how much shift in circumstances can occur before extrapolation has gone too far. Meanwhile, as we have seen, there is no way to ensure against type I and II errors, and multiple factors constrain the experiments scientists can perform. For all these reasons, careful scientists draw only provisional conclusions about all but the simplest phenomena and make only guarded predictions. These limitations apply to even the best science. The situation is much worse when reported results are not reliable, the topic of the next chapter.

Notes

1   Reichenbach, *The Rise of Scientific Philosophy*, 1951, 81–2.
2   Some other hypotheses about the colour of crows can be proven true or rejected with certainty. For example, the hypothesis that *some* crows are black can be confirmed with discovery of one black crow (but could not be rejected with certainty even if one had never seen a black crow after extensive searching). Likewise, the hypothesis no crows are black can be rejected with certainty on the basis of discovery of one black crow, but, like the hypothesis all crows are black, cannot be accepted with certainty even if one has never seen a black crow. Note that the use of the term 'proof' in the context of inductive hypothesis testing is different from its use in the formal deductive reasoning of logic and mathematics, circumstances in which claims can be definitively proven.
3   You may have heard of them as 'water fleas', but I do not like that term because they bear little similarity to fleas – they are neither parasites nor otherwise annoying. I suppose the term is based on their small size and jerky swimming pattern, which roughly approximates the jumping of fleas.
4   Schulze, 'Evidence that fish structure the zooplankton communities of turbid lakes and reservoirs', 2011. (I sought to include two students as co-authors, but they chose not to assist with the necessary follow-up work of drafting and reviewing the report. I recommend that any students who encounter such an opportunity be wary of passing it up.)
5   Hawking, *The Illustrated a Brief History of Time*, 2014, 15–16.
6   Platt, 'Strong inference', 1964.

7 'Theory' is sometimes used (in my opinion too loosely) as a synonym for hypothesis, but in my field of biology, theory is reserved for hypotheses that both have a great deal of empirical support and provide a great deal of explanatory power.

8 Fuller, 'The myth and fallacy of simple extrapolation in medicine', 2019; Fuller and Flores, 'The risk GP model', 2015.

9 Qureshi et al., 'Market withdrawal of new molecular entities approved in the US from 1980 to 2009', 2011, 772.

10 Rabin, 'The drug-dose gender gap', 2013; Whitley and Lindsey, 'Sex-based differences in drug activity', 2009.

11 Gwaltney-Brant, 'Chocolate toxicosis in animals', 2021.

12 Giesy and Hoke, 'Freshwater sediment toxicity bioassessment', 1989, 544–53; Moore and Winner, 'Relative sensitivity of *Ceriodaphnia dubia* laboratory tests and pond communities of zooplankton and benthos to chronic copper stress', 1989; EPA, 'Whole effluent toxicity methods', n.d.

7
Scientific errors

Experiments that cannot be performed, statistical errors and excessive extrapolation are not the only barriers to certain scientific conclusions. Some scientific conclusions are simply wrong. Errant conclusions result from several causes: type I and II errors, hazards of inference, innocent but undetected errors that occur during studies, researcher incompetence, biases that affect study design, data collection, data analysis, decisions whether to publish data, and sometimes even scientific fraud.

Traditional scientific procedures involve multiple safeguards against these errors. Of course, those safeguards do not work perfectly, and the hazards of type I and II errors and uncertainties of inference and extrapolation remain unavoidable. However, the set of precautions often work well, at least eventually. Astronomers no longer think the Earth is at the centre of the universe; microbiologists no longer think life arises routinely from non-living material; and geologists no longer insist the continents' positions are fixed. Because science tends to arrive at correct explanations eventually, we can all routinely take for granted a multitude of scientific insights. That confidence is fostered by ten practices careful scientists employ to guard against reporting errant results (Box 7.1).

Despite these various safeguards, errant conclusions are sometimes, perhaps often, published. False negatives or positives, hazards of extrapolation and undetected, innocent errors all produce errant conclusions on occasion. Such errors are essentially unavoidable. More disconcerting, however, are reports suggesting growing problems due to failure to rigorously apply the safeguards listed in Box 7.1, plus troubling carelessness, corner cutting, statistical incompetence, rush to publication, and various degrees of scientific malpractice, all leading to substantial percentages of irreproducible results, especially in some fields.[1]

Even errors in fields other than environmental research create an obstacle to environmental progress because they erode public confidence

Box 7.1: Conventional procedures for reducing the likelihood of errant scientific conclusions

1 Undergraduate laboratory courses emphasize the importance of obtaining, recording and managing data with integrity and care.

2 Standard experimental design approaches include randomization and other bias-prevention methods in assignment of treatments to replicates, independence of replicates, randomization or standardization of data collection procedures (such as locations, subjects, and identity of data collectors) and replication of experimental treatments.

3 Graduate students, if not undergraduates, learn to identify and consider multiple alternative hypotheses when designing studies, rather than pursuing the first one they imagine, lest they become emotionally attached to a 'pet' hypothesis.

4 Statistical training emphasizes assumptions, proper selection of tests and correct understanding of statistical calculations and their limitations.

5 Data analyses are typically subject to several iterations of review by disinterested parties before submission for publication. For example, results are often first presented to local audiences for critical review, then to a regional, national or international meeting audience, after which a written draft is circulated to local colleagues and other experts for further critique, all before being submitted to a journal for formal peer-review.

6 Following informal reviews, a revised report is submitted to a journal for anonymous peer review. Journal editors send suitable submissions to two or more reviewers whose primary purposes are to assess suitability for publication and identify necessary corrections or other improvements.

7 If a report is important and produces surprising results, others may attempt to reproduce those results. Results that cannot be reproduced garner a great deal of attention.

8 Journals encourage retraction or correction of previously published results when authors or others discover an error after publication.

9 The scientific community shuns authors found guilty of scientific fraud, such as fabricating or misrepresenting data. Clear evidence of such fraud ends careers.

> 10   Perhaps most importantly, scientists take a great deal of pride in being correct – for at least three reasons. First, they genuinely like to advance understanding. (If they did not, why would they embark upon careers that are relatively low-paying given the required schooling?) Second, it is a matter of pride not to steer others astray by publishing incorrect conclusions. Third, they themselves are the ones most likely to build upon their own research reports and therefore they have a strong incentive to avoid errors before proceeding.

in science, as exemplified by a letter to the editor of the *Dallas Morning News* that displayed a remarkably inaccurate impression of the normal scientific process. 'As everyone knows, scientists can and will find numbers to fit their conclusion …'[2] If members of the public do not trust scientists, then warnings of environmental hazards will go unheeded, and the public will not demand environmental progress. This chapter describes causes of errant conclusions.

Innocent errors

Despite best intentions, undetected research errors sometimes occur. Devices can fail inconspicuously, producing values that appear sound. Workers may accidentally err when transcribing data, enter errors into formulae or unknowingly misunderstand the correct steps in a procedure. Such errors are rare because typical scientists are almost compulsively careful. They tend to be the types who double check that the stove is off when leaving home. But with lots of work performed, some innocent errors occur despite the best efforts and intentions.

Some such errors have been spectacular. The Mars Climate Orbiter spacecraft crashed into the red planet in 1999 because workers mixed imperial and metric units in calculations. The NASA Genesis probe crashed on return to Earth in 2004 because a sensor component intended to trigger the parachutes had been installed backwards. The Antarctic ozone hole grew undetected for several years because computers processing satellite data had been programmed to ignore extreme values. The programmers had assumed extreme values must be wrong.[3]

I once labelled a set of experimental containers incorrectly, then followed my errant labels when setting up the experiment. I wasted a week before realizing my error. Fortunately, that mistake was obvious when I collected the data. I wonder whether I have made other, undetected mistakes. That something has gone wrong is obvious when a spacecraft crashes, but if errors do not leave obvious tell-tale signs, resulting data may be treated as sound and errant conclusions may result, as when ozone depletion went undetected for several years.

Incompetence

Incompetence can cause errors in the design of experiments or the analysis of results. Either can lead to false conclusions. Sometimes peer reviewers can detect errors of incompetence before a report is published, but some such errors will not be apparent to reviewers.

Errors in the design of experiments can produce meaningless results that may appear sound. For instance, intended treatments (such as drug versus placebo) should be the only systematic (consistent) differences among experimental units. Otherwise, apparent effects of treatments could be confounded with other differences (such as the average age of subjects in the various treatments).

Numerous, often obscure, methodological details have potential to confound results. Many are sufficiently minor that they would not be included in published descriptions of experimental procedures. Imagine, for example, a test of whether plants grow faster if watered once or twice a week. Only watering frequency should differ between replicates in the two treatments because any other difference could confound effects of watering frequency. It would be easiest to put plants watered once a week in one location, such as on one side of a greenhouse, and plants watered twice a week in another location, such as the other side of the greenhouse. Then one could simply water one side twice as often as the other side. However, one side of a greenhouse might receive more sunlight, get warmer during the day or be superior or inferior in some other way. Thus, any difference between the two sides of the greenhouse could confound the results, either by creating the appearance of an effect from watering frequency when there was none, magnifying an effect of watering frequency, or reducing an effect of watering frequency. Arranging the plants into groups based on their treatments would ease the process of applying those treatments (watering the plants), but that easy procedure would ruin the experiment by confounding the results.

If confounding occurs, data may be misinterpreted as evidence regarding treatment effects. Careful researchers go to great lengths to avoid confounding, but the details of the preventive procedures would not necessarily be included in published descriptions of methods because the necessity of avoiding confounding is so fundamental that competence in its avoidance is assumed, just as competence in calibrating instruments is assumed.[4]

Even if an experiment is properly designed and implemented, incompetent data analysis may introduce errors. Nowadays anyone with a laptop and access to the internet can run statistical tests, but just because one can run a test or operate a machine does not guarantee that one knows what one is doing. Even the most competent data analysts cannot avoid the hazards of type I and type II errors, but those are not the only way statistical tests can lead to errant conclusions. Errant conclusions can also result if statistical tests are misapplied to data that do not meet the test's assumptions or if p-value calculations are not preceded by statements of hypotheses.

You may be aware of several types of statistical tests, such as analysis of variance (often simply called ANOVA), regression and correlation. The correct test in a given situation depends upon the design of the study and features of the data. For example, analysis of variance may be appropriate when independent variable values fall into discrete groups created by the researcher, such as drug v. placebo, while the dependent variable values span a numerical continuum, such as blood pressure. Regression may be appropriate if both the dependent and independent variables span a continuous range of values and the independent variable(s) were manipulated by the researchers. For example, regression might be suitable if subjects were given different amounts of calories per day, and changes in their weights were then measured after a year. Correlation may be appropriate if both variables span a continuous range but neither was manipulated by the researchers, such as when testing for evidence of a relationship between ozone concentrations and reported asthma attacks.

I have written that these tests 'may be' appropriate because each test type makes assumptions about the nature of the input data. Often, however, a computer program will generate results even when data do not comply with a procedure's assumptions. For example, a regression may be run when a correlation would have been appropriate. Experienced data analysts will not make these mistakes, but statistical novices may not realize their errors. In such cases, results may appear satisfactory and thus be treated as such but be meaningless. Peer reviewers will catch many such errors, but not every instance.

Applying the wrong test is only one of many ways to use statistical tests incorrectly. Statistical analyses also require assumptions about designs of experiments and about how measurements of dependent variables vary among replicates. Most statistical tests assume replicate measurements are independent of each other. Many also assume variation in dependent variables is normally distributed at each level of each factor and that those normal distributions have consistent standard deviations across treatments.[5] If these assumptions are violated, calculated p-values are incorrect, but statistical analysis software often generates them anyway. The analyst must know better than to run inappropriate tests.

Yet other pitfalls befall novice data analysts. Recall that statistical tests produce type I errors (false positives) in 5 per cent of cases when variation in data is due to nothing more than random variation. Thus, if one calculates 20 p-values, one can expect at least 1 false positive. Some analyses produce numerous p-values. For example, an analysis that tested for effects of age, sex, diet and exercise regimens on blood pressure, resting heart rate and triglyceride concentration would generate at least 12 p-values, more if the test also checked for interactions among variables or included more than two groups for any independent variable (such as testing three different diets or exercise regimens). Recognizing the higher chance of at least one type I error in such circumstances, competent analysts apply 'multiple-comparisons tests'. Such procedures compensate for the many p-values, and thus many chances of type I error, by effectively reducing the p-value threshold for a finding of statistical significance.[6] A less experienced analyst might run tests without such compensatory corrections and consequently make frequent type I errors.

Perhaps the most common statistical mistake results from attribution of p-values to analyses that were not preceded by hypotheses. Proper attribution of statistical significance requires specification of hypotheses prior to initiation of a study. Tests preceded by prior specification of hypotheses are termed *a priori* ('from the earlier') because they were planned before data were collected. If one predicts a relationship, then collects appropriate data to test for evidence of a relationship, assuming other test assumptions are met, it is reasonable to calculate a p-value.

On the other hand, one should not calculate a p-value or attribute statistical significance to data features not imagined until they were noticed after data were collected. Such *post hoc* ('after this') or *a posteriori* ('in the aftermath') observations are suitable sources of new questions that lead to new hypotheses to be tested in new studies, but p-values attributed to them are meaningless in the present study because many un-hypothesized apparent patterns result from mere coincidence, and innumerable coincidences occur all the time. Calculations of the likelihood of any particular set of cars in a parking lot, vacationers on a beach or students in a class would generate minuscule p-values because each particular set is exceedingly unlikely, but we encounter many such coincidences every day. The great majority are just that – coincidences – not evidence of relationships among variables. Attributing p-values to unanticipated, *a posteriori* observations results in rampant type I errors. A variety of initiatives, such as pre-announcing planned hypothesis tests, have been proposed to guard against this problem.[7]

Unfortunately, *post hoc* application of p-values is common in fields from financial advice to medicine – so common that Professor Uri Simonsohn of the University of Pennsylvania has even given it a name, 'p-hacking'. When false positives resulting from *post hoc* misuses of p-value calculations are contrasted with other correct reports that detect no evidence of a relationship among variables, the contrast gives an impression of tremendous scientific inconsistency. Some refer to this situation as statistical fog. P-hacking and other statistical errors appear responsible for many non-reproducible reports and thus much statistical fog, but most such concerns have arisen from fields other than environmental science.[8]

Decades ago, statistical errors were common in some areas of environmental research,[9] but statistics have been integral to such research for some time, and extensive statistics coursework is typical in environmental fields. One hopes statistical errors in environmental research are rare today, but even if so, errors in other fields are still important because they reduce public confidence in all scientific conclusions.

> We now have a dismissive attitude toward news articles claiming some food or diet or exercise might harm us – we just wait for the inevitable second study some months later, giving exactly the opposite result.[10]

Bias and malpractice

Finally, errant scientific conclusions sometimes result from researchers' biases or even scientific malpractice. A continuum of severity spans from the most innocent of biases that influence conclusions despite the best attempts to prevent them to more severe biases due to financial or other conflicts of interest and finally to outright scientific fraud, such as data fabrication. Biases can influence a study not just in the interpretation of the results, but also in the choice of questions and hypotheses, details of study design and data interpretation, and decisions regarding whether to submit results for publication. Indeed, entire groups of scientists sometimes fail to objectively evaluate evidence, as Thomas Kuhn explained in his book on revolutions in scientific thought.[11]

Even when there are no financial or other conflicts of interest, biases may result from the hope that one's proposed hypothesis is correct. A hypothesis is a type of prediction. Who does not want to make correct predictions? When scientists become emotionally attached to hypotheses, they may fail to objectively design studies or evaluate evidence.

The most fundamental means of avoiding biases in research is to avoid attachment to a particular hypothesis. The standard means of attempting to do so is to develop multiple hypotheses at the outset of a study. If a researcher has created multiple hypotheses, only one of which can be correct, the researcher may avoid emotional attachment to a particular hypothesis because if any proposed hypothesis is correct, the researcher will have been correct. Indeed, the researcher has more chance to have posed a correct hypothesis in this case than if they have posed only one hypothesis, which may very well be wrong. Geologist Thomas Chamberlain identified this concern during the nineteenth century.

> The moment one has offered an original explanation for a phenomenon which seems satisfactory, that moment affection for his intellectual child springs into existence; and as the explanation grows into a definite theory, his parental affections cluster about his intellectual offspring, and it grows more and more dear to him, so that, while he holds it seemingly tentative, it is still lovingly tentative, and not impartially tentative … To guard against this, the method of multiple working hypotheses is urged … The effort is to bring up into view every rational explanation of new phenomena, and to develop every tenable hypothesis respecting their cause and history. The investigator thus becomes the parent of a family of hypotheses: and, by his parental relation to all, he is forbidden to fasten his affections unduly upon any one.[12]

Nowadays Professor Chamberlain's advice is routinely recommended during graduate student training, perhaps especially since it played a prominent role in Professor John R. Platt's 1964 article, 'Strong inference', which, like Dr Chamberlain's original, was prominently published in *Science*, the most prestigious US science journal.[13]

The development of alternative hypotheses, rather than just one, has two major added benefits. First, the initial hypothesis that occurs to a researcher may be incorrect. If one fails to consider other possibilities and proceeds to test only that hypothesis, years or even decades could be spent on relatively unproductive work. Second, it is often possible to test multiple hypotheses in one experiment. All other things being equal, a test of several hypotheses at once is not only more likely to find support for a correct hypothesis, but also more efficient than a sequence of tests of individual hypotheses.

The development of multiple hypotheses is tremendously useful for avoiding emotional attachments to any given idea, but when a practical problem motivates a study, even multiple hypotheses may not eliminate researchers' hopes. Imagine one seeks to develop a better medical treatment or restore an ecosystem. Researchers attempting new treatments or restoration techniques will hope the methods work, even if unmotivated by fame, fortune or glory, simply because they seek improved treatments and more effective techniques.

Thus, while multiple hypotheses are tremendously useful and certainly advisable, they do not guarantee elimination of emotional bias. Furthermore, biases may enter the scientific process before hypotheses are posed, as decisions are made about what to study. These earlier-stage biases cannot be eliminated by posing multiple hypotheses. (This complex, important topic is a focus of the discipline of science studies.)

Scientists use several additional methods besides posing multiple hypotheses to minimize the potential for bias to affect results or conclusions (see Box 7.1 above). Perhaps you are familiar with some particular methods, such as 'double-blind' studies.

'Double blind' refers to experiment designs in which neither the human subject nor the data collector knows the subject's treatment category. For example, in a double-blind test of a new drug, neither the patients nor the researchers who collect data know which treatment was assigned to which patient. When neither the patient nor the data collector has that information, their biases, subconscious or otherwise, about the outcome of the study will not systematically affect the study data.

During graduate school, I agreed to participate in a study of a new decongestant at the university's medical school. The nature of the experiment certainly necessitated double-blind methods. I took a pill. I do not know whether it was the drug being tested or a placebo. The technicians asked how congested I felt on a scale of 1 to 10. Imagine if the technician and I had known I had been given the drug. 'Don't you feel better today?' 'Oh, yes. This stuff is great. I've never been able to breathe so well.' Double-blind procedures prevent this problem. Because I did not know what I had taken, I had no reason to make biased judgments of congestion or lack thereof, and since the technician also did not know, they had no reason to steer me toward any particular response.

Double-blind study designs are not a panacea, however, for two reasons. First, blind designs are often infeasible. Second, data collection is only one step at which bias can affect a study.

Studies of humans can be double blind, but only studies of humans need be double blind. When dependent variables are measured for other species or inanimate objects, a blind data collector would suffice. For example, if treatments of prescribed fire and livestock grazing are applied to experimental fields to test effects on the composition of vegetation, there is no concern about whether fields 'know' which treatment has been applied. However, if the data collectors know which treatments have been applied, that knowledge, combined with some hope or expectation regarding the outcome of the experiment, could bias data collection.

Thus, the potential solution would be to use data collectors who do not know which treatment was applied to which field (blind data collectors), but this is often infeasible because treatments are often unavoidably obvious to data collectors. For example, a person studying the species composition of plants in two field treatments, one grazed by cattle and one not grazed by cattle, will routinely encounter obvious evidence of cattle in some fields but not others. Furthermore, I have never heard of an ecological research budget so luxurious that separate, qualified individuals were hired simply to serve as blind data collectors.

When blind data collection procedures are infeasible, subconscious bias in data collection must be combatted by other means. A variety of complementary techniques exist, such as avoiding measurements that require subjective judgements and randomly or systematically selecting sampling locations.[14] For example, when my students and I measure the abundance of different plants in prairie restoration fields, we walk evenly spaced transects across each field and stop every 10 metres to collect data. This ensures the entire field is evenly represented in our samples. Then we determine precise sampling points by tossing a dart high and backward over a shoulder to one side of the transect, without first observing the landing area and without the thrower watching the dart trajectory. We then collect data from a specified radius around the dart. The sample spacing and dart throwing procedure minimizes the chance of subconsciously selecting specific sampling locations, such as spots with species we hope to find.

The method avoids bias in sampling locations, but measurements themselves could still be biased. A desire to avoid such biases informed our original selection of sampling methods. We considered dozens of potential vegetation and related measurements, tested about two dozen, and eliminated several due to imprecision, inaccuracy, or subjectivity. One potentially very useful measure was simply too subjective for confidence in unbiased measurements.

Assessments of livestock range condition often note whether soil is covered by a 'crust'. Perhaps you have seen dry, barren, soil with curling crust. Crust develops on dry clay soils after raindrops have repeatedly pounded bare soil. The rain breaks large soil particles into smaller fragments that then flow down into the soil with percolating water until they become lodged among pore spaces. Successively smaller pore spaces become filled until the soil surface becomes effectively sealed. In pronounced cases, pieces of crust can be pried up intact. Soil crust is undesirable because it prevents water infiltration, thereby reducing soil moisture and causing runoff and floods, and because it inhibits seed germination and plant establishment.

Severely degraded fields have pronounced crusts, but in our case, few sample locations are in such poor condition, so we found ourselves trying to distinguish minimal crust from none at all. Even though one would ultimately want to classify soil condition correctly to advance understanding of restoration methods, because all of our methods are intended to be helpful, we hoped not to find crust. The risk of that hope interfering with objectivity, combined with the very subtle distinction between minimal crust and no crust convinced me we could not be confident of crust measurements. We therefore abandoned them in favour of more objective measures of prairie recovery.[15]

Such understandable hopes for a particular result are biases of the mildest sort, and the data collection phase of a project is only one of several points where bias can affect conclusions. As noted, biases can also enter at every other stage, from choosing a topic to study, to choosing questions about the topic, through posing hypotheses to designing experiments, interpreting results and deciding whether to publish results.[16]

Sometimes biases against finding evidence are even enacted into law. For example, from 1996 until at least 2018 the US Congress inhibited the ability of the Centers for Disease Control from studying the public health consequences of gun violence. As recently as 2015, the House majority report on the appropriations bill that funded the CDC read as follows:

The Committee reminds [the Centers for Disease Control] that the longstanding general provision's intent is to protect rights granted by the Second Amendment [the US Constitutional amendment that, depending upon one's interpretation, allows individuals to own firearms]. The restriction is to prevent … activities (to include data collection) for current or future research, including under the title 'gun violence prevention', that could be used in any manner to result in a future policy, guidelines, or recommendations to limit access to guns, ammunition, or to create a list of gun owners.[17]

Experiment design details create other, subtler opportunities for bias. For example, a new drug could be tested against a placebo or against the best available drug. If it is effective at all, its efficacy will appear more impressive compared to a placebo than to another effective drug. Likewise, the choice of toxin concentrations can influence experimental results. Many compounds toxic at high concentrations have no detectable effect or may even function as micronutrients at low concentrations, just as people need salt and iron but should not consume too much of either. Thus, one who wishes not to find a toxic effect might simply test low concentrations.

Once research results reach general audiences, experiment design details such as treatment concentrations and whether a drug is compared to a placebo or an alternative drug are often lost in the small print, if mentioned at all. Moreover, general audiences may not appreciate the significance of such details. Obviously, new drugs should be compared to other effective drugs and potential toxins tested at concentrations to which creatures might be exposed. Such experiment-design flaws should be caught by peer reviewers before results are published. However, as we shall see, proliferation of 'predatory' journals have increased the chance of results being published in a source that claims to be 'peer reviewed' without having actually been peer reviewed.

Another source of bias is referred to as positive reporting. Positive reporting bias occurs when results that provide evidence of an association between variables are published but results that fail to find evidence of a relationship are not. Positive reporting bias is often referred to as the 'file drawer' problem. Published results are available for widespread consideration, but results left in a file drawer are not. Positive reporting bias leaves readers with a distorted impression of the complete set of evidence.

Positive reporting bias can occur for either innocent or nefarious reasons. At the innocent end of the spectrum, if researchers find data that support one hypothesis more interesting than data that do not support a *different* hypothesis, and are therefore more likely to find time to write up the former, the literature will disproportionately reflect positive results. Positive reporting bias also occurs if editors more frequently accept for publication reports that provide evidence of a relationship than results that do not provide evidence of a relationship. Such bias is real but relatively innocent if published data address different hypotheses than unpublished data, but other positive reporting bias is more nefarious, such as if reports of a drug's efficacy are published but reports that detect no evidence of efficacy are not published. Positive reporting bias has been a concern for decades. Reviews have concluded that authors are more likely to submit, and journals are more likely to accept, reports of evidence of relationships among variables than reports of no evidence of relationships.[18]

Positive reporting bias is only one of several types of scientific malpractice that can result from conflicts of interest. Conflicts of interest occur if a researcher, or their funder, has a financial stake in a particular conclusion or another incentive beyond advancing knowledge (and the routine professional respect associated with doing so). In the worst case, conflicts are manifested as outright data fabrication. Fortunately, data fabrication appears to be relatively rare, but other forms of scientific malpractice are disconcertingly common.[19]

Brian Martinson, Melissa Anderson and Raymond de Vries anonymously surveyed several thousand US scientists funded by the National Institutes of Health regarding their engagement in a wide range of inappropriate behaviours, from the worst, such as falsifying data, to the mildest, such as inappropriately awarding co-authorship credit. Fortunately, fewer than 1 per cent of respondents reported that they had falsified or 'cooked' data or failed to disclose the involvement of a firm in a study. However, 15 per cent reported that they had changed the 'design, methodology, or results of a study in response to pressure from a funding source', and 11 per cent reported that they had withheld methodological or results details from a publication or grant proposal.[20]

Regrettably, reviews of published literature have concluded that biases associated with conflicts of interest distort the sum total of evidence and conclusions that reach readers. This may involve either positive or negative reporting bias – negative when a researcher or funder with a conflict has a reason to prefer a finding of no evidence of an effect (which they can then misrepresent as 'no effect'). Sheldon Krimsky reviewed published analyses that compare industry-funded studies versus studies funded by non-profit organizations.[21] That literature includes analyses of pharmaceutical drugs, second-hand tobacco smoke and manufactured chemicals, such as bisphenol-A. Krimsky's review found industry-funded studies are much more likely to report positive results for sponsors' medicines and much less likely to find a hazard of exposure to bisphenol-A or second-hand smoke.

Likewise, Shanil Ebrahim and colleagues reviewed published meta-analyses of antidepressant research. They found reports whose authors were not employed by the drug's manufacturer were 20 times as likely to include negative statements about the studied drug as reports whose authors included one or more employees of the manufacturer. Yet others have detected selective data suppression of results from industry-funded studies regarding numerous ailments.[22] Theoretical calculations suggest positive-reporting bias combined with p-hacking may result in quite a few erroneous research reports, at least in some fields. Available empirical results are broadly consistent with such calculations. For example, the biotechnology company Amgen could only reproduce results of 11 per cent of studies of potential new cancer therapies.[23]

> It is difficult to get a man to understand something, when his salary depends on his not understanding it![24]

In theory, peer review before publication should prevent flawed studies from reaching audiences, but peer review, while generally excellent for what it can do, is not a panacea. It works as follows. A researcher submits an article for publication. A journal editor checks whether the article's subject falls within the journal's purview, and if so, whether the article superficially appears suitable. If so, they send the article to qualified but disinterested experts for evaluation (peer review). Ethical codes require invited reviewers to decline requests if they consider themselves unqualified or have a potential conflict of interest, such as being a close friend of, working with, studying under or not getting along with, one or more of a paper's authors. When reviewers decline requests, editors find alternative reviewers.

Reviewers evaluate whether readers are likely to be interested in the question, suitability of study designs, appropriateness of result descriptions and reasonableness of conclusions. Reviewers are normally anonymous and are not paid or otherwise compensated. Reviewers have no stake in whether a paper is published beyond that shared with all colleagues – maximizing the reliability of published reports and thereby advancing understanding.[25]

Reviewers make detailed suggestions for improvements and recommend whether papers should be accepted, revised or rejected. Initial submissions are rarely accepted without at least some revision. Reviewers understand their role as gatekeepers of a process intended to maximize reliability of reports. It is not unusual for reviewers to recommend rejection of the majority of submitted papers. Lately, I have recommended rejection or major revision for almost 90 per cent of papers sent to me for review. (A paper rejected from one journal may later be accepted elsewhere. Journals vary in status; some are more selective than others.)

Peer review is primarily intended to evaluate whether a question would be of sufficient interest to a journal's readers, whether study designs are adequate, results are appropriately presented and described, analyses are appropriate and conclusions are reasonable. However, whereas peer reviewers should be able to detect p-hacking and other basic methodological errors, there is no guarantee that they will do so. (Presumably many do not, otherwise papers based upon p-hacking would be less common and fewer irreproducible reports would be published.) Peer review assumes honesty and absence of scientific malpractice on the part of researchers. Moreover, peer review assumes authors are competent, careful and, aside from any subconscious biases, are motivated by a desire to advance understanding rather than by obvious conflicts of interest, such as a financial interest in the results. (Journals normally require authors to declare any potential conflicts.) Peer review is suitable for detecting errors of rigour, such as excessive extrapolation or flaws in the design of experiments, but is not suited to detecting data fabrication or any sort of data 'cooking'. For example, a peer reviewer would have no way to know if a researcher submitted for publication only a subset of results, rather than all relevant results. Thus, while peer review is tremendously valuable, it cannot be expected to catch all flaws in studies or their conclusions.

Unfortunately, during the last couple of decades another problem with peer review has arisen in association with the proliferation of online, open access publications. Open access strives to make research and other writing available to everyone, which is precisely why this book is open access, but the value of articles and books is severely compromised if open access publications are not rigorously peer reviewed. Unlike rigorously reviewed, legitimate open access publications, 'predatory' journals claim to be peer reviewed but are not.[26] They will publish virtually anything for a fee. Meanwhile, many have impressive sounding names that are often almost identical to the names of established, rigorously reviewed, prestigious journals.

Whereas conventional peer review normally takes a few months for reports on all but the hottest topics, predatory journals accept papers in a few days or less, far too fast for serious peer review. John Bohannon ran sting operations to detect such journals. He received acceptances from more than half of the suspect journals to whom he submitted reports of intentionally flawed studies. For example, within 24 hours multiple journals accepted a report on an intentionally weak study, full of p-hacking, on the health consequences of eating chocolate.[27]

The business model of predatory journals relies on readers' and others' inability to distinguish legitimate, rigorously reviewed journals from predatory journals that will publish more or less anything but give the appearance of and may even claim to be peer reviewed. Experienced authors within a given field will learn which journals are legitimate and which are not, but novices, those reading beyond their field, and those charged with evaluating job candidates outside their own areas of expertise may not.

Why would authors pay to publish in predatory journals when legitimate journals garner more respect and notice and predatory journals often charge higher fees? The simplest explanations are that authors do not realize a journal is predatory or do not believe their report would be accepted for publication in a rigorously reviewed journal but desire publications for the sake of career enhancement or some other reason. If predatory journals only receive submissions from the most naïve authors or authors who do not believe their papers would be accepted elsewhere, predatory journals must disproportionately publish low-quality reports, and their existence must therefore reduce the average quality and reliability of the scientific literature.

During the early 2000s, University of Colorado-Denver librarian Jeffrey Beall maintained a list of journals he considered predatory. He no longer maintains that website, but various other sites list hundreds of journals their website managers consider predatory, and scholarly literature on the phenomenon is proliferating.[28] As noted, experienced researchers know the reputations of their fields' journals and are unlikely to pay much attention to papers published in predatory journals, but novices, members of hiring committees who must evaluate candidates from other fields, and others reading outside their areas of expertise would, absent intentional scrutiny, have little basis for distinguishing two journals with impressive names that both claim to be peer reviewed.

Moreover, once a paper is published in a shoddy journal, its author can then seek to interest media outlets in the 'peer-reviewed' research. It is not reasonable to expect reporters who cover many topics to know which journals are predatory, so they may accept results from predatory journals at face value. Some media then repeat each other's reports, with the result that stories can travel the world at the speed of the internet without ever having been rigorously reviewed. For instance, major magazines and other media outlets rapidly and broadly publicized Bohannon's fake chocolate study, as if to confirm the assertion (often but apparently incorrectly attributed to Mark Twain) that a lie can travel half-way around the world while the truth is still putting on its shoes.[29]

Because reporters without specialized knowledge have difficulty distinguishing reliable research from biased reports, products of p-hacking and articles that falsely purport to have been peer reviewed, both reliable and unreliable research reach the public through news media. The unreliable reports contribute to the public's impression of conflicting conclusions on topic after topic.

Fortunately, errant reports seem more common in other fields than in environmental research, but any science done badly creates an obstacle to environmental progress because errant reports erode public confidence in expert pronouncements. If the public reads that coffee, red wine, high-intensity exercise, sunshine or butter is good for them one year and bad for them the next, they may tend to expect the same flip-flopping regarding climate change, toxins in water, biodiversity loss or any number of other environmental concerns, and thus tune out rather than demand action.

> Before rushing ahead with legal mandates [regarding greenhouse gas emissions], it would be useful to consider 'scientific' predictions from the past that have proven wrong. The government now wants to ban trans fats from our food, but 50 years ago people were told to switch from butter to margarine because it was thought the trans fats in margarine lowered cholesterol levels. Foods such as coffee and chocolate have either been good or bad for us, depending on the 'scientific' study of the moment.[30]

We have now considered seven obstacles to detecting and understanding environmental problems. Problems must first be detected; some are obvious, but others go unsuspected for some time. Even suspected problems are often difficult to confirm. Once a problem is detected, constraints on experiments, uncertainties inherent in statistical procedures, and hazards of inference and extrapolation hinder efforts to understand causes and implications. Finally, reliable reports become mixed with unreliable reports, with the result that the public may lose confidence in expert pronouncements.

Despite these challenges, scientists have developed good understanding of many environmental problems, such as stratospheric ozone depletion and climate change. In the next part of the book I address obstacles to acting upon such problems, beginning with how opponents of environmental protection exploit scientific uncertainty to argue that understanding is insufficient to warrant action.

Notes

1   Altman, 'The scandal of poor medical research', 1994; *Nature*, 'Challenges in irreproducible research', 2018; Ioannidis, 'Why most published research findings are false', 2005; Martinson et al., 'Scientists behaving badly', 2005.
2   Truskey, 'Climate change is just "weather"', 2016, 18A.
3   NASA Science, 'Mars Polar Lander/Deep Space 2', n.d.; NASA Earth Observatory, 'Serendipity and stratospheric ozone', n.d.; Sawyer, 'Mystery of orbiter crash solved', 1999. Numerous other spacecraft destined for Mars have also failed spectacularly, as described by Sample, 'Total recall … of unsuccessful attempts to land on Mars', 2016.
4   Cox, *Planning of Experiments*, 1958 is my favorite text on the design of experiments.
5   A normal distribution is one where a plot of the number of observations of any given value produces a symmetric shape similar to a traditional bell. For this reason, normal distributions are often called bell curves.
6   Unfortunately, using multiple comparisons tests to protect against inflating the chance of type I error (false positive) increases the chance of type II error (false negative). Here again, qualified statisticians understand this and interpret results accordingly, but others may not appreciate that a trade-off is involved.
7   Nosek et al., 'The preregistration revolution', 2018; Wasserstein and Lazar, 'The ASA's statement on p-values', 2016, 131–2.
8   Amrhein et al., 'Inferential statistics as descriptive statistics', 2018; Ioannidis, 'Why most published research findings are false', 2005; Kurzban, 'P-hacking and the replication crisis', 2021; Simmons et al., 'False-positive psychology', 2011; Zwaan et al., 'Making replication mainstream', 2017.
9   Hurlbert, 'Pseudoreplication and the design of ecological field experiments', 1984; Hurlbert and White, 'Experiments with freshwater invertebrate zooplanktivores', 1993.
10 Reinhart, *Statistics Done Wrong*, 2015, 3.
11 Kuhn, *The Structure of Scientific Revolutions*, 1962.
12 Chamberlain, 'The method of multiple working hypotheses', 1965, 755 (originally published 1890).
13 Platt, 'Strong inference', 1964.
14 Cox, *Planning of Experiments*, 1958, 23–90.
15 Schulze et al., 'Fast, easy measurements for assessing vital signs of tall grassland', 2009.
16 Bailar, 'How to distort the scientific record without actually lying', 2006.
17 2015 House of Representatives majority report, quoted in Greenberg, 'Spending bill's gun research line', 2018.
18 Dwan et al., 'Systematic review of the empirical evidence of study publication bias and outcome reporting bias', 2008; Franco et al., 'Publication bias in the social sciences', 2014.
19 *Nature*, 'Challenges in irreproducible research', 2018; Bailar, 'How to distort the scientific record without actually lying', 2006; Fang et al., 'Misconduct accounts for the majority of retracted scientific publications', 2012; Franzen et al., 'Fraud', 2007; Martinson et al., 'Scientists behaving badly', 2005.

20 Martinson et al., 'Scientists behaving badly', 2005.

21 Krimsky, 'Do financial conflicts of interest bias research?', 2013.

22 Ebrahim et al., 'Meta-analyses with industry involvement are massively published and report no caveats for antidepressants', 2016; McGauran et al., 'Reporting bias in medical research', 2010; Michaels et al., 'Selected science', 2006.

23 Begley and Ellis, 'Drug development', 2012; Ioannidis, 'Why most published research findings are false', 2005.

24 Sinclair, U., *I, Candidate for Governor: And how I got licked*, 1994, 109 (originally published 1934).

25 Horbach and Halffman, 'The changing forms and expectations of peer review', 2018.

26 Kolata, 'Many academics are eager to publish in worthless journals', 2017; Sorokowski et al., 'Predatory journals recruit fake editor', 2017.

27 Bohannon, 'I fooled millions into thinking chocolate helps weight loss', 2015; Bohannon, 'Who's afraid of peer review?', 2013.

28 Beall, 'What I learned from predatory publishers', 2017. See also Beall's former website posted to the internet anonymously at https://beallslist.net/, accessed 10 October 2021.

29 Bohannon, 'I fooled millions into thinking chocolate helps weight loss', 2015; Chokshi, 'That wasn't Mark Twain', 2017.

30 Conservative syndicated columnist Cal Thomas opining against efforts to reduce greenhouse gas emissions in Thomas, 'The pope, the globe and the facts', 2015.

Part II

Obstacles to responding to environmental problems

Despite the challenges of detecting problems and understanding their causes, many problems are well understood. Smoking is bad for you. Chlorofluorocarbons destroy stratospheric ozone. Burning fossil fuels acidifies lakes and streams.

Understanding the health consequences of smoking, the causes of acid rain and the effect of chlorofluorocarbons on stratospheric ozone eventually resulted in policies that discourage smoking, reduced acid rain and are healing the ozone layer. But this progress came only after drawn-out battles between proponents of public health and environmental protection and their opponents, many of whom had profited from activities that cause harm and therefore had financial (vested) interests in preventing restrictions on those activities.

Many other problems have been understood for decades but have not received the attention they warrant. Nitrogen and phosphorus pollution from agriculture still causes eutrophication (excessive algae growth and oxygen depletion of waterways), but agriculture remains largely exempt from the Clean Water Act. Children can understand that an aquifer pumped faster than it is replenished will run out of water, yet we continue to deplete aquifers. Overfishing, soil erosion, habitat loss and species endangerment continue, and the concentration of atmospheric carbon dioxide sets a new record each year. These cases demonstrate that adequate progress requires more than scientific understanding; action must follow.

It can be difficult and time-consuming to develop scientific understanding of environmental problems, but the largest barriers to progress are probably not failures of scientific understanding, but failures of political will and hurdles to effective action.[1] Once an environmental problem is recognized and its cause or causes reasonably well understood, there are at least seven obstacles that must routinely be overcome for a response to occur. These are:

- exaggerated impressions of scientific uncertainty
- resistance to restrictions on personal or organizational liberties
- the assumption that the market will overcome problems on its own
- monetary costs of, and biases against, financial investments in environmental progress
- perceived lack of urgency
- impediments to majority rule and passage of new laws
- a tilted playing field of political debate that disadvantages proponents of environmental protection.

The chapters in this section consider these obstacles in turn.

… and you will observe with Concern how long a useful Truth may be known, and exist, before it is generally receiv'd and practis'd on.[2]

Notes

1 Lazarus, 'Environmental law after Katrina', 2007, 1041–53; Lazarus, *The Making of Environmental Law*, 29–43.
2 Benjamin Franklin, 1786 letter to Benjamin Vaughn, quoted in Morgan, *Not Your Usual Founding Father*, 2006, 78.

8
Exaggerated impressions of scientific uncertainty

Environmental progress requires reductions in activities that cause environmental damage, but those activities usually occur for some intentional purpose, often a worthy purpose such as providing food, clothing, shelter, comfort, recreation or convenience. Because the actions are intentional (though their environmental impacts generally are not), proposed restrictions often encounter resistance, especially from those who benefit from the offending activities. Facing such objections, policymakers generally do not restrict activities without widespread public demand to do so. Thus, it is not sufficient for specialists to understand a problem and its causes; public demand for environmental progress must overwhelm opposition to new restrictions on activities. Tremendous public demand was responsible for US environmental progress from the 1960s to the 1980s but has not generally been sufficient since.

Substantial delay often occurs between when experts conclude action is necessary and the public not only agrees but demands action. Much delay results from the public underestimating the rigour of scientific conclusions. For example, the most recent Pew survey comparing scientists' views with the general public showed 87 per cent of scientists but only 50 per cent of the general public agreed with the statement, 'Climate change is mostly due to human activity.'[1] The same circumstance was previously true for stratospheric ozone depletion, acid rain, and the health consequences of smoking.

No one has time or experience to become an expert on every important technical issue, environmental or otherwise. Should we pay more for organic food or worry about toxins in lawn chemicals, air fresheners, tap water or any number of other sources? We have no choice but to rely upon experts. But experts often equivocate, some almost always disagree with any consensus, and it is difficult for laypersons to identify objective, legitimate experts from charlatans.

Relying on expert opinion would be easy if experts made simultaneous, unanimous, definitive pronouncements, but they do not. As previous chapters have explained, careful scientists have several reasons to draw only provisional, tentative conclusions. They understand hypothesis tests can merely support, not prove, hypotheses, and they are aware of the limitations of experiments. They realize research may have involved undetected errors, including statistical errors. And they recognize the inherent uncertainties of extrapolation from experimental results to general circumstances. For all these reasons, careful scientists tend to draw tentative, provisional conclusions.

> A good scientist is never 'certain' ... the good scientist will be ready to shift to a different point of view if better elements of evidence, or novel arguments emerge. Therefore, certainty is not only something of no use, but is in fact damaging, if we value reliability.[2]

Moreover, experts do not reach conclusions simultaneously, and by the time conclusions reach the public, cautious, well-grounded arguments of the most objective experts are mixed with minority opinions or even bogus pronouncements based on shoddy or even sham reports. Vested interests then use conflicting reports and opinions as evidence that the uncertainty is too great to justify action, while minority views receive disproportionate attention because the media often seeks to tell two sides of any story.

For the same reasons that scientists hedge their conclusions, they also avoid making definitive predictions. Pity the poor expert asked to testify before Congress regarding the future climate or any other environmental concern. In day-to-day circumstances, anyone who claims to predict the future is dismissed as delusional, but our friendly scientist is expected to anticipate precisely what to expect with certainty.

They will never state that there is no relationship between variables but rather will state that they know of no evidence of a relationship, recognizing that evidence could always be found later. They will not claim to have proven a cause-and-effect relationship but rather will describe evidence 'consistent with' the hypothesis of such a relationship. In other words, they will not offer definitive conclusions regarding existing data, nor make definitive predictions – they will hedge pronouncements.

This chapter describes how the mixture of cautious expert conclusions, contrasting minority, unreliable or intentionally deceptive claims, and exaggeration of the degree of disagreement among experts leaves the public with an impression of scientific confusion that can prevent demand for action.

Public expectation of certainty

Failure to understand why careful scientists draw cautious, hedged conclusions causes some members of the public to underestimate the rigour of scientists' conclusions. Having seen a simplistic flow chart diagram of the scientific method almost annually in school (see Figure 4.1, p. 45), people could be excused for expecting scientists to methodically prove unequivocal facts, and therefore interpret hedged statements as evidence of substantial uncertainty. The following conclusions read as substantial to experienced scientists but may sound equivocal to members of a public constantly bombarded by more certain but less well-substantiated claims of advertisers, salespeople, pundits, politicians and others (emphases mine):

> Globally averaged precipitation over land has *likely* increased since 1950, with a faster rate of increase since the 1980s.[3]

> The comparison of the rate of carbon release suggests that the ensuing effects on ocean acidification and marine calcifying organisms *will probably* be more severe in the future …[4]

> Children of mothers who live near agricultural areas, or who are otherwise exposed to organophosphate, pyrethroid, or carbamate pesticides during gestation *may be* at increased risk for neurodevelopmental disorders.[5]

Diversity of expert opinion

The public's impression of substantial uncertainty is magnified by lack of simultaneity and unanimity of experts' conclusions. Curiously, the public tolerates or even expects expert disagreement in other policy realms, but in environmental policy many people seem to expect both predictive certainty and expert unanimity or near unanimity before demanding action.[6] Bona fide experts do not speak with one unanimous voice because, while most scientists are highly sceptical in nature, they are not equally sceptical, and any two scientists will view the same evidence from different perspectives.

Scientists' different individual experiences, areas of specialization and conscious or subconscious biases delay achievement of consensus. Different experts do not have the same degree of familiarity or expertise with individual topics. A few are involved in any given study; others work on the same or related topics; yet others work in the same general field; and others study completely different subjects but have experience analysing data. Moreover, as mere humans, they can become emotionally attached to their own hypotheses, hope for a conclusion that would confirm their preferences or, if the study is their own or on a subject of their research, hope new data will confirm an earlier prediction they have made.[7] In addition, publications can affect reputations, future job opportunities, promotions, or pay increases, so authors may find their own data more convincing than do others. Thus, differences in expertise, experience, levels of scepticism, degree of engagement in a study and, in the worst cases, conscious or subconscious biases prevent experts from reaching the same conclusion at the same time, with the consequence that unanimous conclusions are rarely reached and may not occur until evidence is overwhelming.

Climate-change sceptics have for decades exaggerated and distorted the previous lack of scientific consensus. During the 1970s, climatology was not as advanced as today. Several different groups were studying different climate-related processes. One group focused on greenhouse warming. Another group noted a cooling trend from the 1940s to the 1970s due to reflection of sunlight by smog. They projected worsening smog would cause further cooling. A third group realized the planet had been in a longer warm phase than those between the most recent ice ages, and therefore anticipated the next ice age. Finally, a fourth group speculated that nuclear war could lead to a 'nuclear winter' because dust, ash and other particles ejected into the atmosphere by nuclear explosions would reflect sunlight.

Since then, thanks to laws like the US Clean Air Act, smog declined in many places so its cooling effect diminished, concerns about nuclear winter faded after the Cold War, and further study clarified how the warming effect of greenhouse gases can overwhelm effects of cycles in the planet's orbit that cause ice ages. As a consequence, today qualified scientists are nearly unanimous in their agreement that greenhouse gases emitted by human activities are causing climate change.

Though far more peer-reviewed articles raised concerns about warming than cooling during the 1970s, both *Time* and *Newsweek* reported concerns about cooling. For decades thereafter, global warming sceptics distorted the record to suggest a consensus of concern about cooling in the 1970s had later morphed into a concern about warming. The supposed but fictional flip-flop was presented as evidence that climate science is unreliable, but there never was a consensus in the 1970s, just different scientists separately studying different processes, each with its own potential to affect climate.[8]

Even once experts achieve substantial consensus regarding a cause-and-effect relationship, they may not agree about likely future consequences. In other words, they may agree on data interpretation, but not on the resulting predictions. Consequently, some experts will be willing to make more precise, longer-term predictions than others.

Imagine a new question about a complicated phenomenon, such as the situation during the 1950s and 1960s when a substantial number of scientists first became concerned about climate change. How would you expect scientific opinion to develop as evidence accumulates? Initially, no experts will be willing to draw even a tentative conclusion. As evidence accumulates, some experts will find the evidence compelling and recommend policy responses but others will be more reluctant to reach that conclusion. Throughout this process some honest disagreement will persist. As long as a substantial diversity of expert opinion persists, the public is unlikely to demand action, and until they do so, politicians will hesitate to impose restrictions on responsible activities. Thus, diversity of expert opinion serves as an obstacle to action.

Experts' policy aversion

Meanwhile, many experts avoid the policy fray. They may feel a sense of responsibility to engage, but also face strong incentives not to do so. In addition to being trained to be sceptical and understand why results are uncertain, experts also often avoid policy debates out of concern that becoming embroiled in political controversy will compromise their objectivity or others' perceptions of their objectivity. Good scientists strive to be as objective as possible, but policy debates involve questions of what *should* be done – value questions. If I reach a conclusion about what should be done then I may subsequently, consciously or unconsciously, tend to interpret new data as supporting that conclusion. Because some scientists perceive taking a stand as incompatible with objectivity, engagement in policy debates can cause one to lose status within the scientific community.

> Within the scientific community, there is almost a code of honor that you will never transgress the red line between pure analysis and moral issues. But we are now in a situation where we have to think about the consequences of our insight for society.[9]

Columbia University epidemiologist Claire Wang explained her typical reluctance to engage in policy debates as follows:

> Three years ago, I was invited to testify before the New York City Board of Health about a proposed law to cap the portion size of sugary drinks served in restaurants. This request didn't come as a surprise … What did catch me off guard was my reaction: I was horrified at the thought of taking a public position …

> In my field, public health and nutrition, as in many other fields of science, presentations tend to be rich with data and discussions of limitations and caveats, almost always closing with the phrase 'more research is needed'. Testifying before the Board of Health, I would have no such options. Rather I would have five minutes to stake out a clear position. Yes, I believed, as did virtually all of my colleagues, that sugary drinks threatened people's health, but was my belief sufficient to justify policy action? Were a handful of longitudinal studies and two randomized control trials enough evidence?[10]

Moreover, scientists expect and many even enjoy spirited, good-natured debate among peers, but prominent scientists engaged in public policy controversies must often endure something entirely different – aggressive harassment. For example, US climate scientists James Hansen, Michael Mann and others have been subjected to frivolous lawsuits, received mail containing mysterious powders and endured not only death threats but threats to their families.[11] Such tactics will dissuade many from engaging in policy debates.

Far more mundane reasons also disincentivize engagement. Scientists' first encounters with policy often come from reporters' urgent requests that interrupt whatever work is in progress. The potential of such interactions is that public understanding might be advanced, but much can go wrong. Reporters expect brief explanations even though many readers or listeners will have little background in the relevant issues. Complex problems do not lend themselves to brief explanations.

In addition, reporters often lack relevant background knowledge and thus risk misunderstanding scientists' answers without realizing they have done so. One of my colleagues tells reporters he will talk with them if they will give him 30 minutes. They usually call someone else.

Misunderstanding is especially likely when comments are edited to sound bites because unqualified sound bites are often literally incorrect when published out of context. Such errors would not be as substantial a problem if sources could check reports before publication, but because of deadlines, reporters generally do not provide opportunities to do so. Moreover, television reporters do not normally provide questions ahead of time or reshoot answers if an interviewee stumbles. In the worst cases, inexperienced reporters make incredibly egregious errors. I was once quoted as stating something I did not say and would not have said. (The conversation was videotaped so there is no question about what I said.) When I objected to the published quote, the newspaper's editor suggested it was no big deal. When I eventually reached the reporter, she told me that 'I thought you would have said it'.

Anecdotal evidence of disinclination to engage in policy debates comes from a Center for Biological Diversity request for signatures on a letter to the US Fish and Wildlife Service regarding a key passage in the Endangered Species Act. The law prohibits federal agency actions that would 'result in the destruction or adverse modification of habitat' critical to endangered species. Prior to 2014, the precise regulatory definition of 'destruction or modification of habitat' had never been specified. Does the passage forbid destruction of *any* habitat or does it only forbid destruction of *all* habitat? It seems Congress must have intended to forbid destruction or modification of any critical habitat because successive, incremental damages would eventually drive any species extinct. Furthermore, a literal reading of the phrase clearly suggests Congress meant any habitat. But the Obama Administration proposed to interpret the passage to forbid only destruction or adverse modification of all habitat. Any ecologist understands that species only persist where habitat is suitable, so the dire consequence of such a definition to the survival of species would have been obvious to ecologists.

The Center's request for co-signers went to the then 18,000 US subscribers to the ECOLOG email distribution list, the easiest means of reaching the nation's ecologists. Only some twenty recipients endorsed the letter.[12] Even if one assumes half of the recipients disagreed with the letter (which seems highly unlikely), twenty responses from the other

9,000, amounts to 0.2 per cent. All one had to do was read a few pages, decide whether one agreed with the letter and reply with contact information. But for whatever reasons, more than 99 per cent of those who received the request did not allow their names to be added even though the proposed policy change would gut a key protection of the law.

> If scientists choose not to engage in the public debate, we leave a vacuum that will be filled by those whose agenda is one of short-term self-interest. There is a great cost to society if scientists fail to participate in the larger conversation – if we do not do all we can to ensure that the policy debate is informed by an honest assessment of the risks. In fact, it would be an abrogation of our responsibility to society if we remained quiet in the face of such a grave threat [as climate change].[13]

Merchants of doubt

In stark contrast, vested interests fund scientists for the specific purpose of making pronouncements intended to turn public opinion against environmental protection. These hired guns argue hedged conclusions and lack of unanimous agreement among experts (and purported experts) demonstrate too much uncertainty to enact new environmental protections. They often work for think tanks or other organizations that portray themselves as objective entities akin to universities without students, when in reality they are funded by industry to advance a particular agenda.[14] With no other professional responsibilities, think tank experts make themselves available to the media and spend their time writing opinion pieces for broad audiences and briefing papers for policymakers.

Naomi Oreskes and Erik Conway used the term 'merchants of doubt' to describe individuals employed to sow confusion about environmental issues.[15] Merchants of doubt exaggerate diversity of expert opinion, question the reliability of opponents' data and even have the audacity to question opponents' integrity while they themselves are employed specifically to protect profits.[16]

To advance arguments that evidence is too uncertain to act, merchants of doubt blur the distinction between actual experts and others who merely claim expertise. They also call for more research on behalf of 'better understanding'. Who would oppose better understanding? They then argue that as long as scientists are still studying a question, those scientists must not consider understanding sufficient to warrant action (as if research on lung cancer would halt just because cigarettes had been implicated as a cause).[17]

Oreskes and Conway explain how this set of techniques has been repeatedly employed to exaggerate uncertainty and forestall policy. Merchants of doubt successfully prolonged debates over tobacco, acid rain, stratospheric ozone depletion and climate change, with many of the same individuals involved in the different issues.[18] US Representative Sheldon Whitehouse of Rhode Island agrees, arguing that representatives of the fossil fuel industry adopted the tobacco industry playbook. 'The big tobacco playbook looked something like this: (1) pay scientists to produce studies defending your product; (2) develop an intricate web of PR experts and front groups to spread doubt about the real science; (3) relentlessly attack your opponents.'[19]

As we have seen, Congress passed almost all of the nation's major environmental laws during the 1960s, 1970s and 1980s (see Figure 1.3, p. 12). Ever since then, arguments that evidence is not sufficient to require action have helped stymie sufficient political demand to pass major new environmental protections.[20] One major obstacle to environmental progress is thus merchants of doubts' effectiveness at exaggerating scientific uncertainty, confusing the public and thereby diluting demand for political action.

Merchants of doubt employ deceptive arguments that depend on the ability to fool audiences. They focus attention on a fraction of relevant evidence, obscure distinctions between bona fide experts and commenters with vested interests and between peer-reviewed literature and other documents, and exploit the desire of the media to 'tell both sides of the story', all to give the public the impression there is too much uncertainty to act.[21]

The first step is to call attention to selected evidence, thus distracting audiences from other evidence that may be more relevant. This data 'cherry picking' is the equivalent of saying, 'If smoking causes cancer, then how come my father, who smoked, did not die of cancer?' Just because smokers sometimes die of other causes does not mean smoking does not cause cancer.

An example of such cherry picking is the former focus of climate change sceptics on the fifteen or so years following 1998, a period as hot as any in recent history but that, until 2015, could be selectively portrayed as appearing to suggest a lull in warming. To make this argument, merchants of doubt carefully specified the start and end dates under

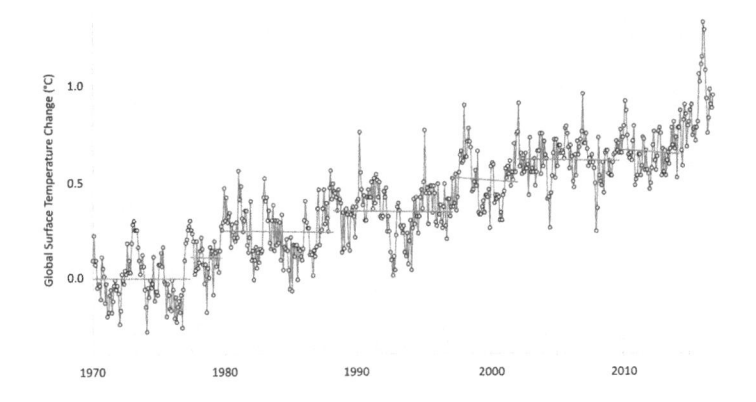

Figure 8.1: *Skeptical Science* graph illustrating how focusing on a particular subset of data can give an erroneous impression. Source: *Skeptical Science*, 'The escalator', n.d.

consideration, the last two periods indicated by blue lines in Figure 8.1, while ignoring all other evidence. Limiting one's perspective to just the period of one or another blue line gives the impression of a lack of warming, but a longer view shows an increasing temperature trend. By focusing on one particular time period and only one of many types of evidence, merchants of doubt sought to distract audiences from more sensible interpretations of the complete collection of evidence (longer-term temperature trends, changes in species' ranges, melting glaciers, changes in sea ice and sea level, and the theoretical reasons to expect greenhouse gases to cause climate change).

Other approaches are even less ambitious, such as calling attention to one snowstorm or a cool spell during summer. Perhaps the most infamous case of relying on a trivial anecdote occurred when Senator James Inhofe of Oklahoma brought a snowball onto the floor of the Senate to suggest a single snowstorm in Washington, DC refuted the evidence of climate change (Figure 8.2). This would have been almost comical, but at the time Senator Inhofe was the Chairman of the Senate's Committee on Environment and Public Works.

Cherry picking data is only one way merchants of doubt employ specious arguments. They also imply existing evidence is unreliable by calling for 'sound science' (which means science with whose results they agree, not science that has been peer reviewed), focus criticism upon opponents' most extreme statements, attack opponents personally rather

Figure 8.2: Image from US public service television channel C-SPAN showing Oklahoma Senator James Inhofe implying that a February snowstorm in Washington DC constitutes meaningful evidence that humans are not affecting the climate during a congressional debate on 26 February 2015. Source: C-SPAN user clip: Inhofe Snowball. Accessed 11 November 2021. https://www.c-span.org/video/?c4529935/user-clip-inhofe-snowball.

than their arguments, and dismiss 'computer models' as if complex calculations have no predictive value whatsoever, or that they have a better way of predicting the future. They also distract audiences from recognizing the folly of demanding certainty before acting when faced with possible catastrophe.

Producing 'studies' that sound good but are not peer reviewed, and funding scientists willing to take minority opinions heightens the effectiveness of cherry picking. The classic US case of combining these techniques is the so-called 'Petition Project' that began in 1998 and persists on the internet.[22]

During 1998, project organizers mailed a slick packet of material to practically every scientist in the country. They sought signatories for a statement that it would be premature to act to prevent climate change. There was no effort to reach qualified scientists with expertise in climate science. Rather, the project was designed to swamp those voices with signatures from any PhDs who would sign on. The project garnered thousands of signatures by combining a bit of fraud, appeals to scientists' characteristic scepticism and such a massive mailing that if only a small proportion of recipients added their signatures, the number would appear impressive.[23]

The packet of material included a letter from a past president of the National Academy of Sciences, Dr Frederick Seitz. Seitz was not a climate scientist, but his cover letter is probably a major reason why some recipients considered the request. Included with the letter was an article precisely formatted to emulate the distinctive appearance of papers published in the prestigious *Proceedings of the National Academy of Sciences* and an op-ed piece by the same authors from the *Wall Street Journal*. The article formatted to look like it was from the well-known journal included numerous examples of cherry-picked data and even a graph with no numbers on its vertical axis, in other words, a graph that was utter nonsense, but at a glance the article looked legitimate. The article is sufficiently complex that I have used it for student practice in detecting deceptive arguments.

The article was published not in the *Proceedings of the National Academy of Sciences* but in the impressive sounding *Journal of American Physicians and Surgeons* (a curious choice for an article on climate change). Stephanie Mencimer, writing in *Mother Jones*, noted that other articles in that journal conclude abortion causes breast cancer, vaccines cause autism and illegal immigrants caused a leprosy epidemic. The journal's editors are evidently less sceptical about some issues than others.[24]

The petition project blurred the distinction between experts and merely purported experts. The authors were affiliated with the impressive-sounding Oregon Institute of Science and Medicine, but its address is a sheet metal building on a farm in a remote rural area of that state. When last checked, its website listed eight 'faculty' members, two of whom are deceased and two of whom are the director's sons. The Institute's 2012 Internal Revenue Service form 990 reported that the sons are also board members and each spends one half hour per week on institute business. The article's third author derives his research funding from the petroleum industry and has failed to disclose conflicts of interest in at least eleven scientific publications.[25] Despite debunking by the National Academy of Sciences and a large number of clearly bogus signatories (such as doctors from the television show *M*A*S*H*) climate change deniers referenced the petition signatories for years to argue that scientists substantially disagreed about anthropogenic climate change, even though consensus among qualified scientists was documented back at the turn of the century when the Petition Project was launched.[26] Rather than relent once there was virtually no question about a consensus among qualified scientists, the merchants of doubt seemed to only increase their efforts.[27]

Both sides of one-sided stories

News reporters' desire to 'tell both sides of a story' further advances the impression of too much expert disagreement to act.[28] Describing alternative perspectives is a valuable service in principle, but it elevates minority views. For example, of more than 3,500 hard news articles about global climate change published by the *New York Times*, *Washington Post*, *Los Angeles Times* and *Wall Street Journal* from 1988 through 2002, the majority covered both sides of the argument regarding whether humans were causing climate change even though a review of more than 900 peer-reviewed articles on the topic from roughly the same period failed to find a single paper that disagreed with the scientific consensus that humans are changing the climate.[29] The map in Figure 8.3 suggests that despite the consensus in peer reviewed research even back in 2002, two decades later merchants of doubt have remained remarkably effective at confusing the public.

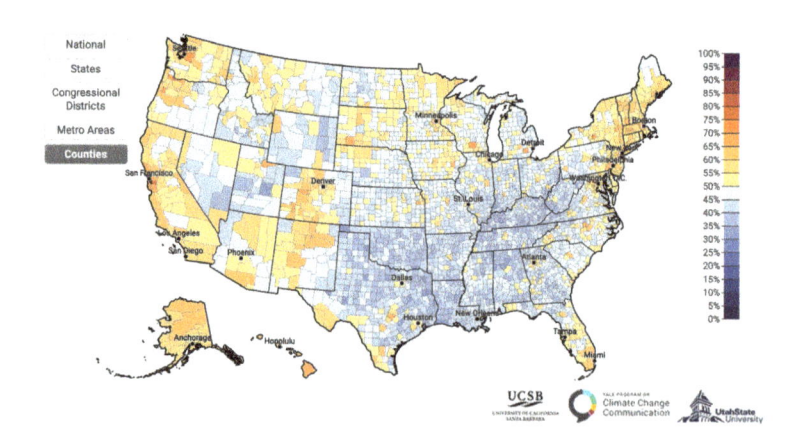

Figure 8.3: Yale Project on Climate Change Communication 2020 county map of estimated percentage of adults who believe most scientists think global warming is happening. (Map provided courtesy of Yale Program on Climate Change Communication. See also Howe et al., 'Geographic variation in opinions on climate change at state and local scales in the USA', 2015.) Source: Marlon et al., 'Yale Climate Opinion Maps'.

Hazard of inaction

Merchants of doubt argue that we should not act until we are certain, but it is foolish to demand certainty before acting. We do not wait to put on seatbelts until an accident is imminent. We do not wait to buy health insurance until we become ill or wait to fund fire departments until a fire occurs. Demands for certainty before acting fail to recognize that inaction is itself a choice – a decision to maintain the status quo, to keep doing whatever may be causing a problem.

Robert Costanza and others use the type of diagram in Table 8.1 to illustrate the possible consequences of policy choices.[30] The left column shows alternative potential true states of the future. The top row shows policy alternatives. The bold text shows possible outcomes. The diagram uses climate change as an example; it illustrates how the worst possible outcome is if climate change is real but there is no effort to prevent it. In other words, rather than being the cautious option, inaction in the face of uncertainty can be the most dangerous option.

Table 8.1: Possible climate change realities, policy options and consequences

	Attempt to prevent climate change	Ignore possibility of climate change
Climate change real	**Minimize damage**	**Disaster**
Climate change not real	**Spend money unnecessarily**	**Lucky**

Possible climate change realities are shown in the left column, policy alternatives in the top row, and consequences in bold type.

The success of exaggerating uncertainty as a reason to delay environmental protection is particularly impressive when one considers that the public does not expect predictive certainty or expert consensus before acting on other issues. We routinely make individual and societal decisions regarding diets, investments, tax policy, foreign policy, welfare policy and other matters despite tremendous uncertainty and expert disagreement. Imagine if unanimity among experts was expected before taking foreign policy action or unanimity among economists was expected before enacting tax policy. Such expectations would be hopelessly naïve, but they are not far from what seems to be expected before acting on environmental policy. Perhaps many members of the public do not expect expert consensus on these other issues because they are not 'scientific' questions whose answers can be readily 'proven'.

As noted in the second chapter's discussion of unintended consequences of new innovations, when harms are familiar, we act cautiously, even when those harms are uncertain. Thus, the US military budget is almost equal to those of all other nations combined, drivers are required to carry automobile insurance even if they have never had an accident, banks require homeowners' insurance before granting mortgages, bridges are so strong they rarely fail, cars must pass safety inspections, and so on. But when environmental harms are uncertain, arguments against caution often carry the day, as is apparent in the contrast between the following examples described by Freudenburg, Gramling and Davidson. Facing uncertainty, the health task force choose precaution while the Forest Service concluded precaution was unnecessary.

> On December 21, 2004, a US federal task force issued its final report on proposals to allow US citizens to import prescription drugs from Canada. Because the task force 'could not be sure' that the imported drugs were safe, its members recommended that the practice remain illegal.

> The next day, a different federal agency, the Forest Service, decided it could not be sure that logging would be bad for the environment. It therefore eliminated the requirements for preparing Environmental Impact Statements in Forest Plans and for protecting 'viable' species from destruction through logging.[31]

The provisional nature of scientists' conclusions, failure of bona fide experts to simultaneously reach unanimous conclusions, intentional efforts to sow confusion and exaggerate uncertainty, and the inclination of the media to 'tell both sides of the story', all cause the public to overestimate the degree of uncertainty regarding environmental threats. As a consequence, members of the public may get the impression that for every PhD there is an equal and opposite PhD, even when for every merchant of doubt there may actually be 100 better-qualified PhDs who draw the opposite conclusion. Under such circumstances, the public can be forgiven for concluding that a topic is just too confusing to know what to do and turn their focus to other concerns. But when that happens, politicians will not act.

Since the 1990s, merchants of doubt have successfully blocked major US environmental protection initiatives, but their tactics eventually failed in the cases of cigarettes, acid rain and stratospheric ozone depletion. The flaws in their arguments eventually became clear to enough people that demand for action prevailed. A return to consistent environmental progress may well require convincing large majorities of the flaws in merchants of doubts' arguments.

Notes

1   Pew Research Center, 'Public and scientist's views on science and society', 2015. By 2020 surveys did at least show that some 70 per cent of respondents thought global warming was happening (Yale Program on Climate Change Communication, 'Yale climate opinion maps 2020').

2   Italian theoretical physicist Carlo Rovelli, quoted in Jha, 'We must learn to love uncertainty and failure, say leading thinkers', 2011.

3   Intergovernmental Panel on Climate Change, 'Summary for policymakers', 2021, SPM-6.

4   Zeebe and Zachos, 'Long-term legacy of massive carbon input to the Earth system', 2013, 12.

5   Shelton et al., 'Neurodevelopmental disorders and prenatal residential proximity to agricultural pesticides', 2014, 1108.

6   Lovejoy, 'Let science set the facts', 2013; Z. Smith, *The Environmental Policy Paradox*, 2004, 12.

7   Platt, 'Strong inference', 1964.

8   Peterson et al., 'The myth of the 1970s global cooling scientific consensus', 2008.

9   Hans Joachim Schellnhuber, Chairman of the Potsdam Institute for Climate Impact Research, quoted in Yardley and Goodstein, 'Pope Francis, in sweeping encyclical, calls for swift action on climate change', 2015.

10 Wang, Y., 'The dangerous silence of academic researchers', 2015.

11 American Association for the Advancement of Science, 'Statement of the board of directors of the American Association for the Advancement of Science regarding personal attacks on climate scientists', 2011; Milman, 'Climate scientists face harassment, threats and fears of "McCarthyist attacks"', 2017.

12 Center for Biological Diversity, 'Letter to U. S. Fish and Wildlife Service', 2014. Lori Burd, Endangered Species Campaign Director, Center for Biological Diversity, estimated the number of signatories (personal communication, 9 October 2014).

13 Mann, 'If you see something, say something', 2014.

14 Beder, *Global Spin*, 2002, 75–89.

15 Brulle, 'Institutionalizing delay', 2014; Farrell, 'The growth of climate change misinformation in US philanthropy', 2019; Oreskes and Conway, *Merchants of Doubt*, 2010.

16 Cushman, 'Industrial group plans to battle climate treaty', 1998.

17 Salzman and Thompson, *Environmental Law and Policy*, 2014, 19.

18 Oreskes and Conway, *Merchants of Doubt*, 2010, 36–215.

19 Whitehouse, 'The fossil fuel industry's campaign to mislead the American people', 2015.

20 Beder, *Global Spin*, 2002, 15–25; Z. Smith, *The Environmental Policy Paradox*, 2004, 17.

21 Farrell, 'The growth of climate change misinformation in US philanthropy', 2019.

22 Anonymous, 'Global Warming Petition Project'. This website has links to the list of signatories, the paper formatted to appear as if it was published in the prestigious *Proceedings of the National Academy of Sciences of the United States*, copies of the mailing's cover letter from Dr. Seitz, etc.

23 It is curious that the Petition Project obtained so many signatories but the previously cited Center for Biological Diversity letter obtained only a few. But there are important differences between the two cases. The Petition Project's letter is still available to sign many years later whereas the Center for Biological Diversity's signatories had only a few days to respond. The Petition Project sent a whole packet of material with a highly-credentialed scientist as the first

author. Their expensive, showy mailings arrived in presumably thousands of mailboxes on the same day. (My Austin College colleagues and I all received them at the same time.) The Petition Project letter was distributed to far more people. And perhaps importantly, the Petition Project asked recipients to sign a letter saying it was too early to take various hypothetical actions whereas the Center for Biological Diversity letter required signatories to agree that a specific policy already proposed by a government agency would be a mistake. In other words, the Petition Project appealed to the natural scepticism of scientists whereas the Center for Biological Diversity letter required drawing a specific, firm conclusion about a policy decision.

24 Mencimer, 'The Tea Party's favorite doctors', 2009.
25 Center for Media and Democracy, 'Oregon Institute of Science and Medicine', n.d.; Gillis and Schwartz, 'Deeper ties to corporate case for doubtful climate researcher', 2015.
26 Oreskes, 'The scientific consensus on climate change', 2004.
27 Frontline, *Climate of Doubt*, 2012.
28 Boykoff and Boykoff, 'Balance as bias', 2004.
29 Boykoff and Boykoff, 'Balance as bias', 2004; Oreskes, 'The scientific consensus on climate change', 2004.
30 Costanza et al., *An Introduction to Ecological Economics*, 1997, 150.
31 Freudenburg et al., 'SCAMming environmental policy', 2008, 7.

9
One-sided perspectives on liberty

I do not like to be told what to do. Perhaps you feel the same way. But living together in society requires restrictions on what each of us may do. For example, we have chosen to restrict our impacts on the environment. We may not dump garbage in the local river, burn waste in a barrel, kill endangered birds or use outlawed pesticides. In all of these cases, we have agreed to restrict our individual freedoms as a means of protecting all of us from the harms those freedoms can cause.

When new environmental protections are proposed, opponents argue that new rules would conflict with liberty, one of the tenets on which the United States was founded. Those opponents refer to the US *Declaration of Independence*, which reads, 'We hold these truths to be self-evident, that all men are created equal, that they are endowed by their Creator with certain unalienable Rights, that among these are Life, Liberty and the pursuit of Happiness', and to the US Constitution's preamble, which describes the objective of securing 'the Blessings of Liberty to ourselves and our Posterity'. Not surprisingly, both major political parties espouse freedom. The Democratic Party platform perennially refers to working to expand rights, while Republican platforms highlight protecting freedoms. The Republican platform preambles of 2016 and 2020 stated, 'We believe political freedom and economic freedom are indivisible. When political freedom and economic freedom are separated – both are in peril; when united, they are invincible. We believe that people are the ultimate resource – and that the people, not the government, are the best stewards of our country's God-given natural resources.'[1] In practice, both parties seek to expand some rights or freedoms and restrict others, but their official statements emphasize protection and expansion of freedom, not restriction. Thus, restrictions on environmental damage can be portrayed as being in conflict with not only the goals of the *Declaration of Independence* and the Constitution, but also major political objectives.

Freedom to versus freedom from

Opponents of environmental protection are partially correct. Environmental protection does restrict one sort of freedom. It restricts freedom to damage the environment. But that is only one consequence. Environmental protection restricts some liberties to protects others. When I am not free to smoke in a restaurant, you are free to dine without breathing my smoke. When I am not free to pollute the air, you are free to breathe unpolluted air. Environmental protection restricts freedom *to damage the environment* to protect freedom *from a damaged environment*. President Franklin Delano Roosevelt prominently articulated the combination of freedoms *to* and freedoms *from* in his address on four freedoms: freedom of speech, freedom of worship, freedom from want and freedom from fear.[2] Environmental protection contributes to both freedom from want (continued availability of natural resources) and freedom from fear (avoidance of hazards due to environmental damage such as climate change, toxin exposure and loss of ecosystem services, which are the free goods that we require from ecosystems, such as oxygen generation, soil formation, pollination, water cycling and climate regulation). Proponents of environmental protection must ensure that discussions of freedoms are comprehensive, including both freedoms foregone and freedoms protected.

Blinkered appeals to freedom arise in all sorts of environmental debates. Among the most vociferous are land-use disagreements. For example, wealthy landowners on Massachusetts's Cape Cod objected to proposed 'Cape Wind' offshore electricity-generating wind turbines because the machines would be visible from shore and therefore would interfere with the landowner's freedom to enjoy a view of the ocean. Whereas you may perceive wind turbines as aesthetically pleasing, climate change-preventing, dynamic, modern techno-art, those Cape Cod residents perceived them as ugly industrial installations. The project was eventually abandoned. The wind farm developers blamed extended litigation from opponents.[3] At least that disagreement was peaceful.

Cliven Bundy grazed his cattle on federal land in Nevada for twenty years without paying the contracted grazing fees. Eventually, federal officials attempted to remove Bundy's cattle, but they were met with armed resistance from Bundy and his supporters. His son Ammon subsequently led another armed standoff at the Malheur National Wildlife Refuge in Oregon.[4] In both cases, the notion of individual rights to exploit the environment were taken to an extreme; proponents claimed a right not only to use public lands, but to do so for free.

Even modest new restrictions encounter opposition. The railway industry objected to a requirement that they notify the US Department of Transportation when transporting more than a million gallons of volatile Bakken Shale oil – even after a fire from a Bakken oil train killed forty-seven people in Lac-Mégantic, Quebec.[5] Indeed, some objections are frankly preposterous. When the Berkeley, California city council drafted an ordinance requiring gasoline pumps to bear stickers noting that burning gas causes climate change, the Western States Petroleum Association complained about the plan, 'imposing onerous restrictions on businesses and forcing unwanted speech in violation of the First Amendment [of the US Constitution]'.[6] None of these objections noted the freedoms protected when other freedoms are restricted.

Reproductive freedom

Population growth concerns raise perhaps the most acute conflicts, or apparent conflicts, between individual freedom and environmental protection. One indication of the subject's sensitivity is the absence of any mention of it by prominent environmental organizations. For example, the Natural Resources Defense Council lists eight priorities, all noble: climate change, communities, energy, food, health, oceans, water and the wild. They make no mention of population.[7] The Friends of the Earth website lists six priorities: climate and energy, democracy, finance and economic systems, food and agriculture, forests and oceans.[8] The Sierra Club lists three major programmes: climate and energy; lands, air, water, and wildlife; and people and justice. Population issues and family planning receive attention only deeper in their webpages.[9] Most remarkably, the environmental group formerly known as Zero Population Growth changed its name to Population Connection, apparently to create a more positive 'brand identity'.[10] At least they give explicit priority to population issues, as does the Center for Biological Diversity.[11]

That the issue of population size is sensitive does not reduce its critical importance. The product of population size and per capita environmental impact is the root of all environmental problems.[12] Indeed, the most parsimonious hypothesis for the many examples of nonsustainability is that the planet cannot sustainably support so many of us living as we do. Thus, efforts to achieve sustainability must grapple with the uncomfortable subject of population growth.

At least five reasons make this subject particularly delicate. (1) Any suggestion that a population is too large, or that population growth is undesirable, has potential implications for individual fertility choices, among the most personal of decisions. (2) Until recently, virtually every government effort to reduce population growth was an atrocious ethical disaster. (3) Contraception is controversial or forbidden in some cultures and by some religions. (4) Population concerns are sometimes used as a convenient cloak for racist and anti-immigrant motivations. (5) Finally, typical systems for funding retirees, such as the US Social Security system, depend upon an ever-increasing supply of new workers to support an ever-increasing number of new retirees.

Writers since Aristotle have raised concerns about manageable population sizes, but Western attention did not galvanize until the publication of Thomas Robert Malthus's 1798 *Essay on the Principle of Population*.[13] Malthus wrote in response to other Enlightenment authors who postulated that social reform could overcome all deprivation. Perhaps most notably, the Marquis de Condorcet had suggested that 'all will be able, by the development of their faculties, to procure the certain means of providing for their wants', arguing that 'nature has no fixed limits to our hopes'.[14]

Malthus did not think social reform alone could prevent poverty and misery. Rather, he was concerned that exponential population growth could overwhelm any increases in agricultural production, resulting in widespread misery. He reasoned as follows:

> Through the animal and vegetable kingdoms nature has scattered the seeds of life abroad with the most profuse and liberal hand; but has been comparatively sparing in the room and the nourishment necessary to rear them. The germs of existence contained in this earth, with ample food, and ample room to expand in, would fill millions of worlds in the course of a few thousand years. Necessity, that imperious all-pervading law of nature, restrains them within the prescribed bounds. The race of plants and the race of animals shrink under this great restrictive law; and the race of man cannot by any efforts of reason escape from it.[15]

He concluded that unless 'preventative checks' limited birth rates, the population would expand as fast as agricultural production, food would never be abundant relative to demand and every bad harvest would cause famine. Some eighty years later, Cornelius Walford's tally mentioned several hundred famines over the course of history, including more than 150 in Great Britain.[16] Because contraception was not well developed and was widely considered immoral in Malthus's day, the only available preventative check was delaying marriage and thus procreation.[17]

Malthus sought to avoid misery, but his prescription for doing so was cruel. He advocated phasing out England's Poor Laws. He thought the guaranteed support of the poor laws increased the number of births to parents who lacked the wherewithal to raise children, thereby increasing the number and proportion of individuals living in poverty.

> The poor-laws of England tend to depress the general condition of the poor in these two ways. Their first obvious tendency is to increase population without increasing the food for its support. A poor man may marry with little or no prospect of being able to support a family without parish assistance. They may be said, therefore, to create the poor which they maintain; and as the provisions of the country must, in consequence of the increased population, be distributed to every man in smaller proportions, it is evident that the labour of those who are not supported by parish assistance, will purchase a smaller quantity of provisions than before, and consequently more of them must be driven to apply for assistance.[18]

Malthus reasoned that without fear that their children would go hungry, some males would reproduce earlier than otherwise, population would rise faster, food prices would climb higher, malnutrition would spread to a larger proportion of the population and the taxation necessary to provide for the poor would push the poorest employed labourers onto government support, creating a positive feedback that would continually increase the proportion of the population in poverty and dependent on government assistance. Malthus realized that if the Poor Laws were eliminated, some children and their mothers would starve unless rescued by private charity, but concluded that this ghastly circumstance would be the price of less misery, suffering and starvation in the long run. He concluded: 'If the plan which I have proposed were adopted, the poor's rates in a few years would begin very rapidly to decrease, and in no great length of time would be completely extinguished.'[19] Thus, the first prominent argument for government policy to reduce birth rates was recognized, even by its proponent, as likely to cause suffering or even starvation.

Though not universally accepted, Malthus's logic was widely appreciated and became a major influence on British thought and policy. Though the English Poor Laws persisted despite Malthus's objections, he influenced Britain's nineteenth-century administration of India. Malthus considered India's long history of famines an inevitable consequence of relatively early marriage and attendant high birth rates, combined with crop failures during years of unfavourable weather.[20] Malthus taught at Haileybury, the East India Company College that trained young men destined for work in the company's administration in India. Some of those administrators applied Malthus's logic, combined with Adam Smith's enthusiasm for free markets,[21] to argue that interfering with the grain market to alleviate famines would only make matters worse in the long run.

Meanwhile, Britain began importing Indian grain. The new source of demand raised Indian market prices above what the lowest-paid Indian labourers could afford. When drought struck, millions starved.[22] Thus, although Malthus intended to prevent starvation, Malthusian logic became associated with starvation in both Britain and India during the nineteenth century, not exactly an auspicious start for efforts to prevent population growth. Then the situation got worse before it got better.

Food shortages continued after India gained independence in 1947. In response, Prime Minister Jawaharlal Nehru initiated the world's first national family planning programme in 1951. The programme was initially based on encouragement, but eventually became coercive. Beginning in the 1960s, Indian women were encouraged to accept intrauterine device (IUD) implants. During the 1970s, mobile field hospital 'vasectomy camps' were introduced. Incentive payments were offered to adults who agreed to sterilization, but popular resistance grew as side effects of intrauterine devices and botched sterilization procedures became widely known. Nevertheless, in 1975 Nehru's daughter, Prime Minister Indira Gandhi, further increased the pressure to accept sterilization, initiating 'negative incentives'. In some states, food rations and other government benefits were withheld if families had more than three children or could not present official sterilization certificates. Objection to these policies led to Gandhi's defeat in the election of 1977.[23]

Such disastrous, inhumane consequences of coercive national population control policies led to the 1994 United Nations International Conference on Population and Development, at which 179 nations agreed that individual rights and well-being, rather than numerical population targets, should serve as the goal of development programmes. Unfortunately, despite the United Nations (UN) plan, practices in India have not met international standards. As recently as 2014, thirteen women died of complications when a surgeon performed over 80 sterilizations in six hours, apparently repeatedly using nonsterile equipment. The women had been paid $23 to undergo the procedure. Only a year earlier some 100 semi-conscious women were left outdoors with no assistance following tubal ligations.[24] Coercive sterilizations under inadequate conditions are not the only tragedy of modern Indian family planning. The natural human sex ratio at birth is about 1.05 males per female. As of 2021, India's ratio was 1.11.[25] The simplest explanation of such a skewed ratio is selective abortion or infanticide of females.

Coercive policies have also skewed the sex ratio of Chinese newborns. China maintained a one-child policy from the 1970s until 2016. When that policy was initiated, the sex ratio of Chinese babies was approximately 1.05 males per female. As of 2001 it was 1.17. In other words, by the late 1990s almost six Chinese boys were born for every five girls. During 2016, China abandoned the one-child policy. As of 2021, the ratio had declined to 1.11[26]

Unfortunately, the US has its own horrible history of government-run sterilization programmes, a topic reviewed in detail by Professor Paul Lombardo in his 2008 book *Three Generations: No imbeciles*, upon which the next three paragraphs are based. During the latter half of the nineteenth century, Francis Galton developed the study of eugenics – controlled breeding of humans to sculpt the genetic composition of future generations. The idea generated great enthusiasm, but the practice of eugenics took off with little attention to the rights of individuals or even much scientific basis for which characteristics of individuals were genetically determined. Various proponents used anecdotal evidence, such as a track record of criminality in a particular family, as the basis for concluding that undesirable behaviours were genetically based and used that reasoning as a rationale for advocating sterilization of individuals with characteristics deemed undesirable. The Carnegie Institute of Washington's Station for Experimental Evolution at Cold Spring Harbor, New York undertook eugenics research in 1904. Dr Harry Laughlin became the managing director of the institute's Eugenics Record Office and a leading proponent of eugenic sterilization. He encouraged states to adopt involuntary sterilization laws. One state to do so was Virginia, which passed the Virginia Sterilization Act of 1924. The Virginia law provided for involuntary sterilization of 'feebleminded' persons.

Virginia subsequently ordered Carrie Buck sterilized while she was a resident of the state's institution for epileptics and the feebleminded. When 17, Ms. Buck had been committed to state care by her foster parents after their nephew raped her and she became pregnant. She was ostensibly committed for feeblemindedness, incorrigibility and promiscuity, not because she had been raped.

An infamous 8–1 Supreme Court decision upheld the constitutionality of the Virginia law in the 1927 case *Buck v. Bell*. Writing for the majority, Chief Justice Oliver Wendell Holmes wrote, 'It is better for all the world, if instead of waiting to execute degenerative offspring for crime, or to let them starve for their imbecility, society can prevent those who are manifestly unfit from continuing their kind'.[27] Prior to *Buck v. Bell*, 17 states had sterilization laws. After the ruling, 30 states eventually adopted sterilization laws. Based on a review of the eugenic Human Betterment Foundation's surveys, geneticist Philip Reilly estimates state laws accounted for some 60,000 sterilizations.[28]

Incredibly, non-consensual sterilization did not cease in the United States until the 1970s. The Relf sisters of Mississippi were sterilized without consent in 1973 at the ages of 12 and 14. After presiding over their lawsuit, Judge Gerhard Gessell estimated that US federal programmes had sterilized more than 100,000 low-income women. Moreover, those sterilization laws and coerced contraception policies disproportionately harmed women of colour.[29] Given the track record of coercive, racist and sexist national birth control policies in the United States and elsewhere, it is no wonder any talk of government-organized population control policy encounters extreme wariness.

Fortunately, since the 1990s the best national programmes have abided by the goals of the 1994 UN International Conference on Population and Development – increasing individual reproductive freedom by providing voluntary contraceptive choices to women who desire to limit their pregnancies. Various programmes have increased availability of contraception, but tremendous unmet demand remains.[30] Indeed, some 120 million unintended pregnancies per year substantially exceed the annual increase in global population of about 80 million. Those pregnancies result in about 50 million births and 70 million abortions.[31]

Even entirely voluntary programmes are controversial. For example, though the American Academy of Family Physicians, the American Academy of Pediatrics, the American College of Obstetricians and Gynecologists, the Centers for Disease Control and the World Health Organization all recommend long-acting reversible contraceptive implants for prevention of unintended pregnancies among adolescents, a successful Colorado programme based on satisfying demand for those contraceptives was so controversial it required funding from an anonymous foundation rather than the state.[32]

Even when family planning programmes are not coercive or discriminatory, they face other cultural, religious or ethical objections. Some cultures favour large families and some religious doctrines consider contraception an affront to God's wishes. Some people believe teaching children about contraception encourages promiscuity. Many consider abortion unacceptable in all or almost all circumstances.[33]

As if those were not enough reasons to consider the issue of population too difficult to touch, two other complications remain. One is the relationship of immigration to population. Populations of nations obviously can grow from either births or immigration. Thus, one means of reducing population growth is to limit immigration. Nations routinely restrict immigration, but proposals to increase restrictions face resistance for several reasons. Immigrants wish to immigrate, so both they and their supporters favour immigration. Immigrants contribute to economies and enrich cultures. Some industries hire large numbers of recent immigrants. Finally, because calls to restrict immigration have often been racially motivated, opposition to such restrictions may be motivated by an assumption that those who wish to restrict immigration have racist intent. Unfortunately, the latter concern is justified because those who oppose immigration out of prejudice often couch their arguments in concerns regarding population growth.[34]

Population control efforts also complicate retiree funding systems, such as the US Social Security system. Many such systems fund current retirees with current workers' contributions. If birth rates decline, then, for a few decades, the ratio of retirees to workers increases, leaving fewer workers to support each retiree. In such a circumstance, either workers must sacrifice more of their income to retiree funding, funding per retiree must decline, the retirement age must increase, or funding systems must borrow money.[35] None of those options is popular, and the retiree funding problem is more immediate than population growth concerns. Thus, retiree funding tends to receive more attention. News headlines routinely express concern about short-term economic consequences of birth-rate declines, such as 'Overpopulation isn't the problem: it's too few babies', and 'Fear of economic blow as births drop around the world'.[36] But a positive feedback system of an ever-increasing number of retirees supported by an ever-increasing number of workers would require continual – and because it would be exponential, continually accelerating – population growth.

A halt to population growth compatible with care for retirees would require financial sacrifices during a period of adjustment. Thus, this presents another case of not simply reducing freedoms, but trading freedoms. Sacrifices in the near term would enable a more sustainable population in the long term – and therefore protect the freedom of future generations to enjoy a world not overcrowded. Ultimately, compared to continual population growth, reworking retirement systems would create less hardship, but short-term concerns about retiree support have so far taken precedence.

We have considered five objections to intentional efforts to slow or prevent population growth: understandable extreme wariness of government efforts to influence personal reproductive choices; the despicable history of early national population programmes; cultural and religious resistance to contraception; concerns about motivations for and consequences of restricting immigration; and concerns about funding retirement systems. Meanwhile, the world's population is now some 7.9 billion, has gained 500 million since I wrote the first draft of this paragraph, and if I live to be 90 and present projections are correct, will have tripled over the course of my lifetime.

As nations have industrialized, child and overall mortality have declined, women's rights and control over their own lives have expanded, access to contraception has increased and population growth rates have declined. Indeed, population growth has halted or nearly halted in many wealthy nations. This shift in industrialization, mortality rates and birth rates is referred to as the demographic transition. In theory, therefore, one way for the world's population to stabilize would be for every nation to achieve an income level at which rich nation's birth rates have fallen to or below the replacement level. However, many environmental scientists doubt the planet can provide the resources to provide so much wealth to everyone.

The alternative is to achieve low birth rates in lower-income countries while respecting individuals' reproductive rights. Figure 9.1 shows that some countries have quite low fertility rates despite modest incomes. Nepal and Bhutan, for example, combine modest per capita gross domestic product (GDP) with relatively low fertility rates and, assuming programmes are implemented as described in policy documents, enlightened population policies.[37] Such data suggest freedom of individual fertility decisions in the present is compatible with protecting future generations from runaway population growth. Indeed, Bhutan has

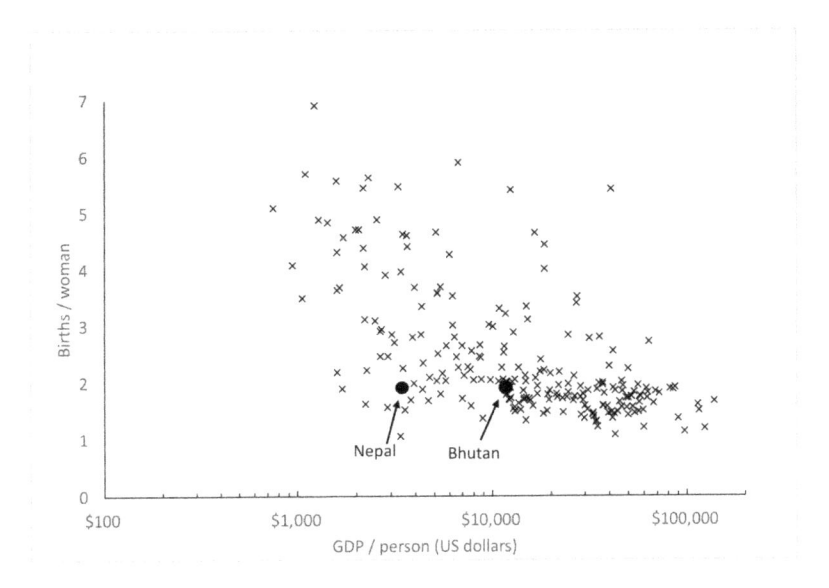

Figure 9.1: Relationship of birth rates to average income for the world's nations. Fertility data are 2021 estimates. Most GDP data are 2019 estimates, with some from earlier during the 2010s. Data source: US Central Intelligence Agency, 'Guide to country comparisons', n.d.

been so successful that their latest (2018) draft national population policy seeks to encourage an increase in fertility sufficient to avoid falling below replacement level.[38]

Freedom trade-offs

Whether the subject is a land-use dispute, an industrial procedure or even birth rates, advocates of freedom from environmental restrictions ignore a critical issue. Rather than simply sacrificing liberty for the sake of environmental protection, environmental protection trades freedom to damage the environment for freedom to enjoy an undamaged environment. Water pollution prevention laws replaced slaughterhouse owners' freedom to throw pig carcasses into rivers with everyone else's freedom from rivers of pig carcasses. The Clean Air Act restricted the freedom to pollute air with freedom to enjoy clearer skies.

Even in the case of individual reproductive decisions, enlightened policy can enhance freedoms. An absence of any policy theoretically maximizes the freedom of individuals to make their own reproductive decisions, but if those individuals lack access to contraception, they may be free only in theory. On the other hand, if a government or some other entity provides access to contraceptives and no oppression or cultural barriers prevent their adoption, those who wish to limit their childbearing have the freedom to do so.

A special case of freedom trade-offs occurs between generations. Future generations benefit from advances made by ancestors, but they also suffer from damage done by ancestors. Might the freedoms of descendants be increased by restrictions on the freedoms of ancestors? Consider some examples.

Today's Grand Banks fishers are not free to catch cod because previous generations were free to catch so many that the fishery is depleted. The same goes for many of the world's other great fisheries. How much freer would today's fishers be if their predecessors had not had the freedom to deplete large ocean fish by 90 per cent.[39] Foresters in many areas are no longer free to harvest old growth trees because those trees were clear cut by their predecessors and those forests have not recovered. Today's potential foresters must seek other work, and you and I have fewer flooring choices, many of which are plastic.[40] More critically, we and other species lack the ecosystem service benefits healthy forests provide, to say nothing of the fate of the trees themselves. Likewise, unless future generations manage to rehabilitate a great deal of land, tomorrow's farmers will not have the freedom to grow food in the astonishing three tons of soil per person that we are annually eroding away.[41] I suspect they will try mightily to rehabilitate land because we have less than 0.2 hectares of cropland per person (less than one half of a football field each, see Figure 9.2), while the Food and Agriculture Organization of the United Nations estimates one in three people did not have adequate food in 2020.[42]

Nor will tomorrow's farmers be free to fertilize their fields with guano from the exhausted mines of Nauru and other Pacific atolls. Past generations exhausted those supplies. Future generations are also unlikely to enjoy the freedom to enjoy a planet with today's climate and sea level because of climate change set in motion by our freedom to burn fossil fuels. Instead, they will pay costs of that damage through expenditures on mitigation of and adaptation to climate change.

These examples represent a common phenomenon and a conundrum. We routinely understand the wisdom of foregoing some expenditures to save assets for the sake of children or grandchildren. Why is the wisdom of doing the same with ecosystem assets less well appreciated? Robert Costanza and others describe our current trajectory as depleting a 'one-time inheritance of natural capital', like a university

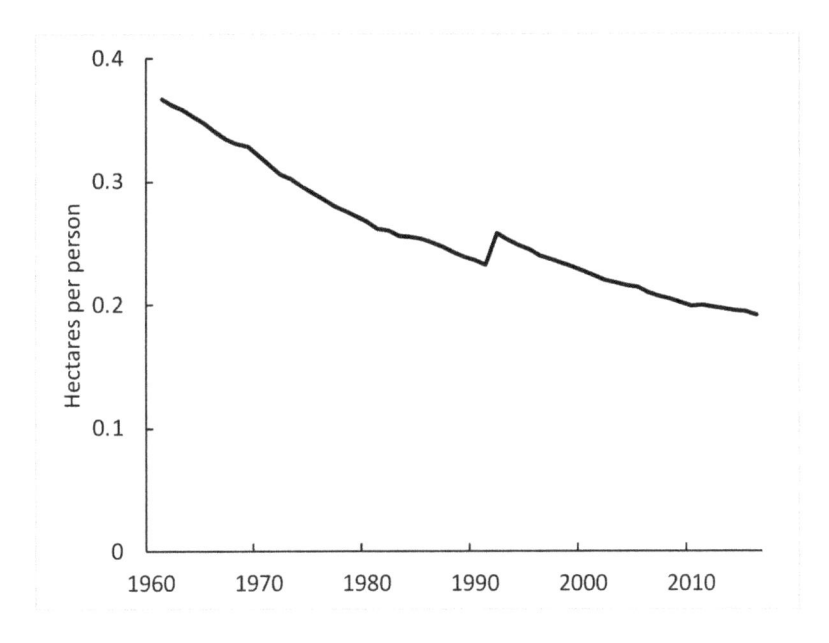

Figure 9.2: Worldwide arable land per person, 1961–2018. Data source: World Bank, 'Arable land (hectares per person)', n.d.

that depletes its endowment or a family that depletes its inherited wealth. We readily grasp the folly of eating into endowments or wasting an inheritance. It seems there is much less appreciation of the folly of depleting natural capital. Some will object that descendants would not enjoy advances developed by ancestors if those ancestors' freedoms were restricted, but perhaps there is a happy medium where beneficial innovation and progress can occur without collateral damage to the life-support potential of the planet.

Might any of today's areas of chronic conflict be less troubled if past generations had better preserved the potential for plant growth? Is it a coincidence that sites of military conflict so often contain few growing plants? I do not mean to be simplistic about the causes of conflict or ecosystem damage, ascribe blame to people of any particular area (let alone the regions of the most ancient farming cultures), or imply I would have done any better, and I realize the productivity of US farmland has been degraded at astonishing rates, but what if desertified lands still enjoyed productive ecosystems? How much more freedom and opportunity might todays' citizens of such places enjoy?

In general, the freedom of earlier generations to unsustainably use a resource precludes subsequent generations from enjoying that same freedom, but earlier generations do not always cause damage. The anthropological literature suggests many indigenous peoples at least implicitly understood the relationship between present and future freedoms. For example, the Dene, Cree, Naskapi, Inuit and other indigenous peoples of North America traditionally believe happiness and well-being depend on proper relationships with other species and the environment.[43] The Quichua, Maasai, Samburu and indigenous peoples of the Philippines hold similar attitudes. An Amazonian indigenous leader noted their forest management is so careful that visitors mistake their managed forests for wild, natural habitat.[44] Such norms are not surprising from the perspective of evolution by natural selection. Any indigenous culture that used its land unsustainably would have gone extinct before contact with people from distant lands.[45] When today's members of remaining indigenous cultures have the freedom to benefit from their environments, it may be because their ancestors did not assume the freedom to destroy those environments.

When you walk outside in an American city on a clear day, look up at the blue sky, recall the photo of Los Angeles in the introduction to this book and be thankful for the Clean Air Act, which, by restricting freedoms to pollute the air, has protected your freedom to breathe (relatively) clean air. But be prepared, meanwhile, for opponents of environmental protection to make appeals to freedom and liberty as a tactic for blocking further environmental progress. They will continue to do so until their audiences realize protecting freedom to damage the environment destroys the freedom of a healthy environment, and the net effect of environmental protection is often, and perhaps usually, an increase in freedom.

> A person with less need for vigilance against poisoned food or toxic drinking water, a consumer who doesn't have to spend hours or weeks making sure that the mortgage company is not corrupt, a worker protected from the risk that the industrial machinery could kill him – these are freer citizens.[46]

Notes

1   Democratic National Convention, '2020 Democratic Party Platform'; Republican National Committee, 'Republican Platform 2020'.
2   Baker, 'Freedom from inspiration', 2019.
3   O'Sullivan, 'Two utilities opt out of Cape Wind', 2015; Sellye, 'Koch brother wages 12-year fight over wind farm', 2013.

4 Martinez et al., 'Oregon standoff', 2016; Nagourney, 'A defiant rancher savors the audience that rallied to his side', 2014.

5 Robertson and McNish, 'Inside the oil-shipping free-for-all that brought disaster to Lac-Mégantic', 2014; Tate, 'Rail industry pushes feds to drop crude-oil reporting rule', 2014.

6 Reilly, 'Berkeley may put climate change warnings on gas pumps', 2014.

7 Natural Resources Defense Council, 'Our work', n.d.

8 Friends of the Earth, 'Issues', n.d.

9 Sierra Club, 'Explore issues', n.d.

10 Population Connection, 'Why population?', n.d.; Simon Does, 'Population Connection brand identity', n.d.

11 Center for Biological Diversity, 'Programs', n.d.

12 Mora, 'Revisiting the environmental and socioeconomic effects of population growth', 2014; Schulze, 'I = PBAT', 2002.

13 Kreager, 'Aristotle and open population thinking', 2008.

14 Condorcet, *Outlines of an Historical View of the Progress of the Human Mind*, 1796, 252–3.

15 Malthus, *An Essay on the Principle of Population*, 1992, 14 (originally published 1798).

16 Walford, *The Famines of the World, Past and Present*, 1879, 4–19.

17 Caldwell, 'Malthus and the less developed world', 1998, 678.

18 Malthus, *An Essay on the Principle of Population*, 1992, 100.

19 Malthus, *An Essay on the Principle of Population*, 1992, 266–7, 380.

20 Malthus, *An Essay on the Principle of Population*, 1986, 119–20.

21 A. Smith, *The Wealth of Nations*, 2000 (originally published 1776).

22 Davis, *Late Victorian Holocausts*, 2001, 25–33.

23 Gwatkin, 'Political will and family planning', 1979, 51; Harkavy and Roy, 'Emergence of the Indian national family planning program', 2007, 310–12; Tarlo, *Unsettling Memories*, 2003, 147–77.

24 Das and Contractor, 'India's latest sterilisation camp massacre', 2014.

25 US Central Intelligence Agency World Factbook, 'India', n.d.

26 Hesketh et al., 'The effect of China's one-child family policy after 25 years', 2005, 1172; US Central Intelligence Agency World Factbook, 'China', n.d.

27 *Buck v. Bell*, 1927, paragraph 4.

28 Lombardo, *Three Generations*, 2008; P. Reilly, 'Involuntary sterilization in the US', 1987, 161.

29 Hornblum et al., *Against Their Will*, 2013, 193–209; Stern, 'Sterilized in the name of public health', 2005, 1131–6.

30 Freedman and Isaacs, 'Human rights and reproductive choice', 1993; Mwaikambo et al., 'What works in family planning interventions', 2011, 67–9; Schlanger and Wolfson, 'How to defuse the population bomb', 2014.

31 Bearak et al., 'Unintended pregnancy and abortion by income, region, and the legal status of abortion', 2020.

32 Ricketts et al., 'Game change in Colorado', 2014.

33 Bill and Melinda Gates Foundation, 'Family planning', n.d.; Doughton, 'Gates birth-control initiative could fire up its critics', 2012.

34 Huang, 'Anchor babies, over-breeders, and the population bomb', 2008; Kulish, 'Dr. John Tanton, quiet catalyst in anti-immigration drive, dies at 85', 2019; Kulish and McIntire, 'Why an heiress spent her fortune trying to keep immigrants out', 2019.

35 Reznik et al., 'Coping with the demographic challenge', 2005/2006.

36 Condon, 'Fear of economic blow as births drop around world', 2014; Kotkin, 'Overpopulation isn't the problem', 2011.

37 Government of Nepal Ministry of Health and Population Department of Health Services, 'Annual Report, 2019/2020', 101–2; Royal Government of Bhutan, 'Draft National Population Policy', 2018, 4–8.

38 Royal Government of Bhutan, 'Draft National Population Policy', 2018, 8.

39 Myers and Worm, 'Rapid worldwide depletion of predatory fish communities', 2003.

40 One of those choices is flooring made from reused boards taken from dismantled buildings. The reused wood is expensive but interesting and supposedly even trendy. The supply is, however, extremely limited.

41 Food and Agriculture Organization of the United Nations, *Status of the World's Soil Resources*, 2015, 101.

42 Food and Agriculture Organization of the United Nations, *The State of Food Security and Nutrition in the World*, 2021, xvi.

43 Brody, *Living Arctic: Hunters of the Canadian North*, 1987, vii and 75–6; Manning, *Grasslands*, 1995, 28.

44 Bennagen, 'Tribal Filipinos', 1993, 68–74; Chirif et al., *El Indígena y su Territorio Son Uno Solo*, 1991, 181 (English translation from Macdonald et al., 'The Quichua of eastern Ecuador', 1993, 13); Lochgan, 'The Samburu of Kenya', 1993, 46–8; Matampash, 'The Maasai of Kenya', 1993, 35–6.

45 For example, the agricultural communities of Chaco Canyon in present-day New Mexico and Mesa Verde in south-western Colorado were both apparently abandoned at least partly due to depletion of trees in the vicinity of their remarkable communities. See Kohler and Matthews, 'Long-term Anasazi land use and forest reduction', 1988; Lentz et al., 'Ecosystem impacts by the ancestral Puebloans of Chaco Canyon, New Mexico, USA', 2021.

46 Kuttner, 'Obama's Obama: the contradictions of Cass Sunstein', 2014, 88.

10
Market freedom

A parallel of the misplaced notion that individual liberty is maximized by lack of rules and restrictions is that society and its individuals will be better off if individuals can participate freely in markets as they see fit – that people and markets should be entirely free. By restricting behaviours (of individuals and organizations), environmental protection restricts markets. Therefore, free market enthusiasts often oppose environmental protection.

The most extreme free-market proponents frame environmental problems merely as cases of resource scarcity. They expect the economic logic of supply and demand, combined with freedom of entrepreneurs to produce innovations, to overcome any shortage, arguing scarcity causes price increases that reduce demand and inspire innovation. Innovators either find more of a resource, devise a way to extract previously technically or economically inaccessible stocks, or devise substitutes for the resource. In any case, entrepreneurs alleviate shortages by innovating in response to free market incentives.[1] Historian David Wootton summarizes this perspective as follows: 'The triumph of capitalism derives from its willingness not to plan but to venture into the unknown, trusting (perhaps unreasonably) that we will solve problems as fast as we generate them.'[2]

For example, when the price of oil rises, entrepreneurs have an incentive to devise better exploration and extraction technologies. These new technologies, like fracking and horizontal drilling, make previously inaccessible stocks accessible (thus maintaining the supply), provide profit for the entrepreneurs and counteract the earlier increase in the price of oil. If the price remains high, other entrepreneurs devise other innovations that provide the same service with less requirement for the resource (such as more fuel-efficient cars) or develop innovations that do not require oil (such as electric cars). Here again, the service in demand, such as transportation, continues to be available without any need for government intervention in the market. Markets combined with entrepreneurship and technological innovation often do have these effects. For example, Teslas and other electric cars can run on electricity generated by solar panels or wind turbines. Extreme free marketers assume that such entrepreneurship and innovation will *always* overcome resource scarcities.

Enthusiasts apply the same logic to accumulation of wastes (pollution). If wastes accumulate to the point that people are burdened, those people will be willing to pay for clean-up of the wastes. Thus, entrepreneurs enjoy an opportunity to profit by developing clean-up mechanisms. Here again, innovations will satisfy market demand, solving the problem without requiring government interference.

Market fundamentalism

Perhaps the most extreme proponent of this view was Julian Simon, who channelled the Marquis de Condorcet's argument from two hundred years earlier when Simon wrote:

> There is no physical or economic reason why human resourcefulness and enterprise cannot forever continue to respond to impending shortages and existing problems with new expedients that, after an adjustment period, leave us better off than before the problem arose. Adding more people will cause us more such problems, but at the same time more people will be available to devise means of tackling problems, ultimately leaving us with lower costs and less scarcity in the long run.[3]

A 2017 *Wall Street Journal* editorial reflected this perspective when the editors wrote: 'The best form of climate-change insurance is a large and growing economy so that future generations can afford to adapt to whatever they may confront.'[4]

This is an appealing vision because it avoids any need for regulations, bureaucracies to implement regulations, legal systems to resolve disputes regarding regulations or taxes necessary to operate bureaucracies. No one has to go out of their way to either overcome environmental problems or avoid causing them. Entrepreneurs and their collaborating engineers will more or less automatically take care of everything by responding to market forces.

Indeed, market fundamentalists argue, any interference in this process through regulations, taxes or other means will make the market less efficient, destroy incentives and reduce general welfare. The Cato Institute, a libertarian think tank, articulates free-market enthusiasts' anti-regulatory perspective: 'Environmental goods and services, to the greatest extent possible, should be treated like other goods and services in the marketplace. People should be free to secure their preferences about the consumption of environmental goods such as clean air or clean water regardless of whether some scientists think such preferences are legitimate or not. Likewise, people should be free, to the greatest extent possible, to make decisions consistent with their own risk tolerances regardless of scientific or even public opinion.'[5]

The intellectual roots of such sentiments are often attributed to Adam Smith's 1776 *Wealth of Nations*, in which he argued that the 'invisible hand' of the market will 'frequently' cause individuals motivated by their own economic interests to take actions that benefit society at large. Enthusiasts often paraphrase Smith as if he said individual actors in free markets *always* benefit society, rather than claiming this 'frequently' occurs in one specific aspect of market activity, an aspect that true free-marketers often abhor (preferring 'the support of domestic to foreign industry').[6]

Appeals to free markets provide convenient cover for those seeking to protect their own freedom to profit from environmentally damaging activities. They cannot argue that 'we want to continue to make money from damaging the environment', so they must make some other argument. Thus, they distort evidence to support the claim that scientists have not reached consensus that a problem exists, object to infringements on liberties restricted (while ignoring liberties protected), extol the wonders of the free market and its potential to create jobs while ignoring the potential of environmental protection to create jobs, and implying free markets can accomplish virtually anything (except tolerate environmental regulation). An internet search of 'restrictions', 'jobs', and a reference to any extractive industry, such as coal or logging, will return a multitude of examples like the following:[7]

These newly mandated fees will add burdensome new costs on our independent producers, taking investments away from developing new American-made energy, much-needed job creation and economic growth.[8]

The war on coal is a war on jobs.[9]

If we do the things they want us to do, cap and trade, you name it, how much will that change the pace of climate change vs. how much will it cost to our economy? ... Scientists can't tell us what impact it would have on reversing these changes. But I can tell you with certainty it would have a devastating impact on our economy.[10]

Compliance with the terms of the Paris Accord and the onerous energy restrictions it has placed on the US could cost America as much as 2.7 million lost jobs by 2025 according to the National Economic Research Associates.[11]

The Clean Air Act's unduly stringent and extremely costly provisions could seriously threaten this nation's economic expansion.[12]

These arguments about environmental protection causing job losses not only tend to be exaggerated, they require two double standards. First, they tend to ignore simultaneous job creation in clean energy and environmental protection industries even though various estimates suggest many more jobs have been or will be created in those industries than lost due to environmental protection.[13] Second, those who object to job losses due to environmental progress tend not to object to job losses due to business or technological innovation in non-environmental realms, as occurs when formerly popular products fall out of favour (such as digital versus film cameras, Uber and Lyft v. taxis, newspapers v. websites, news talk shows v. investigative reporting, today's latest fad v. yesterday's), nor do they object to workers being left unemployed by automation. Those cases are attributed to the creativity and ingenuity of the free market, the invisible hand or even 'creative destruction', and accepted under the assumption that their net effect will advance welfare.

I do not wish to make light of the severe personal, family and community disruption associated with economic changes, but merely wish to highlight the double standard of objecting to job losses due to environmental protection but not due to other societal or market changes. (Ideally, effective interventions could minimize disruptions to lives and livelihoods in all such cases.) Where jobs are concerned, it is also important to recognize that losses in extractive industries such as mining, logging, and fishing, are inevitable when resource extraction depletes non-renewable supplies, renewable resources are harvested faster than those resources recover, or automation replaces workers.

Proponents of markets free of environmental regulation justify their expectations by reference to the trend of increasing material welfare that some have enjoyed for the last few hundred years. However, that argument requires assuming that trend can continue and spread to all. In other words, the missing fish, forests, soils, species, and ecosystem services will not matter because future people will enjoy other benefits due to 'progress' and thus have no need for fish, forests, soils or obscure species.

Can free-market incentives really overcome all resource shortages and clean up wastes? If so, then why do environmental problems persist? When presented with evidence of persistent pollution problems or resource shortages, free-market enthusiasts argue the market would work its magic but has never had the opportunity because it has never been entirely free. Failures are the result of burdensome regulations and other interference.

In contrast, sceptics of free-market responses to environmental problems not only note continuing shortages and accumulations of waste and pollutants such as greenhouse gases, but also point to environmental damage done by profit-seeking businesses as evidence that free markets do not protect the environment.

Markets are remarkable. Combined with technological innovation (the origins of which have generally depended not on markets but on taxpayer-funded, government research),[14] and massive supplies of natural resources, markets have provided a remarkable supply of goods to consumers who can afford them. That they have done so despite the attendant depletion of resources such as copper, phosphorus, forests, soils and aquifers superficially suggests we can count on market ingenuity to overcome resource depletion. Indeed, thanks largely to market freedom, humble college professors and many of their students enjoy luxuries unknown even to royalty of the past. Queens and kings of past ages could not travel in airplanes, eat fruit out of season or communicate immediately with people on other continents. But the existence of these luxuries does not guarantee eventual freedom from all scarcities for everyone.

The presumption that a free market could provide such luxury to everyone indefinitely requires a leap of faith from the observation that free markets have *overcome some shortages in the short term for some people* to the conclusion that markets can *overcome all shortages in the long term for all people* (and also that overcoming those shortages would have no consequence besides meeting the immediate demands of human consumers). Professor Liam Heneghan refers to this sort of wishful thinking as a lullaby.[15] My friend Kelby Archer refers to it as hopium. As far back as 1982, the President of Exxon Research and Engineering was also sceptical:

But faith in technologies, markets, and correcting feedback mechanisms is less than satisfying for a situation such as [climate change]. The critical problem is that the environmental impacts of the CO_2 buildup may be so long delayed. A look at the theory of feedback systems shows that where there is such a long delay the system breaks down unless there is anticipation built into the loop.[16]

Fundamentalists' assumptions

In addition to common assumptions of basic supply and demand theory, such as that consumers are rational and have perfect knowledge of available goods, that trading involves no transaction costs, and that markets are competitive, the free-market fundamentalist argument depends upon optimistic assumptions about the potential of technology to extract previously unavailable resources and discover, extract or produce substitutes for exhausted resources, all without generating harmful quantities of pollutants or causing other undesirable consequences.[17] It would be one thing to find substitutes for all resources, but the market argument must also assume technological substitutes can be developed for the free ecosystem services we require. Environmental scientists tend to be sceptical; many consider ecosystem services non-substitutable because of their scale and complexity.[18]

Furthermore, market enthusiasts tend to overlook the dependence of market miracles not just on relatively free markets, but also upon depletion of the planet's life-support potential. In the course of generating monetary wealth, markets have depleted soils, old-growth forests, concentrated stores of elements such as phosphorus and copper, and perhaps most notably fossil fuels. What has been depleted cannot be depleted again.

Consider the ingredients in a typical mass-produced cookie. They often include palm oil, which is largely harvested from trees planted in South-East Asia after first removing the native tropical rainforest. Thus, with each bite of such a cookie, one contributes to the destruction not only of the forest itself, but of indigenous societies, orangutans, birds of paradise and other species that have caused us no harm, and reduction in the production of ecosystem services. Markets alone have not produced the luxuries so easily taken for granted. Rather, that production caused environmental damage and depleted resources.[19]

It seems risky to bet future generations' welfare on the assumption that the continual increase in production of marketed products, which some people in some places have enjoyed for a limited time, can spread to everyone everywhere forever when the production of those goods has depleted resources it has depended upon. Future generations might prefer we not make that bet.

When the Cato Institute writes that 'People should be free to secure their preferences about the consumption of environmental goods', they must mean that if you want to consume clean air at your factory and turn it into dirty air, you should be allowed to do so. Or if you want to use mountaintop removal mining to extract coal, then throw the overburden and other wastes into nearby valleys, you should be allowed to do so. Then if the neighbours do not like it, they can express their preferences about consumption of environmental goods by buying untainted property somewhere else.

The technologically optimistic arguments of market fundamentalists also require no ethical prohibitions on doing whatever we want to the planet in the interest of finding resources to satisfy market demands. If oil extraction from the Arctic endangers Inuit hunting grounds, then the Inuit should express their preference by moving somewhere else. If palm oil plantations destroy the forest homes of the Dayak and other indigenous peoples of Borneo, that is just collateral damage in the process of making cookies and chocolates available to others. If mountaintop removal coal mining not only forces people out of valleys filled with mine spoils, but buries valley streams and the species that live in them, then so it goes. And if forest destruction drives other species extinct and destroys the production of ecosystem services, then that's the price of progress. Some future innovation will solve the problem.

If pushed on these matters, market enthusiasts will argue that meeting demands for goods is often more important than the collateral damage. That might be the case in some instances when true needs are at stake and damages are minimal and temporary. But only the staunchest free market enthusiast would posit that future humans will not need the services provided by healthy ecosystems. Moreover, the market does not distinguish between meeting true needs and satisfying mere wants (and, in fact, converts mere wants into needs as we saw in Chapter 2's discussion of systems perspectives).

Logical inconsistency

Curiously, extreme market fundamentalists assume market-driven technological innovation can overcome any resource scarcity and any waste problem, but fret about whether the same ingenuity and entrepreneurial spirit can overcome constraints of environmental regulation. This inconsistency has been noted by Nobel-Prize-winning economist and *New York Times* columnist Paul Krugman.

> Normally, conservatives extol the magic of markets and the adaptability of the private sector, which is supposedly able to transcend with ease any constraints posed by, say, limited supplies of natural resources. But as soon as anyone proposes adding a few limits to reflect environmental issues – such as a cap on carbon emissions – those all-capable corporations supposedly lose any ability to cope with change ...[20]

Market fundamentalists also tend not to explain *when* the market will achieve its miracles. If pressed, they argue political hurdles have interfered, as if a day will soon come when there are no political hurdles. One manifestation of this perspective occurs in the argument that there is plenty of food; people only go hungry because food is unevenly distributed. Such arguments routinely ignore that most food production, dependent as it is upon fossil fuels, soil erosion, fertilizer inputs and other non-renewable resources, is non-sustainable. Market fundamentalists would explain away this concern by arguing that technology will devise substitutes for shortages of those materials, as if a plant can just use more iron if it doesn't have enough phosphorus (it cannot), meanwhile assuming it is fine for humans to grind up the planet however they see fit if doing so meets some market demand. In other words, non-sustainability itself would be a non-issue if we would just let the market work its wonders. It is difficult to find an adherent of this position who has an educational background that includes ecology, the requirements of chemical elements for the functioning of cells, or the thermodynamics of energy and material transformations.

For our purposes, the critical point is that free-market purists will resist environmental protection, arguing that markets provide goods best when they are unrestricted. Thus, if trees become scarce, floors will be made with plastic boards that look like wood (forests only being good for making floors). If fish become scarce, people can eat beef, chicken or

Figure 10.1: *Top*: A natural resource. Photograph by the author. *Bottom*: A market response to scarcity of places to swim. Photograph by Wade Morgen. Original photo cropped. Accessed 16 November 2021. https://www.flickr.com/photos/lash9420/7505370490/. CC BY 2.0.

synthetic meat (consequences for the ocean and the fish themselves being irrelevant). As Figure 10.1 illustrates, if wilderness and swimming holes become scarce, we will have Disneyland and swimming pools (wilderness being nothing more than a place for backpacking, which can always be substituted for with fake cliffs with built-in hand holds in shopping malls). And famously, if palm trees will not grow in the shallow soil of a highway median they can be replaced with plastic trees (since the only value of trees is to improve the view, and of course a fake tree is just as good as a real tree for that purpose).[21]

Uncompromising market fundamentalism is probably rare. I suppose few people would argue soil erosion is of no consequence. But the default position that markets will work best when unfettered remains prominent, at least in public if not scholarly discourse, and proponents of these ideas strongly resist efforts to restrict environmentally damaging activities. When pressed, opponents of environmental regulation might admit that soil erosion is not desirable, but in practice we have done precious little about it.[22]

Most members of the public presumably would not claim to be economic theorists, but many nevertheless implicitly subscribe to the assumptions of free-market enthusiasts through what Zachary Smith calls the Dominant Social Paradigm, '... those clusters of beliefs, values, and ideals that influence our thinking about society, government, and individual responsibility'. Smith writes, 'The most important components of the [Dominant Social Paradigm] are free-market economics, faith in science and technology, the [economic] growth orientation common in Western democracies, and a sense of separation from the natural environment.'[23] Some early expressions of faith in science and technology were quite remarkable, including the following.

The only thing we can be sure of about the future is that it will be absolutely fantastic.[24]

Our children will enjoy in their homes electrical energy too cheap to meter.[25]

Nuclear energy promises to restore the balance between the 'have' and 'have not' nations of the world by providing an abundant, virtually limitless source of energy, enough to raise the standard of living of every nation in the world to heights undreamed of. In addition, nuclear energy also offers the greatest promise in history to increase greatly the world's food supply, to prolong life, to conquer disease, and, in general, to create a better life for the world's millions everywhere.[26]

Machinery, the New Messiah.[27]

The assumptions of free-market enthusiasts create obstacles to environmental progress because members of the public who trust markets and technology to overcome environmental problems are likely to oppose further environmental protections that would restrict economic activities.

Jared Diamond, while discussing his book *Collapse: How societies choose to fail or succeed*, wondered about the thoughts of the person who cut down the last tree on Easter Island. He imagined these possibilities.

'This is our clan's land. Don't tell us what to do.'

'Restricting cutting would be premature. There may be more trees we have overlooked.'

'I'm sure we will come up with a technological substitute for trees.'

'Restricting cutting would hurt the economy and cause a loss of jobs.'[28]

Notes

1   Barbier, *Economics, Natural-Resource Scarcity and Development*, 1989, 22–6.
2   Wootton, '"Origin Story" review', 2018.
3   Simon, *The Ultimate Resource,* 1996, 580.
4   Wall Street Journal Editorial Board, 'Trump bids Paris adieu', 2017.
5   Cato Institute, 'Environmental regulation', n.d.
6   Schlefer, 'Today's most mischievous misquotation', 1998; A. Smith, *The Wealth of Nations*, 2000, 484–5 (originally published 1776). I was alerted to the frequent out-of-context paraphrasing of Adam Smith's 'invisible hand' comment by Jonathan Schlefer's 1998 article. Describing how individuals in a market economy employ their capital, Smith writes, 'By preferring the support of domestic to that of foreign industry, he intends only his own security; and by directing that industry in such a manner as its produce may be of the greatest value, he intends only his own gain, and he is in this, as in many other cases, led by an invisible hand to promote an end which was no part of his intention. Nor is it always the worse for the society that it was no part of it. By pursuing his own interest he frequently promotes that of the society more effectually than when he really intends to promote it.' Note that Smith wrote *'frequently* promotes that of the society', not *always* promotes that of the society and made that statement in the context of preferring domestic to foreign industry.
7   The Tongass Forest in Alaska has been a chronic setting for such a dispute between logging and old-growth forest protection, as described in Wines, 'In Alaska, a battle to keep trees, or an industry, standing', 2014.
8   Barry Russell, CEO, Independent Petroleum Association of America in response to proposed hydraulic fracturing regulations, as quoted in Cama, 'Drillers file lawsuit to challenge Obama's new fracking rules', 2015.
9   Competitive Enterprise Institute Vice President Iain Murray, in his 'Obama's climate plan: it's for the kidz', 2013.
10 2016 Republican Presidential Candidate Senator Marco Rubio commenting on proposed climate change policies, as quoted in Carroll, '"With certainty" cap-and-trade would wreck the economy, Rubio says', 2015.
11 President Donald Trump citing a study funded by fossil fuel interests while ignoring jobs that would be created, as quoted in Milman, 'Fact check: Trump's Paris climate speech claims analyzed', 2017.
12 Nobel Prize-winning economists James Buchanan, Milton Friedman, George Stigler and others famously overestimating economic costs of the Clean Air Act in 1990, at the start of a period of rapid conventional economic growth, as quoted in D. Cohen, 'Climate regulations a job killer?', 2011; see also Gleick, 'Will new climate regulations destroy the economy? (Hint: No)', 2017.
13 Calderón Hinojosa, 'The restoration revolution', 2017; Ettonson, 'US clean energy jobs surpass fossil fuel employment', 2017; Garrett-Peltier, 'Green versus brown', 2017; US Department of Energy, 'US energy and employment report', 2017, 22.
14 Michael Hanlon, 'The Golden Quarter', n.d. refers to the 'Golden Quarter' of a century of technological innovation from 1945 to 1971, describing how major innovations were rooted in

publicly funded research, not private investment in science and technology. He writes: 'During the Golden Quarter, we saw a boom in public spending on research and innovation. The taxpayers of Europe, the US and elsewhere replaced the great nineteenth-century venture capitalists. And so we find that nearly all the advances of this period came either from tax-funded universities or from popular movements. The first electronic computers came not from the labs of IBM but from the universities of Manchester and Pennsylvania. (Even the 19th-century analytical engine of Charles Babbage was directly funded by the British government.) The early internet came out of the University of California, not Bell or Xerox. Later on, the world wide web arose not from Apple or Microsoft but from CERN, a wholly public institution. In short, the great advances in medicine, materials, aviation and spaceflight were nearly all pump-primed by public investment. But since the 1970s, an assumption has been made that the private sector is the best place to innovate.'

15 Heneghan, 'Is there need for "The New Wild"?', 2015.

16 E. E. David Jr., President of Exxon Research and Engineering Company, remarks at the Fourth Annual Ewing Symposium on climate processes and climate sensitivity, Tenafly, New Jersey, 1982, as quoted in David, 'Inventing the future', 1984, 1.

17 R. Ayres, 'On the practical limits to substitution', 2007.

18 Daily and Ehrlich, 'Population, sustainability, and Earth's carrying capacity', 1992; Millennium Ecosystem Assessment, *Ecosystems and Human Well-being*, 2005, 1.

19 Ponting, *A New Green History of the World*, 2007, 185–6.

20 Krugman, 'Crazy climate economics', 2014. Also see Krugman, 'Making ignorance great again', 2017.

21 Tribe, 'Ways not to think about plastic trees', 1974, 1315–17.

22 Reusser et al., 'Quantifying human impacts on rates of erosion and sediment transport at a landscape scale', 2015.

23 Z. Smith, *The Environmental Policy Paradox*, 2004, 7.

24 Clarke, 'The Knowledge Explosion', 1964, 4:33–7.

25 Lewis Strauss, Chairman of the US Atomic Energy Commission, quoted in *New York Times*, 'Abundant power from atom seen', 1954, 5.

26 Laurence, 'Nuclear history due to be made in Geneva parley', 1955, 3.

27 Ford, 'Machinery: The new messiah', 1928.

28 Jared Diamond, speech at the Dallas Museum of Art, 22 February 2006.

11
Paying for protection

Environmental protection often comes at a price. Moreover, its future benefits often incur present costs. Improving building insulation reduces environmental damage associated with future energy consumption, but the insulation must be paid for now. Preventing overharvesting protects ecosystems and future harvests but requires restricting today's harvest and income. Installing pollution control devices reduces future pollution, but the devices must be purchased and installed now. We have no choice but to replace fossil-fuel-based energy infrastructure with cleaner, renewable alternatives, but doing so incurs substantial near-term expense. In other words, like a traditional investment, environmental protection often requires initial expenditures. Thus, a decision to increase environmental protection hinges upon an expectation that future benefits will justify their costs.

Initial costs of environmental protection

Even if people agree that environmental protection is warranted, individuals or organizations may be unwilling or unable to make the necessary initial investment. This is often true even when financial benefits are certain or nearly so. For example, under many circumstances, the initial additional cost of better attic insulation, an electric car, or rooftop solar panels will be exceeded by long-term energy cost savings, but many who could afford to add insulation, purchase such vehicles, or install solar panels have not done so. Initial costs are an important barrier. Long-term cost savings are obscure, hidden in energy bills, but up-front cost premiums are certain, obvious and immediate.

Overgrazing, excessive logging, overfishing and other non-sustainable consumption of renewable resources involve the same conflict of present benefits v. future costs. Too much present extraction reduces recovery of the resource and therefore future harvests. Despite the ease of understanding this trade-off and despite Plato's warning thousands of years ago (see Chapter 1, p. 5) and many others since, overharvesting continues.

Ranchers know restricting grazing now will produce more future grass. Loggers and fishing-boat captains understand an excessive harvest this year will reduce future harvests. But bills are due now. Those bills incentivize present overharvesting.

Discounting the future

Behaviours such as purchasing inefficient electrical appliances may occur either because people are unaware of alternatives, unaware of alternatives' advantages, or value present cost savings more than future savings. People do not always behave as if they value the present more than the future, but they often do, especially with regard to market decisions. Such behaviour is referred to as discounting the future.

Prioritizing the present over the future can be rational. Economists, psychologists and evolutionary biologists have identified several reasons one might do so.[1] In acute situations, such as those with immediate life-or-death consequences, unless the present is prioritized, the decision maker will have no future. Even when lives are not at stake, such as when a bill is due, paying the bill may make sense even if that choice requires borrowing money and thus having to pay a larger debt in the future. If the higher cost of paying back the loan seems preferable to the consequences of not paying the present debt, a loan may make sense. Meanwhile, where financial investments are concerned, present money often literally is worth more than future money because successful investments convert a smaller sum today into a larger sum tomorrow, so having one dollar now enables one to convert it into more than one dollar later.

In general, present problems are immediate and certain, but future problems are uncertain and distant. That distance, moreover, affords time to find solutions, but acute present problems demand immediate solutions. We may even be genetically programmed to prioritize the present over the future. Those alive today are descended from billions of years of ancestors, each of whom successfully solved all of their short-term problems and consequently survived until their offspring could fend for themselves. In contrast, potential ancestors who failed to solve immediate problems left no descendants. Thus, evolution by natural selection may have predisposed us to favour present over future concerns.

Of course, we do not always prioritize the present and we do not always behave as selected for in our ancestors. Many routinely forego present ease for the sake of the long term. People exercise, buy insurance and avoid junk food. Those who can, save for retirement. Indeed, many cultures hold in high regard the ability to defer gratification, presumably because doing so, just like overcoming immediate acute threats, has historically led to well-being. However, the foresight to make present sacrifices becomes more challenging as the future payoff becomes more distant or less certain. Indeed, long or uncertain delays before benefits accrue can lead to remarkable decisions with dire long-term consequences.[2] Many would argue that US federal inaction on climate change is an example of such extreme future discounting.

Just as discounting the future encourages short-term exploitation, such as non-sustainable harvesting or production of greenhouse gases, it simultaneously discourages investment in long-term environmental benefits. A September 2016 Associated Press-University of Chicago poll found 71 per cent of Americans preferred federal government action on climate change, but only 57 per cent preferred action if it cost them $1 per month and only 2 per cent preferred action if it cost $50 per month.[3]

Thus, discounting the future serves as an obstacle to environmental progress because it encourages environmental damage and discourages investment in future environmental quality. Consuming copper to make wire now comes at the costs of having less copper available in the future. Deep well injection of hazardous waste now comes at the cost of potential future groundwater contamination. Buying less-expensive, inefficient appliances causes not just higher electricity bills, but more pollution from power plants. As long as the future is discounted, these activities are easy to rationalize, but future generations might object.

Reasonable people will agree that actions should be worth their costs, but whether that will be the case is often difficult to determine because the future is uncertain and decisions have numerous consequences, only some of which are anticipatable and quantifiable. Moreover, differences in perspectives and value systems cause individuals to disagree about the relative importance of various consequences. Given all of these complexities and uncertainties, how might one predict whether the benefits of a decision will exceed its costs?

Cost–benefit analysis: basics

Rules restrict behaviour. People reasonably expect benefits of new rules to outweigh costs of such restrictions. But how can this be determined ahead of time? Any attempt to assess whether benefits will outweigh costs requires considering the collective effects of immediate and future consequences. In the case of government actions, those consequences are often numerous, disparate and unevenly borne by different people.

A calculation procedure called cost–benefit analysis provides a method for tallying present and future anticipated consequences of an action. The procedure, which is based upon assigning all consequences a monetary value, produces a precise result that projects whether benefits will exceed costs. Proposed environmental protections are often expected to pass such cost–benefit analyses.[4] For example, the monetary value of the health benefits of pollution control might be expected to surpass the monetary costs of controlling harmful pollution.

Given the apparent utility of the procedure, it is not surprising that many environmental laws mandate cost–benefit analysis of proposed regulations. Such analyses have been in favour for decades. For example, the Toxic Substances Control Act, the Safe Drinking Water Act and the Federal Insecticide, Fungicide, and Rodenticide Act of the 1970s all explicitly require comparisons of economic costs and benefits when developing regulations. Four decades after those laws were written, in 2015, the Supreme Court determined that the Clean Air Act also requires monetary cost–benefit analysis.[5] Moreover, every president from Ronald Reagan to Joe Biden signed or abided by an existing executive order requiring tallying costs and benefits of proposed regulations.[6]

Many cost–benefit analyses conclude that environmental protection would be worth the cost. For example, Hope and Hope estimate the cost of carbon emissions as greater than $100 per ton whereas activities that prevent greenhouse gas emissions can be financed for about $20 per ton.[7] Analyses of other environmental concerns, however, sometimes reach the opposite conclusion – that environmental protection would not be warranted. Unfortunately, scepticism is warranted whenever a cost–benefit analysis leads to the conclusion that environmental protection would not be worth its cost. This is because, as we shall see, *six features of cost–benefit analysis bias it against environmental protection*.[8]

Cost–benefit analysis is based upon forecasting annual monetary costs and benefits of a potential project. A project's 'net present value' is then calculated from those annual costs and benefits. The calculation discounts future projected costs and benefits, then tallies the resulting discounted annual values. (Inflation does not affect such analyses because inflation affects costs and benefits equally.)

Net present value is calculated as follows:

$$NPV = \Sigma \, \frac{b_t - c_t}{(1 + d)^t}$$

where

NPV	=	net present value (a unit of currency, such as dollars)
b_t	=	benefits in year t (same currency)
c_t	=	costs in year t (same currency)
d	=	discount rate (proportion per year)

When the estimated net present value is negative, the analysed action is projected to cost more than it returns.

Do you discount the future? Imagine I offered to give you either $100 now or some other amount a year from now. How much would I have to offer to give you next year for you to consider the offers equivalent? If you consider today's $100 equivalent to $110 received next year, then you use a discount rate of 10 per cent per year (d = 0.1 in the above equation).

The choice of discount rate has tremendous implications for net present value calculations. High discount rates severely reduce the present value of future benefits (and the present cost of future environmental damage), but have little effect on near-term costs. An increase in discount rate can thus shift a projected net present value from positive to negative.[9] But just as there is no theoretical basis for choosing a correct p-value for statistical calculations, there is no theoretically correct discount rate (though there is a tremendous amount of academic debate about correct rates).

Together, the choice of a discount rate, decisions regarding which costs and benefits to include in an analysis, and estimates of future monetary values dramatically affect net present value calculations. Thus, the assumptions and underlying decisions of cost–benefit analyses require careful scrutiny.[10] In the worst cases, their manipulation is a complete sham, as in this example:

> EPA employees say that in mid-June [2017], as Mr. Pruitt [the agency Administrator] prepared a proposal to reverse the [Clean

Water Act] rule, they were told by his deputies to produce a new analysis of the rule – one that stripped away the half-billion-dollar economic benefits associated with protecting wetlands.

'On June 13, my economists were verbally told to produce a new study that changed the wetlands benefit,' said Elizabeth Southerland, who retired [in July 2017] from a 30-year career at the EPA, most recently as a senior official in the agency's water office.

'On June 16, they did what they were told,' Ms. Southerland said. 'They produced a new cost–benefit analysis that showed no quantifiable benefit to preserving wetlands.'[11]

The Clean Water Act rule is only one example of the Trump Administration making a farce out of cost–benefit analyses. Whereas the Obama Administration concluded that a rule to limit mercury emissions would cost $9.6 billion to implement but provide $40–90 billion in annual savings due to reduced emissions of mercury and other pollutants, the Trump Administration recalculated that projection after arbitrarily excluding all benefits not directly attributable to reduced mercury exposure (in other words, excluding all benefits of simultaneous reductions in other associated pollutants). On that basis, the Trump Administration concluded the rule would provide only $4–6 million in annual benefits, or 1/10,000th of the benefits estimated by the Obama Administration. The Trump EPA later went on to formalize the same analytical procedure as a matter of policy – forbidding consideration of any benefits other than those directly attributable to reduced exposure to the target pollutant, even when the action that reduced the target pollutant also reduced other pollutants.[12] During May 2021, the Biden Administration announced it had begun the process to repeal that Trump rule.[13] This example illustrates how easily cost–benefit analyses can be manipulated by selection of what to include or omit from tallies. Imagine if engineering calculations were similarly manipulated. Bridges would collapse.

Cost–benefit analysis: biases

Cost–benefit analysis is instructive for projecting estimated net present values of private investments, such as whether a new widget factory would be profitable,[14] but six features cause the procedure to overestimate costs and underestimate benefits of environmental protection. The method is also susceptible to gross manipulation, as the mercury example illustrates. Environmental protection is often deemed worthwhile despite these problems, but in other cases cost–benefit analysis leads to the conclusion that protection would not be worthwhile.[15] Surely the disadvantages of some proposed environmental protections would outweigh the benefits, but, because of the six biases (outlined in Box 11.1), one should be wary of any such conclusion based upon a conventional cost–benefit analysis.

Whereas it is reasonable to expect an initiative to be worth the necessary investment, that is a broader question than whether a net present value calculation is positive. Cost–benefit analysis is not an adequate tool for judging the wisdom of major societal decisions because it is insufficiently comprehensive, requires numerous questionable assumptions, gives no consideration to the distribution of costs and benefits across a population, ascribes extreme priority to the present over the future, and is prone to manipulation. Its simple, precise results obscure these inherent biases and uncertainties, resulting in what Professor Mark Leighton calls masquerading precision.

Cost–benefit analysis is useful for helping when individuals and organizations evaluate potential investments, while a variation on the procedure, cost-effectiveness analysis, can assist with comparing the most economically efficient means of achieving a given objective. But because of its six biases, cost–benefit analysis is not adequate for evaluating the wisdom of major societal decisions with long-term, potentially irreversible implications. It is like most tools, such as a hammer, useful for some tasks but not adequate for others. Hammers are useful for driving nails, but not for installing screws or windows; misused hammers can do serious damage.

The method's biases are presumably why Driesen concluded: 'Environmentalists generally oppose cost–benefit analysis (CBA) and regulated industry generally supports it.'[16] Just as a skilled carpenter needs to understand the proper uses of tools, those who seek environmental progress must understand how cost–benefit analyses are biased against environmental protection, so they can defend against their uncritical or even intentionally biased use.

Imagine if other societal decisions hinged upon net present value calculations. Few would suggest making decisions regarding gun control, reproductive rights, or public education on the basis of narrow monetary calculations that discount the future. What if society expected efforts in space exploration, medical research or foreign policy to be demonstrably,

Box 11.1: Six features that bias cost–benefit analyses against environmental protection
(see Appendix, p. 294, for more complete explanations and references)

1. Discounting the future. Environmental protection typically provides long-term benefits but imposes short-term costs. Discounting reduces the value of distant benefits but not immediate costs, thereby prioritizing immediate costs. For example, at a modest 4 per cent discount rate, $100 of benefit that would accrue 100 years from now has a present value of less than $2. Thus, by the logic of cost–benefit analysis it would not be worth spending $2 today for the sake of $100 of environmental protection 100 years from now, or to put it more tangibly, it would not be worth letting two fish go free today to enable harvest of 100 fish a century from now. Moreover, fish are not the only creatures whose future lives are devalued. Cost–benefit analyses often incorporate dollar values for human lives saved or lost; thus, at a 4 per cent discount rate two people alive today would be ascribed equal value to 100 people of some future generation. I cannot imagine those 100 people would agree.

2. Cost–benefit analyses ignore who benefits and who pays. Costs and benefits are not evenly distributed across generations or populations. If the two fish in the above example are harvested today, the present generation enjoys all the benefits, but a future generation pays all the long-term cost. It seems unlikely that those who would have eaten the 100 future fish would agree to sacrifice their consumption for the sake of two fish caught today. Similarly, the cost of environmental damage often affects the population as a whole while the benefits of the damaging activity accrue primarily to the owners and customers of select industries. Therefore, if a pollution control proposal, for example, is not enacted because it fails a cost–benefit analysis, the population at large will suffer from the resulting pollution (with the poorest members of the population often suffering the most) but the financial savings of avoided regulations will disproportionately accrue to the relevant industry and its customers.

3. Overestimation of costs of environmental protection. Potentially affected industries routinely overestimate costs of compliance with proposed environmental protections. This happens for two reasons. First, those who would have to comply with a new policy have an incentive to overestimate costs because that will strengthen their argument against the proposed requirements. Second, initial compliance cost estimates do not benefit from efforts to find the least expensive means of compliance. Once regulations are imposed, those who must comply have an incentive to minimize, rather than overestimate, costs. Consequently, actual costs are often lower than estimated costs, but the higher estimated costs serve as the basis for cost–benefit analyses.

4. Contingent valuation. Market prices provide the basis of cost–benefit analyses, but many environmental goods are not traded in markets and thus lack such prices. To enable their inclusion, analysts ascribe 'shadow' prices. For example, a cost–benefit analysis of a plan to prevent a species' extinction would need a shadow price for survival of the species, and an analysis of river pollution prevention would need a dollar value for an unpolluted river. What shadow prices should be ascribed to clean water or species survival? One might ask experts what they think, but typical cost–benefit analyses use a different procedure called contingent valuation – surveys of the general public regarding the value of environmental protection. The rationale for contingent valuation is that market prices are based on what consumers are willing to pay, so consumers should also determine shadow prices. In other words, people who may know nothing about a circumstance are asked to place a monetary value on it. We base other technical decisions on expert judgements, not surveys of laypersons. Would you use a survey to decide what medicine to take when you are sick or how much steel to use in a bridge? If we would not expect members of the general public to make informed decisions regarding other technical matters, we should not expect them to do so regarding environmental protection, but conventional contingent valuation does just that.

5. Underestimation or omission of environmental protection benefits. It is impossible to anticipate all future consequences of a present action (or inaction). Imagine cost–benefit analyses had been applied to whether to use chlorofluorocarbons for refrigeration or fossil fuels for energy. No costs would have been included for the destruction of the stratospheric ozone layer or climate change because these consequences were not appreciated when the technologies were first used. Cost–benefit analyses' default assumption is an absence of unanticipated, undesirable environmental consequences, but such consequences are common.

6. Price does not equal value. Because people are often irrational, price is not a good measure of value. For example, according to the market, heroin is worth more than water. Such a valuation mechanism may be acceptable for letting individuals or firms make their own purchasing and investment decisions (or mistakes), but it is not a good basis for societal decisions. Imagine if quantities that had been affected by irrational decisions were used as the basis of calculations in other circumstances. If experts used irrational inputs for their calculations, bridges would collapse, drugs would be administered at poisonous doses and spacecraft would blow up on launch pads. (This issue has tremendous implications beyond the realm of environmental protection.)

predictably profitable on the basis of a number at the bottom of a simple spreadsheet? Rockets would not be launched. Cures would not be found. Embassies would not be staffed. No one using cost–benefit analysis calculations would have built the beautiful stone house in Figure 11.1 because its value after the first couple of decades would have been discounted to a present value of approximately zero.

Fortunately, we are not always so short-sighted. We staff embassies, cure diseases and launch spacecraft – because society judges these investments on a broader basis than net present value. The Romans built the beautiful Pont Julien so well that traffic still crossed it 2,000 years later (see Figure 11.2). Such appreciation of long-term value needs to extend to include protection of the planet's life-support potential. Then we will be less inclined to discount the future.

The expectation that environmental protection proposals will pass a net present value test is like the expectation of 95 per cent statistical confidence before guarding against a hazard and an expectation of unanimity of experts before acting upon an environmental threat. All three apply unreasonable standards to environmental protection – standards not expected in other realms.

In his essay 'Goose Music', the great ecologist Aldo Leopold asks what a wild goose is worth? Sixty years later, in response to the BP Horizon oil drilling platform explosion, Shamarr Allen's song 'Sorry Ain't Enough No More' asks the same question a bit more brutally when he

Figure 11.1: A charming home whose durable stone construction would have failed a cost–benefit analysis. Discounting would have limited the estimated benefits to the home's first few decades, overlooking its long-term value. Photographer: Peter C. Schulze.

Figure 11.2: Romans built the Pont Julien in the Luberon region of southern France some 2,000 years ago. It remains durable and was used by modern vehicles until this century. Photographer: Peter C. Schulze.

sings, 'How much is this dead pelican worth?'[17] I doubt either would have found a net present value calculation compelling.

Leopold's best-known essay, 'The Land Ethic', describes the history of ethics as beginning with relationships among individuals, then later extending to relationships between individuals and society.[18] He explains how the realm of purely utilitarian decision making has contracted over the course of human history while ethical considerations have expanded. He advocates another extension of this process – using ethical rather than utilitarian criteria for evaluating actions that affect our relationships to other species and the planet itself.

Some progress has occurred since Leopold wrote, but society does not yet routinely base environmental choices in ethical considerations. Rather, we still often apply the biased, short-sighted approach of cost–benefit analysis. Indeed, as we have seen, many US laws prescribe its use. Until Leopold's dream of a land ethic is broadly adopted, those who seek environmental progress should understand not only the limited utility, but also the severe biases and potential for manipulation of cost–benefit analyses. Otherwise, assessments of net present value will serve as uncritically accepted, unreasonably high barriers to environmental protection, and the discounting that its calculations entail will exclude the needs and concerns of future generations, as well as the long-term future of all other species and the planet's life-support potential.

The previous few chapters have described arguments that opponents use to deter environmental protection. They claim scientific evidence is too uncertain, environmental protection would infringe upon freedoms, free markets alone will solve environmental problems, and environmental protection would not be worth its cost. These arguments reinforce each other. If there is no real problem, then freedom from rules is desirable. If the free market alone can solve a problem, then restrictions on the market would be counterproductive. And if there is no hazard to avoid, there is no reason to invest in doing so. These same chapters have sought to explain the flaws in each of these arguments. The next three chapters describe related obstacles rooted in features of the US political system.

Notes

1. For instance Jason Collins et al., 'Evolutionary biology in economics', 2016, 294–6; Koffarnus et al., 'Changing delay discounting in the light of competing neurobehavioral decision systems theory', 2013, 32–3; Lazarus, 'Environmental law after Katrina', 2007, 1035–6; Rogers, 'Evolution of time preference by natural selection', 1994, 460–1.
2. Lazarus, 'Environmental law after Katrina', 2007, 1041–53.
3. Borenstein, 'Poll', 2016.
4. Driesen, 'Is cost–benefit analysis neutral?', 2006; Hahn and Sunstein, 'A new executive order for improving federal regulation?', 2002; Nordhaus, 'An optimal transition path for controlling greenhouse gases', 1992.
5. *Michigan v. EPA*, 576 US 6 (2015); Salzman and Thompson, *Environmental Law and Policy*, 2014, 38–40.
6. Shapiro and Morrall, 'The triumph of regulatory politics', 2012, 189–90; Sunstein, 'Biden chooses a pragmatic path for regulation', 2021.
7. For instance Attina et al., 'Exposure to endocrine-disrupting chemicals in the USA', 2016; Dennis and Eilperin, 'EPA to make it harder to tighten mercury rules in the future', 2018; Eilperin and Dennis, 'The EPA is about to change a rule cutting mercury pollution', 2020; Hope and Hope, 'The social cost of CO_2 in a low-growth world', 2013.
8. See for example Heinzerling et al., 'Applying cost–benefit analysis to past decisions', 2005; Shapiro and Morrall, 'The triumph of regulatory politics', 2012, 189–90.
9. See for instance Schulze et al., 'Enrichment planting in selectively logged rain forest', 1994.
10. See further in Dennis and Eilperin, 'EPA to make it harder to tighten mercury rules in the future', 2018; Eilperin and Dennis, 'The EPA is about to change a rule cutting mercury pollution', 2020; McGarity et al., *Sophisticated Sabotage*, 2004, 163–213.
11. Davenport and Lipton, 'Scott Pruitt is carrying out his EPA agenda in secret, critics say', 2017.
12. Dennis and Eilperin, 'EPA to make it harder to tighten mercury rules in the future', 2018; Eilperin and Dennis, 'The EPA is about to change a rule cutting mercury pollution', 2020.
13. Friedman, 'Biden Administration to repeal Trump rule aimed at curbing EPA's power', 2021.
14. Schulze et al., 'Enrichment planting in selectively logged rain forest', 1994.
15. For examples of different choices regarding which costs and benefits to consider, compare these three analyses: Bollen et al., 'Local air pollution and global climate change', 2009; Nordhaus, 'An optimal transition path for controlling greenhouse gases', 1992; Risky Business Project, 'The economic risks of climate change in the US', 2014.
16. Driesen, 'Is cost–benefit analysis neutral', 2006, 1.
17. Leopold, *Round River*, 1993, 168; Allen, 'Sorry Ain't Enough No More', 2010. According to Kraus ('Halliburton to pay \$1.1 billion to settle damages in Gulf of Mexico oil spill', 2014) as of August 2014, Halliburton and BP had paid or agreed to pay almost \$30 billion in claims and fines as a result of the BP Horizon oil rig blowout, but those payments only compensate other humans. The dead pelicans get nothing.
18. Leopold, *A Sand County Almanac*, 1949, 201–4.

12
Perceived lack of urgency

One rarely has the time or resources to do everything one wishes. Therefore, we do some things but not others. We choose. Moreover, our different perspectives and values create different priorities, and disagreement about the wisdom of alternative choices. One person may perceive an issue as important while another does not, or a choice as foolish that another considers wise.

Because of time and resource constraints, worthy concerns frequently receive little attention. I have hundreds of emails with little red flags next to them. I have meant to address them, but have not found or made the time to do so. I have prioritized other things. Like individuals, organizations must also make such choices. Well-run organizations set priorities. What should a college president prioritize – providing an excellent education, attracting students, attracting faculty, raising funds, balancing the budget, reducing the institution's environmental impact? Likewise, government representatives contend with multiple worthy objectives, some of which compete with each other. City councils at the very least must simultaneously foster public safety, maintain local transportation systems and ensure water supplies and sanitation. Federal governments manage similar operations, plus others, such as immigration, foreign relations and national security. I imagine many people sympathize when Elton John sings that there is 'more to do than can ever be done.'[1]

Meanwhile, leaders need supporters in order to retain their positions. College and university presidents seek to stay in the good graces of students, faculty, trustees, alumni and donors even while members of these different groups likely have different priorities and different perspectives on the wisdom of various choices. Likewise, chief executive officers depend on the support of corporate boards, and elected representatives depend on public support for re-election. All these people wish to be perceived as satisfying constituents' concerns. Unfortunately for those of us concerned about environmental problems, and for future generations and other species, environmental problems often seem less urgent than other concerns and are therefore susceptible to repeatedly deferred attention.

Gradualness of environmental problems

Environmental problems are problems of scale. They result from too much or too little of something. If only a few cars were on the road, their exhaust would not warrant concern. As the number of vehicles increases, so does their collective impact. Likewise, a little aquifer depletion, fishing, logging or release of greenhouse gases has little impact, but as the scale of these activities increase, they eventually overwhelm the regenerative capacity of the environment. Some environmental problems involve qualitative changes or critical thresholds, such as when overgrazing leads to desertification or when non-native species upend food webs, but gradual, incremental deterioration is common, especially before thresholds are reached. A little soil damage is undesirable but its effects are negligible. The same damage repeated for generations appears to have destroyed numerous ancient civilizations.[2]

Environmental deterioration is not only often gradual, but often imperceptible to casual observers. Years or even decades may be insufficient for individuals to perceive damages like biodiversity loss, decline in soil fertility, aquifer depletion or desertification. In other cases, such as the effects of invisible water pollutants or unfamiliar invasive species, casual observers will not detect any change at all.[3] These are perhaps among the quieter elements of the 'quiet crisis' that Secretary of the Interior Stuart Udall warned about in 1963 when he noted that Robert Frost's 'West-Running Brook' had become an automobile junkyard.[4] Even professionals often have difficulty detecting some problems. Climate change is an obvious example. Researchers with sophisticated measurement systems and vast data-collection operations took decades to confidently distinguish anthropogenic climate change from normal multi-year weather variation.

The creeping, sometimes nearly invisible growth of environmental problems creates two related obstacles to action. First, because problems grow slowly, sometimes almost imperceptibly, public demand is often insufficient to achieve enough political momentum for action. Second, leaders desire tangible, objective, rapid progress with which to maintain constituents' support, but effort devoted to avoiding a distant future problem provides no such immediate improvement. Thus, it is difficult for those seeking re-election (or facing financial reporting deadlines) to incur short-term costs for the sake of benefits that will accrue years or decades later. Moreover, polls indicate that although most citizens express environmental concerns, electoral choices tend to be driven by more immediate concerns, such as the present state of the economy, healthcare or safety and security.[5] 'Re-elect me; I reduced your medical bills' is an easier sell than, 'Re-elect me; I ensured a toxin you have never heard of will not poison your unborn great-grandchildren.'

The policy process

Where federal and state governments are concerned, the decision whether, and if so how, to act depends on the outcome of struggles among competing interest groups (see Chapter 14) and proceeds through three basic phases: agenda setting, policy development and policy implementation. More detailed descriptions distinguish six stages: problem identification, agenda setting, policy formulation, policy adoption, policy implementation and policy evaluation.[6] As this and subsequent chapters explain, success requires effective completion of the first five of these stages, and its confirmation requires completion of the sixth.

Agenda setting refers to the choices and negotiations that establish political priorities. Proponents of action push to achieve sufficient public support. Such demand for environmental protection repeatedly overwhelmed opposition during the 1960s–1980s, the heyday of US environmental progress, but advocates of environmental protection have not had similar success since.

Political scientists consider policy change likely only when three circumstances coincide – a problem is recognized, a solution is imagined and sufficient political will for action exists.[7] They note that public interest is often fickle, with strong demand likely only during a narrow window of time when recognition of a new problem alarms people.[8] For example, since the 1980s, the problem of climate change has been widely recognized and potential solutions identified, but in the United States sufficient public demand has not materialized. Using arguments described in the preceding four chapters, opponents have successfully dampened public demand, thereby rendering leaders' collective political will inadequate to achieve substantial environmental policy change and allowing those leaders to focus upon other issues. Whether increased attention of the late 2010s and early 2020s is the beginning of a sea change remains to be seen.

Roles of government branches

In combination with a perceived lack of urgency and narrow windows of opportunity for policy action, the division of power among the three branches of the US federal government (legislative, executive, and judicial) can further delay environmental progress because US national legislation requires support from all three branches. The legislative branch (Congress, made up of the House of Representatives and the Senate) passes legislation that authorizes agencies to develop and implement policy. The president, as head of the executive branch, signs or vetoes legislation and chooses leaders of the agencies responsible for implementing legislation. Together, Congress and the president set agency budgets. Once legislation is passed, the judiciary settles disputes about statutes' constitutionality and policy implementation.

Environmental legislation typically prescribes goals but leaves policy details up to agencies such as the EPA, the Bureau of Land Management or the Fish and Wildlife Service. For example, the Clean Water Act mandated a halt to the discharge of pollutants into the nation's waterways but did not specify how to achieve that goal.[9] Congress delegates such details to administrative agencies because it lacks expertise and because policy needs to be responsive to new information that becomes available after laws are passed. Also, it is easier to attract votes for legislation with ambiguous wording that allows legislators to claim their own preferred interpretations.[10] This delegation of authority gives agencies great discretion and thus great power (see Chapter 18), but is limited by laws such as the Administrative Procedures Act.[11] Agencies must, for example, describe a rational, factual basis for promulgating or altering rules. Even within the constraints prescribed by the Administrative Procedures Act, disagreement about Congress's intent can delay environmental protection as subsequent presidential administrations apply different interpretations when developing policy, or the courts become involved in settling disputes about appropriate interpretations of Congress's intent.

When major US environmental laws were passed, champions of the legislation recognized that agencies would face pressure to develop only weak regulations and avoid aggressive implementation. To prevent that, legislators included 'citizen suit' provisions in many laws. Whereas one cannot normally sue the federal government, such laws authorize citizens to sue federal agencies for failing to implement legislation as intended, follow required procedures, or provide a plausible basis for decisions. (The EPA employs many attorneys because it gets sued almost regardless of what it decides – either by those who consider policy too lenient or those who deem it too strict.)

For example, extended debate has surrounded the question of just what water falls under the jurisdiction of the Clean Water Act. Because water molecules cycle among the atmosphere, surface and groundwater, and the law repeatedly refers to protection of surface water and underground water, many (including me) conclude Congress must have intended to protect all of the nation's water. Indeed, this is the interpretation the EPA applied during multiple administrations. However, the first statement of the law's objective reads, '… it is the national goal that the discharge of pollutants into navigable waters be eliminated by 1985'. Some interpret the specification of navigable waters to indicate that Congress only intended to protect waterways large enough for navigation.

After years of debate, the Obama EPA developed regulations sympathetic to the traditional interpretation that the law was intended to protect all surface and groundwater. However, those regulations were soon rejected by the Trump Administration, which favoured a narrower interpretation. The Trump EPA was immediately sued for changing the interpretation. Then, after a few months in office, the Biden Administration began the process of restoring the stronger, previous policy.[12]

Courts rescind rules when they determine agencies have failed to follow Congress's intent, abide by required rulemaking procedures, or base rules on reasonable interpretations of relevant information. The Trump Administration announced some hundred environmental-protection rollbacks and was sued dozens of times by organizations such as the Natural Resources Defense Council, the Center for Biological Diversity, and Earthjustice. By January 2020, the Trump Administration had lost most of the resolved suits.[13]

Repeated deferral

Lawsuits regarding interpretation of statutes become relevant only after legislation has been passed into law. As we have seen, however, no major US environmental legislation has been adopted since 1990. Since then, interest groups opposed to new legislation have prevailed, assisted by the

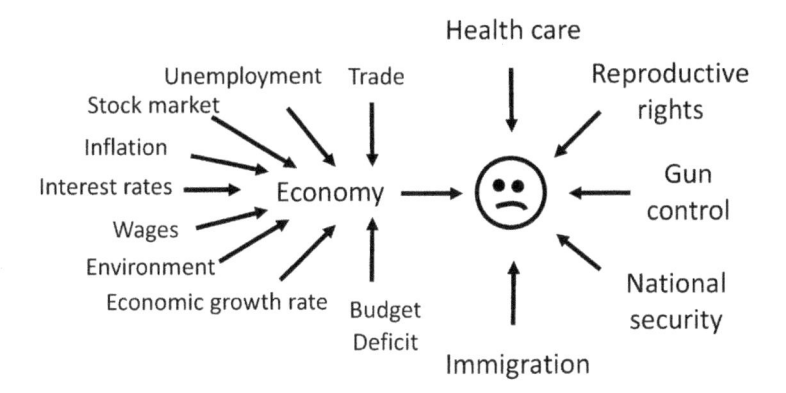

Figure 12.1: One way a member of Congress might perceive concerns, with the environment as just one of many. Figure by the author.

various obstacles described in this and other chapters. Public demand has not been sufficient to overcome the obstacles to new federal environmental protection statutes.

The gradual, incremental nature of environmental problems is partially, and perhaps largely, responsible for the inadequate public demand. Absent sufficient demand for attention to one issue, representatives and others authorities will prioritize others their constituents (or funders) consider more urgent (see Figure 12.1).

Although that short-term behaviour is understandable, it often leads to repeated deferral of action on critical but slow-moving problems, such as climate change, species extinction and the loss of productive ecosystems. Furthermore, even if many understand the necessity of action, if a problem worsens only incrementally, and especially if the worsening is difficult to perceive, it may seem acceptable to defer action temporarily while attending to other problems perceived as more urgent. But such deferrals may be repeated year after year as a situation worsens. Some problems eventually become insurmountable when irreversible damage occurs, as is the case for species extinction and may be the case if positive feedbacks cause runaway climate change.

> I don't really think we want a commander-in-chief who's battling climate change instead of terrorism.[14]

Ascribing priority to acute, easily understood problems such as terrorism risks relegating environmental problems to chronic low priority even as they worsen. If such situations persist long enough, consequences are sometimes profound. Problems such as soil erosion and deforestation have persisted for millennia despite warnings since at least Plato. Consequently, large areas of the planet are desertified, their soils having been ruined. Even today, with so much hindsight, we continue to allow soil erosion.[15]

Erosion provides an easily understood example of how repeated deferral makes problems worse. If erosion is halted next year, the soil will suffer more than if erosion had been halted this year, and overcoming its consequences will be harder. How much difference could one year make to a process as slow as erosion? According to the US Department of Agriculture, the country's 180 million hectares of cropland lose some 1.6 billion metric tons of soil per year, or almost *ten metric tons per hectare per year*.[16] In other terms, the US is losing almost *five metric tons of soil per person per year* just from cropland. That statistic is hard to comprehend. It amounts to more than 13 kilograms of soil per person per day. Thus, for each pound of food grown, the US loses several pounds of soil. Imagine the consequences of doing that in a garden. Imagine also the benefits for future agricultural production if we had long ago limited the rate of soil erosion to the rate of soil formation. The same cost of delay applies to many other problems, such as aquifer depletion, biodiversity loss, deforestation, failure to recycle non-renewable resources and climate change.

In contrast to Figure 12.1, a different perspective on priorities results from Herman Daly's diagram (Figure 12.2), which accurately portrays the economy as a subset of the planetary ecosystem.[17] Daly's diagram avoids the error of portraying the environment as just one of many special interests, depicting it instead as the source of all material goods. But this view of the economy as a subsidiary of the environment is not yet dominant. As long as a perspective akin to that of Figure 12.1 remains common, lack of perceived urgency may continue to stymie environmental progress.

Many people and some members of Congress have consistently prioritized environmental protection, but since the 1980s an inadequate sense of urgency and associated inadequate political demand have prevented major new legislation. Meanwhile, attention has focused on other concerns, such as the economy, foreign relations and healthcare. The combination of the gradual nature of environmental damage plus effective opposition have kept environmental protection low on the political agenda. As a consequence, action has repeatedly been deferred. Sustainability cannot be achieved, or even approached, until this pattern is overcome – a challenge made even larger by circumstances described in the next two chapters.

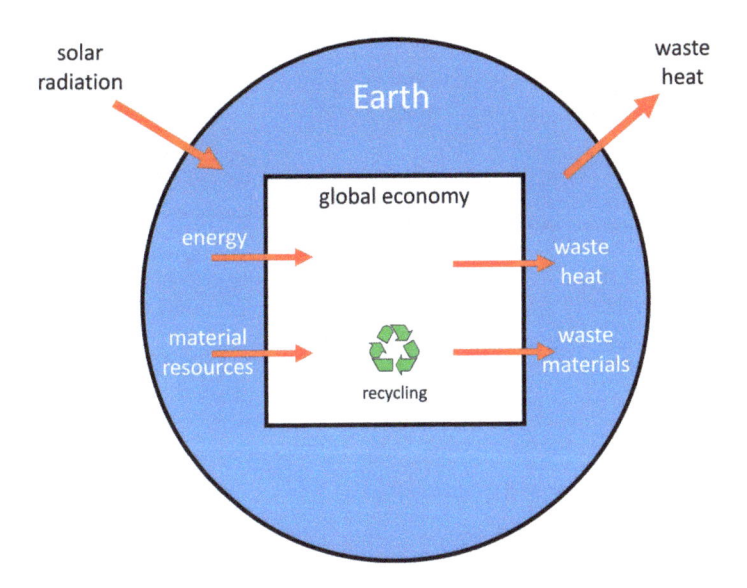

Figure 12.2: The economy as a subset of and wholly dependent upon the planetary ecosystem. Source: *Beyond Growth* by Herman E. Daly, 49. Copyright © 1996 by Herman E. Daly. Reprinted by permission of Beacon Press, Boston.

Notes

1   John, 'Circle of Life', 1994.
2   Dale and Carter, *Topsoil and Civilization*, 1955; Ponting, *A New Green History of the World*, 2007, 67–86.
3   Likewise, we may not recognize declines in our expectations for what constitutes a precious natural setting. Aldo Leopold describes encountering paradise when he and his brother camped in the delta of the Colorado river in 1922: '…we had not for weeks seen a man or a cow, an axe cut or a fence' (Leopold, *A Sand County Almanac*, 1949, 141). In striking contrast, during the 1990s some local birdwatchers asked me to speak at a Bethlehem, Pennsylvania City Council meeting regarding a plan to convert a small, unmanicured pie-piece-shaped corner of a city park into a mown area with picnic tables. The birders preferred the area as it was because the unmanicured vegetation attracted birds. One speaker pleaded with the City Council not to alter the area, describing it as her 'little piece of paradise', tears streaming down her cheeks as she spoke. She loved that piece of the park, but it was a far cry from the Colorado delta Leopold described only 70 years earlier. (By the way, the delta of the Colorado is chronically bone dry now except during flood years – so much water having been diverted to Las Vegas, Los Angeles, Phoenix and elsewhere.)
4   Udall, *The Quiet Crisis*, 1963, vii–viii.
5   Z. Smith, *The Environmental Policy Paradox*, 2004, 20–4.
6   Rosenbaum, *Environmental Politics and Policy*, 2002, 46–9.
7   Kingdon, *Agendas, Alternatives, and Public Policies*, 2003, 165–70.
8   Downs, 'Up and down with ecology: the issue-attention cycle', 1972, 38–44.
9   Salzman and Thompson, *Environmental Law and Policy*, 2014, 38–40.

10 Salzman and Thompson, *Environmental Law and Policy*, 2014, 77–9.

11 Breyer et al., *Administrative Law and Regulatory Policy*, 2017, 466–75 and 791–809.

12 Beitsch, '14 states sue EPA over rollback of Obama-era water rule', 2019; Friedman, 'Biden Administration to restore clean-water protections ended by Trump', 2021; Friedman and Davenport, 'Trump Administration rolls back clean water protections', 2019; EPA, 'About waters of the US', n.d.

13 Earthjustice, 'Three years battling the Trump Administration's attacks on our health and environment', 2020.

14 US Senator Rand Paul, quoted in Leber, 'What's Rand Paul's position on climate change?', 2015.

15 Dale and Carter, *Topsoil and Civilization*, 1955; Montgomery, 'Soil erosion and agricultural sustainability', 2007; Ponting, *A New Green History of the World*, 2007, 67–86; Reusser et al., 'Quantifying human impacts on rates of erosion and sediment transport at a landscape scale', 2015.

16 Lubowski et al., 'Major uses of land in the US, 2002', 2002, 5; Natural Resources Conservation Service, '2007 National Resources Inventory', 2010, 1–2.

17 During 1986, when the global population was less than 5 billion, Vitousek et al. ('Human appropriation of the products of photosynthesis', 1986) estimated that humans were appropriating 41 per cent of terrestrial plant growth. By appropriation they meant not only the consumption of food, paper, fibre and construction materials, but also reduction of plant growth from converting land to human uses such as farms, roads and cities, and otherwise preventing plant growth through damage such as desertification, overgrazing and pollution. Assuming that, on average, per capita appropriation is the same today, with nearly 8 billion people, we must be appropriating more than 60 per cent of terrestrial plant growth. One hundred per cent is the absolute upper limit, but 100 per cent appropriation is not tenable because that would leave only human-dominated landscapes for the land-based provision of the 'ecosystem services' on which all life depends – oxygen generation, stratospheric ozone creation, air purification, water cycling, water purification, soil production, pollination and so forth. Indeed, the authors of the Millennium Ecosystem Assessment (*Ecosystems and Human Well-being: Synthesis*, 2005, 1) and Rockström et al. ('Planetary boundaries', 2009), conclude that our demands already exceed the planet's support capacity.

13
Flawed democracy

If, despite obstacles already discussed, a large majority of US citizens demand action, they may not get their wish because the US system of government imposes many barriers to majority rule. The US is generally referred to as a representative democracy, but some citizens are much better represented than others and government policy often reflects minority, rather than majority, opinion. Therefore, even if most people prefer greater environmental protection, a small, determined opposition may thwart that desire.

Numerous factors combine to afford some citizens better representation than others. Gerrymandering (strategically altering the boundaries of state voting districts to favour the party in power) disenfranchises supporters of states' minority parties, while impediments to voting disenfranchise citizens of low socio-economic status and persons of colour. Meanwhile, lenient campaign finance laws afford wealthy citizens and organizations disproportionate influence, not only upon elections but also upon public opinion, legislation and the vigour with which agencies implement rules and regulations. Others have extra influence because they live in states with small populations (and thus disproportionate influence on the Senate), states with early presidential primaries (which are especially important to the viability of presidential candidates), or 'swing' states whose Electoral College votes could conceivably be won by either party (which causes such states to receive disproportionate attention from candidates). Given these many problems, it is not surprising the Economist Intelligence Unit does not include the US in its most robust democratic category, 'full democracy', with Canada, Ireland, Norway and the UK, but in its second tier, 'flawed democracy', with Argentina, Mongolia, the Philippines and South Africa.[1]

It is especially easy for a minority view to prevail when the minority objects to proposed legislation, such as a proposed new environmental law, because the US Constitution imposes barriers to expansion of federal government power. Thus, although most citizens prefer higher taxes on the wealthy, stricter privacy laws and regulation of greenhouse gases, such policies have not been adopted.[2] This chapter considers the many reasons majority support for environmental protection does not necessarily suffice to ensure action, first by reviewing the reasons some citizens have more influence than others and then by reviewing the hurdles to passing new laws.

Disenfranchisement and environmental injustice

Life is more than fair to some and exceedingly unfair to others. One manifestation of unfairness is individuals' unequal influence upon government. Socio-economic and sociocultural factors strongly advantage some over others. The situation has become so pronounced in the US that whereas many understand the nation's democracy as based on the concept of one person, one vote, others have suggested a more accurate description is one dollar, one vote. Meanwhile, that wealth inequality has strong demographic patterns. For example, 2018 US Census Bureau data show households held by men have higher net worth than those held by women and households held by white individuals have an astonishing *fifteen times* the average net worth of households held by black individuals.[3] The roots of the latter situation in systemic racism is receiving substantial political, media and scholarly attention, and injustices will hopefully be eliminated. Presently however, individuals experience extreme differences in financial wealth, and thus dramatic differences in potential to influence policy because those who are occupied making ends meet have little if any time or money to invest in influencing political decisions, whereas the wealthy can afford to make contributions and invest time influencing policy.

Extreme variation in financial wealth and political power not only interferes with majority rule, but also fosters, and prevents overcoming, unequal exposure to environmental harms. For example, persons of colour disproportionately live near facilities that handle toxic chemicals, and suffer exposure to high concentrations of pollutants.[4] These patterns are rooted in a history of systemic racism, explicitly manifested in such policies as redlining (where banks refused to offer loans for persons of colour to buy properties in wealthier neighbourhoods) and zoning decisions and deed covenants that prevented persons of colour from purchasing homes in 'white' areas.[5] Meanwhile, because those suffering from economic hardship have little time or money to devote to influencing political decisions, they are often unable to prevent dirty industries from moving into their neighbourhoods, or to achieve the political power necessary to remedy disproportionate pollution exposure.[6] These same people generally cannot afford to move to less polluted, more expensive areas.

> Today, hundreds of studies conclude that, in general, ethnic minorities, indigenous persons, people of colour, and low-income communities confront a higher burden of environmental exposure from air, water, and soil pollution from industrialization, militarization, and consumer practices.[7]

Perhaps the most fundamental impediment to majority rule is the set of laws, policies and procedures that create barriers to voting. Incredibly, major efforts in various state legislatures seek to maintain or even raise those barriers. For instance, from January to October 2021, 19 states enacted 33 laws that, according to the Brennan Center for Justice, impede voting.[8]

Several aspects of election procedures and voter eligibility rules make it more difficult for some citizens to vote than others. These include the number, locations and hours of polling places, obscurity of information on poll locations and procedures, identification requirements, proof of citizenship requirements, aggressive purging of registered voter rolls, and prohibitions against felons voting.[9] Because members of some groups face more impediments than others, votes cast do not accurately represent the wishes of a representative cross section of eligible voters, and therefore do not reflect the will of the people.

Limited voting hours create one impediment. For example, in many areas, polls are open from about 7 am to only 7 pm – shorter hours than are routinely offered even by many retailers.[10] Relatively narrow time windows for voting have potential to disproportionately hinder hourly workers who would be penalized for absence from jobs. For instance, as a salaried college professor, I can leave campus to vote practically any time other than when my classes are in session. My compensation is not affected; I need not seek permission; and no one will object. In contrast, a daytime hourly worker, such as a roofer or landscaper, may lose pay and could be put in the uncomfortable position of seeking permission from a supervisor to be absent to vote.

Restrictions on voting times are relieved somewhat by the option of early voting or voting by mail or online. According to the National Council of State Legislatures, as of late 2020, a handful of states provided mail-in ballots to all registered voters and four fifths of states offered some sort of early voting. Still, only about two thirds of states allowed every registered voter who wished to vote by absentee (mail-in) ballot to do so. Other states require an excuse. Many states relaxed their rules and enabled more voting by mail for the 2020 election due to the coronavirus pandemic, and more and more states have been moving to convenient mail-in voting, but the ease of mail-in voting continues to vary from state to state.[11]

Once one arrives at a polling place, many states now require state-issued photographic identification. Again, wealthier individuals face less hindrance. The most common form of such identification is a driver's license, but only those who can afford to drive have a reason (besides voting) to obtain a license. States offer alternative forms of photo identification, but these are usually only available at central offices. Adults who cannot afford a car lack both their own means of easily travelling to such offices and the dual incentives of doing so to satisfy requirements for both driving and voting. Empirical analyses suggest strict voter identification laws disproportionately reduce voting by racial and ethnic minorities and benefit right-wing candidates.[12]

Photographic identification will not suffice, however, if one's registration has been purged from the voter rolls. Many states have aggressively purged rolls, ostensibly to eliminate registrations of individuals who have died, moved, are registered under more than one name or are otherwise ineligible to vote in a given precinct. However, reviews have found the most aggressive purges have occurred in states with a history of racial discrimination that, until the 2013 Supreme Court *Shelby County v. Holder* (570 US 529 [2013]) decision, were required to obtain federal Department of Justice Civil Rights Division approval for changes to their voting procedures. Various authors who have examined the criteria for and timing of voter roll purges have raised concerns that the real motivation is often to suppress voting by members of visible minorities and other select groups.[13]

Finally, many states do not allow those convicted of felonies to vote, in some cases even after completion of sentences. Though some restrictions on felon voting have been eased, six million Americans remain ineligible to vote because of felony convictions. This interferes with majority rule because felons are not a representative cross section of the population. Compared to the population at large, felons tend to be less able to afford private legal representation and more likely to be members of minorities who may be victims of racial profiling or other biases in the US justice system.[14] (In Ferguson, Missouri, for example, police were almost twice as likely to stop black drivers as white drivers and twice as likely to arrest black drivers as white drivers even though white drivers were found in possession of contraband 50 per cent more often than black drivers.)[15] Prohibitions on voting by felons skews the rolls of eligible voters toward wealthier, whiter populations.

These various obstructions to voting disproportionately hinder members of groups who have traditionally favoured Democratic candidates, and they therefore advantage their Republican opponents. Thus, even if those most hindered are not motivated primarily by environmental concerns, the restrictions function as an obstacle to environmental progress because, as of the early twenty-first century, Republican candidates tend to oppose government efforts to increase environmental protection while Democratic candidates are more supportive.

Gerrymandering

Gerrymandering refers to the process of drawing electoral district boundaries, especially boundaries of congressional districts, to favour the current majority party. Gerrymandering further reduces the match between the preferences of citizens and the positions of elected officials.

By law, Congressional district boundaries are arranged such that each representative has approximately the same number of constituents. Maintaining roughly equal populations per district requires adjusting boundaries as populations grow or decline. Each state is responsible for revising its districts on the basis of each decennial census. Independent commissions revise districts in some states, but in most states the legislature sets the boundaries.[16]

Gerrymandering occurs when dominant parties arrange districts to maximize their prospects of winning elections. Gerrymandered districts have boundaries that are carefully engineered either to divide the minority party's likely voters thinly across many districts, none of which they can dominate ('cracking'), or concentrate minority party voters in a minimum number of districts ('packing'), thereby increasing the likelihood of wins by the majority party in the other districts. Many states' district boundaries incorporate both packing and cracking.[17] Nowadays, importing detailed census data into geographical information system mapping software enables precise gerrymandering.

By disenfranchising supporters of the minority party, gerrymandering reduces the match between the composition of

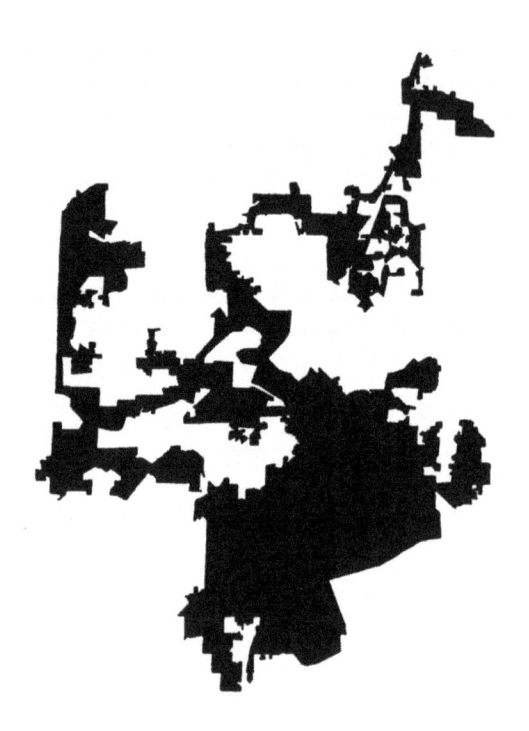

Figure 13.1: The boundaries of the Texas 30th Congressional district created after the 1990 census. Source: *Bush v. Vera* (94–805), 517 US 952 (1996), 987.

legislatures and overall support for a party among a state's voters. In other words, it interferes with the 'representative' intention of democracy. Figure 13.1 provides an extreme example of a Texas district during the 1990s. The situation had not noticeably improved as of 2021.[18]

Imbalances between the percentage of the vote received by each party and the percentage of elected officials from each party provide evidence of effective gerrymandering. For instance, in the 2016 US House of Representative elections, Republican candidates received 49 per cent of votes but won 55 per cent of seats while Democratic candidates received 48 per cent of votes but won only 45 per cent of seats.[19] A difference of a few members has major consequences because a simple majority determines the outcome of House votes, majority-party members chair all committees and subcommittees, and the leader of the majority party controls which bills are brought up for a vote. Imbalances between vote totals and number of seats won also occurs in state legislatures. For example, 2018 Republican candidates for the Wisconsin House of

Representatives received 48 per cent of votes and won 64 per cent of seats.[20]

The Supreme Court has ruled racially motivated gerrymandering unconstitutional, but has decided federal courts have no jurisdiction over partisan gerrymandering. On the other hand, the Court has decided voters can prevent gerrymandering by using state constitutional ballot referenda to shift districting power from the legislature to independent commissions.[21] Several states, including Arizona and California, have created independent, non-partisan redistricting commissions. Comparison of Arizona and California election results to national averages suggests the commissions have created more competitive districts, as would be expected if their district boundaries are less influenced by gerrymandering. Establishment of nonpartisan redistricting commissions may become more common because both parties' voters object to gerrymandering,[22] but as long as legislatures set district boundaries, gerrymandering will presumably continue to prevent elections from representing the will of the voters.

Campaign finance

Running for office is expensive. The average senator elected in 2016 spent more than $10 million and the average winning candidate for the House of Representatives spent about $1.5 million. Hillary Clinton's presidential campaign spent more than $700 million.[23] A small fraction of candidates are independently wealthy and willing to fund their own campaigns. Others must raise funds.

Following the Federal Election Campaign Act amendments of 1974 and the related Supreme Court decision in *Buckley v. Valeo* (424 US 1 [1976]), individuals could give only limited amounts of money to any particular candidate in any election. This kept candidates from being heavily beholden to any particular supporter. However, a variety of Supreme Court decisions since, culminating with *Citizens United v Federal Election Commission* (558 US 50 [2010]) and *McCutcheon v FEC* (134 US 1434, 1437 [2014]) effectively removed limits on donations, either from individuals or organizations. As a consequence, wealthy individuals, organizations and corporations can provide tens of millions of dollars in support of particular candidates. They may even do so anonymously.[24]

Multimillion dollar donations interfere with majority rule in two ways. First, huge expenditures enable wealthy individuals and organizations to influence campaigns through advertising and other publicity favourable to their preferred positions and candidates. Second, election winners are indebted to supporters. Elected 'representatives' are especially attuned to the concerns of major donors for multiple reasons. First, they may have a conscious or unconscious sense of gratitude or bias. Second, they may spend enough time talking with wealthy donors to be disproportionately influenced by donors' views. Third, they may treat donations as quid-pro-quo arrangements (bribes), as if donors have implied that they expect a return on their investment and will provide more money in the future but only for as long as the candidate supports the donors' preferred policies.

Such corruption of democracy seems to me an inevitable consequence of allowing large donations. Imagine how you would behave if you could make large donations and wished to influence policy. To which candidates would you send donations? Presumably to the ones who support your preferred policies. That's what I do with my trivial donations. Now, if the recipients of your donations subsequently do not support your preferred policies, would you give them more money in the future? I would not.

One may contribute directly to individual candidates' campaigns, to any of various committees under the auspices of a candidate's party, to political action committees (PAC) or to so-called Super PACs. Parties and political action committees can coordinate their actions with candidates and share resources. In theory, Super PACs cannot participate in such coordination, but as we shall see, that restriction is exceedingly weak in practice.

Table 13.1 lists the 2021–22 limits on contributions to and from various entities. (Super PACs are not included in the table because there are no limits on contributions to Super PACs, as explained below.) Even without contributing to Super PACs, wealthy individuals and organizations (functioning as political action committees) can give tens or hundreds of thousands of dollars per year to their preferred candidates and party. These amounts may influence candidates, but they pale in comparison to contributions that may be made to Super PACs.

Super PACs work on behalf of particular issues, parties and/or candidates, but are prohibited by law from coordinating their actions with candidates or parties. Their efforts are often referred to as 'independent expenditures' because they are supposed to be made independently of any coordination or communication with a candidate or party, but decisions about what qualifies as 'coordination' have rendered this restriction almost meaningless. For example, Super PACs run by candidates' former aides or advisers have been set up to support those same individual candidates without objection from the Federal Elections Commission. Likewise, the Commission allows candidates to help Super PACs raise money as long as the candidate and Super PAC do not coordinate how that money is spent.[25]

The *Citizens United* and *McCutcheon* decisions and their predecessors have created a situation where individuals, corporations and other organizations may contribute unlimited sums,[26] either directly to Super PACs or to certain other types of non-profit entities that are not required to identify donors.[27] The latter may directly advocate for policies or pass those anonymous donations on to super PACs.[28] Super PACs must reveal their donors, but because donors to super PACs are not required to reveal *their* donors, individuals or organizations can anonymously funnel unlimited sums to super PACs. The Center for Responsive Politics estimates super PACs spent more than $5 billion to influence US elections between 2010 and late 2021, with more than $1 billion having come from undisclosed donors.[29]

Justices in the majority on these split Supreme Court decisions have defended the allowance of unlimited contributions on the basis of the free speech protection of the Constitution, arguing that electioneering is a type of speech that cannot be restricted by the government, and protection of free speech is a greater concern than the fear of undue influence of wealthy donors, but massive contributions provide wealthy individuals bullhorns that are unavailable to typical citizens. Dismissing the latter concern, Justice Kennedy seemed surprisingly certain when he wrote:

> Independent expenditures, including those made by corporations, do not give rise to corruption or the appearance of corruption. That speakers may have influence over or access to elected officials does not mean that those officials are corrupt. And the appearance of influence or access will not cause the electorate to lose faith in this democracy.[30]

Bill McKibben articulates an opposing perspective. He uses, as an example, a Congressional vote to expedite review of the proposal to build the Keystone XL tar sands pipeline. Oil companies favoured quick approval of the pipeline while most environmentalists favoured rejection. McKibben noted the 234 members who voted in favour of rapid review had received $42 million from the fossil fuel industry while the 193 who voted against rapid review had received $8 million. He concluded as follows.

Table 13.1: US political contribution limits

		Recipient				
		Candidate committee	Political action committee†	Party committee: state/district/local	Party committee: national	Additional national party committee accounts
Donor	Individual	$2,900 per election	$5,000 per year	$10,000 per year	$36,500 per year	$109,500 per account, per year
	Candidate committee	$2,000 per election	$5,000 per year	Unlimited transfers	Unlimited transfers	
	Multicandidate political action committee	$5,000 per election	$5,000 per year	$5,000 per year (combined)	$15,000 per year	$45,000 per account, per year
	Single candidate political action committee	$2,900 per election	$5,000 per year	$10,000 per year (combined)	$36,500 per year	$109,500 per account, per year
	Party committee: state/district/local	$5,000 per election	$5,000 per year	Unlimited transfers	Unlimited transfers	
	Party committee: national	$5,000 per election*	$5,000 per year	Unlimited transfers	Unlimited transfers	

We've reached the point where we're unfazed by things that should shake us to the core. So, just for a moment, be naïve and consider what really happened in that vote: the people's representatives who happen to have taken the bulk of the money from those energy companies promptly voted on behalf of their interests.

They weren't weighing science or the national interest; they weren't balancing present benefits against future costs. Instead of doing the work of legislators, that is, they were acting like employees. Forget the idea that they're public servants; the truth is that, in every way that matters, they work for Exxon and its kin. They should, by rights, wear logos on their lapels like NASCAR drivers.

If you find this too harsh, think about how obligated you feel when someone gives you something. Did you get a Christmas present last month from someone you hadn't remembered to buy one for? Are you going to send them an extra-special one next year?

And that's for a pair of socks. Speaker of the House John Boehner, who insisted that the Keystone approval decision be speeded up, has gotten $1,111,080 from the fossil-fuel industry during his tenure. His Senate counterpart Mitch McConnell, who shepherded the bill through his chamber, has raked in $1,277,208 in the course of his tenure in Washington.

Table 13.1
2021–22 limits on contributions to federal candidates and party committees from individuals, campaign committees, and political action committees (PACs). Except for a few omitted details, the information in this table has been reproduced verbatim from Federal Election Commission websites https://www.fec.gov/help-candidates-and-committees/candidate-taking-receipts/contribution-limits/, and https://www.fec.gov/help-candidates-and-committees/registering-pac/understanding-nonconnected-pacs/, accessed 30 December 2021. Refer to Federal Election Commission websites for further details.

Notes to Table 13.1
*Additionally, a national party committee and its senatorial campaign committee may contribute up to $51,200 combined per campaign to each senate candidate.
† 'PAC' here refers to a committee that makes contributions to other federal political committees. Independent-expenditure-only political committees (sometimes called 'Super PACs') may accept unlimited contributions, including from corporations and labour organizations.

If someone had helped your career to the tune of a million dollars, wouldn't you feel in their debt? I would. I get somewhat less than that from my employer, Middlebury College, and yet I bleed Panther blue. Don't ask me to compare my school with, say, Dartmouth unless you want a biased answer, because that's what you'll get. Which is fine—I *am* an employee.

But you'd be a fool to let me referee the homecoming football game. In fact, in any other walk of life we wouldn't think twice before concluding that paying off the referees is wrong. If the Patriots make the Super Bowl, everyone in America would be outraged to see owner Robert Kraft trot out to midfield before the game and hand a $1,000 bill to each of the linesmen and field judges.[31]

The Supreme Court's removal of limitations on contributions to political campaigns is why some commentators argue that democracy in the US is based on one dollar, one vote rather than one person, one vote. To the extent that this is accurate, huge political donations distort the ideal of equal representation for all citizens.

Of course, the same anonymous, unlimited contributions can also be used to confuse public understanding regarding environmental issues, to argue that environmental protection restricts freedoms or would be too costly, or to resist the passage of proposed laws or rigorous implementation of policies. Freedom to speak is protected but freedom to be assured that public speech is accurate or even basically true is not, so unlimited sums can be spent on confusing the public and distorting their understanding of environmental issues. As we shall see in the next chapter, compared to proponents of environmental protection, opponents are generally able to bring substantially more funding to bear on such debates.

Disproportionate influence of selected states

While some individuals have disproportionate political influence because they are wealthy, others have outsize influence because of where they live. If voters in states with disproportionate influence are less motivated by environmental concerns than voters in other states, then elected representatives will be less motivated than the public at large. This creates an obstacle to environmental progress because of the disproportionate influence of rural states with small populations whose voters often oppose further environmental protection.[32]

Small state voters have a tremendous influence on the Senate because each state has two senators but states vary widely in population. The most populous state, California, has one senator for every 20 million residents while the least populous state, Wyoming, has one senator for every 300,000 residents. In other words, a Wyoming voter has more than sixty times as much impact on the Senate as a California voter.

Efforts to halt debate and vote on legislation in the Senate have traditionally required not just a majority of 51 of 100 votes, but a supermajority of 60 votes. With few exceptions, unless 60 senators vote to halt debate, any single senator can filibuster – prevent the end of debate and thus prevent a vote on legislation.[33] Therefore, 41 senators can prevent the passage of any legislation. For example, although the Capitol was invaded by a mob on 6 January 2020, a proposal to create a Senate commission to investigate the incident enjoyed majority support (54 of 100 possible senators) but not the 60 required to end a filibuster, and thus the proposal failed and the proposed commission was not formed.[34]

As of 2020, the 21 least populous states – who between them can supply the required 41 senators to block a vote – collectively had about 37 million residents, roughly 11 per cent of the national total and two million fewer than California alone. Thus, 41 senators representing about 10 per cent of the country and fewer people than the residents of California, could prevent the passage of any bill. That is unlikely, however, because the 21 least populous states' senators are unlikely to vote as a block. On the other hand, the 21 least populous 'red' states (states in which the Republican presidential candidate won at least three out of four of the 2004–16 presidential elections) could conceivably vote as a block. (Republican senators voted as a block 89 per cent of the time from 2000 to 2016.)[35] Those 21 states hold only 22 per cent of the national population but their representatives cast 42 per cent of Senate votes.[36] Many of those states have economies heavily dependent on oil and gas, mining, logging, farming or ranching, and thus many residents who will be wary of any sort of environmental protection that involves restrictions on land use, ecosystem damage or greenhouse gas emissions. Thus, the power of small states in the Senate serves as an obstacle to environmental progress.

States with early presidential primaries also have special influence. In particular, Iowa, with the earliest primary, and New Hampshire, with the second primary, are most important.[37] Strong performance in Iowa, New Hampshire or both has historically been critical to winning a party's presidential nomination. For example, since 1996 only one major party candidate, Joe Biden, has won either party's nomination without winning

Iowa or New Hampshire. During 2020, Pete Buttigieg, from nearby Indiana, won in a crowded Iowa field and Bernie Sanders, from neighbouring Vermont, won in New Hampshire. The eventual nominee from both major parties won at least one of these states in every other election since 1996.[38] Presidential candidates therefore have a strong incentive to appeal to the concerns of Iowa and New Hampshire voters.

The last major reason why some states have a disproportionate influence is the role of the Electoral College. The candidate who receives 270 Electoral College votes becomes president. Because all states except Maine and Nebraska award all of their Electoral College votes to the state's popular-vote winner, the Electoral College interferes with majority rule in two ways, both of which provide some states' voters with disproportionate influence.

First, presidential candidates pay disproportionate attention to voters in competitive states, practically ignoring states consistently won by one party or the other. Presidential candidates rarely campaign in reliably red or blue states, such as Wyoming or New York. They either take such states for granted or write them off as a lost cause, spending their time instead appealing to voters of 'purple' states – those that have not consistently been won by either party.

Second, a candidate may win many states by narrow margins but lose others by wide margins, thereby losing the popular vote but still winning the Electoral College and becoming president. When Donald Trump defeated Hillary Clinton in 2016, he became the most recent of five presidents who have won the Electoral College while losing the popular vote. In 2000 George W. Bush also lost the popular vote to Al Gore but still became president. The three previous occasions were all in the nineteenth century.

Though Hillary Clinton received almost three million more votes than Donald Trump, Trump won the Electoral College because he won many states by narrow margins while losing others by large margins. Together, Clinton and Trump received almost 130 million votes, but if as few as about 40,000 voters had switched their votes in Michigan, Pennsylvania and Wisconsin, Clinton would have been elected. In other words, because most states award all of their Electoral College votes to the state's popular-vote winner, Clinton lost despite receiving almost three million more votes nationwide and could have won if just 0.03 per cent of all voters had switched their votes.[39]

Together, the disproportionate influence of states with small populations, Senate filibusters, the timing of states' presidential primaries, and the rules of the Electoral College give some states disproportionately large influence upon US law and policy and therefore impede simple majority rule. Furthermore, because many small states are largely rural with economies heavily dependent on agriculture, ranching or extractive industries, representatives from these states tend to be especially wary of new rules or regulations that would impact those industries, and therefore often oppose new environmental protections. To the extent those representatives oppose strengthening environmental protection, differential influence of such states serves as an obstacle to environmental progress. A closely related obstacle derives from the many federal mechanisms that make it much harder to pass legislation than prevent passage of legislation.

> The American political system has a variety of counter-majoritarian features, most importantly the Electoral College, the Senate, and a powerful appointed judiciary, that have few parallels in other democracies. These are meant to preserve minority rights against a tyrannical majority.
>
> Gerrymandering and the bias of the Senate and the Electoral College, however, means that instead of protecting minority rights, they can enable minority *rule*.[40]

How a bill does not become law

Once the voting is done and representatives have been elected, those representatives may seek to alter existing laws and policy. Major strengthening of federal environmental protection requires passage of new laws or amendments that strengthen existing laws. Therefore, any hurdles to passing laws can function as obstacles to environmental protection.

The nation's founders' wariness of government power led them to construct numerous constraints on expansion of that power. In addition to adopting the Bill of Rights to protect minorities from the tyranny of the majority, they enacted multiple hurdles to passing laws.

New laws must pass both houses of Congress and enjoy the support of the president, or pass both houses with supermajorities. Later, if challenged, their constitutionality must pass muster with the judiciary. Collectively, the necessity of supermajority support from two legislatures plus the support of the judiciary, or support from all three branches of the federal government, creates a substantial hurdle to passage of new laws.

Rules, traditions and customary procedures for debating legislation raise the bar much higher. Indeed, one scholar has concluded that the United States has the 'most intricate lawmaking system in the world'.[41]

The Constitution does not specify House and Senate procedures; those procedures are somewhat malleable and evolve over time, but House bills generally proceed as follows.[42] Introduced bills are assigned to one or more committees whose chairs typically refer them to one or more subcommittees.[43] Committee or subcommittee chairs then decide whether to consider proposed legislation. This is a competitive process because Congress lacks time to address all bills. Most bills do not get considered – they 'die in committee'.[44] If a subcommittee does debate a bill, it may seek input from agencies, experts and the public at large. Subcommittee members modify bills, either of their own volition or on the basis of such testimony, then return the modified bills to their larger committees with a favourable or unfavourable recommendation, or a recommendation that the bill be tabled (not acted upon).

The full committee may table a bill indefinitely, remove it from consideration or amend it further and report it to the full House. If a bill is reported to the House by all relevant committees, it is given a 'calendar number'. Just getting this far is an accomplishment. During some congresses, as many as a hundred subcommittees have had jurisdiction over the EPA and thus an interest in environmental bills.[45]

Bills are not necessarily considered in the order they reach the full House. Under the guidance of the Speaker of the House (the leader of the majority party), the Committee on Rules controls the order. If a bill does come up for consideration by the whole House, members debate it, often adding amendments. Some bills acquire as many as a hundred amendments. Finally, a vote may be taken.

The Senate employs similar procedures, except a supermajority is normally required to pass a bill. Senate convention, and only convention, dictates that 60 votes are required to end debate – that is, to stop a filibuster. Historically, and still today in some deliberative bodies, a filibuster occurs when a legislator speaks at great length, thereby preventing the close of debate and thus preventing a vote. Senators are not required to actually speak; merely announcing an intent to filibuster has the same effect. If one member threatens a filibuster, under normal procedures a bill will not come up for a vote unless 60 senators announce they will vote to end debate. Recognizing this, the Senate does not normally consider bills with fewer than sixty supporters. Few controversial bills enjoy so much support; therefore, many bills die just because one senator threatens a filibuster.[46]

… the Senate's treasured tradition is not efficiency but deliberation. One of the body's central purposes is making new laws earn broader support than what is required for a bare majority in the House. The legislative filibuster does not appear in the Constitution's text, but it is central to the order the Constitution sets forth. It echoes James Madison's explanation in Federalist 62 that the Senate is designed not to rubber-stamp House bills but to act as an 'additional impediment' and 'complicated check' on 'improper acts of legislation.' It embodies Thomas Jefferson's principle that 'great innovations should not be forced on slender majorities.'[47]

Because the requirement of 60 votes to end debate is rooted merely in tradition, not specified in the Constitution, the Senate majority leader can waive the rule, a tactic often referred to as the 'nuclear option'. During 2013, when Republican senators routinely refused to approve Obama Administration nominees for agency posts, the Democratic leadership abandoned the requirement of 60 votes to close debate on nominees for all but the Supreme Court. During 2017, the Republican leadership abandoned it for approval of Supreme Court nominees.[48] The future of the filibuster is presently under debate.

A bill may pass in the House but not the Senate or vice versa. For example, 2010 legislation to address climate change was passed in the House but never voted upon in the Senate.[49] Because the Senate never voted, the bill died.

A bill cannot become law until the House and Senate pass identical versions. When bills are originally introduced in the two chambers, ostensibly for the same purpose, they are nevertheless generally not identical. Furthermore, both bodies typically amend proposed legislation. Thus, similar bills are rarely identical when first passed in each chamber. A Conference Committee involving members of both the House and Senate seeks to resolve differences and agree on a common text, usually through compromises. Then both the full House and Senate must pass the revised bill.

Throughout this process, House and Senate leaders have tremendous power over which bills come up for a vote. Since the mid-1990s, Republican speakers of the House have refused to allow a vote on any bill not supported by a majority of their party's representatives. This is often referred to as the Hastert Rule after its initiator, former Speaker of the House Dennis Hastert.[50] Insisting on majority support of the members of the party in power raises the bar for new laws yet farther and inhibits passage of legislation with broad bipartisan support of moderate representatives from both parties but lacking support of the Republican party's less moderate members. Together, the Hastert Rule in the House plus the Senate requirement of 60 votes to close debate are largely responsible for Congress's recent decades of relative stalemate.

When both chambers pass the same bill, it is sent to the president, who then has ten days to sign or veto it. If the president signs the bill or takes no action for ten days (not including Sundays) it becomes law – unless Congress is not in session at the end of the ten days, in which case the bill is considered vetoed. (The latter is referred to as a 'pocket veto'.) A vetoed bill may be sent back to committees, amended, passed in a modified form and returned to the president for reconsideration. Alternatively, the House and Senate may override the veto, but an override requires two-thirds majorities in both chambers. Controversial bills rarely garner such support.[51]

Both legislatures can suspend rules to streamline processes, but they rarely do so for controversial bills or bills perceived as non-urgent.[52] Finally, a bill must complete this entire process during one Congress (two annual Congressional sessions of about 160 working days each). Any failed bill must return to the first step of subcommittee consideration during the next Congress. Given so many hurdles, it is not surprising the great majority of bills never become law.

Opponents of a new law need merely halt a bill at *any* step in either the House or Senate, but supporters must prevail at *every* step. Thus, it is much harder to pass new legislation than to prevent its passage. This creates a barrier to new environmental protections (and a barrier to the removal of existing environmental protection).

> There is, in short, a strong structural bias within our existing lawmaking institutions in favor of government acting slowly and incrementally. Whatever their ideological bent, sweeping law reforms in response to new information or values are very difficult to accomplish without institutional change, yet those same institutions that need reform resist just that possibility.[53]

This chapter has explained why US government decisions do not always reflect majority preferences and how legislative procedures impose barriers to new environmental legislation. As we shall see in the next chapter, those wishing to pass new environmental protections must not only achieve sufficient demand for action, overcome impediments to majority rule and prevail at each legislative step; they must win those battles despite being outspent by their opponents.

Notes

1 Economist Intelligence Unit, 'Democracy index 2020', 2021.
2 Marlon et al., 'Yale Climate Opinion Maps 2020', 2020; Wu, 'The oppression of the supermajority', 2019.
3 US Census Bureau, 'Wealth, asset ownership, and debt of households detailed tables', 2018.
4 Brulle and Pellow, 'Environmental justice', 2006, 103–7; Bullard et al., 'Toxic wastes and race at twenty, 1987–2007', 2007, x–xi, 38–83; Rosenbaum, *Environmental Politics and Policy*, 2002, 143–8.
5 Mohai et al., 'Environmental justice', 2009, 413–16; Moskowitz, 'SCOTUS 101', 2018; Vose, *Caucasians Only*, 1959, 5–13.
6 Salzman and Thompson, *Environmental Law and Policy*, 2014, 43–6.
7 Mohai et al., 'Environmental justice', 2009, 406.
8 Brennan Center for Justice, 'Voting laws roundup', 2021.
9 Brennan Center for Justice, 'Voting laws roundup', 2021; Herron and Smith, 'Race, party, and the consequences of restricting early voting in Florida in the 2012 general election', 2014; D. Smith, 'Voter suppression policies in the 2016 campaign cycle', 2018, 33–8.
10 I mean this as no criticism of poll workers who typically work long shifts for minimal compensation and heroically did so during 2020 despite the coronavirus pandemic.
11 National Conference of State Legislatures, 'Voting outside the polling place', 2020; Swasey, 'Map', 2020.
12 Hajnal et al., 'Voter identification laws and the suppression of minority votes', 2016; Highton, 'Voter identification laws and turnout in the US', 2017; Kuk et al., 'A disproportionate burden', 2020.
13 Lerner, 'States purged 16 million voters from the roles before the 2016 election', 2018; S. Levine, 'Voter purges', 2019.
14 Chung, 'Voting rights in the era of mass incarceration', 2021; Nellis, 'The color of justice', 2021; D. Smith, 'Voter suppression policies in the 2016 campaign cycle', 2018, 36.
15 Ghandnoosh, 'Black lives matter', 2015, 6–7.
16 Brennan Center for Justice, 'Who draws the maps?', 2019.
17 Bazelon, 'The new front in the gerrymandering wars: democracy vs. math', 2017; Daley, 'New poll', 2017.
18 Corasaniti et al., 'How maps reshape American politics', 2021; Corasaniti et al., 'How Texas plans to make its house districts even redder', 2021.
19 History, Art and Archives, US House of Representatives, 'Election statistics', 2021; Reynolds, 'Republicans in Congress got a "seats bonus" this election (again)', 2016.
20 Corasaniti et al., 'How maps reshape American politics', 2021.

21 See summaries of *Miller v. Johnson*, 515 US 900 (1995), *Arizona State Legislature v. Arizona Independent Redistricting Commission*, No. 13-1314, 576 US, 135 S. Ct. 2652 (2015) and *Rucho v. Common Cause*, 139 S. Ct. 2484 (2019) in National Conference of State Legislatures, 'Redistricting and the Supreme Court', 2021.

22 Daley, 'New poll', 2017; Soffen, 'Independently drawn districts have proved to be more competitive', 2015.

23 Ingraham, 'Somebody just put a price tag on the 2016 election', 2017; Kim, 'The price of winning just got higher, especially in the Senate', 2016; Malbin and Glavin, 'CFI's guide to money in Federal elections', 2018, 11.

24 Alschuler, 'Limiting political contributions after *McCutcheon*, *Citizens United*, and *SpeechNow*', 2016, 392, 409–17; Klumpp et al., 'The business of American democracy', 2016, 6–10; Polsby, 'Buckley v. Valeo', 1976, 2.

25 M. Wang, 'Uncoordinated coordination', 2011.

26 Alschuler, 'Limiting political contributions after *McCutcheon*, *Citizens United*, and *SpeechNow*', 2016, 392, 409–17.

27 Such as those defined in the following tax classes: 501(c)4, 'social welfare' organizations such as the National Rifle Association Political Victory Fund and Planned Parenthood Action Fund; 501(c)5, labour and similar organizations, such as the American Federation of State, County, and Municipal Employees; 501(c)6, business organizations such as the US Chamber of Commerce and the American Medical Association. See Charity Navigator, 'Types of nonprofits', n.d.; Open Secrets, 'Dark money basics', n.d.; S. Sullivan, 'What is a 501(c)4, anyway?', 2013; US Internal Revenue Service, 'Public disclosure and availability of exempt organizations returns and applications', 2021.

28 Good, 'Don't blame Citizens United', 2010; Open Secrets, 'Dark money basics', n.d.

29 Open Secrets, 'Dark money basics', n.d.; Open Secrets, 'Outside spending', n.d.

30 Quoted in Edsall, 'The high cost of free speech', 2014.

31 McKibben, 'Armed with naïvete', 2012.

32 Kennedy, 'Public support for environmental regulations varies by state', 2016.

33 As of early 2022 the Democratic Senate majority was considering abandoning the filibuster. Since 1917, sixty votes have been required to prevent a filibuster of most Senate debates (see Binder, 'The history of the filibuster', 2010).

34 Nobles et al., 'Senate Republicans block January 6 commission', 2021.

35 Brookings, 'Vital statistics on Congress', 2021 (see data table 8.3, 'Party unity votes in Congress, 1953–2016').

36 US Census Bureau, 'National population totals: 2010–2020'.

37 Furthermore, Iowa uses precinct caucuses to select candidates. Caucus meetings take hours. Thus, individuals' scheduling constraints may have especially large effects on caucus participation. Though results are somewhat mixed, some authors have found evidence that caucuses (versus polls) select for disproportionate participation by individuals with extreme political views (Karpowitz and Pope, 'Who caucuses?', 2015). This is not surprising given the time required for caucus participation. It seems reasonable to expect those with unusually strong sentiments to be most likely to take the necessary time.

38 US Federal Election Commission, 'Election and voting information', n.d.

39 US Federal Election Commission, 'Election and voting information', n.d.

40 Mukunda, 'Long crisis ahead', 2020.

41 Charles Jones, *The Presidency in a Separated System*, 1994, 297.

42 B. Sinclair, *Unorthodox Lawmaking*, 2017, 10–46; S. Sullivan, 'How our laws are made', 2007.

43 Procedures exist to bypass House committees. This generally occurs either when 218 or more members vote in favour of 'discharging' a bill from committee consideration; when an emergency or perceived emergency exists; or when the majority party seeks advantage by either rushing or generating publicity for a particular bill. B. Sinclair, *Unorthodox Lawmaking*, 2017, 18–21.

44 US Capitol Visitors Center, 'Committees', n.d.

45 Lazarus, *The Making of Environmental Law*, 2004, 80.

46 An exception is budget 'reconciliation' bills that allow passage with a bare majority of 51 votes for some tax, spending and debt limit legislation. Controversy surrounds when bills may be considered under reconciliation rules. See for example Rampell, 'No one in their right mind would design a government that works like ours', 2021, and Heniff, 'The budget reconciliation process: the Senate's "Byrd Rule"', 2016.

47 McConnell, 'The filibuster plays a crucial role in our constitutional order', 2019.
48 Flegenheimer, 'Senate Republicans deploy "nuclear option" to clear path for Gorsuch', 2017.
49 Goldsmith, 'A wrong turn on climate change', 2010.
50 Because the members of the majority party elect the Speaker and the Speaker can be removed at any time, Speakers have an incentive to please the majority of their party. Golshan, 'The "Hastert Rule," the reason a DACA deal could fail in the House, explained', 2018.
51 J. Sullivan, 'How Our Laws Are Made', 2007.
52 Schneider, 'House and Senate rules of procedure', 2008.
53 Lazarus, 'Super wicked problems and climate change', 2009, 1180.

14
An endless uphill battle

As we have seen, proponents of environmental protection encounter opposition. Both sides organize into groups. The two types of groups, those pushing for more environmental protection and those resisting new environmental protections, have various advantages. Those who seek further environmental protection may enjoy the moral high ground and have more supporters, but their opponents tend to have highly motivated supporters with livelihoods at stake. As a consequence, those opponents, drawing on the resources of well-established industries, can often raise more money for their cause. Moreover, for many battles, such as over resource extraction, they have another advantage. Opponents need win only once to gain access to a resource while protectors of a resource must win every time or the resource can be lost, in some cases forever.

This chapter describes the two main types of groups engaged in environmental debates, the approaches that those opposed to further environmental protection use to influence legislators and the public, the funding disadvantage of those favouring environmental protection, and the need for those protecting the environment to win some battles over and over, not just once. Having to win over and over while out-funded is akin to playing ball uphill in a game that ends only if the opponent takes the lead.

Interest groups

Various groups seek to influence US environmental policy. Dozens of organizations, such as the Center for Biological Diversity and the Natural Resources Defense Council, represent interests of those in favour of strong environmental protection. Meanwhile, dozens of others, such as the Competitive Enterprise Institute and the Heartland Institute, represent those generally opposed to further, or even existing, environmental protection.

Zachary Smith and others identify two general categories of interest groups, public non-economic groups and private economic groups. Private economic groups seek benefits that accrue primarily to their members, though they often cast their arguments as in the interest of the public at large. Public non-economic groups seek benefits that accrue to the public at large or to other species, not exclusively to their members. Private economic groups offer their members direct economic benefits while public non-economic groups only offer the benefit of supporting what they perceive as a public good. Public, non-economic groups cannot offer a financial return on membership. The expectation of a financial gain associated with membership provides private groups a fundraising advantage.[1]

Public non-economic groups often favour environmental protection while private economic groups oppose it. For example, the American Petroleum Institute favours drilling on the Alaskan North Slope while the Center for Biological Diversity opposes it. Private economic groups often seek to maintain the legality of resource extraction or other environmentally damaging activities. They have a financial incentive to do so.[2] Conversely, members of environmental organizations generally do not have a personal financial stake in environmental debates. For example, many who advocate restrictions on coal burning do not work in related industries and thus have no direct financial stake in the outcome of that debate, so their incentives are not as acute as those of opponents whose incomes depend upon coal. Therefore, because of members' financial motivations, groups that oppose environmental protection are often able to raise more funds than their opponents.[3]

Opponents of environmental protection routinely spend several times as much money as supporters of protection. For example, Monsanto, DuPont, Bayer CropScience, Dow Agrosciences, the Grocery Manufacturers Association and other agribusinesses spent $37 million to defeat a 2013 Washington State ballot initiative to label genetically modified foods (GMOs). Collectively they outspent proponents of labelling by more than 3:1. A year later, labelling proponents were outspent 20:1 during debate over a similar Colorado ballot initiative.[4]

During 2009, when Congress was considering a bill to curb greenhouse gases, supporters of the bill spent $22.4 million on federal lobbying while the oil and gas industry alone spent eight times as much, $175 million, resisting the legislation. The bill passed the House but was never voted upon by the Senate. Over the longer period of 2000–16, opponents of climate change action invested approximately ten times as much on lobbying as proponents.[5] Spending by hedge-fund manager and 2020 Democratic presidential candidate Thomas Steyer was an exception. Steyer has invested some $100 million advocating climate change action, but his contributions on behalf of environmental advocacy are unprecedented.[6] The norm is for environmental groups to be substantially outspent by their opponents, as when oil industry interests outspent environmental activists 40:1 opposing a 2018 Colorado ballot measure that would have imposed new restrictions on oil and gas projects.[7]

Manipulating political debate

Chapter 8 describes how opponents of environmental protection seek to confuse the public regarding the need for further environmental protection. They spend millions of dollars on such efforts, employing the latest public relations techniques, such as creating 'front groups' that falsely appear to be grassroots movements of ordinary citizens, and providing material for news outlets designed to appear as if reporters and editors had developed the material themselves. Such motivations are evident in an internal General Motors document that boldly explained, 'GM Public Relations helps to make GM so well-accepted by its various publics that it may pursue its corporate mission unencumbered by public-imposed limitations or regulations.'[8] Sharon Beder documents such tactics in detail in *Global Spin: The corporate assault on environmentalism*, on which the remainder of this section is based.[9]

Corporations and their trade organizations realize the public will be sceptical of obviously self-serving industry pronouncements, so they often use sophisticated public relations techniques to obscure their motivations and create the impression that grassroots, populist objections are responsible for opposition to new environmental protections. Beder describes one technique in which a radio talk show hosts gets listeners agitated about some issue, then during a commercial break a free telephone number is announced where callers can get more information. After callers speak with others who provide further information, they are patched through to their representatives' offices to voice their opinions on the issue. The effect is to give their representatives the impression of spontaneous grassroots concern. This may fool representatives and, even if it does not, it may fool enough constituents to provide political cover for representatives opposed to environmental protection.[10]

Knowing that politicians consider a constituent's letter a stronger message than a phone call, public relations consultants and their clients also work to give the impression that members of the public have spontaneously chosen to write to their representatives. One public relations consultant, John Davies, claimed that his firm would even prepare handwritten letters after obtaining agreement from the sender over the telephone. 'We hand write it out on "little kitty cat stationery" if it's a little old lady. If it's a business we take it over to be photocopied on someone's letterhead. [We] use different stamps, different envelopes ...'[11] Environmental groups also attempt to generate messages to representatives. For example, readers may be familiar with emails asking for signatures on electronic petitions. But a handwritten letter on kitty cat stationery will impress a politician much more than an electronic signature on a petition because the letter suggests a higher level of commitment on the part of the constituent. Email petitions are cheap; handwritten letters – in bulk – are expensive.

Trade associations go beyond giving the impression of spontaneous grassroots objections from individuals. They routinely create front groups – organizations intended to appear to be independent grassroots organizations but funded and organized by the trade associations or their public relations consultants. The names of front groups often suggest their goal is environmental protection when in fact their objective is the opposite. Some of the earliest front groups were particularly brazen in their choices of misleading names. For example, the Global Climate Coalition fought restrictions on greenhouse gas emissions while the National Wetlands Coalition defended the opportunities of fossil fuel companies to drill in wetlands. The latter's logo was a duck flying over a wetland.

Both of those groups have disbanded, but plenty of others remain. Citizens for Recycling First is funded by the coal industry to argue coal ash should serve as fill rather than be treated as hazardous material. Energy Citizens is funded by the American Petroleum Institute to oppose restrictions on greenhouse emissions. The National Center for Policy Analysis and the National Consumer Coalition both advocate for free market responses to public-policy problems – they oppose regulations. The Oregon Institute for Science and Medicine was the source of the petition project described in Chapter 8. Idaho for Wildlife holds 'derbies' to see who can shoot the most wolves and coyotes. The Center for Media and Democracy's SourceWatch website describes these and dozens of other front groups.[12] Clearly, the name of an organization is often no clue to the organization's true objective.[13]

In addition to conventional advertising, public relations consultants produce glorified press releases dressed up to look like reporting by independent journalists. They provide material the media can directly incorporate into stories or use without any editing, but not labelled as a press release. These materials give audiences the impression of being generated by independent news organizations. Approximately half of the material in US newspapers is based upon such disguised press releases.[14] Public relations offices also provide video material for use by local television stations who are often hard pressed to generate their own. Beder notes:

> It is popular nowadays to accompany the fully edited piece ready to be broadcast (A-roll) with unedited footage (B-roll) and a script so the television station crew can put together and edit the story as if they had shot it themselves, inserting their own journalist's voice over or adding their own material.[15]

When you watch, listen to or read news, see if you can detect apparent press releases masquerading as products of independent reporting.

Public relations professionals also provide material for their supportive lawmakers to use as those lawmakers attempt to influence policy. Some letters from lawmakers, or key sections of them, have been written by industry public relations officers. For example, North Dakota Governor Doug Burgum and several North Dakota state legislators used text provided to them by oil industry representatives in letters to the Federal Energy Regulatory Commission advocating approval of a company pipeline.[16]

Now even Instagram 'influencers' are discretely employed for this purpose, publishing posts praising gas cookstoves with no indication they have been paid to do so and no indication the stoves can pollute indoor air to levels above outdoor standards. Indeed, various reports suggest the natural gas industry has been using entertainers to use the phrase 'now we're cooking with gas' (which to a US audience means doing well) since the 1930s when homeowners were shifting from wood to either gas or electric stoves and ovens.[17]

When most of the major US environmental laws were passed during the 1960s and 1970s, public support for environmental protection prevailed, probably at least partly because private economic interest groups and public relations efforts were not as well-organized or effective as they have subsequently become.[18] Since then, a few other federal laws have been passed, but for the most part financial advantages, combined with sophisticated public relations efforts and numerous opportunities to prevent or derail new legislation, have enabled opponents to prevent major new environmental protection, such as a law addressing climate change.

Provisional protection

Despite disadvantages, proponents of environmental protection sometimes prevail, but they often achieve only temporary protection. They may have to wage the same battle again and again. In cases where environmental damage could be irreversible, protectors of the environment must prevail every time opponents seek access to a resource or authorization to otherwise modify the environment. As David Brower has noted, 'All a conservation group can do is to defer something. There's no such thing as a permanent victory. After we win a battle, the wilderness is still there and still vulnerable.'[19]

The Alaskan National Wildlife Refuge provides an example of the need to repeatedly defend a particular resource. Congress debated drilling for oil in the refuge some fifty times over the course of decades. Anti-drilling forces prevailed over and over, but eventually lost when the Tax Cuts and Jobs Act of 2017 was passed (using the Senate budget reconciliation procedure to prevent a Democratic filibuster).[20] None of the earlier victories were permanent. Those who wish to protect old growth forests, endangered species or any intact ecosystem face the same predicament. They must win every time. If they lose just once, the forest may be logged, the species may go extinct or the land may be 'developed' or otherwise damaged.

Like those who wished to drill in the Alaskan National Wildlife Refuge, those who wished to extract Albertan tar sands needed only achieve legal access once. But those who wished to protect the boreal forest above the tar sands would have had to deflect every attempt to allow mining because mining tar sands destroys the forest ecosystem. They failed to do so. The forest might perhaps recover over geological time, or a few trees may grow back, but the ecosystem will not be restored anytime soon. (Ecological restoration is a booming field, but its practitioners do not claim to be able to restore severely degraded ecosystems to full health.)[21]

The same situation pertains for soil, wetlands, and perhaps climate change. Once soil is lost, its natural recovery is so slow that, for practical purposes, soil should be considered a non-renewable resource. Artificial wetlands can be useful, but they are unlikely to have the complexity or biodiversity of natural wetlands or provide as many ecosystem services. Open space can be protected, but once it has been developed it is effectively lost. If greenhouse gases reach a concentration that initiates overwhelming positive climate feedbacks, as may already be occurring in areas losing permafrost, even a habitable climate may be permanently lost, at least in some regions of the globe.

We have now considered seven reasons why society may fail to respond to a newly understood environmental problem. Members of the public may not appreciate the strength of scientific evidence. Proposed protections will be portrayed as interfering with individual freedoms even though their net effect may be to expand freedoms. Efforts to influence the market will be resisted by those who believe markets should operate without hindrance. Costs of protection may be perceived as prohibitive. The incremental nature of problems may consign them to chronic low priority, as may voter disenfranchisement, especially in cases of environmental injustice. If an issue does achieve political priority, it is harder to pass new protections than block them, and financially motivated opponents of protection enjoy three advantages. They have more money, need block protection at only one stage in a lengthy process and if they fail, can try again. When, despite all these hurdles, a decision to protect the environment does occur, the challenge then turns to devising and implementing a successful response, the topic of this book's third and final section.

Notes

1   Levine and Forrence, 'Regulatory capture, public interest, and the public agenda', 1990, 174–6; Z. Smith, *The Environmental Policy Paradox*, 2004, 57.

2   Highly motivated small groups have had a history of public policy success, often attributed to the 'concentrated benefits–dispersed costs phenomenon' where a small group benefits tremendously (e.g. through access to oil drilling on federal lands or offshore) while the cost, which may be much larger (e.g. of oil spills, air pollution or climate change), is dispersed among a much larger group, indeed potentially the entire population, each individual of whom therefore perceives themselves to have much less to lose than proponents have to gain, leading to a permanent asymmetry of motivation. An extensive literature addresses collective action in politics, including the advantages of small, highly motivated groups. Key ideas are often attributed to Friedrich Hayek (*The Road to Serfdom*, 1944), Mancur Olson (*The Logic of Collective Action*, 1965) and E. E. Schattschneider, who wrote: 'The protective tariff is well established because large areas of adverse interests are too inert and sluggish to find political expression while an overwhelming proportion of the active interests have been given a stake in maintaining the system' (*Politics, Pressures, and the Tariff*, 1935, 163).

3   Z. Smith, *The Environmental Policy Paradox*, 2004, 57–8.

4   Gillam, 'GMO labeling foes spend big on campaigns in Oregon, Colorado', 2014; Washington Public Disclosure Commission, 'Follow the money', n.d. [see Initiative Committees (Statewide), 2013, Committees, Ballot 522; Washington State ballot initiative I-522, 2013]; Wilson,

'Initiative spending booms past $1 billion as corporations sponsor their own proposals', 2013. GMO supporters often portray opponents as irrationally concerned about hazards of consuming GMO ingredients. Some opponents may harbour concerns unsupported by available evidence, but other opposition is rooted in concerns about implications for organic agriculture, evolution of socio-agricultural systems toward greater corporate control, or high herbicide use on some GMO crops.

5   Brulle, 'Institutionalizing delay', 2014; Brulle, 'The climate lobby', 2018; Mackinder, 'Pro-environment groups outmatched, outspent in battle over climate change legislation', 2010.

6   Davenport, 'Billionaire environmentalist to spend $25 million to turn out young voters', 2016.

7   McKibben, 'Up against Big Oil in the midterms', 2018.

8   Blyskal and Blyskal, *PR*, 1985, 76.

9   Beder, *Global Spin*, 2002, 15–139.

10   Beder, *Global Spin*, 2002, 27–45.

11   Beder, *Global Spin*, 2002, 36; Stauber and Rampton, *Toxic Sludge is Good for You!*, 1995, 91.

12   Beder, *Global Spin*, 2002, 27–45; Center for Media and Democracy, 'SourceWatch', n.d.

13   This is not a solely environmental phenomenon. For example, wealthy backers funded 'grassroots' protests against government mandated lockdowns during 2020 in response to the Coronavirus pandemic (Vogel et al., 'The quiet hand of conservative groups in the anti-lockdown protests', 2020).

14   Beder, *Global Spin*, 2002, 112–18.

15   Beder, *Global Spin*, 2002, 116.

16   Parrish, 'Revealed', 2020. See also Lipton, 'Energy firms in secretive alliance with attorneys general', 2014.

17   Barba, 'IE questions', 2014; Leber, 'The gas industry is paying Instagram influencers to gush over gas stoves', 2020.

18   Beder, *Global Spin*, 15–25; Z. Smith, *The Environmental Policy Paradox*, 2004, 17.

19   McPhee, *Encounters with the Archdruid*, 1971, 61.

20   Comay et al. 'Arctic National Wildlife Refuge (ANWR)', 2018. Senate budget 'reconciliation' bills allow passage with a bare majority of 51 votes for some tax, spending and debt limit legislation. Controversy often attends decisions regarding whether a bill qualifies. See for example Rampell, 'No one in their right mind would design a government that works like ours', 2021, and Heniff, 'The budget reconciliation process', 2016.

21   See for instance Valek, 'Challenges of Utilizing Municipal Compost as an Amendment in Boreal Forest Reclamation Subsoil Material', 2018.

Part III
Obstacles to effective responses

Even after a problem is detected, its causes are understood and those involved decide to take action, effective responses can be difficult to design, fund or implement. Effective action requires overcoming several challenges. It is often difficult to design responses that would reduce one problem without creating or exacerbating others. Compromises can doom the effectiveness of promising ideas. Boundaries of authority often do not match the geographical scales of problems. Intended responses may not be implemented correctly. Finally, and perhaps most importantly, other societal priorities may overwhelm the effects of new policies.

Furthermore, those who oppose new environmental protections continue their resistance despite widespread support for a response. After new policies or procedures are adopted or new laws passed, opponents shift to resisting vigorous implementation. They will push for weak regulations in response to new laws and, once new federal regulations are implemented, will file lawsuits arguing new policies are excessive, or regulatory agencies have overstepped their authority.

15
Devising effective responses

The examples of environmental improvements mentioned in the introduction demonstrate that progress is possible. As we have seen, however, major progress does not come easily. Even when a problem is understood and society, or a relevant group, decides to act, means of effectively responding may not be obvious.

Fortunately, the potential of some responses is obvious. Hazardous concentrations of lead in the atmosphere resulted almost entirely from burning leaded gasoline. A technical response, unleaded gasoline, was readily available, so the choice of response was straightforward: phasing out of leaded gasoline. EPA regulations created under the authority of the Clean Air Act reduced combustion of leaded gasoline by 95 per cent between 1980 and 1999, during which time atmospheric lead concentrations declined 94 per cent (see Figure 1.2, p. 4).

In other cases, problems result from multiple sources, each of whose contributions are imprecisely known, and the hazard may not be sufficient to justify banning all responsible activities. In this common situation, effective responses may be especially elusive.

Consider a polluted stream. The obvious solution is to stop delivering pollutants to the stream, but what is polluting it? What are the sources of those pollutants? What specific change or changes would halt the pollutants' release? Must all types of pollution be prevented, or are some far worse than others? Must all harmful pollution be prevented or is there some tolerable level?

Proposed responses must not only overcome obstacles discussed in other chapters, such as how to cover initial expenses and how to achieve success despite compromises, they must also achieve the desired changes while contending with five common challenges. First, imaginable technical solutions are often unavailable. Second, specialists may recognize only some, not all, causes of problems, and even where causes are known, precise quantitative relationships among variables often remain uncertain, in which cases the relative importance of different causes also remains uncertain. Third, affected parties often seek exemptions from policies and regulations. Fourth, like new technologies, new environmental policies and procedures often have their own undesirable, unanticipated, consequences.[1] Fifth, responses must avoid the unintended but often predictable consequence of overcoming a shortage for a small number of people in the short term by creating a shortage for more people in the long term. After considering two examples, this chapter discusses each of these challenges in turn.

Even relatively simple problems sometimes defy effective responses. For example, Austin College, where I work, strives to continually reduce its environmental impacts. Students of environmental studies write proposals to do so. Several students have envisioned a set of bicycles available for anyone to use on campus. The environmental motivation would be to provide a readily available, quick alternative to driving a car from a dorm on one side of campus, around the campus perimeter to a classroom on the other side, a few hundred steps away, thereby reducing emissions from cars. We have not, however, managed to design a suitable system.

We could check bikes out like library books. They would then usually be secured and returned, but would be available only to whoever checked them out. This would be a valuable service for some students, but it would not substantially address the problem at hand. The obvious alternative is to make bikes freely available to the entire campus, but we have not identified a system that would prevent bikes from gradually disappearing when, for example, students take them off-campus but return by some other means, say in a friend's car. Tracking devices exist, but the types designed for small objects, such as a set of keys, have inadequate ranges. We are unaware of tracking devices of reasonable cost, small enough to hide on a bike, with sufficient range. So far, we have not identified any way to make bikes available to everyone while preventing them from gradually disappearing. We are hardly trying to prevent global climate change and yet we have failed to design a promising solution. (Please send suggestions.)

The present state of US municipal recycling provides a more consequential example of an inadequate response to a problem. US municipal recycling is in near crisis, with some programmes closing, largely because of new restrictions on the amount of contamination that China and other nations tolerate in imported recycled materials. But why are recyclables contaminated? Households typically have a recycling bin and a trash bin. What could be simpler?

Though recycling sounds simple, many residents put contaminants (materials that sorting facilities are not designed to process and for which there is little or no recycling market) into recycling bins. This apparently occurs for three reasons. First, some people wishing to recycle as much as possible but, unsure precisely what is recyclable, place contaminants in bins. This is so common that it has a name, 'aspirational' recycling. (Please do not do it. Recycle only what you know to be acceptable to your recycling system.) Second, at least here in Sherman, Texas, some residents had been treating recycling carts as second trash carts rather than paying for an additional proper trash cart. Such people presumably did not realize, or perhaps care, that they were contaminating entire truckloads of otherwise recyclable material. (The perverse incentive in the city's fee structure was eventually overcome by changing to an opt-in recycling system that charged residents the same fee for either one trash cart and one recycling cart or two trash carts.) A third group may not have realized that certain carts were for recyclable materials only. For example, new residents and those who do not speak English may not have understood the colour-coded lids the city used to distinguish recycling and trash bins (see Figure 15.1).[2]

All three errors stemmed from design problems. The first and third resulted from inadequate investment in participant education. The second resulted from a perverse financial incentive for residents who produced large quantities of trash – to save money by contaminating the city's recyclable material rather than paying for a second trash bin. Better participant education plus enforcement of bin contents or earlier implementation of the opt-in system would have reduced these problems. But education takes effort and costs money, and enforcement involves examining bin contents, which may be considered a privacy violation and therefore could create ill will between city officials and residents. The opt-in system avoided the privacy concern, but lost many participants who previously recycled correctly but did not continue to do so once they were required to opt in to the system.

Because of these and similar problems in other cities, the nation's municipal recycling systems are desperate to prevent contamination. System designers, myself included, made two errant assumptions: that people would understand what should and should not go in their carts, and that people would cooperate, not intentionally put trash in recycling carts. Those assumptions were invalid.

Figure 15.1: A Sherman, Texas household recycling bin, the visible contents of which consist entirely of contaminants – materials the sorting facility was not equipped to recycle. Photographer: Peter C. Schulze.

Successful, effective environmental protection programmes are important not merely for the fate of any particular project, such as ensuring recycling actually occurs, but also for receptivity to future proposed actions. In addition to failing to make progress on the immediate concern, ineffective responses engender cynicism regarding future proposals. Even small failures foster resistance to future initiatives. Austin College's new science building achieved Gold certification from the US Green Building Council's Leadership in Energy and Environmental Design programme, but early in the design phase several science faculty members were resistant to green design criteria. Some of their resistance resulted from a failure of earlier green technology on campus. In particular, a passive solar water heater plumbed to the school's swimming pool had long occupied dozens of choice parking spaces but never worked properly. Those panels became a monument to a good idea poorly implemented. Memories of the failed pool heater made people wary of other new-fangled green ideas.[3]

Loans to the solar energy company Solyndra provide a more important example. A Department of Energy programme to spur clean energy development loaned Solyndra $535 million. Shortly thereafter, Solyndra went bankrupt. The Solyndra loan was only one of forty clean energy development loans, but the failure of that one loan was the big news and was even touted as the first financial scandal of the Obama Administration. Almost all other loans were repaid on schedule and the programme provided net revenue to taxpayers, but those other cases have received far less attention.[4] Another failure, the horrific designs of twentieth-century national birth-rate reduction efforts described in Chapter 9 are probably responsible for the extreme reluctance of many people and organizations to even consider any intentional efforts to use government policy or programmes to foster low birth rates.

Failures of these sorts play into the hands of those looking for reasons to oppose greening efforts. Theirs is a weak argument of extrapolating from occasional failure to all future cases – equivalent to arguing that because some bridges fail, bridges are a bad idea – but weak arguments often have great influence. The lesson for those who would make environmental progress is that careful design of proposed responses is critical to both the immediate project's success and receptivity to future efforts. Devising satisfactory solutions requires avoiding five design challenges.

Technical limitations

Just as my colleague Professor Hugh MacIsaac imagines learning everything about a lake by sticking a finger in the water, one can imagine amazing but non-existent technical solutions to environmental problems. Contamination of recycling would be a trivial matter if facilities that process material had inexpensive sorting robots. Controlling particulate air pollution would be much easier if sensors could automatically and inexpensively detect concentrations of all pollutants from all pollution sources. Preventing water pollution would be easy if industries could be fitted with devices that automatically removed all pollutants from their outflows. No such devices exist, and if they did they might cause other problems (see Chapter 2). Innovations occur and technology advances, but some technical challenges will remain thermodynamically or otherwise daunting, and those seeking environmental progress now must work with technology available today or in the near future.

Partial knowledge

Incomplete knowledge of relevant circumstances and processes routinely hampers the development of effective responses. Imagine the uncertainties involved in attempting to regulate a marine fishery sustainably. First, managers cannot directly see the fish so it is hard to determine how many are in the ocean. Next, they cannot know precisely the relationship between a harvested species' population size and its population growth rate, let alone how that relationship is affected by interactions between the harvested species and other species. When some fish are caught, there is more food for others, so the remaining individuals may grow faster or have more offspring. But how much faster will they grow and how many more offspring will they have? Might the extra food be consumed by other species instead? Finally, fish often cross into international waters where no single nation has authority, or responsibility, to regulate harvests, so regulations imposed only in one nation's waters are often insufficient, while international cooperation has repeatedly failed.[5]

In the face of this uncertainty, managers have the unenviable job of choosing such things as net mesh sizes, allowable fishing techniques and the means of limiting catches (such as direct catch quotas, season duration limits, catch permits or prohibitions on fishing in nursery areas). Then, a year or more may pass before it becomes apparent whether too large a catch has been allowed, so errors may be compounded before they are detected and corrected. Thus, it is no simple matter to regulate a fishery sustainably. Yet, compared to some other environmental management challenges, fishery management is relatively simple.

Consider the task of setting air-quality standards. Richard Lazarus's excellent book on the history of US environmental law describes the challenge of managing airborne particulate matter:

> National ambient air quality standards for particulate matter ... have to take into account not just one source of particulate matter, but all possible sources, both regulated and unregulated, natural and manmade. There are many types of pollutants that contribute to the presence of particulate matter in the atmosphere, and their respective contributions are highly dependent on the occurrence of chemical reactions between various chemical compounds in the atmosphere. Wind, temperature and atmospheric pressure are accordingly relevant. Moreover, the adverse impact of particulate

matter on human health depends on the size of the particle and the duration of the exposure. That impact, of course, varies considerably among persons with different susceptibilities rooted in personal physical and biologic differences, as well as lifestyle differences. The challenge for a government agency responsible for promulgating a national ambient air quality standard for particulate matter is to choose a legal standard that sensibly accounts for all these variables without being overwhelmed by the associated scientific complexity.[6]

Similar challenges occur in determining acceptable grazing pressure on federal grasslands, the extent and type of habitat necessary for the recovery of endangered species, quantities of pollution that can be withstood without diminishing water quality, atmospheric gas concentrations that will result in a given global temperature increase, risks of carcinogens, and sustainable limits for countless other variables.

Regulators must act despite only partial understanding of problems. Even if regulators understand the hazard of inhaling fine particulates, they cannot possibly know the quantitative relationships between all plausible mixtures of particle size and chemical composition and the health consequences of those mixtures. But those regulators must still define acceptable concentration limits just as fisheries managers must set fishing restrictions, because the alternative – delaying action indefinitely – will allow harms to persist and the problem may even worsen.

Exemptions

Once regulators determine a maximum acceptable concentration of particulate matter in air, they must develop policies to bring concentrations below that limit. They could require installation of pollution control devices, limit allowable emissions from facilities, create pollution permit markets or use some combination of these or other approaches. Moreover, these choices must be made recognizing that as soon as new regulations or policies are promulgated, members of the regulated community will attempt to avoid having to comply, either by claiming they are exempt for some reason or by altering their operations to receive an exemption or otherwise reduce their regulatory burden.[7]

The oil pipeline company Enbridge provides an example of a bold effort to skirt the intent of a regulation. President G. W. Bush's Executive Order 13337 required that the State Department approve '… the construction, connection, operation, or maintenance, at the borders of the US, of facilities for the exportation or importation of petroleum, petroleum products, coal, or other fuels to or from a foreign country'.[8] The necessity of such State Department approval had delayed TransCanada Corporation's proposed Keystone XL pipeline. Seeking to avoid the same delays, Enbridge announced plans to connect its Alberta Clipper pipeline to another of its pipelines, Line 3, just before Line 3 crosses into the US from Canada in eastern North Dakota, then reconnect Line 3 to the Alberta Clipper after crossing the border. Enbridge argued that this plan did not require State Department review because the flow in Line 3 would be within the already permitted limit. The State Department agreed the plan did not require a new permit and approved the plan.[9]

> ... the greatest challenge in drafting regulations can lie in trying to fulfill the statute's intent while knowing full well that the regulated community will act strategically to take advantage of any possibility of favorable treatment.[10]

Unintended consequences

Even if responses to environmental problems achieve their intended effects, they may have undesirable, unintended consequences that cause or exacerbate other problems, including other environmental problems. Some such consequences are unanticipated, while others are anticipated and accepted as necessary trade-offs. For instance, better air-pollution control requires landfilling of the toxic waste from air pollution control devices. Such conflicts are almost ubiquitous. Other examples include mining rare-earth metals in countries with lax environmental rules or perhaps even from the ocean floor to supply electric vehicle batteries, renewable fuel mandates that have led to clearing tropical rainforest to grow oil-palm monocultures, and harvesting of trees to make fuel pellets.

I routinely encounter minor examples of such conflicts, as when cutting invading trees to foster prairie restoration, and attempting to restore native grass in the presence of established, invasive, non-native grasses. We could plough or poison the non-native grass and thereby assist establishment of seeded natives, but either procedure would hasten soil erosion until native species establish, and who knows what legacy effects the poison would have. Even the most modest efforts can involve such conflicts. For instance, trees in our yard partially shade solar panels on our roof. I want the panels to generate electricity, but not enough to cut down the trees. The trees stay. That trade-off was easy to anticipate and is trivial. Others have been unanticipated and momentous.

A classic example occurred when Indonesia used DDT to control mosquitoes that transmit malaria. The DDT apparently also killed parasites of moth larvae. Freed from their parasites, moth populations increased and ate thatched roofs. The DDT also killed cats, fostering rodent outbreaks.[11]

During the late 1960s and early 1970s, the US Department of Agriculture attempted to eradicate non-native fire ants by spraying 60 million kilograms of bait poisoned with the pesticide Mirex over 45 million hectares of the southern US. Subsequent analyses suggested that, while the Mirex initially killed ant species indiscriminately (as well as mammals, birds and fish), fire ants were the most aggressive recolonizers of the treated areas and, with other ant species suppressed, ended up more abundant than before Mirex had been sprayed.[12]

The introduction of Nile Perch to Africa's Lake Victoria during the mid-twentieth century provides yet another example. Nile Perch were apparently introduced to create a commercial fishery, but the large, predatory fish decimated smaller native fish that had served as the basis of an artisanal fishery and were one of the world's most spectacular examples of evolutionary diversity.[13] Similarly, early European Union (EU) requirements to use biofuels as a substitute for petroleum made profitable the destruction of tropical rainforests to grow oil palm and led to the cutting of forests to make wood pellets.[14] Upon recognition of such unintended consequences, the European Union (EU) altered its policies, but some analysts believe the revised policies will also have unintended consequences.[15]

Two of the saddest cases of unintended consequences resulted from digging wells to improve water supplies. Who would oppose provision of clean, reliable water supplies? The goal seems obviously worthy, but in these cases the unintended consequences have been catastrophic.

During the 1970s, the United Nations Children's Fund (UNICEF) and the Bangladesh Department of Public Health Engineering constructed wells as an alternative to consumption of polluted surface water that was causing tremendous infant mortality. But water from many of the wells is naturally contaminated with arsenic, often in carcinogenic concentrations. World Health Organization experts estimate that more than 70 million people are at risk from these wells.

Even though the well digging was intended to improve water quality, the water was not tested for arsenic contamination because naturally occurring arsenic contamination was not yet recognized as a potential problem. Detection of arsenic in the water did not occur until residents developed symptoms a decade later. Even more tragically, once the arsenic contaminated wells were painted red, many people continued to use them because they lacked safe, alternative sources.[16]

A similarly tragic story occurred in the Sahel where nomadic pastoralists had subsisted for thousands of years by moving livestock in synchrony with seasonal rains. During the 1960s, international aid agencies constructed wells and clinics, while newly independent nations sought to restrict border crossings. Herders understandably remained near wells. Where the herders remained, livestock remained as well. Consequently, the livestock overgrazed the vegetation that was the backbone of the subsistence system. Without vegetation, the area desertified and both livestock and people starved.[17] These Bangladeshi and Sahelian tragedies demonstrate that even efforts to ensure a goal as noble as a safe and reliable water supply can cause disastrous unintended consequences.

Proposed environmental protection is a type of innovation, and as for any other innovation, a systems perspective may reduce the chance of undesirable, unintended consequences. As discussed in Chapter 2, a systems perspective will not permit perfect anticipation, but it probably would have resulted in awareness that big fish added to Lake Victoria might kill off little fish, cattle kept around Sahelian wells would kill the nearby grass, and a programme to dig wells for millions of people should test at least a subset of those wells for every plausible contaminant.

Perhaps the worst of all unintended consequences of an environmental 'solution' could come from 'geoengineering'.[18] Geoengineering refers to altering major planetary processes to counteract an environmental problem. Geoengineering is most often contemplated to prevent climate change. One proposal would add white particles of sulphur dioxide to the atmosphere to reflect incoming solar radiation, thereby preventing warming. Another would add iron to areas of the ocean where lack of iron limits the growth of algae. The latter idea presumes faster growth would cause algae to take more carbon dioxide from the water. Natural physical equilibria would then replace that carbon dioxide with carbon dioxide from the atmosphere, in a milder but much more extensive reversal of the process of bubbles leaving a carbonated beverage. Some algae cells would sink to the sediments, where they would remain, sequestering carbon that had been in the atmosphere. This is an appealing notion. Sprinkle a little iron and get rid of global climate change.

If these ideas sound too good to be true, your intuition is probably correct. Side effects are almost certain. For example, sulphur dioxide, the compound that reflects solar radiation, is a primary cause of acid rain. Any number of other 'side effects' are also plausible. Adding iron to the ocean might shift competition among algal species, potentially altering the ocean food web in ways no one can predict, but that could include changing the abundance or species composition of the zooplankton that eat algae, which could potentially reduce the abundance of algae and thus the amount of carbon sequestered to the ocean floor. In other words, the effort might not only fail, but backfire.

Perhaps some other reflective agent would not cause acid rain? Warming might be prevented, but what else would happen when light was blocked from reaching the surface? How would a reduction in sunlight affect other processes? Photosynthetic rates might decline, in which case plants would grow more slowly, counterproductively taking less carbon dioxide out of the atmosphere. If photosynthesis declines, crop growth could decline, native and domestic herbivores would have less food and ocean food chains might also become less productive. These are just a few plausible consequences. Any ecologist could list many more.

The point is not only that unintended consequences of geoengineering are virtually certain, but also that no one can confidently predict which unintended consequences would occur or how severe they would be. For this reason, some refer to geoengineering scenarios as 'betting the planet', a bet too big for many. Despite the stakes, as greenhouse gas concentrations keep increasing, more people seem to be seriously considering geoengineering.

'Solutions' that exacerbate problems

A qualitatively different sort of unintended consequence occurs when a perceived shortage is relieved by an increase in supply – as when roads are expanded to reduce traffic congestion. Adding lanes initially reduces congestion, but as discussed in Chapter 2, it attracts more traffic to the larger road and development to the surrounding area. Thus, the system responds by causing larger and larger traffic jams on larger and larger roads. In such circumstances, a short-term 'solution' worsens a long-term problem. Increase in supply seems like an obvious response to increase in demand, but the traffic example illustrates how such a response can create a positive feedback that makes the original problem worse. Positive feedbacks are not sustainable. Some are more critical than traffic jams.

For example, water shortages often inspire reservoir construction. These may seem like obvious responses, and they help for a while, but a bit of reflection shows that, *by themselves*, they are likely to make problems worse in the long run. More water in an arid area allows local population growth and thus causes a future, larger population to depend on an ever more complex water system.

Consider the example of southern California. The Los Angeles and San Diego metropolitan areas rely on an elaborate system of canals, pipes and pumps to deliver water from remote reservoirs, including the Shasta Reservoir, north of San Francisco, hundreds of kilometres away. One component of the system, the Edmonston Pumping Plant, uses fourteen 80,000-horsepower pumps to lift water almost 600 metres over the Tehachapi Mountains. Each of those pumps is about a hundred times as powerful as the most powerful production Ferrari. This remarkable feat of engineering enables twenty million people to live in the southern California desert, but it has made that large population entirely dependent on a technologically complex, reservoir-based water-delivery system vulnerable to drought and climate change in an area known for earthquakes. A short-term 'solution' (finding water for a small population) has created a larger long-term problem (sustaining a water supply for a large population).

That adding water supplies will facilitate population growth and thus eventually cause a water shortage for an even larger population is as easy to anticipate as a widened highway leading to larger traffic jams, but officials continue to propose supply increases anyway. For example, the Texas Water Development Board 2022 State Water Plan proposes numerous new reservoirs.[19] Those new reservoirs will initially increase the water available per person, just as added lanes initially alleviate traffic jams. But they will also facilitate population growth, just as lanes increase traffic, until demand again exceeds supply.

In the case of reservoirs there is another problem. Dams are often constructed in arid regions. Arid region streams are typically muddy because of sparse watershed vegetation and consequent soil erosion during rains, a problem exacerbated yet further when watersheds are overgrazed. Upon reaching a reservoir, muddy flows slow and sediment sinks. Thus, reservoirs slowly but surely fill with sediment, reducing their capacity and rendering them temporary, not permanent, means of storing water. Therefore, reservoir construction to meet water demand facilitates population growth, those new residents become dependent on the reservoirs, but the reservoirs represent only temporary supply increases.

Loss to sedimentation is substantial. Texas Water Development Board staff estimate sedimentation will reduce Texas reservoir storage capacity by some 100 million cubic metres per year by the middle of the twenty-first century. The US Geological Survey estimates average annual domestic water consumption as 100 cubic metres per person.[20] By that estimate, Texas reservoirs will lose enough storage capacity each year to account for the household consumption of about a million people (see Figure 15.2).[21]

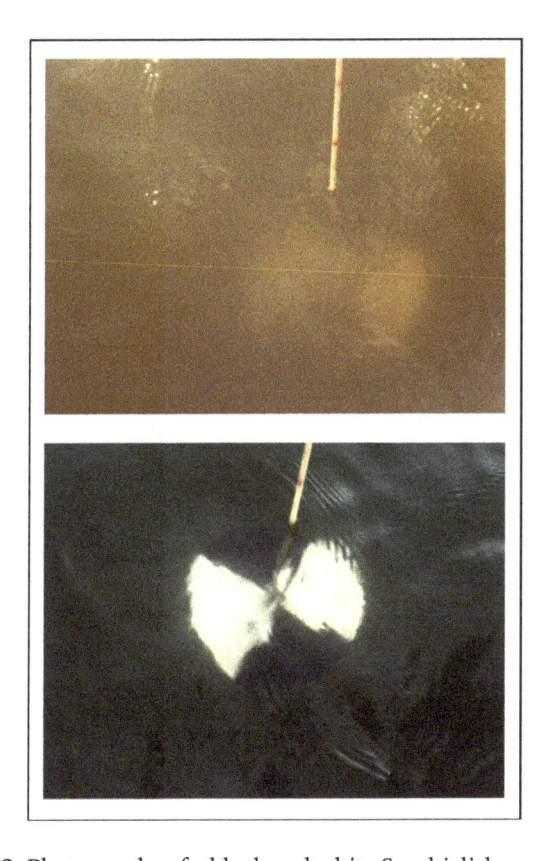

Figure 15.2: Photographs of a black and white Secchi disk suspended 20 cm below the water surface of Lake Texoma (on the Texas–Oklahoma border). The top photo is from an upstream location near the Red River inflow while the bottom photo is from the downstream end of the lake near the dam. Except during floods, as water moves downstream through the reservoir, suspended material responsible for the turbidity in the upper image sinks to the lake bottom, thereby displacing water storage capacity. Photographer: Peter C. Schulze.

In the (ecologically) relatively short term of a few decades, reservoir construction can alleviate perceived water shortages, but in the longer term of a century or so, reservoirs can make the problem worse by causing a much larger population to depend on what turns out to be a temporary and thus non-sustainable 'solution'. This is fundamentally the same problem as increasing food production to meet increased demand without avoiding further population growth (see Figure 15.3). If the only response to hunger is increased food production, then alleviation of a critical, immediate problem may foster a larger long-term problem of even more hungry people in the future. Once the long-term problem is apparent, it becomes clear that future generations would benefit from more sophisticated responses that satisfy short-term needs without creating larger long-term problems. These are complex, dire issues and I do not wish to be simplistic, but public transit, bicycles, working from home, water conservation and universally meeting desired access to contraception quickly come to mind.

Imperfect understanding complicates the development of environmental protection mechanisms. Some apparently good ideas backfire, but others work. Air and water pollution have been reduced without causing serious undesirable side effects. Species have been kept from going extinct without causing disastrous side effects. Success is possible. But those who design responses to environmental problems should study the history of failures, learn to apply a systems perspective and do their best to anticipate and avoid serious, unintended, undesirable consequences.

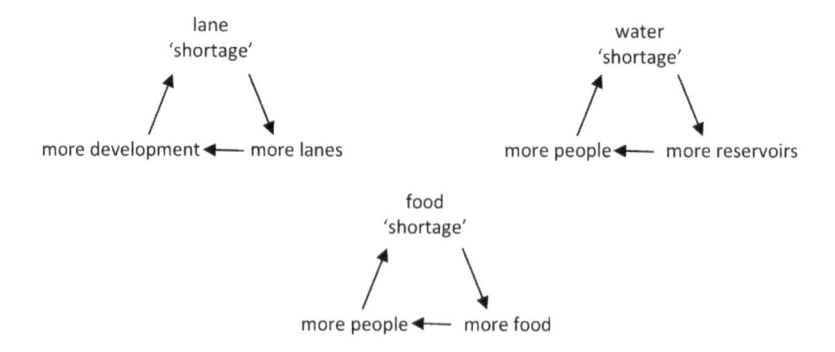

Figure 15.3: Three similar, nonsustainable positive feedbacks that result from attempting to overcome shortages by increasing supplies without considering system-level effects. Figure by the author.

Failure to confirm success

Because policies are developed with imperfect knowledge, they may not have the intended effects. Therefore, once implemented, their effects should be monitored. Often, however, there is little or no effort to check whether a policy has been effective or has caused unintended consequences. In such cases, no one may know whether a policy has worked. This can occur because managers lack funding for follow-up studies or because managers are disinclined to track whether policy has been effective or has had undesirable, unintended consequences.[22]

For several decades, the ecologist C. S. Holling and his colleagues have encouraged 'adaptive management' of natural resources.[23] Adaptive management is predicated on the notion that environmental protection efforts may not have the intended consequences and are likely to have unanticipated consequences.[24] Adaptive management tests for both intentional and unintentional effects of management and then adjusts procedures based on insights from those tests. A large adaptive management literature has developed, but practice has yet to catch up with theory. For example, wildlife management plans routinely espouse the benefits of adaptive management but do not actually include procedures for its implementation.[25] Likewise, Bernhardt et al. determined that only about ten per cent of river restoration projects have been monitored to assess success.[26] If the effects of management are not studied, or not adequately studied, then there is no way to be confident of success. Future projects should include the necessary investments to determine success or failure and detect unintended problems.

These examples illustrate some of the many challenges of designing effective responses to environmental problems. Unfortunately, that is not the final hurdle to environmental progress. Responses must withstand political compromises, work when problems cross political boundaries, be implemented as intended and be compatible with other societal objectives, the topics of the following chapters.

Notes

1   Holling, 'What barriers? What bridges?', 1995, 18–34.
2   Regrettably, during 2020 the City of Sherman halted curbside recycling.
3   I never met anyone who had detailed knowledge of the system. As far as I know, those with the relevant knowledge had retired before I arrived, but apparently there was a problem with the fluid used in the pipes intended to transfer heat from the panels to the pool. I suspect a much larger backlash has resulted from the requirement to add ethanol to gasoline. Ethanol added to gasoline causes problems for small motors that sit unused for extended periods, such as

those in lawnmowers and chainsaws. I wonder how many owners of such devices, frustrated by motors that will not start, have been made skeptical of other environmental efforts as a consequence. One motivation for mixing ethanol into gasoline was to reduce fossil fuel imports, but it was also defended as a means of reducing greenhouse gas emissions and shifting to renewable energy sources (though analysts disagree about both).

4   Groom, 'Exclusive', 2014; Lott, 'Solyndra', 2011.
5   During the 1970s, NATO allies Britain and Iceland nearly came to blows over fishery disputes. Iceland rigged their coast guard boats to cut the nets off British trawlers, which were themselves accompanied by British naval vessels. More recently, aggravation with EU fishing rules were a major consideration in some British voters' 2016 vote to leave the EU. See De Freytas-Tamura, 'In Brexit debate, English fishermen eye waters free of EU', 2016; Kurlansky, *Cod*, 1997, 92–106 and 144–233.
6   Lazarus, *The Making of Environmental Law*, 2004, 17.
7   Salzman and Thompson, *Environmental Law and Policy*, 2014, 236–7.
8   Bush, 'Executive Order 13337: Issuance of Permits with Respect to Certain Energy-Related Facilities and Land Transportation Crossings on the International Boundaries of the US', 2004.
9   Reuters, 'Enbridge plans Alberta Clipper pipeline boost despite US delays', 2014; Marcetic, 'The other Keystone', 2016.
10 Salzman and Thompson, *Environmental Law and Policy*, 2014, 236.
11 O'Shaughnessy, 'Parachuting cats and crushed eggs', 2008, 1942–3.
12 Tschinkel, *The Fire Ants*, 2006, 45–57, 73–4. See also Carson, *Silent Spring*, 1962, 162–70.
13 Balirwa et al., 'Biodiversity and fisheries sustainability in the Lake Victoria basin', 2003, 706–8.
14 Abt et al., 'Effects of policies on pellet production and forests in the US South', 2014, 6–11; Drouin, 'Wood pellets', 2015; Koh and Wilcove, 'Is oil palm agriculture really destroying tropical biodiversity?', 2008; Rulli et al., 'Interdependencies and telecoupling of oil palm expansion at the expense of Indonesian rainforest', 2019, 499–500.
15 European Parliament, 'Directive (EU) 2018/2001 of the European Parliament and of the Council of 11 December 2018', 2018, 328/94–7 and 328/129–33; Rulli et al., 'Interdependencies and telecoupling of oil palm expansion at the expense of Indonesian rainforest', 2019, 499–500; Searchinger et al., 'Europe's renewable energy directive poised to harm global forests', 2018.
16 Rahman, 'An interview with Mahmuder Rahman', 2008; Flanagan et al., 'Arsenic in tube well water in Bangladesh', 2012; A. H. Smith et al., 'Contamination of drinking-water by arsenic in Bangladesh', 2000.
17 Sinclair and Fryxell, 'The Sahel of Africa', 1985.
18 Temple, 'What is geoengineering – and why should you care?', 2019.
19 Texas Water Development Board, '2022 State Water Plan', n.d.
20 Dieter et al., 'Estimated use of water in the United States in 2015', 2018, 23; Zhu et al., 'Projected reservoir rating curves based on sedimentation surveys and its application in water planning in Texas', 2018, 2.
21 It might seem sensible to dredge reservoirs to prevent loss of storage capacity, but dredging is generally impractical because of the scale involved, the need for a location to deposit voluminous spoils, and the cost of dredging and transportation. When harbours are dredged the spoils are generally dumped offshore in deeper water, but dredging a reservoir requires moving the spoils out of the reservoir to another location. For example, a small reservoir in a wealthy area of Dallas, Texas has been periodically dredged to remove some accumulated sediments. The most recent effort in 1998 cost $18 million to make the lake about 1 metre deeper. Even that was much less expensive than would otherwise have been the case because a landowner desired the material to fill an abandoned quarry. Nevertheless, the quarry was nearly 20 km from the lake, so the slurry had to be pumped through temporary pipes the entire distance (Dunaway-Seale, 'The dredge report', 2019). After doing research on reservoir zooplankton for more than a decade, I have never heard of any proposal to dredge a large reservoir.
22 Buzbee, 'Contextual environmental federalism', 2005, 128.
23 Holling, *Adaptive Environmental Assessment and Management*, 1978.
24 Savory, *Holistic Management*, 1988, 17–27.
25 Fontaine, 'Improving our legacy', 2011, 1406–7.
26 Bernhardt et al., 'Synthesizing US river restoration efforts', 2005, 637.

16
Compromises that doom responses

Even if it is possible to design a law or policy whose implementation would prevent an environmental problem, any law eventually passed, or regulation promulgated, is likely to differ from original proposals because of compromises. Compromises are often necessary to achieve agreements, but the same compromises can doom efforts to failure.

Passage of practically any environmental law or development of any regulation will require identification of an acceptable limit of human impact. Management of public grazing lands requires limiting grazing. Air pollution regulation requires preventing pollutants from reaching harmful concentrations. Endangered species will survive in the wild only if sufficient habitat is protected. Whether the subject is fish catches, greenhouse gas emissions or pumping from an aquifer, knowledgeable specialists must identify a suitable level of protection.

As discussed, some who would have to comply with new laws resist their passage. If laws are passed despite objections, these opponents may then turn to resisting the development of strong implementation policies, arguing that proposed policies would be excessive.[1] For example, in response to spills from trains transporting liquid fuels, the Obama Administration proposed retrofitting existing rail cars to standards set for new cars, but industry representatives contended that compliance would be too expensive. The same industry previously objected to using double-hulled oil freighters and improving oil pipeline safety.[2] Such complaints are routine. Some objections are remarkably farfetched, like the Petroleum Association's complaint mentioned earlier about the 'onerous' requirement to put stickers on gasoline pumps. Any reader of the news can readily find similar examples of objections to proposed regulations. Objections often carry the day when laws are debated, in which case new laws are not passed. In other cases, objections result in compromises that render responses to problems inadequate to achieve their environmental purposes. The exemptions mentioned in the previous chapter commonly result from such compromises.

Compromise between biologists' recommendations and desires of land users routinely affect Endangered Species Act critical habitat designations. Timothy Beatley describes the US Fish and Wildlife Service process of designating critical habitats as a 'negotiated process, typically involving compromise on all sides'. He explains, for example, how the Fish and Wildlife Service proposed to designate 440 square kilometres as critical habitat for the Coachella Valley Fringe-toed Lizard, but ended up designating only 50 square kilometres. 'Despite the large area of potentially occupiable habitat, and a wide distribution of recorded sightings of lizards, the [Fish and Wildlife Service] chose to designate a relatively limited area of critical habitat. To many observers these boundaries were selected primarily to avoid areas slated for development and in direct response to vociferous local opposition [to designating a larger area].'[3]

The map in Figure 16.1 shows how some habitat protected for the endangered northern spotted owl forms a checkerboard with unprotected habitat. Close inspection of satellite or other aerial images of the same area shows that the unprotected squares are subject to logging. I cannot imagine a biological basis for designating a checkerboard of critical habitat. Rather, as Beatley describes, the decision must have been a compromise. No doubt logging companies were unhappy to be restricted from one half of the area, but at the same time, if half of the land is not enough for the owl to persist, or if the fragmentation of suitable habitat caused by the checkerboard logging pattern harms the owl, then the policy may fail.

The history of Clean Air Act implementation has been rife with compromises. When metropolitan areas are out of compliance with the laws and regulations, states must develop 'state implementation plans' designed to achieve compliance. State implementation plans result from compromises between states and the EPA. Often the EPA pushes for strong air pollution control measures and the states argue for weaker measures. (Chapter 18 explains why some state officials tend to be less enthusiastic about environmental protection than federal officials.) The Dallas-Fort Worth, Texas metropolitan area has chronically failed to achieve ozone standards despite dozens of state implementation plan revisions since 1972.[4] The simplest explanation for that failure is that the plans have been too weak. The most obvious explanation for that weakness is that compromises have allowed too much pollution.

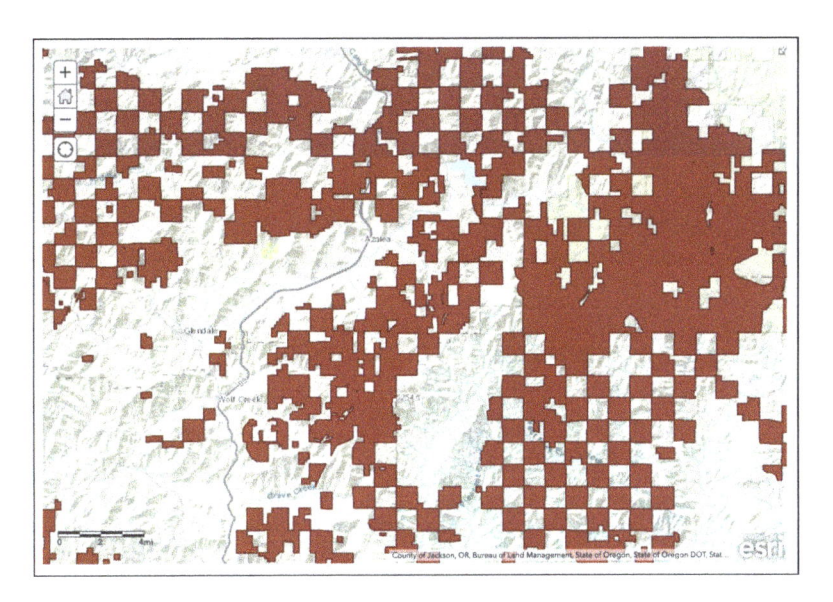

Figure 16.1: Designated critical habitat for the northern spotted owl, *Strix occidentalis caurina*, in areas northwest and east of Azalea, Glendale, and Wolf Creek, southwestern Oregon, US. Source: US Fish and Wildlife Service, 'Endangered and threatened wildlife and plants', 2021.

Another manifestation of compromise occurs when selected industries or types of facilities receive exemptions from laws or regulations that would logically apply to them. For example, 'return flows' from agriculture (water flowing from agricultural fields to waterways) are exempt from the Clean Water Act. Therefore, the nation's premier water pollution control law does not appreciably address pesticide and nutrient runoff from agriculture. Likewise, the fossil fuel industry is exempt from various sections of the Clean Air Act, the Safe Drinking Water Act and the Resource Conservation and Recovery Act. Meanwhile, narrow interpretation of the word 'facility' and allowances for confidential protection of trade secrets exempt many aspects of oil and gas operations from Toxics Release Inventory requirements of the Community Right-to-Know Act.[5] Such exemptions typically result from compromises made when laws are written as their sponsors seek sufficient support for passage.

Though conventional air and water pollution in the US is better now than a few decades ago, in many locations water remains too polluted for drinking, or even swimming, while many live where air quality is chronically out of compliance with standards. These cases of improvements with lingering problems are evidence of a broader sort of compromise. Society has been willing to expend some effort to reduce air and water pollution, but not enough to prevent harmful air and water pollution.

Compromises also occur elsewhere. Describing the history of negotiations to prevent damage from acid deposition in Europe, Reis et al. write, 'Inevitably, financial and political realities constrained negotiations with respect to scientific objectives.'[6] European rain is less acidic than it was before control efforts began, but acid deposition remains a concern. On a yet larger scale, analysts conclude that nations' Paris Agreement climate pledges are inadequate to prevent global warming beyond 1.5°C.[7] Greenhouse gas concentrations continue to rise despite existing international agreements.

Consider a common circumstance in more detail. Imagine an unregulated fishing harvest has declined from 1,000 to 300 tons per year while fishing has intensified. A declining harvest despite increased fishing effort is strong evidence that the stock of available fish is declining – the fish are being overharvested. Now imagine that experts estimate the fishery can sustainably withstand harvests of only, say, 100 tons per year, and propose that limit. Industry representatives will object. The decline in yields that has already occurred will have reduced revenues, and operators will face hardship due to ship payments and other fixed expenses. Industry representatives will argue further yield restrictions will not be affordable.[8] Proponents of higher catch limits may base their arguments on uncertainties in relevant data. Politicians or regulators then weigh the various arguments, compromise and set the catch limit at something more than 100 tons. After all, reasonable people routinely compromise, and politics is often referred to as the art of compromise.[9]

But what happens if the technical specialists are correct that the sustainable limit is 100 tons? In that case, the larger limit will cause more fish to be caught than the population can sustain, which will suppress the fish population further. If natural processes produce only 100 tons of harvestable fish per year, but the annual catch exceeds 100 tons, the fish population will decline whether regulators, politicians, members of the fishing industry or others like it or not.

> The laws of Congress and the laws of physics have grown increasingly divergent, and the laws of physics are not likely to yield.[10]

Environmental processes have finite rates that such political compromises do not respect. As the cartoons show, big fish eat small fish that eat smaller fish. The number of big fish in the ocean is ultimately limited by the abundance of their prey, which cannot exceed the amount supported by the abundance of *their* prey, all the way down to the phytoplankton and other microscopic organisms. Tyler Miller has described the same constraint on the growth of trout in a stream.

> Three hundred trout are needed to support one man for a year. The trout, in turn, must consume 90,000 frogs, that must consume 27 million grasshoppers, that live off of 1,000 tons of grass.[11]

Regardless of anyone's wishes, the growth rate of fish in the ocean is limited, as are the growth rates of forest trees and pasture grasses, the rate at which aquifers recharge and the environment's ability to break down pollutants. If compromises allow impacts greater than what the environment can withstand, that environment (and future harvests) will not be protected. For this reason, two of Herman Daly's three guidelines for sustainability are that renewable resources should not be depleted faster than they are regenerated and wastes should not be released faster than they are assimilated (rendered harmless).[12]

Moreover, the relevant processes are more complicated than cartoons showing big fish eating small fish and more complicated than a balance between harvesting and regrowth. For example, if trees or fish are harvested, there is no guarantee the same species will grow back in their place.[13] When the white pines of Michigan were logged, a beech-maple forest grew in their place. The white pines may never return. After overfishing decimated Canada's Atlantic cod, the stock was only starting to recover 20 years later despite a moratorium on offshore fishing.[14] An even scarier scenario may be brewing in the Amazon. Experts have estimated that the Amazon rainforest has so great a role in evapotranspiration, and thus regional rainfall and temperatures, that clearing some forest might doom the rest because reduced evapotranspiration could cause a decline in rainfall, thereby making the climate in that region more suitable for savanna than tropical rainforest.[15] Imagine a decision to protect 20 or 30 per cent of the Amazon. Surely conservation groups would prefer more protection, but they would celebrate protection of 20 or 30 per cent. After all, it is almost unprecedented to protect 20 or 30 per cent of an ecosystem. And yet 20 or 30 per cent might not be enough if projections about resulting rainfall and temperature changes are correct.

Compromise about technical environmental matters is yet another example of a societal double standard in environmental decision making. We do not request compromises with technical recommendations of specialists in other realms. We would not expect engineers to compromise on the amount of cement to use in a bridge or cardiologists to compromise on the number or arteries to bypass. But when it comes to acceptable air or water pollution concentrations, the number of fish to harvest from the ocean or the amount of water to pump from an aquifer, we strike a compromise between the recommendations of experts and the wishes of others, protecting the environment as long as it is not too much trouble.

One of the most striking examples of this attitude occurred before the 1992 Earth Summit in Rio de Janeiro, when President G. H. W. Bush told critics worried about overconsumption: 'The American way of life is not up for negotiations. Period.'[16] Bush's statement was repeated almost verbatim sixteen years later when, in response to concerns about greenhouse gas concentrations, Vice President Richard Cheney declared in 2008 that 'the American way of life is non-negotiable'.[17] The next year, President Barack Obama, in his first inaugural address, appeared open to negotiation on this point when he stated, '... we'll work tirelessly to roll back the spectre of a warming planet', but in the next sentence said that 'we will not apologize for our way of life, nor will we waver in its defense'.[18] When it comes to the magnitude of environmental impacts, these statement are like telling a doctor that 'you may perform surgery on my clogged arteries as long as the surgery will be free, I will not be uncomfortable and I will not miss my afternoon golf game.'

> We'd all like to save the environment, but maybe not when it costs hundreds of dollars per year.[19]

Ecosystem processes upon which all life depends operate at finite rates. Environmental problems result when we impact those processes at excessive rates, such as extracting fish from the ocean faster than they grow back or releasing greenhouse gases into the atmosphere faster than they can be removed by natural processes. Efforts to rein in excessive impacts fail when political compromises result in continued impacts above those that the ecosystem can withstand.

> I have an idea that a large number of us, including even a large number of politicians, believe that it is wrong to destroy the Earth. But we have powerful political opponents who insist that an Earth-destroying economy is justified by freedom and profit. And so we compromise by agreeing to permit the destruction only of parts of the Earth, or to permit the Earth to be destroyed a little at a time – like the famous three-legged pig that was too well loved to be eaten all at once.[20]

Notes

1   See for instance Galloway, 'Controversial changes to fisheries act', 2013; Hemphill and Dunbar, 'DFL lawmaker', 2013.

2   Associated Press, 'Industry fights safety retrofit of older rail cars', 2013; Nalder, 'Big oil spends cash by the barrel to keep double bottoms from becoming a rule', 1989; C. Parker, 'The pipeline industry meets grief unimaginable', 2004, 247–51.

3   Beatley, *Habitat Conservation Planning*, 1994, 52, 74.

4   Environmental Protection Agency, 'Green book national area and county-level multi-pollutant information', n.d.; Texas Commission on Environmental Quality, 'Texas SIP revisions', n.d.

5   Salzman and Thompson, *Environmental Law and Policy*, 2014, 225; T. Stuart, 'Big oil's best-kept secret', 2015.

6   Reis et al., 'From acid rain to climate change', 2012, 1154.

7   For example see Le Page, 'What is the Paris climate agreement?', 2019.

8   See Comeau, 'New endangered species plan unveiled', 1998; Gaines, 'Senate panel hearing set for Magnuson reform', 2012; Goethel et al., 'Closing the feedback loop', 2019, 1895–9.

9   Kolbert, 'The scales fall', 2010; MacKenzie, 'The cod that disappeared', 1995, 29.

10 Bill McKibben, quoted in Hawken, 'Natural capitalism', 1997.

11 G. T. Miller, *Energetics, Kinetics, and Life*, 1971, 291.

12 Daly, 'Economics in a full world', 2005, 102. Daly's third guideline for sustainability is that non-renewable resources should not be depleted faster than substitutes are developed.

13 Benoît and Swain, 'Impacts of environmental change and direct and indirect harvesting effects on the dynamics of a marine fish community', 2008, 2098–9; Whitney, 'An ecological history of the Great Lakes forest of Michigan', 1987, 680–1.

14 Frank et al., 'Transient dynamics of an altered large marine ecosystem', 2011.

15 Sampaio et al., 'Regional climate change over eastern Amazonia caused by pasture and soybean cropland expansion', 2007; Vergara and Scholz, 'Assessment of the Risk of Amazon Dieback', 2011, 61–4.

16 Deen, 'US lifestyle is not up for negotiation', 2012.

17 Lindbergh, 'Apres moi le deluge', 2014.

18 Obama, 'President Barack Obama's inaugural address', 2009.

19 Automobile industry analyst Jessica Caldwell, quoted in Ulrich, 'With gas prices less of a worry, buyers pass hybrid cars by', 2015.

20 Berry, *The Way of Ignorance and Other Essays*, 2005, 25.

17
Mismatched or overlapping authority

Environmental problems often blow over, flow across or otherwise transcend political boundaries. As a consequence, the geographic scope of problems often does not match the jurisdiction of organizations with the potential to address them. Officials in whose districts problems are created face little pressure to tackle problems that only affect others downstream or downwind. Meanwhile, officials in downstream and downwind districts lack authority to alter the practices responsible upwind or upstream.[1]

Geographical mismatch

The distribution of US farm homesteads granted to pioneer settlers is a classic case of artificial boundaries not matching natural boundaries. Properties were allocated based on surveys with regular north–south and east–west boundaries, regardless of the lay of the land. This meant boundaries of homesteads were unrelated to boundaries of watersheds. Some homesteads were high and dry. Others were lower and wetter, but subject to flooding. Downstream landowners could not control erosion and runoff from upstream properties.[2] Thus, an uphill landowner's effects on the environment could harm another landowner downhill, but the lower landowner had no recourse. These nineteenth-century decisions have consequences to this day. For example, one of the most challenging problems for Austin College's Sneed prairie restoration is erosive flash-flood runoff from poorly managed upstream properties.

Downstream homesteaders were in a similar, though less precarious, circumstance to the cities and towns to the southwest when Chicago stopped its river from draining east into Lake Michigan and diverted it west to the Mississippi River. By the late nineteenth century, water pollution in Chicago had reached ghastly levels and threatened Chicago's drinking water from Lake Michigan. To alleviate the problem, city leaders built a canal that rerouted the river water away from Lake Michigan, sending it instead to the Des Plaines River, a tributary to the Illinois River, which flows into the Mississippi (see Figure 17.1). As you might imagine, cities downstream along those rivers did not share Chicago's enthusiasm for this project. The leaders of Joliet, Illinois, threatened to fill in the canal with soil. Missouri sought a court injunction.[3] Missouri Attorney General Edward C. Crow

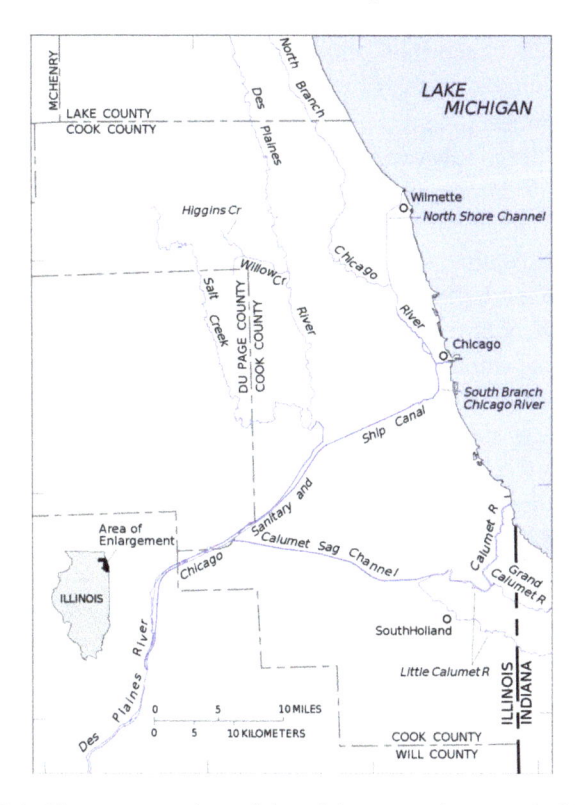

Figure 17.1: The construction of the Chicago Sanitary and Ship Canal enabled the Chicago and Calumet Rivers to drain to the Des Plaines River (and thus eventually to the Mississippi River), rather than to Lake Michigan. Source: Unattributed Wikimedia Commons image, https://commons.wikimedia.org/wiki/Category:Chicago_Sanitary_and_Ship_Canal#/media/File:ChicagoRiver.svg, accessed 16 November 2021, redrawn from original source: Terrio, 'Relations of changes in wastewater-treatment practices to changes in stream-water quality during 1978–88 in the Chicago area, Illinois, and implications for regional and national water-quality assessments', 1994, 5.

exclaimed in 1903, 'The action of the Chicago authorities in turning their sewage into the Mississippi River for the people of St. Louis to drink is criminal, and Chicago knows it.'[4]

Fearing the Missourians would prevail in court and hoping for an engineering *fait accompli* to pre-empt any legal decision, Chicago sanitary trustees dynamited a dam that held back Lake Michigan while the canal was being built, causing water from Lake Michigan to push Chicago River pollution through the canal to the Mississippi River. Confident they would be perceived as local heroes, they even invited reporters to photograph the spectacle. Since then, the Chicago River has flowed not to Lake Michigan, but to the Mississippi River.[5]

The project did protect Lake Michigan from Chicago's sewage and improve Chicago River water quality. A *New York Times* headline at the time even declared with amazement, 'Water in Chicago River ... Now Resembles Liquid.'[6] More than a hundred years later, that same canal serves as a conduit for invasive Asian Carp in the Mississippi River drainage to reach the Great Lakes and from there the lakes' tributaries.[7]

Failure of environmental problems to respect political boundaries also pertains when geographical relationships are more complicated. Fishery management famously suffers from this problem because ocean fish do not respect national boundaries, crossing from near-shore, national waters into offshore, international waters where there is no or little regulatory authority capable of constraining harvests. Thus, once a collapse of its cod fishery was apparent, Canada sought to limit cod catches on the Grand Banks of Newfoundland, but could not prohibit vessels from Spain, China or any other nation from fishing just beyond their boundary in international waters. Restrictions in Canadian territorial waters may not enable recovery of the fishery as long as fishing continues across the boundary (see Figure 17.2).[8]

The dynamics of fish stocks are far more complex than the previous paragraph implies,[9] but with unregulated fishing in international waters, it is not surprising that the abundance of large marine fish declined 90 per cent since the advent of industrialized fishing methods, a classic tragedy of the commons.[10] Similar examples of jurisdictional problems include air pollution from the United States that causes acid deposition in Canada, international acid deposition problems in northern Europe, stratospheric ozone depletion and climate change.

The fundamental problem is that for many transboundary environmental problems no entity has authority to limit the offending activities. Recall the challenges inherent in determining the cause of a fishery decline in the Baltic Sea (Chapter 4). The Baltic receives the flow

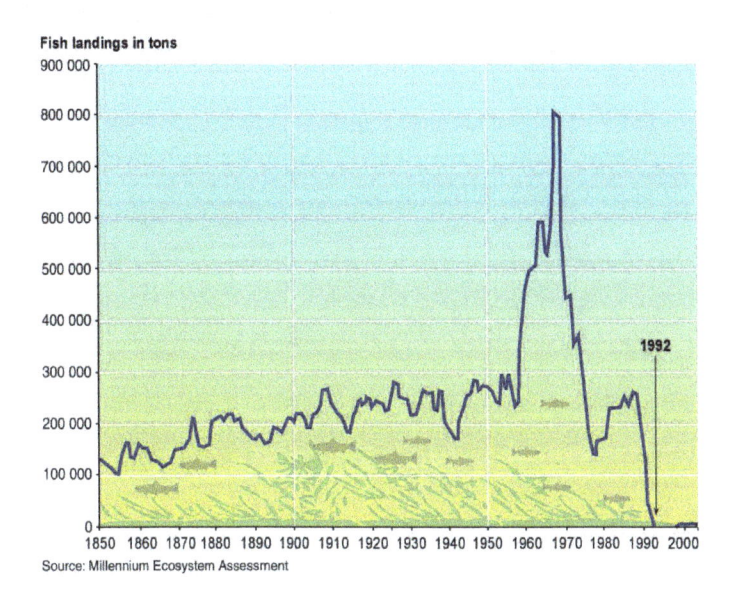

Figure 17.2: Collapse of the cod fishery off Newfoundland, Canada. Source: Millennium Ecosystem Assessment, *Living Beyond Our Means: Natural assets and human well being*, 2005, 18.

of ten major rivers that run through nine industrialized countries.[11] If the fishery decline is attributed to pollution from, for example, Polish factories, only Polish authorities could compel changes in Polish industry. Various EU and regional international agreements and organizations seek to manage and protect water quality, but the members of these organizations are sovereign nations with conflicting interests, and the mechanisms for dispute resolution have limited ability to enforce compliance.[12] The World Wildlife Fund's Baltic Sea Scorecard concludes that compliance with such agreements has been poor, describing the situation as follows:

> The Baltic Sea is in serious trouble. Despite a rich tradition of environmental stewardship, eutrophication, toxic pollution, over-exploitation of fish stocks and irresponsible shipping practices continue to threaten the health of this unique and highly sensitive sea. Moreover, it threatens the quality of life of the entire region, which is home to around 90 million people.

The Baltic Sea is one of the most studied seas in the world. We have excellent scientific knowledge at our disposal, and the world's oldest regional seas convention to guide us. Yet, despite innumerable international and regional agreements and conventions aimed at improving the management and conservation of the Baltic Sea, the situation continues to get worse.

Too often, political statements urging action to protect the Baltic Sea have been countered with decisions taken by policy makers in defiance of scientific recommendations and based on short-term interests. Without strong leadership, many of these threats are going to become more, not less, of a problem in the coming years.[13]

Administrative buck passing

A challenge similar to geographical mismatches occurs when multiple organizations share responsibility for environmental protection. While everyone focuses on their primary responsibilities, some obvious tasks may be neglected.

This situation seems responsible for the lack of a beach monitoring system suitable for warning the people who make the millions of annual visits to Lake Texoma. As explained in Chapter 3, several agencies have responsibility for some aspect of recreation on Lake Texoma, but no single agency has comprehensive responsibility for visitor safety, and public safety is not the primary responsibility of any of the agencies. The US Army Corps of Engineers is the 'Nation's number one federal provider of outdoor recreation', but its mission is to 'Deliver vital engineering solutions, in collaboration with our partners, to secure our Nation, energize our economy, and reduce disaster risk', not test lake water for bacterial contamination. The Oklahoma Tourism and Recreation Department manages a state park on the lake. It promotes tourism. The Texas Parks and Wildlife Department operates a state park, guided by its mission to 'manage and conserve the natural and cultural resources of Texas and to provide hunting, fishing and outdoor recreation opportunities for the use and enjoyment of present and future generations'. The US Geological Survey samples the lake water under its mission to 'provide science about the natural hazards that threaten lives and livelihoods, the water, energy, minerals, and other natural resources we rely on, the health of our ecosystems and environment, and the impacts of climate and land-use change'. The lake is an impoundment of the Red River. The Texas Red River Authority analyses water samples, but its mission is 'the orderly conservation, reclamation, protection, and development of the water resources throughout the Red River Basin for the benefit of the public'.[14]

It may seem there is so much attention to the lake that its every aspect must be well studied, but in fact no agency tests the water for bacterial contamination when and where contamination is most likely to be a concern – at beaches after heavy rains. Indeed, public health is not the primary responsibility of any of these agencies. Given various agency missions, every agency employee may be doing a spectacular job, but because no agency has been charged with ensuring the lake is safe for swimming following heavy summer storms, no one runs the necessary tests. (You may recall from Chapter 3 that a lone undergraduate, Nichole Knesek, sampling when and where contamination would be most likely, detected a chronic pollution source in the lake.[15] Her advantage was a focus on detecting any such source.)

On a grander scale, the same problem of jurisdictional overlaps and gaps complicates environmental protection in mining. Various federal agencies share responsibility for US mining policy, including the Bureau of Land Management, the Forest Service, the Office of Surface Mining, the Geological Survey and the EPA. Despite all the attention, the EPA determined the metal mining industry was the nation's largest toxic polluter, responsible for 47 per cent of national toxin releases, amounting to 3.4 billion pounds of toxic waste in 2000 alone – ten pounds of toxic waste for each person in the United States.[16]

An EPA Office of Inspector General's report explained that the relevant laws and regulations create obstacles that prevent the agency from preventing mining pollution, noting for example that 'the Comprehensive Environmental Response, Compensation, and Liability Act largely allows the Agency to respond [only] after environmental damage has occurred; amendments to the Resource Conservation and Recovery Act exempt some mining wastes from regulation; and EPA has only an advisory role in the development of environmental impact statements for mining operations on Federal lands'.[17]

In yet another example, the US Government Accountability Office determined that the Bureau of Land Management, the US Forest Service and the Department of Energy (the three agencies responsible for uranium mining on federal land), do not know the number or locations of thousands of abandoned uranium mines, and maintain incompatible databases because of problems such as using different definitions of 'abandoned mine site'. It seems obvious situations like these should be reformed, with authority and responsibility given to a single entity, but that objective is replete with political challenges, one of which is that the various regulatory agencies have their own staffs and constituencies who will defend each agency's historical authority.[18]

Even if suitable policy exists, jurisdictional overlaps can cause problems because employees of one agency may assume their counterparts at other agencies will handle a problem. For example, tires thrown in a Texas ditch can simultaneously violate a city ordinance, a health nuisance law, an illegal dumping law and a water pollution law. Municipal code officers handle city ordinances. City health departments are responsible for health nuisances. Local police, district attorneys and Texas Commission on Environmental Quality officers investigate illegal dumping. With so much overlapping jurisdiction, busy employees might be excused for assuming a counterpart at another agency will handle a problem.[19]

Today's most prominent mismatch between an environmental problem and political jurisdictions is global climate change, where the magnitude of a necessary response must be of planetary scale, requiring cooperation of dozens of independent nations. Efforts to reach international agreements began in earnest in 1992 with the United Nations Framework Convention on Climate Change, but three decades later the atmospheric concentrations of greenhouse gases continue to set records. Well-intended agreements have so far been too weak and partial to achieve their objective, largely because the United States' response has been inconsistent and inadequate (because opponents of US action have successfully and repeatedly exploited obstacles discussed in this book). Whether developments associated with the United Nations Paris Agreement, especially successive strengthening of nations' intended contributions to reducing greenhouse gas emissions, will halt the ongoing increase in greenhouse gas concentrations remains to be seen.[20]

Mismatches between geographical scales of problems and political jurisdictions create challenges for environmental progress from the local to the global scale. Similar problems arise when responsible entities share overlapping, non-comprehensive responsibilities. If such problems are avoided, and compromises in the development of policy do not doom resulting efforts, environmental progress may yet be stymied if policies are not implemented as intended or if environmental protection efforts are overwhelmed by other, more-or-less unrelated societal efforts, the topics of the next two chapters.

Notes

1 Salzman and Thompson, *Environmental Law and Policy*, 2014, 25–8.
2 Manning, *Grasslands*, 1995, 102–9.
3 Cahan and Williams, *The Lost Panoramas*, 2011, 18–20; Chagnon and Harper, 'History of the Chicago diversion', 1994; Metropolitan Water Reclamation District of Greater Chicago, 'The District to the MWRD', n.d.; D. Miller, *City of the Century*, 1996, 425–32.
4 *New York Times*, 'Chicago poisons St. Louis', 1903.
5 D. Miller, *City of the Century*, 1996, 425–32. Donald Miller explains that Missourians were not the only neighbours upset about Chicago's engineering feats. Armed residents of Waukesha, Wisconsin failed to prevent construction of a pipe from their famous mineral springs to the Chicago World's Fair of 1893. That water supply was intended to prevent attendee concerns about Chicago's notoriously polluted water. The fairgoers drank the Waukesha water and other purified water, and no cases of typhoid were reported. The contrast between the healthy fairgoers and the history of disease outbreaks in Chicago, combined with the developing field of microbiology, fostered public understanding that polluted water was the source of much disease and thus support for the protection of city water supplies.
6 *New York Times*, 'Water in Chicago River', 1900, 14. For an updated description of the complexities of Chicago's relationship with Lake Michigan and its rivers, see Egan and French, 'The climate crisis haunts Chicago's future', 2021.
7 Jerde et al., 'Detection of Asian carp DNA as part of a Great Lakes basin-wide surveillance program', 2013, 522.
8 Kurlansky, *Cod*, 1997, 144–233.
9 See for example: Folke et al., 'Social-ecological resilience and biosphere-based sustainability science', 2016; Scheffer et al., 'Catastrophic shifts in ecosystems', 2001; Sguotti et al., 'Catastrophic dynamics limit Atlantic cod recovery', 2019.
10 Myers and Worm, 'Rapid worldwide depletion of predatory fish communities', 2003. A tragedy of the commons occurs when individuals have unlimited access to a limited renewable resource (a common property). In such cases, individuals responding to incentives often collectively destroy the resource, thus the 'tragedy of the commons'. For example, when you or I drive a gasoline or diesel vehicle we receive virtually all of the benefits of the convenient transportation but others suffer most of the costs of the resulting air pollution. As I have often explained to students, I would never drive a gas-powered vehicle if the exhaust was routed to the vehicle's interior (that is, if I had to pay the bulk of the pollution cost, rather than foisting most of it off on others). Resource depletion and pollutant accumulation routinely result from tragedies of the commons. Such tragedies may be prevented if a small number of individuals lack potential to appreciably damage an abundant resource, if a community is sufficiently cohesive to police each other's behaviour, if cultural norms forbid abuse of the resource, or if effective laws or policies prohibit such abuse.
11 Jansson and Velner, 'The Baltic', 1995, 295–306.
12 Baltic Marine Environment Protection Commission, 'About us', n.d.; European Commission, 'EU Water Framework Directive', n.d.; United Nations Environment Program Global Marine Oil Pollution Information Gateway, 'Helsinki Convention'.
13 World Wildlife Fund, 'Baltic Sea Scorecard', n.d., 2.
14 Red River Authority of Texas, 'Red River Authority of Texas', n.d.; Texas Parks and Wildlife Department, 'Mission and philosophy', n.d.; US Army Corps of Engineers, 'Mission overview', n.d.; US Geological Survey, 'About us', n.d.
15 Knesek, '*Escherichia coli* concentrations in Lake Texoma', 2000.
16 Copper et al., 'Implementation, information, and statutory obstacles impede achievement of environmental results from EPA's national hardrock mining framework', 2003, 2, 9.
17 Copper et al., 'Implementation, information, and statutory obstacles impede achievement of environmental results from EPA's national hardrock mining framework', 2003, ii.
18 Kamieniecki, *Corporate America and Environmental Policy*, 2006, 207; US Government Accountability Office, 'Uranium mining', 2012, 30.
19 Dr John Ockels, Texas Illegal Dumping Resource Center, personal communication, 20 July 2021.
20 United Nations Framework Convention on Climate Change, 'The Paris Agreement', n.d.

18

Breakdown in policy implementation

If you have ever encouraged simple resource conservation efforts, such as switching off lights or recycling, you may understand how even modest efforts can fail. A few years ago, Austin College students tallied substantial energy waste due to lights left on in unoccupied rooms. They posted stickers on switch plates to encourage turning off of lights when departing. The new stickers were placed directly over faded, fifteen-year-old stickers with the same message. If the earlier effort had created a pervasive culture of energy conservation, the new stickers would not have been necessary. Those earlier stickers, and whatever other effort went along with them, had not had their intended effect.

It is easy to understand the logic of turning off lights, and it is easy to turn lights off, yet lights get left on. Similarly, the town where the college is located, Sherman, Texas, halted its curb-side recycling programme during 2021 because of a drop in market prices for recyclables and excessive contamination of recycling bins. If the implementation of these relatively simple efforts can fail, more complex procedures surely can as well. As we shall see, many pitfalls exist along the way to effective implementation of environmental efforts.

Numerous factors interfere with implementation. Some procedures are difficult to understand or implement; some interfere with other activities, many lack adequate funding, and perhaps most importantly, individuals and organizations often face disincentives to vigorous implementation. In the worst cases, those responsible for implementation may even object to policy goals or procedures. The same implementation hurdles hinder both modest and momentous efforts.

Consider the task of reducing a small college's greenhouse gas emissions. Austin College is a signatory of the Second Nature Carbon Commitment (formerly the American College and University Presidents' Climate Commitment). That commitment requires reduction of net greenhouse gas emissions to zero. The college reduced its emissions by 58 per cent from 2008 to 2020, but has not eliminated them despite a desire and commitment to do so. Why not?

Several factors impede complete success. For example, individual behaviours and preferences impede energy savings and recycling. The college would emit fewer greenhouse gases if it used less natural gas to heat water and regulate building temperatures, but some students have reported taking forty-five-minute showers, and physical plant staff perceive strong resistance to adjusting building temperature settings for the sake of further energy efficiency. During warm seasons, buildings are air conditioned to temperatures that leave many occupants cold because staff are wary of complaints of uncomfortable warmth, while the same concerns keep winter temperatures well above what one would expect in a colder climate. Clearly, we have not convinced everyone on campus of the benefits of energy conservation. Likewise, emissions would be lower if all recyclable materials were diverted from the college's solid waste stream, but despite instructions and ease of recycling, some people continue to put recyclables in the trash. (The college has made substantial progress. As noted, greenhouse gas emissions declined almost 60 per cent since 2008. Electricity and natural gas consumption per square metre of building space declined 25 per cent and 20 per cent respectively from 2004 to 2015. Campus electricity is 100 per cent wind-generated, and in 2019 Environment America determined that the college was second nationally in renewable energy use per student, but the goal of no net greenhouse gas emissions remains to be achieved.)[1]

Progress is primarily hampered by lack of funds. The college could achieve carbon neutrality by buying about $120,000 of carbon offsets per year. (Carbon offsets pay others to take actions that 'offset', or negate, the buyer's greenhouse gas emissions.) That amounts to a little more than 20 cents per person on campus per day[2] (hardly the economy-destroying impact claimed by Senator Rubio during his 2016 presidential campaign).[3] The total annual cost of $120,000 is less than the highest-paid major-league baseball player receives *per game*, but is also the cost of four substantial scholarships. The college's climate action plan specifies ramping up to such purchases by 2035, but the necessary funds remain to be raised.[4] Thus, Austin College has made much progress, but could make more if funding was more readily available. Similar hindrances interfere with more consequential state, federal and international environmental policies.

Even with the best intentions, implementation may not achieve goals due to inadequate budgets, technical challenges or shifts in priorities. The history of the Clean Water Act provides a clear example of a gap between ambition and implementation. The Clean Water Act amendments of 1977 gave the EPA six short years to provide for 'the protection and propagation of fish, shellfish, and wildlife', and 'recreation in and on the water', and (ridiculously) only eight years to eliminate all pollutant discharges into the nation's waters. The law's ambitious objectives provided excellent sound bites for politicians, but were not realistic. Success would have required making the nation's waters safe for swimming and fishing less than twenty years after the Cuyahoga River last burned. The nation has made great progress in improving water quality, but plenty of polluted waterways remain even today. The history of the Clean Air Act is similar: great progress, but goals not met and deadlines extended to accommodate technical, political and budgetary hurdles.

Perhaps the greatest challenge occurs when responsible officials disagree with the goals, methods or consequences of a law or policy. Once a law is passed or an organization adopts a policy, enthusiasm for its implementation may wane as new leaders are elected or appointed, priorities shift or the challenges of achieving the goal become clear. For example, it is relatively easy for one president to commit a college to achieving carbon neutrality. Once the easiest energy- and money-saving steps have been taken, however, it may be much harder several years later for another president to take the more challenging actions necessary to achieve the goal. More critically, because federal environmental laws specify broad goals and assign administrative agencies great discretion for determining how to achieve those goals, if agency leaders lack enthusiasm for those goals, implementation will suffer.[5] The problem is loosely analogous to making a New Year's resolution, keeping it for a few days, and then expecting someone else to keep it for you. It is easy to make such a resolution and may not be too difficult to begin its implementation. It can be much harder to keep a resolution and success would be unlikely if those subsequently responsible oppose the methods or objective.

> What Congress and the President do with much fanfare can quickly and quietly slip away in the ensuing years. This is famously so for environmental law. Subsequent legislative amendments, limited budgets, appropriations riders, interpretive agency rulings, massive delays in rulemaking and simple nonenforcement are more than capable of converting a seemingly uncompromising legal mandate into nothing more than a symbolic aspirational statement.[6]

Inadequate funding

Lack of sufficient funding often prevents achievement of environmental protection goals. Inadequate funding is common because motivation to fund efforts is often weaker than motivation to announce ambitious efforts, and challenges of environmental protection are often underestimated.[7] For instance, during the late-twentieth-century era of strong public support for environmental protection, legislators pleased constituents by passing ambitious laws, but their constituents and subsequent representatives have not been equally motivated to provide necessary funding or impose regulations that have the potential to achieve the stated goals. The lack of enthusiasm for funding is apparent when the EPA budget is compared to others. For example, the budgets for the Departments of Agriculture and Transportation are both twenty times greater than the EPA budget.[8]

Moreover, as time passes, enthusiasm for environmental protection may wane as the worst problems improve, laws' champions retire, the cost of environmental protection becomes clear, or the public and new legislators focus on other priorities. Finally, compared to members of Congressional committees who advance environmental legislation, members of Congressional appropriations committees who draft budgets may have less enthusiasm for environmental protection.[9]

Expectations placed on individual workers make funding limitations apparent. For example, as of 2017 the US Pipeline and Hazardous Material Safety Administration had only 90 pipeline inspectors to ensure the safety of 4.5 million kilometres of oil and gas pipelines, or about 50,000 kilometres of pipeline per inspector.[10] Given the apparent condition of some pipelines (Figure 18.1), and NASA's satellite detection of about one oil spill per day in American waters,[11] it seems unreasonable to expect each inspector to take responsibility for 50,000 kilometres of pipe. Various other examples discussed earlier, such as the limited ability of the EPA to confirm Toxic Release Inventory reports, the minimal scale of water-quality monitoring and the inability of the EPA to run toxicology tests on chemicals proposed for manufacturing, provide yet more evidence of funding limitations.

Lack of funding (or enforcement motivation) is especially common when state agencies implement federal laws.[12] For example, the Texas Commission on Environmental Quality has a staff of about twelve criminal-enforcement officers, which leaves each officer responsible for an average of almost 60,000 square kilometres, or almost the area of West

Figure 18.1: Minimal expenditure on pipeline safety. Oil pipelines at Hagerman National Wildlife Refuge, Grayson County, Texas, US. In wetter weather, water routinely flows over this road while large tree trunks float down the stream that floods this area. Photographer: Peter C. Schulze.

Virginia. With more than 400,000 oil and gas wells in Texas, that is 33,000 wells per officer.[13] Unfortunately, inadequate funding is only one reason laws are not always vigorously implemented.

Implementation disincentives

Environmental efforts can also fail when administrators face disincentives to fulfill mandates, a routine situation for US federal laws. US environmental laws leave much to the discretion of implementing agencies because Congress does not have the expertise or resources to tailor regulations to new understanding or case-specific circumstances, and because it is sometimes easier to generate votes for ambiguously worded statutes that allow supporters to claim their own preferred interpretations.[14] For example, the Clean Air Act requires the EPA to set air quality standards 'requisite to protect the public health' while 'allowing an adequate margin of safety'. Congress charged the EPA with deciding which pollutants to regulate and how strictly to regulate them. Individual members who later consider regulations too strict or expensive can defend their votes in favour of the law with, 'I didn't have in mind that great a margin of safety', or 'Life is risky. We don't need that much protection. The EPA has overreached.' (Which pollutants would you regulate? How would you decide how much air pollution is compatible with protecting public health? What would you consider an adequate margin of safety?) Likewise, the 'multiple-use' mandate of the US Forest Service dictates national forests be managed sustainably for the competing interests of recreation, wildlife protection, preservation and logging. Forest Service administrators have a great deal of discretion (and face a real challenge) in determining how to balance those conflicting objectives.[15]

As if the technical challenge of choosing an 'adequate margin of safety', or balancing wildlife protection and logging are not daunting enough, administrators work in a political environment. Once laws are passed, opponents attempt to prevent vigorous implementation (a relatively easy task if the dominant political party opposes regulations or the political agenda shifts to other issues). Such political pressure incentivizes weak implementation.

Differences between Obama and Trump administration policies provide numerous examples of the power of administrative discretion. For example, whereas the Obama Administration valued carbon emissions at $50 per ton, the Trump Administration proposed to value the emissions at $1–7 per ton. The difference obviously affected cost–benefit analyses of pollution-control efforts. Similarly, the Obama Administration proposed to protect the Greater Sage Grouse over 3.6 million more hectares than what the Trump Administration proposed, a difference almost ten times the size of Rhode Island. These are just two of many discretionary differences.

As of May 2020, the Trump Administration had planned to loosen 100 environmental rules.[16] Many such changes were defeated in court, or became moot after Trump lost his bid for re-election and the Biden Administration began reversing its predecessor's changes, but these examples illustrate striking differences in law and policy implementation from one administration to another.

The lawsuits in response to Trump Administration loosening of rules and regulations were based upon the 'citizen suit' provisions of environmental laws described in Chapter 12. Weak implementation is so common that environmental organizations such as the Center for

Biological Diversity and the Natural Resources Defense Council are kept busy filing, and often winning, such suits.

The EPA's historic reluctance to regulate greenhouse gases under the authority of the Clean Air Act provides a rich example of the effect of political disincentives on vigorous implementation and thus the importance of citizen suits. It also illustrates the influence of the courts.

The Clean Air Act requires the EPA to identify and regulate air pollutants that endanger public health. The agency has designated six such 'criteria' pollutants, carbon monoxide, sulphur dioxide, nitrogen oxides, lead, ozone and particulates. The legislators who drafted the law in the 1970s were focused on materials harmful to inhale. Greenhouse gases are not toxic at atmospheric concentrations, and during the 1970s few were concerned about climate change. But by the 1990s, concern about climate change had grown and members of the public began to push the EPA to regulate greenhouse gases. The agency declined to do so, however, apparently to avoid political controversy. (It may seem curious that an agency charged with environmental protection would seek to avoid such controversy, but that is understandable. If their implementation is more rigorous than most members of Congress prefer, the EPA risks retaliatory budget cuts and thus reductions in their ability to implement any laws.)

During 1999, a group of environmental organizations petitioned the EPA to set standards for greenhouse gases emitted by motor vehicles, arguing the gases endanger public health when rising temperatures raise sea levels and foster the spread of tropical diseases. The EPA rejected the petition four years later in a decision that hinged on subtle interpretations of the term 'air pollutant'. The petitioners, plus several states, responded by filing a citizen suit. Because Massachusetts was the lead plaintiff, the case is known as *Massachusetts v. EPA*. A panel of three appellate judges in the District of Columbia Circuit upheld the EPA determination two to one in 2005, but the Supreme Court overturned that decision five to four in 2007. Writing for the majority, Justice Stevens found the EPA had authority to regulate greenhouse gases under the Clean Air Act and its decision not to do so had been 'arbitrary and capricious' (a legal designation for inadequately grounded in evidence or reasoning).[17]

Having been ordered to do so by the Supreme Court, and soon under the more enthusiastic leadership of the Obama Administration, EPA staff developed a plan to regulate greenhouse gas emissions, the 'Clean Power Plan'.[18] (This was no simple task. How would you regulate greenhouse gases given their multitude of sources?) That plan depended on a section of the 1990 Clean Air Act amendments that authorizes the

EPA to regulate 'any air pollutant' not regulated under other provisions of the law. However, the relevant text of the law contains two conflicting statements regarding when the EPA may impose regulations. Conflicting language is normally removed before bills become law, but Congress erred in this case and the president signed the bill as written, including the internal inconsistency. Some interpret the text passage from the House version as prohibiting the regulatory mechanisms of the Obama Administration's proposed Clean Power Plan.[19]

As you might imagine, environmentalists and industry representatives disagree about the proper interpretation of the statute's conflicting language. Just as predictably, a group of states and companies sued to block implementation of the plan. Before the new lawsuit was litigated, the Supreme Court, in yet another five to four decision (but after a change in the membership of the Court), took the unprecedented step of 'staying' (halting) the plan's implementation until after the lawsuit was decided. Before the case was resolved, the Trump Administration came into office and rejected the Obama Administration plan, thus rendering the stay moot.[20] As this book went to press, the Supreme Court had just further limited the EPA's climate policy authority in the case *West Virginia v EPA*.[21] The court did not prohibit the EPA from regulating greenhouse gas emissions, but restricted the options for doing so. Precisely what will be allowed remains to be determined, but in the absence of new legislation, this most recent decision further constrains the EPA's, and therefore any presidential administration's, options for regulating greenhouse gases. This example not only illustrates the role of citizen suits, it also illustrates the conflicting pressures on regulatory agencies, the importance of regulatory discretion, constraints upon that discretion, and how much environmental authority rests with judges, presidents and political appointees, not scientists or technical experts.

The 1973 Endangered Species Act provides another example of how policy may falter, either because of limited resources or political disincentives against vigorous implementation.[21] The Act is administered by two agencies. The National Marine Fisheries Service is responsible for marine species. The Fish and Wildlife Service is responsible for all others. The law is based upon 'listing' (designating) species, subspecies, or 'distinct population segments' as threatened or endangered, and then developing plans for their recovery. When the law was passed in 1973, many members of Congress apparently had showy species like bald eagles and peregrine falcons in mind, but biologists have since documented endangerment of little-known plants, insects and other obscure creatures.

As of May 2022, the Fish and Wildlife Service website listed 2,367 taxa as threatened or endangered.[22] (Experts estimate perhaps ten times as many US species are in danger of extinction but have not yet been proposed for listing.[23]) Few listed species have gone extinct, but meanwhile few have recovered enough to be delisted.

Listings involve several required steps. First, a petition for listing is filed, often by an independent biologist or an organization whose mission includes protecting endangered species, such as the Center for Biological Diversity. The relevant agency then has three months to determine whether the petition warrants review. If a petition is deemed worthy of review, the agency has a year to make an initial determination. If that analysis finds the species is threatened or endangered, the species becomes a 'candidate' for formal listing. The agency then has another year to publish a proposed rule (announce in the Federal Register a tentative plan to list the species as endangered), hold public hearings and reconsider the proposed rule on the basis of public comments and any new evidence on the species' conservation status.[24] Listing proposals generate controversy because it is illegal to damage the habitat of listed species, and therefore listing restricts activities where species occur, including on private land. Consequently, the agencies face strong political pressure not to list species.

Historically, many species have remained at the candidate stage of evaluation for longer than a year. Species may linger at that stage either because agency staff simply have not had time to complete the formal listing process or because of a disinclination to make a listing decision. A disinclination to make a formal listing could be motivated by desire to avoid the controversy associated with enforcing the resulting land-use or other restrictions, or to give a species a chance to recover and not need listing. Several species have been deemed to have recovered while candidates, often as a result of state, local or even private conservation efforts that may have been inspired by the candidate status and its attendant threat that the species might be formally listed and regulated by the federal government. Such species are removed from listing consideration.[25]

By the early 2000s, hundreds of species awaited a final decision at the candidate stage, some having done so for decades. The Center for Biological Diversity filed suit to force the Fish and Wildlife Service to make listing decisions. The Center won its suit in 2011, and the court required the agency to make several hundred listing decisions by 2019, by which time the agencies had listed 292 additional species.[26]

The law also requires the agencies to identify critical habitats when doing so is 'prudent and determinable', but habitats have been designated for only about thirty per cent of listed species.[27] Some delays are probably due to agency resource limitations, but it seems likely political resistance to land use restrictions is responsible for others.

Anecdotal evidence of the power of administrative discretion is also apparent from the different rates at which species have been listed during different presidencies (Figure 18.2). Multiple factors could influence listing rates. For example, when a statute is adopted, the agency responsible for its implementation needs time to develop policy and procedures. That could potentially account for relatively few listings during the Nixon and Ford administrations when the law had only recently been passed. Later, once a species is listed as endangered, it is not available to be listed again. Such factors cannot, however, account for the variation in listing rates under the Clinton, G. W. Bush, Obama and Trump administrations. These seem most easily attributable to administrative discretion.

The G. W. Bush and Trump administrations not only listed few species, they also changed or sought to change accepted definitions of key terms. The Endangered Species Act requires basing listing determinations

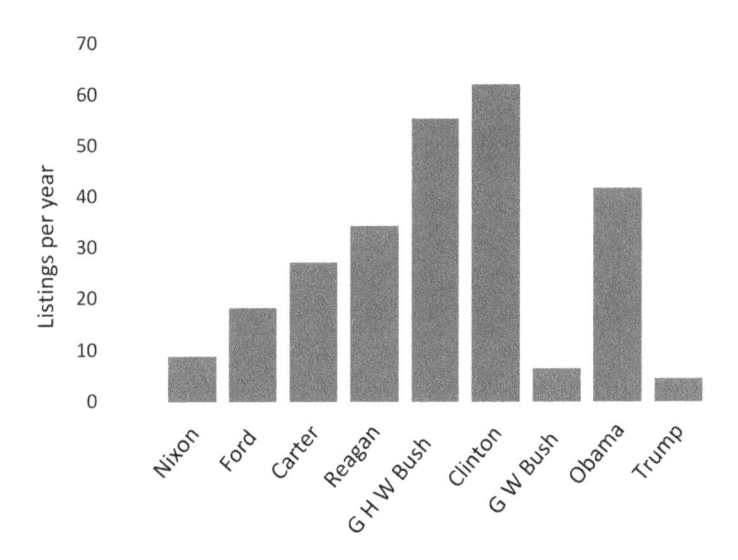

Figure 18.2: Average annual number of taxa newly listed as threatened or endangered per year per US presidential administration from 1970 through 2020. Data source: US Fish and Wildlife Service, 'US federal endangered and threatened species by calendar year'.

on whether a species is imperilled *over a significant portion of its range*. Prior to the G.W. Bush Administration, 'range' had been interpreted to mean the species historical range, but that administration redefined it to refer only to a species' current range — the few remaining locations where an endangered species survives. Eliminating the bulk of the historical range from analysis and instead considering only where a species still exists substantially weakens the law. Under this curious definition, a species could have a healthy population in one small reserve but be extinct over 99 per cent of its former range, and be deemed not imperilled 'over a significant portion of its range', and thus not listed as endangered even though the species is indeed in danger of extinction. Unfortunately, the Obama Administration maintained the same narrow definition of 'range'.[28] Later, the Trump Administration sought to further weaken the Endangered Species Act by, among other things, considering economic costs when determining whether a species is endangered and restricting the definition of critical habitat.[29]

Political interference with scientific conclusions

The history of the Endangered Species Act demonstrates not only how administrative discretion can influence the vigour of implementation, but also the potential for political interference with scientific conclusions. For example, Reagan Administration Fish and Wildlife Service officials in Washington, DC pressured the agency's Portland, Oregon staff to conclude that northern spotted owls were not facing extinction, in direct contradiction to the agency's own scientists. The Government Accountability Office's review of that issue reads as follows:

> [US Fish and Wildlife Service] management substantively changed the body of scientific evidence presented in the study team's status report ... The revisions had the effect of changing the report from one that emphasized the dangers facing the owl to one they could more easily support denying the listing petition.[30]

Such interference with science and scientific conclusions is unfortunately common.[31] Officials from both the G. H. W. Bush and G. W. Bush Administrations watered down their scientists' analyses of the seriousness of climate change.[32] The Texas Commission on Environmental Quality deleted references to climate change in a report on Galveston Bay.[33] Trump Administration officials pressured an independent scientist to alter her planned Congressional testimony regarding dismissals of experts from the EPA's scientific review board. The president simply explained that he did not believe his agencies' scientists' reports.[34] Trump Administration officials also altered pesticide licence reviews, even in ways that staff scientists found nonsensical. Some career scientists refused to sign off on the finalized analyses.[35] Even the Obama Administration overruled its own scientists' advice when that administration decided not to designate wolverines as threatened, a decision later thrown out when Defenders of Wildlife sued.[36] Interference in technical analyses often come from non-environmental offices, such as the Office of Management and Budget, and are fostered by appointing former industry officers to those agencies. Such individuals often eventually return to their industries through the 'revolving door' between government agencies and the industries they regulate.[37]

When you mix science and politics, you get politics.[38]

Lax enforcement

Lack of enthusiasm for regulations can also result in lax enforcement. Decades of evidence of poor compliance suggest frequent lack of effective enforcement. For example, Bethlehem Steel violated the Clean Water Act more than 700 times during the late 1970s and early 1980s.[39] Such repeated violations suggest either that the chance of a penalty was too low or the penalties were too weak to affect business practices, but that was decades ago.

Little seems to have changed. Oil and gas companies spilled salty oil-field brine 20,000 times from 2009 to 2014. Various industries violated environmental regulations some 10,000 times from 2011 to 2015.[40] Forty per cent of companies that mine and haul fracking sand in Wisconsin have broken state rules. Perhaps this is because it takes three rule violations before fines are issued, and some fines are only hundreds of dollars.[41] During 2019, Formosa Plastics agreed to pay $50 million to settle a lawsuit for polluting Lavaca Bay on the Texas Coast. Judge Kenneth Hoyt found Formosa guilty of Clean Water Act violations daily for four years, calling the company a 'serial offender'. Previously, the Texas Commission on Environmental Quality had fined Formosa a paltry $121,000, which amounted to $64 per violation.[42] (The latter is not unusual. State fines tend to be especially low.[43])

We all make mistakes, but we do not repeat mistakes 20,000 times. Surely corporate managers could institute policies and procedures to prevent such violations if they chose to do so? The most logical explanation for lengthy records of persistent violations is that some businesses make intentional choices to violate laws and regulations, considering modest fines simply part of the cost of doing business.

Just as funding constraints on implementation can be stronger at the state and local level than the federal level, so too political disincentives to enforcement are often stronger. State legislators are often less enthusiastic about new regulations than their federal counterparts because states and municipalities compete to attract business. Moreover, many states have less public support for environmental protection than is typical nationwide.[44]

West Virginia provides one example. Tap water near the capital, Charleston, sometimes contains arsenic, barium, lead and manganese at concentrations suspected of damaging kidneys and nervous systems. Even though courts determined companies had illegally pumped chemicals into groundwater, those companies were never fined or otherwise punished.[45] Texas provides another example. A 2018 analysis by Environment Texas found that the Texas Commission on Environmental Quality acted on only three per cent of unpermitted air pollution emission events from 2011 to 2018. Whereas the law would have allowed $2.3 billion in fines for the violations logged, the agency collected only $1.3 million, less than a thousandth of the allowed maximum and equating to just 4.5 cents per kilogram of unpermitted releases. As you may recall from Chapter 3, during Hurricane Harvey, when numerous oil and gas facilities caught fire in the Houston area, releasing 3.8 million kilograms of harmful chemicals, NASA offered to operate an air pollution monitoring plane in the area. Texas officials rejected the offer, arguing the extra data might cause 'confusion'.[46] In another instance, when the US Court of Appeals overturned an EPA rule intended to reduce thousands of premature deaths, the Texas Attorney General at the time, Greg Abbott, tweeted, '#EPA overlords suffer another defeat to #Texas: The power to regulate is the power to destroy.'[47] Abbott was subsequently elected Governor.

Unfortunately, West Virginia and Texas are not the only states with less than aggressive enforcement of environmental laws. Nationwide from 2004 to 2009, industrial facilities broke water pollution laws more than 500,000 times. In the great majority of cases the polluters were not punished.[48] During 2014, attorneys general from at least a dozen states worked with energy industry representatives to resist federal environmental regulations.[49]

Enforcement cannot be assumed at the local level either. Enforcement failures can result from lack of effort to detect violations, disinclination of local officials to enforce laws or prosecutors' lack of familiarity with relevant statutes. District attorneys do not have the resources to prosecute every crime. Thus, they select which cases to pursue. Political pressure often infringes on these decisions. Other officials or members of the public may push for a focus on violent crimes or drug offences, or may pressure prosecutors to go easy on local employers. Furthermore, prosecutors are often more familiar with the procedures for prosecuting traditional crimes than environmental crimes, so they can make faster progress on the former.[50]

Moreover, local officials live in the same cities, towns and even neighbourhoods as those subjected to laws and regulations, so they face the prospect of interfering not just with activities of businesses in the abstract, but with livelihoods of their neighbours and even friends. John Ockels, the Director of the Texas Illegal Dumping Resource Center, explains the problem as follows: 'The closer you get to the local level, the greater the personal risk to individuals in charge of enforcing regulations and prosecuting violators. This creates resistance to enforcing environmental regulations and prosecuting environmental crimes because doing so can upset the apple cart, cause local controversy and animosity, and thus can create a political problem for whoever takes the initiative to enforce the law. It is understandable that poorly paid, low level government employees, such as sheriff's deputies or city code enforcement officers, are reluctant to put themselves in such situations.'[51]

Other failures of enforcement occur because potentially large penalties make fines controversial, especially when imposed on small companies or individuals, rather than giant corporations. For example, penalties for Resource Conservation and Recovery Act violations are often per day. A facility that has been found in violation for a long period could potentially face astronomical fines. Likewise, the Texas water code provides for fines of $1 million or more, prison terms of up to 30 years and civil penalties up to $25,000 per day for persistent violations. If a Texan dumps used motor oil on the ground, they can theoretically be sentenced to a year in jail, fined $50,000 or both, but it is hard to imagine a prosecutor pushing for such a sentence.[52] Thus, small fines can result in chronic violations, while excessive allowable fines may influence decisions not to prosecute.

Meanwhile, overlapping jurisdictions can result in enforcement gaps. As explained in Chapter 17, tires thrown in a Texas ditch could simultaneously break four health and environmental regulations for which multiple agencies have investigative authority. It is easy to imagine staff of each agency being overworked and choosing to assume a colleague at another agency will handle a case.[53]

Industry capture

In the most extreme cases, agencies not only fail to vigorously enforce laws, but become so close to the regulated industries that they end up being 'captured' by those they are supposed to regulate. Captured agencies promote, rather than regulate, industry. Their decisions are often motivated not by public interest but by personal sympathies or even benefits, such as future employment opportunities in the regulated industry.

Numerous agencies with environmental responsibilities have been accused of industry capture. Various analyses have concluded that the livestock industry has captured the Bureau of Land Management; the oil and gas industry the Office of Pipeline Safety; and in Canada, the tar sands oil industry the Alberta Energy Resources Conservation Board.[54] When he was a senator, Barack Obama concluded that the nuclear industry had captured the Nuclear Regulatory Commission.[55] Author Norman Miller concludes that the EPA was captured during the Administration of President G. W. Bush, and the Trump EPA's track record suggests capture under the leadership of Scott Pruitt, who made his name as Oklahoma Attorney General by suing the EPA on behalf of the oil and gas industry, and who appointed to his staff many former staff members of Senator James Inhofe, one of the Senate's most prominent climate change deniers.[56] Regulatory capture is also the simplest explanation for the reluctance of officials from the Texas Railroad Commission (the state's oil and gas regulator) to accept that disposal of hydraulic fracturing ('fracking') wastewater caused earthquakes, even after the US Geological Survey, the Oklahoma Geological Survey and numerous independent seismologists had reached that conclusion.[57]

It is also hard to escape the conclusion that the former Minerals Management Service (now the Bureau of Ocean Energy Management, Regulation, and Enforcement) was captured by the oil industry when the Service approved BP's Gulf of Mexico Deepwater Horizon drilling rig emergency plan. That plan included procedures to protect walruses in case of an accident.[58] Walruses live in the Arctic, not the Gulf of Mexico. This suggests the regulators did not even read the plan before awarding their approval.

Shortly after the 2010 BP Deepwater Horizon spill, President Obama described the Minerals Management Service's track record as follows: 'Over the last decade, this agency has become emblematic of a failed philosophy that views all regulation with hostility – a philosophy that says corporations should be allowed to play by their own rules and police themselves. At this agency, industry insiders were put in charge of industry oversight. Oil companies showered regulators with gifts and favours, and were essentially allowed to conduct their own safety inspections and write their own regulations.'[59]

President Obama broke up the Minerals Management Service and assigned its responsibilities to separate entities,[60] but that reorganization did not solve the problem. During 2014, the Ninth Circuit Court of Appeals found in favour of Earthjustice and other plaintiffs who sued one of the newly created agencies, the Bureau of Ocean Energy Management, over its approval of Shell's application to drill in Alaska's Chukchi Sea. The court found the Bureau had based its projections of potential environmental harms on 'the lowest possible amount of oil that was economical to produce', and therefore based its analysis on minimum potential harms. The court agreed with the plaintiffs that the analysis was arbitrary and capricious. Those analyses, moreover, were so rushed that numerous Bureau employees complained of unreasonable time pressure and six quit or retired early in objection to the Bureau's effort to complete its analysis in time for Shell's open-water drilling season.[61]

Finally, one of the more startling cases of apparent industry capture is the US Army Corps of Engineer's historically routine permitting of 'valley fills' associated with mountaintop coal mining. Section 404 of the Clean Water Act requires a permit from the Corps of Engineers for discharges of material into wetlands. A discharge is 'categorically prohibited if it would significantly degrade water quality'.[62] Mountaintop coal mining is based on dynamiting mountain tops above Appalachian coal seams, then pushing the exploded 'overburden' into adjacent valleys to gain access to the coal on the now flat, exposed plateau. It is hard to comprehend a conclusion that water quality is not significantly impacted when valley streams are buried under hundreds of metres of mining overburden, and yet until a few years ago the Corps routinely granted section 404 permits for stream burial. Such dumping impacted 6,700 valleys between 1985 and 2001.[63] During 2016, the Obama administration developed new regulations for protecting streams from mining waste, but then in early 2017 President Trump signed a bill overturning the Obama era regulations.[64]

Environmental progress can falter if policies are not implemented as intended, such as if inadequate budgets or political disincentives hinder implementation. Given these considerable obstacles, and the many others discussed in previous chapters, it is remarkable that air and water in the United States are so much cleaner than a few decades ago. But it is not surprising that there has not been yet more progress, especially considering the final obstacle, the many ways that efforts to achieve other societal goals conflict with or overwhelm environmental protection.

Notes

1   To date, the college's cost premium for the wind-generated electricity has been modest – about 5 per cent of the simultaneous cost savings from energy conservation. Austin College, 'Austin College sustainability plan', 2018, 6; Bradford et al., 'America's top colleges for renewable energy', 2019, 2; SIMAP, 'Austin College', n.d.

2   The college's net annual greenhouse gas emissions, as these things are conventionally calculated, were about 6,000 metric tons of carbon dioxide equivalent in 2020 (SIMAP, 'Austin College', n.d.). Carbon offsets cost about $20 per metric ton. There are some 1,600 students, faculty and staff on campus. (6,000MT/yr)($20/MT)/(1600 people)(365 days/yr) = $0.205/person/day.

3   Wolf, "'America is not a planet'", 2015.

4   Austin College, 'Climate action plan and greenhouse gas reports', n.d.

5   Rosenbaum, *Environmental Politics and Policy*, 2002, 9–10, 70–5, 100–1, 185–6.

6   Lazarus, 'Super wicked problems and climate change: restraining the present to liberate the future', 2009, 1153.

7   Salzman and Thompson, *Environmental Law and Policy*, 2014, 34, 39–40, 78, 232–44, 266, 277–87, 289.

8   US Department of the Treasury, 'Spending explorer'.

9   Downs, 'Up and down with ecology', 1972, 39–40.

10 US Department of Transportation Pipeline and Hazardous Materials Safety Administration, 'Advancing the safe transportation of energy and hazardous materials', n.d.; US Department of Transportation Pipeline and Hazardous Materials Safety Administration, 'PHMSA and pipelines FAQs', n.d.

11 Migliozzi and Tabuchi, 'After Hurricane Ida, oil infrastructure springs dozens of leaks', 2021.

12 Flatt, 'Dirty river runs through it', 1997, 2–6, 15–21, 27–8; Flatt and Collins, 'Environmental enforcement in dire straits', 2009, 60–2; Salzman and Thompson, *Environmental Law and Policy*, 2014, 89–91.

13 DrillingEdge, 'Oil and gas production in Texas', 2021; Johns Ockels, Texas Illegal Dumping Resource Center, personal communication, 8 October 2021.

14 Rosenbaum, *Environmental Politics and Policy*, 2002, 70–5; Salzman and Thompson, *Environmental Law and Policy*, 2014, 77–9.

15 Fischman, 'The divides of environmental law and the problem of harm in the Endangered Species Act', 2008, 678.

16 Davenport, 'Trump Administration loosens sage grouse protections, benefitting oil companies', 2019; Plumer, 'Trump put a low cost on carbon emissions', 2018; Popovich et al., 'The Trump Administration is reversing 100 environmental rules', 2020.

17 Justice Scalia, writing for the minority, argued greenhouse gases are not air pollutants. Heinzerling, 'Climate change in the Supreme Court', 2008; Salzman and Thompson, *Environmental Law and Policy*, 2014, 233.

18 EPA, 'Overview of the Clean Power Plan', 2015.

19   Davenport, 'Obama climate plan, now in court, may hinge on error in 1990 law', 2016.
20   Liptak and Davenport, 'Supreme Court deals blow to Obama's efforts to regulate coal emissions', 2016; Friedman and Plumer, 'EPA announces repeal of major Obama-era carbon emissions rule', 2017.
21   Ando, 'Waiting to be protected under the Endangered Species Act', 1999, 52–3; Salzman and Thompson, *Environmental Law and Policy*, 2014, 287–309.
22   US Fish and Wildlife Service, 'Listed species summary (boxscore)', 2022.
23   D. Evans, et al., 'Species recovery in the US', 2016, 6.
24   Salzman and Thompson, *Environmental Law and Policy*, 2014, 292–4.
25   US Fish and Wildlife Service and US National Marine Fisheries Service, 'Policy for evaluation of conservation efforts when making listing decisions', 2003.
26   Center for Biological Diversity, 'Landmark agreement moves 757 species toward federal protection', 2011; Center for Biological Diversity v. Salazar, 'Stipulated settlement agreement', 2011; US Fish and Wildlife Service, 'U.S. federal endangered and threatened species by calendar year', n.d.; Wines, 'Endangered or not, but at least no longer waiting', 2013.
27   Salzman and Thompson, *Environmental Law and Policy*, 2014, 298; US Fish and Wildlife Service, 'USFWS Threatened & Endangered Species Active Critical Habitat Report', n.d.
28   Eilperin, 'Since '01 guarding species is harder', 2008; Vucetich and Nelson, 'Conservation, or curation?', 2014.
29   Friedman et al., 'Law that saved the Bald Eagle could be vastly reworked', 2018; US Fish and Wildlife Service and National Oceanic and Atmospheric Administration, 'Endangered and threatened wildlife and plants', 2018, 35194.
30   US Government Accountability Office, 'Endangered species: spotted owl petition beset by problems', 1989, 1.
31   See for instance Donahue, 'Western grazing', 2005, 772–89; Lipton, 'Ties to Obama aided in access for big utility', 2012; Mooney, 'Beware "sound science."', 2004.
32   Revkin and Seelye, 'Report by EPA leaves out data on climate change', 2003; Shabecoff, 'Scientist says budget office altered his testimony', 1989.
33   Sheppard, 'Perry officials censored climate change report', 2011.
34   Cillizza, 'Donald Trump buried a climate change report because "I don't believe it"', 2018; Davenport, 'EPA official pressured scientist on Congressional testimony, emails show', 2017.
35   Katz, 'EPA admits to altering science under Trump, pledges new course', 2021; EPA, 'Report: EPA deviated from typical procedures', 2021.
36   Brown, 'Feds reverse course on wolverine protections', 2014; *Defenders of Wildlife v. Jewell*, 2016.
37   Beder, *Global Spin*, 2002, 84–5, 118–19, 200–1, 267–73.
38   Barry, 'Politics won't stop the pandemic', 2020.
39   Z. Smith, *The Environmental Policy Paradox*, 2004, 128.
40   Flesher, 'AP Exclusive', 2015; Thomson et al., 'Green crime havens', 2020, 509–10.
41   Hirji, '40% of Wisconsin "frac sand" producers violated environmental rules, study says', 2014.
42   Collier, 'Federal judge rules against Formosa Plastics in pollution case', 2019; Fernández, 'Plastic company set to pay $50 million settlement in water pollution suit brought on by Texas residents', 2019.
43   Atlas, 'Enforcement principles and environmental agencies', 2007, 964.
44   Atlas, 'Enforcement principles and environmental agencies', 2007; Buzbee, 'Contextual environmental federalism', 2005; Flatt, 'Dirty river runs through it', 1997; Flatt and Collins, 'Environmental enforcement in dire straits', 2009; Natter, 'States move to roll back environmental rules in Trump's wake', 2019; Rosenbaum, *Environmental Politics and Policy*, 2002, 110–15.
45   Davenport and Southall, 'Critics say spill highlights lax West Virginia regulations', 2014; Duhigg, 'Clean water laws are neglected', 2009.
46   Environment Texas, 'Polluters spewed 63 million pounds of unauthorized air pollution in 2017', 2019; Phillips, 'Preparing for the next storm', 2018; Rust and Sahagún, 'Must reads', 2019.
47   Tresaugue, 'Court overturns EPA's cross-state pollution rule', 2012.
48   Duhigg, 'Clean water laws are neglected', 2009.
49   Lipton, 'Energy firms in secretive alliance with attorneys general', 2014.
50   John Ockels, Texas Illegal Dumping Resource Center, personal communication, 12 October 2021; Weale, *The New Politics of Pollution*, 1992, 17. See Kendall, 'Revealed', 2020 for a similar situation in a different context.

51 John Ockels, Texas Illegal Dumping Resource Center, personal communication, 12 October 2021.
52 Ockels, *Illegal Dumping Enforcement*, 2022, 242.
53 John Ockels, Texas Illegal Dumping Resource Center, personal communication, 12 October 2021.
54 Donahue, 'Western grazing', 2005; Nikiforuk, *Tar Sands*, 2010; C. Parker, 'The pipeline industry meets grief unimaginable', 2004, 247–50.
55 Elliott, 'Ex-regulator flacking for pro-nuke lobby', 2011.
56 Davenport, 'Counseled by industry', 2017; N. Miller, *Environmental Politics*, 2009, 55–7; Lipton, 'Energy firms in secretive alliance with attorneys general', 2014.
57 Anonymous, 'Energy executives question SMU-led quake study at Austin meeting', 2015; Thompson and Kuchment, 'Seismic denial?', 2016.
58 Mohr et al., 'BP's gulf oil spill response plan lists the walrus as a local species', 2010.
59 Obama, 'President Obama's Oval Office address on the BP oil spill', 2010.
60 Hogue, 'Reorganization of the Minerals Management Service in the aftermath of the Deepwater Horizon oil spill', 2010.
61 Yeoman, 'The inside story of Shell's Arctic assault', 2016.
62 Copeland, 'Mountaintop removal mining', 2016, 3.
63 S. Clark, 'In the shadow of the Fourth Circuit', 2008, 144; Palmer et al., 'Mountaintop mining consequences', 2010.
64 US Department of the Interior Office of Surface Mining Reclamation and Enforcement, 'Stream Protection Rule', n.d.

19
Conflicts with other societal objectives

Environmental problems result from an excessive scale of one or more actions. Too many greenhouse gas emissions. Too much aquifer pumping. Too much habitat loss. Consequently, environmental sustainability depends upon reducing the scale of harmful impacts, such as by avoiding logging adjacent to streams, shifting to clean renewable energy sources or reducing the nutrient content of treated wastewater. But even improved practices impact the environment. Therefore, if scales of activities increase more than the environmental impacts of those activities decline, cumulative environmental damage increases despite reduction of impact from the individual activities. For example, if average fuel efficiency of gasoline-powered cars improves but the number of miles driven by such cars increases even more, cumulative gas consumption and greenhouse gas emissions from cars increase despite improved fuel efficiency. Sometimes major design changes – such as electric cars run on renewable energy, efficient public transportation, or the ability of employees to work from home – achieve revolutionary reductions in the environmental impact of a good or service, but even then, the benefit of greening practices can be overwhelmed if the scale of activities increases dramatically.

Increases in scale are a major obstacle to environmental progress because society routinely seeks to increase the scale of activities. In particular, efforts to increase wealth or welfare through increases in economic activity routinely and unintentionally have the 'side-effect' of increasing environmental impacts. Moreover, those who seek to protect the environment and those who seek to improve the functioning of the economy often fail to coordinate their efforts.[1]

Separate agencies, departments, and organizations specialize in energy, land, food, air, water, wildlife, economy, finance, building regulations, urban policy, technology, health, and transportation – as if each were unrelated to the others. So, one agency pushes hard to grow the economy while another is charged to clean up the resulting mess and so forth, which is to say that the right hand and left hand seldom knows – or cares – what the other is doing. The results are often counter-productive, overly expensive, risky, sometimes disastrous, and most always ironic.[2]

Economic growth

Need for jobs and desire for increased individual wealth and general welfare create demand for increased economic production. Those who lack employment or have inadequate employment need better employment. The poor need basic needs met. Others wish to satisfy more wants.

There are two ways to meet the material needs of the poor – transfer wealth among individuals or increase overall economic production. Wealth transfers are controversial because they depend upon drawing from some individuals (in the form of taxes or fees) to provide for others. Increased economic production, on the other hand, at least seems to have potential to make everyone wealthier.[3]

A desire to meet basic needs is only one of several motivations for increased economic production. A perhaps more powerful force is demand for increased wealth from those whose basic needs have been met. Furthermore, corporations seek increased sales, both for the sake of stockholders and profits and because their ability to attract employees depends on offering prospects of rapid promotion up an expanding corporate hierarchy. Finally, population growth creates yet further motivation for economic growth lest a growing number of potential workers suffer unemployment and the same amount of goods and services be divided among more people.

Economic growth has been associated with important improvements in quality of life, such as clean drinking water, effective sanitation systems, more comfortable housing, and reductions in toxic air pollutants (for the latter see Figure 1.2, p. 4). Many such changes resulted from prioritizing federal investment in public health aspects of environmental quality (thanks to environmental laws passed in the 1960s, 1970s, and 1980s).

More generally, however, increased economic production has caused increased resource consumption and waste production. Edward Ayres illustrated why this is so with the example of a simple cup of coffee.[4]

Consumption of two cups of coffee per day requires about seven kilograms of beans per year, or the combined output of 18 coffee plants. As with most other agriculture, natural ecosystems are largely or entirely removed to provide space for coffee bushes, so one impact of the coffee is loss of native vegetation, ecosystems, and their ecosystem services.[5] Conventional growers typically spray coffee bushes with pesticides several times per year, causing multiple undesirable consequences. Pesticides typically kill non-target organisms and may leach into waterways where they do more damage. Farmworkers may inhale them or otherwise be exposed, and their production pollutes air and water. Meanwhile, processing each kilogram of beans results in about two kilograms of pulp that may be dumped in a local river where its decomposition will foster eutrophication, deplete oxygen, and harm aquatic species. Later, freighters transporting beans burn bunker fuel, a particularly dirty form of fuel oil, while marketers and purveyors fly in airplanes and work in climate-controlled offices and cafés. The coffee itself is often sold in bags that have both plastic and metal layers, a combination that renders the bags unrecyclable. Brewing coffee consumes energy. The grounds make great compost, but some people dispose of them with trash, where they often end up in a landfill, decomposing anaerobically as microbes convert their carbon to methane, a strong greenhouse gas. Others dump grounds down garbage disposal units in kitchen sinks, converting them into water pollution or increasing the work of wastewater treatment systems. Finally, washing cups consumes detergent and energy to heat water, produces wastewater and, depending on the energy source, air pollution.

As coffee consumption increases, so do all of these impacts. Coffee consumption is just one of countless products and processes that have increased with population and economic growth. A little reflection will identify similar lists of impacts from other products. (The relatively new fields of industrial ecology and [product and process] life-cycle assessment employ professionals who attempt to rigorously and quantitatively identify all environmental impacts of a product or process and use that information to inform efforts to devise less-damaging alternatives.)

Communities occasionally resist economic growth. For example, whereas cities often compete to attract the Olympics, Colorado voters opposed Denver's bid to host the 1976 Winter Olympics due to concerns about added alpine infrastructure. On a smaller scale, residents of Petoskey, Michigan opposed local road expansions due to concerns about attendant increases in traffic and environmental damage. Both areas sought to protect their environmental quality.[6] Examples like these are, however, relatively rare exceptions to the rule.

Business leaders and politicians routinely advocate for, encourage, and in the case of politicians, often subsidize conventional economic growth. Individuals and political parties may disagree about the best policies to foster such growth, but the objective of growth generally receives strong bipartisan support – a dynamic that is not limited to capitalist democracies. Indeed, cities, states and even nations compete to attract businesses by offering tax exemptions, infrastructure and other incentives. This attitude was captured when presidential candidate John Kasich argued: 'Economic growth is the key to everything.'[7]

As we saw in the discussion of a systems perspective (Chapter 2), efforts to increase economic production create a positive feedback where demand for more goods and services leads to the production of new goods and services, the marketing of which fosters further demand for yet more goods and services. For the purposes of this chapter, the key point is that increased production of all of those goods and services has historically caused increased resource consumption and waste production, and those increases can overwhelm simultaneous environmental protection efforts.

Figure 19.1, for example, shows how greenhouse gas emissions per dollar of gross domestic product declined by 50 per cent since 1960 as processes became more fuel efficient and thus less carbon intensive, but the same figure shows today's total greenhouse gas emissions are almost four times the 1960 quantity. In other words, consumption of materials and consequent production of greenhouse gases increased much more than the efficiency of that consumption and production improved.

The impacts of individual products, such as coffee, combined with increases in their production, result in strong correlations between economic output and environmental impacts.[8] Figure 19.2 shows how greenhouse gas emissions from various economic sectors correlate with per capita economic production. As economies have grown, resource consumption and waste production have increased.

As the coffee example illustrates, the wastes we personally throw in the trash are a small fraction of the waste our consumption causes. Individuals typically produce about two kilograms of garbage (or more technically, municipal waste) per day, but that does not include wastes produced in supplying raw materials or manufacturing, transporting, marketing, trading, consuming and recycling of products. The collective magnitude of those wastes is incredible but rarely estimated.

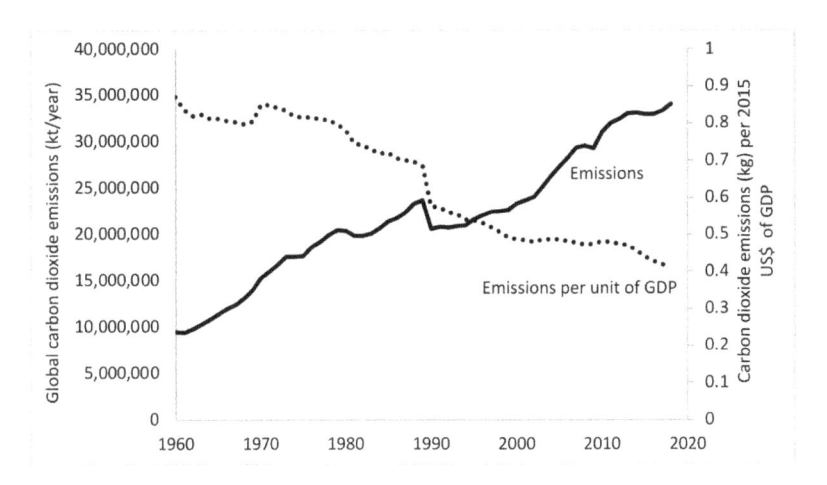

Figure 19.1: Worldwide annual greenhouse gas emissions from burning fossil fuels and cement production (solid line) and the same variable per US dollar of 2015 gross domestic product (GDP) (dotted line). Data source: World Bank, 'CO2 emissions (kt)' (https://data.worldbank.org/indicator/EN.ATM.CO2E.KT) and 'CO2 emissions (kg per 2015 US$ of GDP)' (https://data.worldbank.org/indicator/EN.ATM.CO2E.KD.GD). Emissions per dollar of GDP have declined but total emissions have nevertheless increased.

Two research teams independently tallied per capita US waste production around 1990. Both estimated the sum as about 150 kilograms per person per day, not including water. Seventy-five per cent of that was overburden from coal mining, but even without coal mining, the average would have been more than 30 kilograms per person per day, or roughly one's weight in waste every couple of days. A subsequent study that involved one of the same authors calculated some 180 kilograms per person per day as of 2000.[9]

Major innovations sometimes dramatically reduce the environmental impacts of some types of production. For example, scientists at the Land Institute are working to grow perennial grains that would avoid the annual ploughing and soil erosion associated with growing corn, wheat and rice. Similarly, the Savory Institute, Holistic Management International, and others work on developing livestock grazing practices that restore, rather than damage, range vegetation and soil health.[10]

In other cases, innovations reduce one sort of impact but increase another. Over a century ago, the shift from horses for urban transportation to internal combustion engines freed cities from tremendous quantities of

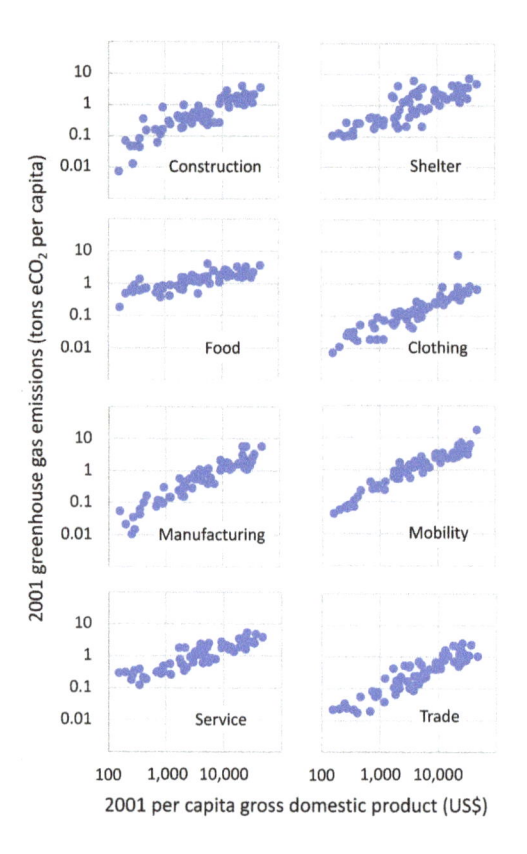

Figure 19.2: Greenhouse gas emissions (2001 tons of CO_2 equivalent per capita) of various economic sectors in various countries as a function of per capita expenditures. Each point represents one nation. Source: Redrawn from the data used for Figure 3 of Hertwich and Peters, 'Carbon footprint of nations: a global, trade-linked analysis', 2009, 6418. Requests for further permission to reuse this figure or its contents should be directed to the American Chemical Society.

manure. However, the new motors caused different environmental impacts of their own. Sometimes such trade-offs represent an improvement. If today's fleet of personal vehicles is completely converted to electric or hydrogen-powered engines run on solar energy, the number of cars on the road could increase while gas consumption, like horse manure before it, dramatically declines. But as with the shift from horses to internal combustion engines, other types of consumption will increase, such as the demand for, and environmental damage associated with, mining of rare earths and other metals used in electric motors and batteries. (This shift seems necessary and desirable despite the environmental impacts of electric vehicles.)

In theory, modern economies could evolve to emulate natural ecosystems – running entirely on current solar energy and producing only materials that can be recycled, composted or directly returned to the environment in harmless form. Necessity dictates that we make this transition, and the sooner the better. The relatively young field of industrial ecology takes natural ecosystems' dependence on solar energy and thorough material recycling as a model and goal. Industrial ecologists have achieved much in just a few decades, and their approach has tremendous potential for further progress, which will be necessary to break free from dependence on depletion of both renewable and non-renewable resources, and non-sustainable waste production.

While industrial ecologists, life-cycle analysts, and others help us emulate natural ecosystems' reliance on current solar energy and comprehensive materials cycling, those of us interested in reducing environmental impacts must remember that as long as processes have harmful environmental impacts, increases in the scale of those processes have potential to overwhelm other environmental progress. In other words, improved efficiencies alone cannot achieve sustainability if the scales of activities increase faster than efficiencies improve.

Free trade

International trade is one contributor to increases in the scale of economic activity. The implications of international trade are complex and controversial, but, like economic growth, free international trade has been widely supported by proponents of various political philosophies. For example, prior to the Trump Administration, both Democratic and Republican presidents routinely worked to increase international free trade agreements. The motivations for international trade include potential for increasing economic production in trading countries and a chance that trading partners are less likely to go to war against each other.[11] Meanwhile, individual economic actors, such as corporations, often favour free trade because trade can increase their markets and thus profits, and many economists favour free trade because they expect resulting competition among producers to improve the quality of products while reducing consumer prices.

A thorough discussion of international trade and its implications is beyond our scope,[12] but trade cannot be entirely ignored here because international trade agreements create obstacles to national environmental progress. International trade is largely regulated by the World Trade Organization (WTO). WTO rules generally forbid imposition of tariffs due to production methods in exporting nations. For example, importing countries cannot impose tariffs on products from countries that employ child labour. The basic rationale is that such tariffs could be concocted by importing countries when the real motivation is protection of domestic industries from international competition.[13]

WTO rules create an obstacle to environmental progress because disallowance of tariffs based on production practices disincentivizes domestic environmental protection. If one nation proposes to protect, for example, its waters by regulating waste from factories, its manufacturers may argue the regulations would be unfair because foreign corporations would not have to meet the same standards and would therefore enjoy lower manufacturing costs. Those lower costs would enable foreign corporations to undercut domestic producers' prices such that domestic manufacturers might go bankrupt, putting their employees out of work.

The US Senate's Byrd-Hagel resolution opposing the 1997 Kyoto Protocol exemplified this concern. The Kyoto Protocol set limits on greenhouse gas emissions for wealthy countries, but not 'developing' countries. That year, the Senate voted 95 to 0 in opposition to the Kyoto Protocol. The Senate resolution included the following passage.

> Whereas the [United Nations Framework] Convention [on Climate Change], intended to address climate change on a global basis, identifies the former Soviet Union and the countries of Eastern Europe and the Organization For Economic Co-operation and Development (OECD), including the US, as 'Annex I Parties', and the remaining 129 countries, including China, Mexico, India, Brazil, and South Korea, as 'Developing Country Parties' ... Whereas the 'Berlin Mandate' calls for the adoption, as soon as December 1997, in Kyoto, Japan, of a protocol or another legal instrument that strengthens commitments to limit greenhouse gas emissions by Annex I Parties for the post-2000 period ... Whereas the 'Berlin Mandate' specifically exempts all Developing Country Parties from any new commitments in such negotiation process ... the Senate strongly believes that the proposals under negotiation, because of the disparity of treatment between Annex I and Developing Countries and the level of required emission reductions, could result in serious harm to the US economy, including significant job

loss, trade disadvantages, increased energy and consumer costs, or any combination thereof ...

Byrd-Hagel Resolution
105th Congress, 1st Session, Senate Resolution 98, 25 June 1997

The senators objected to the US being bound by commitments to reduce greenhouse gas emissions if developing countries were not also required to reduce emissions. They feared this disparity would give an economic advantage to other nations and therefore cause economic problems for the US. Even though a majority of senators had previously endorsed an earlier UN Convention that called upon signatories to develop policies to limit greenhouse gas emissions, no senator voted in favour of an agreement they perceived would disadvantage the US in international trade.

Though the senators seemed confident that the protocol would have put domestic industries at a competitive disadvantage, whether strong domestic environmental policy generally has this effect is unclear. Strong environmental laws might actually benefit producers, for instance by spurring innovation that leads to resource use efficiency and therefore reduces long-term costs. Moreover, other factors, such as labour costs, government stability and transport costs may be more important to business finances. A 2015 review suggests various authors have reached disparate conclusions regarding how domestic environmental regulation affects competitiveness.[14]

For our purposes, the actual economic effect of international differences in environmental regulations may be less important than perceived differences because perceptions can serve as an obstacle to domestic environmental protection. Ten years after the Byrd-Hagel resolution, the US Chamber of Commerce argued that climate change legislation proposed by senators Lieberman and Warner (2007) would give an unfair advantage to corporations operating in other nations – precisely the same argument that had been made by the 95 senators who voiced their opposition to the Kyoto Protocol a decade earlier. Such sentiments consistently motivate opposition to anti-pollution efforts.[15]

The track record of WTO decisions reveals subtle distinctions regarding when the organization approves of domestic environmental regulations versus when it authorizes retaliatory tariffs in response to such rules. That leaves future WTO decisions hard to predict, which causes concern that new domestic environmental laws might result in retaliatory tariffs upon national exports.

An instructive WTO case involves tuna fishing methods. Bottlenose dolphins often school at the surface of the ocean above yellowfin tuna. Some boat captains, aware of this behaviour, fish for tuna in the vicinity of the dolphins. Dolphins end up being killed in their nets. In response to public concerns about dolphin deaths, the US imposed an embargo on tuna imports from nations that used this fishing technique. Mexico objected, arguing that trade rules prohibited import restrictions based on production methods. A 1991 decision by the WTO's predecessor found in favour of Mexico, though the finding was never implemented because rules were being renegotiated at the time. Shortly thereafter, the US and several tuna-fishing nations entered into a separate multilateral agreement regarding tuna fishing methods and the US devised rules for labelling tuna 'dolphin safe'. However, later in 2013 the US lost a subsequent WTO dispute with Mexico which concluded the US labels violated WTO rules. Yet later, after a subsequent US labelling change in 2016, the WTO concluded the US was no longer out of compliance with WTO rules.[16] The relevance of this example for our purposes is that labels are far weaker measures than import bans, so the WTO rulings weakened US policy intended to protect dolphins.

A similar consequence resulted in 1996 when the EU sought to ban imports of US beef from cattle treated with certain hormones. The WTO ruled that there was inadequate evidence to conclude the meat was harmful and awarded the US retaliatory tariffs of some $120 million. Subsequently, in 2003, the EU argued it had provided more and sufficient evidence of harm, but again the WTO deemed the scientific evidence inadequate and reauthorized the penalty. (Recall earlier discussions about scientific uncertainty and type II statistical errors.) Finally, in 2009 the EU and the US agreed to a system where the EU would prohibit the imports but the US would impose retaliatory tariffs in compensation.[17] Here again, a WTO decision penalized national (or in this case EU) environmental protections.

More recent WTO decisions have had the same basic effect of disincentivizing strong national environmental laws. During 2008, Canada objected to US laws requiring that pork and beef be labelled with their country of origin. The WTO panel found the label requirement amounted to a technical barrier to trade and was thus unacceptable. On appeal in 2012, an appellate panel confirmed the initial decision on the basis that the labelling requirement 'has a detrimental impact on imported livestock because its recordkeeping and verification requirements create an incentive for processors to use exclusively domestic livestock'. In 2015, the WTO authorized Canada to retaliate. Thus, even though the US law made no production process requirements, but merely sought to provide source information to consumers, the WTO found the law unacceptable due to the record-keeping burden.[18]

Yet more recently, during 2019 the WTO ruled against a US state law designed to encourage domestic green energy production. Given its prior rulings, the WTO not surprisingly sided with India in their objection to a Michigan law that would have given renewable energy generators extra credit if they used Michigan labourers or equipment manufactured in the state.[19]

Recent WTO documents suggest sensitivity to the need to reconcile environmental protection and trade concerns, and describe a desire of some members for more emphasis on environmental sustainability,[20] but the history of WTO decisions and the tentative nature of the more recent documents leave reason to wonder how WTO panels would rule in future cases. Thus, the risk of retaliatory tariffs continues to create an obstacle to domestic environmental protections.

Other trade agreements also hinder strong domestic environmental policy. In particular, so-called 'investor–state dispute settlement provisions' in various bilateral and multilateral trade agreements (such as the former North American Free Trade Agreement and its successor the US–Mexico–Canada Agreement) allow foreign investors to sue importing nations if importing nations' policies discriminate against foreign investors' potential to profit.

When the Obama Administration rejected the proposed Keystone XL tar sands pipeline, which was intended to move fossil fuels from Alberta in Canada to Texas in the United States, TransCanada, the corporation that planned to build the pipeline, invoked the North American Free Trade Agreement's investor–state dispute settlement provisions to sue the US for $15 billion. That suit was dropped when the Trump Administration later approved the pipeline, but a new suit, again seeking $15 billion, was filed when the Biden Administration again blocked the pipeline. Commentators suspected the US would have lost the initial lawsuit as other nations have lost similar challenges.[21]

Enthusiasm for trade agreements that disincentivize domestic environmental protection may be waning. The Obama Administration participated in negotiations to develop a trade agreement that, if finalized, would have been called the Trans-Pacific Partnership. The draft agreement included investor–state dispute settlement provisions. When those provisions gained publicity, tremendous opposition developed, at least partially out of concern for the effect of such provisions on domestic US environmental policy. By the time of the next presidential election in

2016, both major candidates, Donald Trump and Hillary Clinton, expressed opposition to the Trans-Pacific Partnership.[22] The Trump Administration subsequently refused to sign the agreement and the Biden Administration's trade representative, Katherine Tai, has called for focusing trade rules on climate change concerns.[23]

Imagine the potential environmental benefits if future WTO decisions and other international trade agreements allowed restrictions on trade for the sake of protecting the environment. Tariffs on products from countries with weak environmental laws would eliminate the cost disadvantages of industries in nations with strong regulations. Moreover, and perhaps even more importantly, allowing tariffs based on production practices might replace the 'race to the bottom' (forcing a focus on price) that WTO policy currently encourages with a 'race to the top' (privileging the best environmental practices) as nations that lack strong environmental protections improve their environmental standards to avoid more progressive countries' tariffs. But such is not yet the case, and thus existing free trade rules create an obstacle to strong domestic environmental protection, both in the US and elsewhere.

In the long-term, when the environment collapses, economies collapse, as occurred on Easter Island and in Mesopotamia, the Indus Valley, the Roman breadbasket of North Africa, and elsewhere.[24] In the short term, however, environmental protection routinely conflicts with, and is overwhelmed by, other societal objectives, especially economic growth. Therefore, those who propose further environmental protection must not only demonstrate reason for concern, marshal a consensus for action and devise suitable responses; proponents of protection must explain why further environmental protection is worth any trade-offs that restrict other societal objectives. Protection of whales must be worthwhile despite impacts on the Navy's abilities to detect submarines. Restriction of the spread of invasive species must be worth encumbrances on international trade and travel. Protection of pollinators must be worth consequences for agricultural methods. More generally, restrictions on environmental impacts must be seen as worth any concomitant reductions in conventional economic growth because reducing per-unit environmental impacts will not suffice if those improvements are overwhelmed by increases in the cumulative scale of activities.

Notes

1   Other activities can also interfere with or prevent environmental progress. Perhaps most notably, environmental progress can be infeasible or reversed in active conflict zones and areas that lack stable governance (International Union for the Conservation of Nature, 'Conflict and conservation', 2021).

2   Orr, 'Systems thinking and the future of cities', 2014.

3   General welfare does not necessarily correlate with economic production, as conventionally measured by gross domestic product (GDP) or gross national product (GNP). Welfare may even decline as economic production increases. Recognizing the limitations of GDP as a measure of welfare, a succession of refinements has been devised, including Bhutan's effort to track Gross National Happiness (Aitken, 'Measuring welfare beyond GDP', 2019; Managi, 'Accounting for the inclusive wealth of nations', 2018, 3–6; Schultz, 'In Bhutan, happiness index as gauge for social ills', 2017).

4   E. Ayres, 'The history of a cup of coffee', 1994.

5   Shade-grown coffee is a bit less harmful in this regard. Shade-grown cultivation involves leaving some tropical rainforest trees growing amongst coffee bushes.

6   Moore, 'When Denver rejected the Olympics in favour of the environment and economics', 2015; Puit, 'Existing roads', 2007; Puit, 'Survey finds little support for new roads', 2007.

7   John Kasich, Governor of Ohio 2011–19, quoted in *Washington Post*, 'Annotated transcript', 2015.

8   Hertwich and Peters, 'Carbon footprint of nations', 2009; Weinzettel et al., 'Affluence drives the global displacement of land use', 2013.

9   R. Ayres, 'Use of materials balances to estimate aggregate waste generation in the US', 1999, 150–1; Wernick and Ausubel, 'National material metrics for industrial ecology', 1999, 158; Rogich et al., *Materials Flows in the US*, 2008, 10. Such analyses require a tremendous amount of work. I am not aware of a more recent estimate. Entire government agencies exist to tally all manner of economic production, but tallies of waste production have depended on a few scholars with the knowledge and skills to combine economic and chemical engineering data to calculate production of all forms of waste.

10   Holistic Management International, 'Healthy land, healthy food, healthy lives', n.d.; Land Institute, 'Transforming agriculture, perennially', n.d.; Savory Institute, 'Our mission', n.d.

11   Conflicting schools of thought disagree about the actual effects of trade on international conflict. The political science literature includes dozens, or maybe even hundreds, of theoretical and empirical analyses of the question. The topic is too complex for a simple yes or no conclusion. See the following articles for an introduction to the question: Cohen, 'Economic ties among nations spur peace. Or do they?', 2022; Krugman, 'Trade and peace', 2022.

12   Various authors raise concerns that, rather than raising well-being of people in all trading nations, international trade can trap some countries in production of low-value commodities that disadvantage the long-term trajectories of their economies, may disadvantage lower-wage workers in trading nations, and reduce self sufficiency, as was apparent when supply chains broke down during the COVID-19 pandemic in 2021. See for example discussions in: Daly and Cobb, *For the Common Good*, 1989, 209–35 and Ponting, *A New Green History of the World*, 2007, 171–98.

13   McBride et al., 'What's next for the WTO?', 2021.

14   D'Agostino, 'How MNEs respond to environmental regulation', 2015.

15   Carroll, '"With certainty" cap-and-trade would wreck the economy, Rubio says', 2015; Miller, *Cases in Environmental Politics*, 2009, 173–5; Selin and VanDeveer, 'Global climate change', 2013, 288.

16   Inter-American Tropical Tuna Commission, 'International Dolphin Conservation Program (IDCP)', 2016; Miles, 'Mexico loses 10-year WTO battle over US tuna labeling', 2018; WTO, 'Mexico etc versus US: "tuna-dolphin"', n.d.; WTO, 'US – restrictions on imports of tuna', 1994.

17   WTO, 'DS26: European communities – measures concerning meat and meat products (hormones)', n.d.

18   WTO, 'DS384: US – certain country of origin labelling (COOL) requirements', n.d.

19   Tucker, 'There's a big new headache for the Green New Deal', 2019.

20 Okonjo-Iweala, 'Launch event of ministerial statements on trade, environment and sustainable development', 2021; WTO Committee on Trade and the Environment, 'Communication on trade and environmental sustainability', 2021.

21 Tucker, 'TransCanada is suing the US over Obama's rejection of the Keystone KL pipeline', 2016; Zacks Equity Research, 'TC Energy (TRP) files $15B suit against U.S. over Keystone XL', 2021.

22 Taylor, 'A timeline of Trump's complicated relationship with the TPP', 2018; Warren, 'The Trans-Pacific Partnership clause everyone should oppose', 2015.

23 Reuters and Andrea Shalal, 'USTR Tai calls for bold action to put climate at center of trade policy', 2021.

24 Dale and Carter, *Topsoil and Civilization*, 1955; Ponting, *A New Green History of the World*, 2007, 67–86.

20
Recapitulation, reasons for optimism, and recommendations

Improvements in US air and water pollution since the 1960s demonstrate that major environmental progress is possible. But such success requires sustained effort to overcome numerous obstacles. As explained in Chapter 1, I perceive three sets of obstacles: limits on our ability to understand and control the world around us; obstacles rooted in value systems that deprioritize environmental protection, and the obstacles discussed in this book (those immediate, practical factors often held responsible when environmental efforts fail). Real progress will require addressing all three sets: advancing predictive and management ability towards their ultimate limits; shifting societal norms such that more and more people prioritize environmental protection and recovery; and systematically overcoming the immediate obstacles to progress on existing environmental problems.

Recapitulation

The first requirement for progress on an existing problem is recognition that the problem exists, but so far, we have not been systematically on the lookout for new problems, and some problems are difficult to detect even when we try. Meanwhile, despite a history of unpleasant surprises such as stratospheric ozone depletion, we cavalierly continue to adopt new technologies with precious little analysis, only to later encounter unanticipated 'side effects'.

Once a problem has been detected, its cause or causes must be identified, but this is often difficult. Complexities of human and ecosystem health; ethical, logistical and financial constraints on experiments; and limitations of analytical procedures individually and collectively obscure causes. Meanwhile, controversy frequently surrounds appropriate data interpretation, especially when extrapolating from particular studies to general circumstances. Collectively, limitations on experiments, uncertainties of extrapolation and the possibility of scientific errors result in tentative conclusions, not certain predictions. Fortunately, despite these challenges, expert consensus eventually coalesces regarding the causes and significance of a new problem.

Once such consensus develops, several political barriers then hinder action. Scientists' hedged conclusions leave members of the public confused about whether a problem exists or its causes are understood. This is especially so because media reports, in seeking to tell both sides of the story, give disproportionate attention to minority judgements, and because those opposed to action exaggerate uncertainty. Meanwhile, proposed restrictions on activities engender resistance from vested interests and those who perceive such infringements as restrictions on freedoms.

Free-market enthusiasts contend environmental protection is economically inefficient and unnecessary because an unfettered market can overcome almost any problem. Though such a default position is hard to defend, it will be made, either by true believers in unfettered free markets or by others whose real motive is to protect their ability to engage in profitable activities responsible for the problem at hand. In the course of such debates, environmental proposals will be critiqued with simplistic, biased cost–benefit analyses.

Even if proposed efforts pass cost–benefit analyses, they may not be implemented if required funds are not forthcoming or other issues are perceived as more urgent and thus enjoy political priority. If an environmental issue does receive attention and a consensus for action develops, those interests that stand to be regulated will work to block the passage of new laws, an easier task than passing them. Moreover, opponents of environmental protection will usually enjoy much better funding than those who seek environmental progress.

Even when sufficient support for action exists despite the above obstacles, several other hurdles remain to be overcome. It is often difficult to design effective procedures or policies that would not have their own undesirable, unintended consequences. Once designs are proposed, opponents will seek to inject compromises that may doom effectiveness. Or, the geographical extent of the problem may not align with political jurisdictions, in which case there may be no entity with clear responsibility for and authority over the problem.

If potentially effective laws and regulations are passed and promulgated, inadequate implementation budgets, opposition to effective implementation, or political incentives for lax implementation or enforcement may cause breakdowns in implementation. Finally, environmental protection efforts often conflict with other societal objectives, especially efforts to foster traditional economic growth and international trade. So far, these other objectives have usually been given priority, often resulting in increasing scales of activities that overwhelm the benefits of new environmental protections or improved technical efficiencies.

Reasons for optimism

Reading through the many obstacles could give an inaccurate impression of hopelessness, especially if one focuses on US federal policy since the 1990s. Indeed, I know many students observe the record during their short lifetimes and struggle to resist the conclusion that problems are overwhelming. If you are inclined towards that conclusion, it may be helpful to remember that environmental problems had millennia to grow into today's resource depletion, destruction of biodiversity, habitat loss, global-scale pollution, climate change and other problems.[1] By contrast, it has been only about a century since popular support for environmental protection became widespread, and in the meantime, there have been two world wars and various other major concerns. Thus, the environmental sustainability that our indigenous ancestors apparently prioritized is effectively a new idea to be relearned by industrialized, agricultural societies. By the scale of a bristlecone pine's lifetime, striving for environmental sustainability in an industrial society is a brand-new concept.

Such a shift does not happen quickly, but it may be starting. Less than two centuries ago, the lifetime of an oak, a Pennsylvania railroad company commissioned George Inness's painting of trains and factories belching smoke amid clearcuts as if to suggest prosperity (Figure 20.1). Only one century ago (not that long — my mother celebrated her one hundredth birthday the week I wrote this), Aldo Leopold noted that many still considered a tree stump a sign of progress.[2] Early 1960s municipal guidance instructed citizens to dump refuse adjacent to a waterway (Figure 1.1, p. 3), while a prominent magazine recommended pouring used motor oil into the ground (Figure 20.2). Such actions are considered abhorrent today, only a few decades later. Indeed, wide majorities support

Figure 20.1: *The Lackawanna Valley* by George Inness c. 1856. Oil on canvas, 86 × 127.5 cm. Source: National Gallery of Art, Washington, DC (1945.4.1).

environmental protection, at least in principle.[3] And the evolution of views and norms continues: we still send burned fossil fuel into the atmosphere, but that causes angst today and before long may be considered as ghastly as pouring oil on the ground or dumping at the water's edge.

The present stalemate in Washington is discouraging, but federal policy is among the hardest to shift. A longer historical view and a more comprehensive assessment that includes other nations, selected US states, municipalities, corporations, industries and non-governmental organizations provides much more reason for hope. Worldwide, countless institutions and individuals have been overcoming all of the obstacles they have encountered and making inspiring progress.

A bit of internet searching produces extensive lists of remarkable examples, such as the recipients of the Goldman and Tyler prizes.[4] Any list of names I give will only be partial, but if you seek inspiration or encouragement, you could read about the successes of Jane Goodall, Kimiko Hirata, Sharon Lavigne, Gene Likens, Wangari Maathai, David Schindler, Greta Thunberg or countless others. These people persisted or still persist today despite any obstacles, as have those involved in the following, less-well-known cases with which I happen to be familiar. As with the people listed above, those involved in each of the following cases

Disposing of used engine oil can be a problem. Solution: Dig a hole in the ground with a posthole digger and fill it with fine gravel. Then pour in the oil. It will be absorbed into the ground before your next change. Cover the spot with soil.

166 POPULAR SCIENCE JANUARY 1963

Figure 20.2: Early 1960s recommendation for motor oil disposal. Reproduced with permission of *Popular Science* magazine. Of course, the magazine would not recommend such a procedure today; many recent *Popular Science* articles explore more sustainable options. Source: *Popular Science*, 'Hints from the model garage', 1963, 166.

identified a problem and its causes, marshalled community cooperation and support for responding (including financial support), and then devised and implemented an effective response, overcoming each obstacle they encountered in the process. Moreover, I am not aware of any of these cases causing undesirable, unintended consequences.

As a young man, J. David Bamberger read Louis Bromfield's account of restoring a farm to its former productivity.[5] Bamberger dreamt of doing the same for a degraded ranch. Five decades ago, he purchased the most damaged ranch he could find in the central Texas hill country and, with a few full-time employees and a handful of others, began working 'with mother nature instead of against her'.[6] Eventually donated to a non-profit foundation he created, the ranch preserve named Selah has grown to 2,200 hectares and been transformed into one of the finest US examples of ecosystem restoration.[7]

Where the ground was formerly covered with caliche (mineral sediment exposed after soil erosion) and invasive ashe juniper trees that together caused most rain to run off, soil and native vegetation are recovering. With the return of deep-rooted, perennial grasses, the land once again captures rainwater. When Bamberger began there was no surface water, and seven 150-metre wells he drilled reached no water at all. He and his crew have worked constantly since then, among other things wearing out dozens of chainsaws removing the invasive trees.[8]

Today, with the vegetation again capturing rainfall and enabling it to percolate, eleven springs feed several small lakes and ponds. Some springs flow even during the most severe droughts. The rainwater infiltration facilitated by restored grass has enabled the return of hundreds of species of wildlife, supplies the few families who live at the ranch and even contributes to the Austin, Texas water supply. More than 150 bird species have returned, deer grow approximately twice as large as before, and the ranch has the potential to support twice as many cattle as previously (if Bamberger and his team chose to do so). Meanwhile, numerous scientists and thousands of visitors use the property as a research site and outdoor education centre each year.

This was all possible because Bamberger prioritized ecosystem restoration, identified the causes of ecosystem damage, attracted support for the project and devised and implemented creative, effective means of fostering vegetation recovery that did not require massive resource inputs or expense. Meanwhile, he was determined and therefore stuck with it, along the way accumulating a team of like-minded collaborators.

Also in Texas, Dr John Ockels detected a problem (various types of illegal dumping), identified its causes (which were numerous), recognized that existing prohibitions were not being enforced, and devised an effective response. He saw an opportunity to clean up and prevent pollution by helping municipal officials and others learn and implement the state's public health, nuisance and environmental laws. Virtually singlehandedly, and with a remarkable ability to quickly develop rapport with people from all sorts of backgrounds and perspectives, he created the Texas Illegal Dumping Resource Center and began teaching classes to anyone who would listen, from city managers, to county commissioners, police officers, sheriff's deputies, prosecutors, local civic groups, oil company employees and others.[9] Since developing his first course on illegal dumping in 1997, he has created a dozen related courses on environmental topics.

Some fifteen thousand participants have attended those courses. His students include not only municipal officials all over the huge state, but also many civic volunteers and employees of companies who wish to ensure their operations comply with regulations. All of his courses are approved for State of Texas continuing education credits. Given that he has educated thousands of people around the state on how to use existing laws to prevent and clean up various forms and sources of pollution, and most of these people have professional responsibilities to ensure such work is done, he may have done as much as anyone for pollution prevention in Texas (which has a population approximately equal to the Benelux countries but spread over an area larger than France). Like Bamberger, Ockels deserved to retire long ago, but he persists. Like Bamberger, he recognized a need and an opportunity, devised a creative response that leverages his own effort, developed a feasible and economical funding mechanism, and has never quit. Perhaps one of you will take over for him and ensure that his small but so effective organization continues to thrive and is replicated elsewhere.

A little farther north in Kansas, the Land Institute breeds perennial grains.[10] This effort, the brainchild of Dr Wes Jackson, has the potential to transform agriculture, thereby reducing multiple environmental problems. Grains, especially corn, wheat and rice, provide the bulk of human calories.[11] Because all three are annuals (completing their life cycle within one year), fields must be prepared and planted every growing season. That preparation often leaves bare soil exposed to wind and water erosion for many months each year. Even when annual grains are growing, their short, young roots do little to hold what soil remains, while leaving the plants vulnerable to drought.

Jackson realized perennial grains could obviate the need for annual ploughing, planting and cultivating, thereby reducing fuel consumption. Meanwhile, deeper roots would hold soil and impart drought resistance. If grown with legumes, whose symbiotic bacteria capture nitrogen from air, perennial grains might even reduce the need for fertilizer. But wild perennials tend to produce much smaller seed crops than long-since domesticated annuals.

Whereas generations of ecologists learned that a plant could maximize investment in seeds or roots but not both, Jackson realized that was only a broad generalization. Annual plants, such as corn, wheat and rice, have limited potential for both because they complete their life cycle within a single year. But long-lived perennials have the potential to grow extensive, deep roots and also produce large crops of seeds. He and his collaborators thus began hybridizing and selectively breeding various grasses and wildflowers, and have continued ever since. He has also masterfully advocated for this approach, and devoted his life's effort to making it happen. As a consequence, since the 1970s, the Land Institute has capitalized on his insight to experimentally breed perennials that produce large crops of edible seeds. Along the way, they have attracted both financial supporters and scientific collaborators all around the world who are multiplying their successes.

When he spoke at Austin College, Jackson suggested one's goals should be bigger than what one can accomplish in a single lifetime. He certainly set such a goal for himself – transforming agriculture. That task is not yet finished, but today one can bake bread with perennial grain developed at the Land Institute.[12] Before long, foods from multiple perennial grasses and wildflowers may be widely available.

Yet farther north, in the area where Lakes Huron and Michigan meet, the dedicated volunteers and few staff of the Little Traverse Conservancy have protected more than 25,000 hectares of land of unusually high conservation value, largely by working with private landowners who donate or sell deed restrictions called conservation easements.[13] Conservation easements transfer land development rights to a land trust, in this case the Conservancy, thereby preventing future real estate development and ensuring conservation of the properties even after they change hands. The Conservancy capitalizes on the combination of landowners' interests in conservation plus tax reductions that result from easement donations, but the required formal documentation is substantial. The small but tireless group of Conservancy staff have helped landowners understand the potential and benefits of the easements, guided owners through the steps required for a donation, and in the process leveraged their modest budgets to conserve a tremendous amount of land in a manner affordable to its owners. In addition to conserving lands, the Little Traverse Conservancy has also provided their community with educational programmes for 150,000 students and almost 200 kilometres of public hiking trails.

Also in the Great Lakes region, collaboration among Professors Hugh MacIsaac and Anthony Ricciardi, their colleagues, government agencies and shipping companies has stemmed the introduction of non-native species. Environmental monitoring of the lakes detected numerous non-native species and identified various harmful effects on native food webs. Researchers considered the possible routes of introduction of non-native species, quickly identified ballast water of oceangoing ships as the likely culprit, and detected such species in ballast water. Species were transferred when fresh water containing plankton and other creatures were pumped into ballast chambers at Eurasian ports then pumped out again at North American ports (and presumably vice versa as well).

Because most freshwater species cannot survive in salt water, an obvious potential solution was to flush ballast chambers with enough salty ocean water to kill any organisms in the tanks. Early 1990s regulations allowed ship captains to simply declare they were not transporting ballast water. Once research confirmed those requirements were inadequate – that substantial numbers of species continued to be introduced and ballast water or sediments were almost certainly responsible – Canada and the United States developed more rigorous, and rigorously enforced, requirements. Species transfers have since declined by some 85 per cent. This success depended on cooperation among university scientists, regulatory agencies, and companies that allowed tests on their ships, and even retrofitted one ship to facilitate experiments.[14]

Here again, the keys to success included detecting an environmental problem, identifying its cause, designing a feasible, effective response, attracting community support by means of a compelling argument, and leveraging the effort and resources of supporters and collaborators. A common theme through all of these examples is persistence through whatever obstacles pertained until substantial progress was achieved. Thus, each example exemplifies one of Bamberger's favourite sayings: 'The only place success comes before work is in the dictionary.'[15]

In addition to these and other examples like them, I have found the progress of many colleges and universities inspiring,[16] especially because so much has been accomplished by students making their first efforts at influencing an organization. For example, Austin College students have convinced the administration to adopt some thirty different actions and policies to reduce the college's environmental impact. The list includes many items that are routine today, but which were not routine, at least in our area, when they were first proposed a decade or two ago. They all involved overcoming obstacles, from identifying a problem or the cause of a problem to devising responses compatible with other community priorities and from funding any necessary expenditures to effective implementation and subsequent management of the response. In the process, the college has reduced all sorts of environmental impacts, including cutting greenhouse gas emissions some 60 per cent at a substantial net saving thanks to increased energy efficiency and great cooperation from people all across campus.[17]

These are but a tiny fraction of some of the people and groups making progress despite obstacles. Paul Hawken estimates that, worldwide, there are between one and two million groups – not individuals, but groups – working towards the interdependent goals of ecological sustainability and social justice. He concludes that there has never before been so large a collective effort of any kind.[18] If you find these issues compelling and wish to get involved, you can probably find kindred spirits in your community.

Are such examples the first few decades of a massive worldwide movement that will eventually accomplish the unprecedented task of bringing industrial societies into harmony with the planet's life-support systems? Will success breed success? Will the expectations of Martin Luther King Jr., Aldo Leopold and others be borne out such that more and more issues will be considered ethical matters and justice will have more and more influence over human affairs? Will more and more people learn to resist the marketing that creates wants and then turns wants into perceived needs? Perhaps they will. The answers to these questions depend on decisions not yet made.

We may not yet understand just how much change will be necessary to achieve sustainability, and only hindsight will tell whether such a goal is ever achieved, but as Aldo Leopold observed, over the course of history, 'ethical criteria have been extended to many fields of conduct, with corresponding shrinkages in those judged by expediency only'.[19] If that trend continues, more and more people will perceive environmental damage as wrong and support for environmental protection and restoration will continue to grow, perhaps faster than you or I imagine.

Assume, for the sake of discussion, that all environmental problems could be tallied under one measurement, such as a unit of planetary life-support potential. Assume also that all activities can also be measured with the same unit, such that all environmental impacts represent either damage to or repair of that potential. (Ignore for the moment that harms suffered by a person or other creature at one time cannot be undone by preventing similar harms to others later.) Now imagine the historical trajectory of damages and repairs, and their cumulative effects. How would such a graph appear?

Little can be predicted with precision at this broad scale, and any attempt at such a summary glosses over numerous critical issues and makes a plethora of assumptions, but a few observations seem safe. Damage began before repair. Repair is accelerating, if not yet keeping up with damage. Neither's future has been determined; rates of both damage and repair will depend upon decisions yet to be made.

I imagine trajectories something like Figure 20.3, with repair accelerating and damage slowing until the rate of repair exceeds that of damage such that, eventually, as much damage as possible has been undone. Such a future presumes major shifts in individual and societal priorities, plus tremendous advances in how to prevent and repair

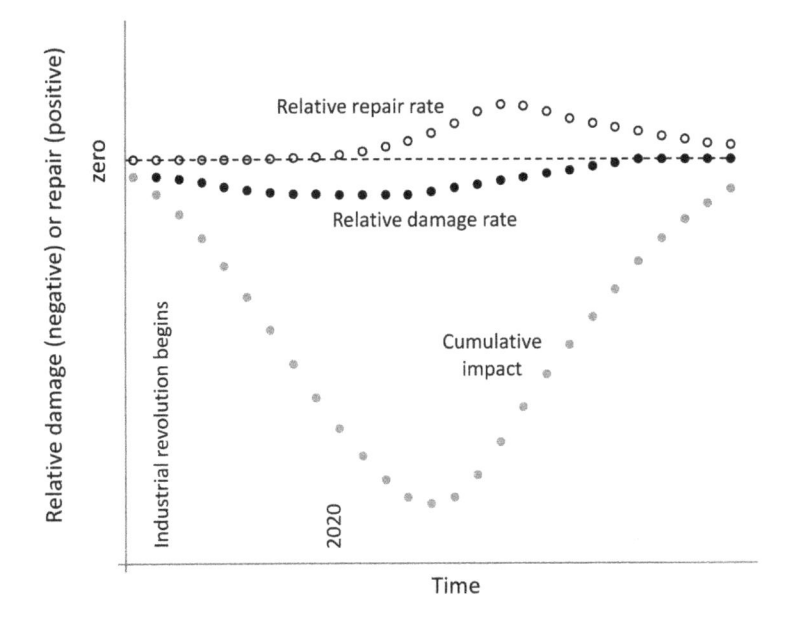

Figure 20.3: Hypothetical potential trajectories of environmental damage to (negative values) and repair of (positive values) the planet's life-support potential, showing some damage preceding the start of the industrial revolution, higher rates of damage than repair as of the early-twenty-first century, but future reduction in damage rate and increase in repair rate until repair exceeds damage and society learns to avoid new damage (damage rate becomes zero). As that situation continues, the cumulative impact approaches zero but remains negative because some damage is never successfully repaired. Figure by the author.

damage, and may be unrealistic given the potential for runaway positive feedbacks of climate change or other processes not yet recognized. But such a trajectory seems an appropriate, necessary goal, and within the realm of possibility. Given the stakes – the future of the only place in the universe known to have any life-support potential at all – that goal seems worth the effort.

Achieving anything like the trajectory of Figure 20.3 will require much more than overcoming obstacles to progress on individual existing environmental problems, but overcoming those obstacles is necessary. Faster success in doing so could come from systematic lowering of the obstacles and from better procedures for overcoming obstacles as they are encountered. Here I offer a few suggestions that might be useful, not as any sort of comprehensive list but in the spirit of encouraging others to correct, refine and expand upon these partial notions.

Recommendations for systematically dismantling obstacles

Four societal changes that are warranted in their own right would also contribute to reducing the significance of the obstacles: (i) overcoming injustices that cause some to suffer greater environmental burdens than others and create tremendous inequities in political influence; (ii) greater investment in understanding environmental problems, their causes and how damage can be undone; (iii) improvements in the general level of critical thinking, especially with regard to understanding the nature of scientific evidence, making decisions despite uncertainty and detecting specious arguments; and (iv) aligning thresholds for action on environmental concerns to match thresholds in other realms, rather than applying double standards that raise the bar for environmental action.

As many others have noted in a variety of contexts, contemporary US society suffers from extreme economic inequality, disenfranchisement of many citizens, legacy effects of, and continuing, discrimination, and tremendous structural obstructions to majority rule. The US Constitution, existing laws, economic advantages of some, and political power structures make overcoming these problems a formidable task, but doing so is nevertheless critical. Components of a solution include removing impediments to representative political participation, such as gerrymandering and structural racism, voter disenfranchisement, and unequal opportunity to influence political decisions rooted in existing campaign finance laws and grotesque economic inequality. It seems obvious to me that we should change campaign finance laws, eliminate the Electoral College, outlaw gerrymandering, alter the tax code to reduce disparities in wealth, and change procedures for presidential primaries, but others are much better qualified than I to identify societal changes that would most reduce unfairness and injustices and thus improve lives and strengthen US democracy. I can, however, offer somewhat more specific suggestions regarding a few changes that would reduce the significance of the obstacles discussed here.

We should invest far more in anticipating consequences of new technologies, detecting environmental change, understanding the causes of environmental change, maximizing the reliability and public understanding of scientific results, and understanding how to undo environmental damage. Such investments would almost surely enable avoidance of some potential problems before they occur and earlier detection and reduction of other problems as they arise. More investment in undoing environmental damage would hasten repair and recovery. Moreover, dissemination of the resulting improved environmental knowledge would foster increased demand for preventing and undoing damage.

In particular, we should fund a multiplication of efforts in systems thinking and predictive forecasting like those of the Santa Fe Institute, the New England Complex Systems Institute and others who use systems thinking to advance forecasting in environmental and other realms, such as Britain's geopolitical prediction market, the Cosmic Bazaar.[20] Such efforts would enable detection and prevention of some potential problems before they occur or grow. Systematic efforts of this sort might have anticipated consequences of well drilling in the Sahel, the use of lead in gasoline or perhaps even the effect of chlorofluorocarbons upon stratospheric ozone. We should not count on contemporary Ben Franklins, Elisha Footes or Sherwood Rowlands to happen upon such concerns, but rather should fund cadres of scouts on the lookout for unintended consequences of new technological developments and other changes. When those scouts identify potential concerns, well-funded, organized teams should immediately follow through with comprehensive evaluations.

Similarly, we should invest far more heavily in life-cycle analysis of products, potential products, activities and systems, and in related efforts to achieve green designs of products and systems. We should not only re-establish and expand the Office of Technology Assessment, but should make interdisciplinary programmes in systems dynamics, socio-environmental forecasting, environmental design, industrial ecology and life-cycle assessment as ubiquitous at colleges and universities as environmental studies has become since the 1970s. Together, much greater investment in advancing and applying systems perspectives, life-cycle assessment and environmental analysis of designs would surely improve anticipation and thus enable avoidance of some potential environmental problems. The same efforts could also identify available precautions against less certain potential problems, would advance nascent efforts to judge products and processes on the basis of their environmental impacts, would help consumers make environmentally friendly choices, and would reduce the frequency with which environmental efforts have unanticipated, undesirable consequences.

Meanwhile, we should dramatically increase investment in environmental monitoring and science so that the necessary data for detecting problems and determining their causes becomes available sooner. It is absurd that only a few people are able to identify rainforest tree species, that states depend on volunteers to monitor stream water quality, that the world's finest ecosystem experiments are based upon tiny plots of land, that budding environmental scientists must often build credentials with unpaid internships, and that we rely upon industry to self-report pollution releases. I do not doubt that most report faithfully and accurately, but we do not expect drivers to self-report highway speeds even though most might do so accurately.

Parallel efforts should seek to improve public understanding of scientific results. All elements of critical thinking should be emphasized throughout formal and informal education, including abundant practice in making decisions despite uncertainty, and detecting logical errors and specious arguments. Such improvements in critical thinking would benefit all sorts of societal problems, not only with regard to the environment. High school graduates should be able to explain why science is usually reliable but cannot be expected to eliminate uncertainty and sometimes errs, should understand the concept of a false negative, and should be able to distinguish between the value of statistical significance to a research programme and the wisdom of precaution against uncertain hazards. Improvements in critical thinking would foster better collective decision-making about environmental problems and would reduce the ability of merchants of doubt to deceive the public and thus reduce demand for environmental progress.[21]

Such demand would probably also result from giving environmental science higher status in both high school and university education, rather than treating it as a low-priority elective subject once students have studied biology, chemistry, physics and ten or more years of mathematics. Any defenders of focus on traditional scientific disciplines rather than 'applied' fields should recognize how environmental science provides outstanding opportunities for using math while bringing fundamental physics, chemistry and biology concepts alive and providing experience in how science actually works in realistic, complex circumstances. Given that our lives depend on an amenable climate and the provision of numerous other ecosystem services, students should not enter college without having heard of ecosystem services, being able to explain why Earth is cooler than Venus and warmer than Mars, or cavalierly assuming technology can substitute for anything in short supply.

Unfortunately, it seems that we also need to fund more deliberate efforts to reduce scientific errors and maximize the reliability of scientific results. Undergraduate and graduate science curricula should include formal study of scientific ethics, fraud and incompetence with the goal of helping students understand how much their lives depend on others behaving honourably, and on prevention of errors and ethical transgressions by both current and future scientists.[22] Meanwhile, institutional structures should eliminate any perverse incentives to engage in such behaviours, as when hiring and promotion committees cannot readily distinguish legitimate from predatory journals. Expanding the small network of specialists who have taken it upon themselves to identify predatory publications and detect faulty scientific reports would increase the rate at which both are detected.[23] Together, such efforts would foster public confidence in scientific results and obviate the need for individual scientists to independently evaluate the rigour of various publications.

We should also eliminate five double standards in societal decision-making that presently magnify various obstacles. Each of the five create higher thresholds for environmental protection than we apply in other, more familiar realms. First, we should apply precaution in environmental circumstances as we do elsewhere, learning the lessons of how modest safety measures such as seat belts and ships' navigational aids often provides great returns. Safety features add to the cost of vehicles but reduce the chance of catastrophe. Similar opportunities exist where the environment is concerned. For example, carbon fees and dividends have potential to reduce the risk, rate, or magnitude of climate change for a modest cost.[24]

We should also apply precaution when there is a risk of crossing uncertain but potentially catastrophic thresholds of environmental impact as we do in other realms. Sensible people would consider it crazy to use rope rated for 100 kg when lifting 80 kg overhead or build a bridge to hold just slightly more than the maximum expected vehicle weight. Stronger rope and bridges cost more but are worth the extra expenditure because they are so much safer. Yet, we routinely base resource consumption and waste production guidance on uncertain estimates of maximum sustainable limits. Thus, we estimate maximum stocking rates for ranches, harvest rates for trees and fish, and water withdrawal rates for aquifers. Moreover, we often exceed such rates. We know better than to make such errors in more familiar circumstances with faster and more familiar consequences, such as ropes and bridges. We should extend the same logic to our dependence on the planet's life-support potential. If we did, we would set all such limits at some fraction of estimated sustainable maxima, especially because environmental limits are less certain than rope and bridge capacities, and because the most basic ecological theory indicates that exceeding maximum sustainable yields can drastically reduce future yields.

Second, we need to overcome a tendency to expect certainty before taking environmental action when we know better than to expect certainty before acting in other circumstances. In other realms, we understand that an ounce of prevention is often worth a pound of cure, but we have not yet applied that wisdom to environmental problems. We should respect the cost of delay, understand why some disagreement among scientists is to be expected, and learn to distinguish real experts from charlatans. Better decision-making under uncertainty would result from more widespread understanding of why neither science nor statistical analyses can be expected to eliminate uncertainty, and why all scientists and purported scientists do not simultaneously reach identical conclusions. Such understanding would foster more appropriate considerations of the strength of evidence and the wisdom of precaution.

Third, we need to eliminate the unreasonable expectation that environmental protection will turn a conventional profit by the sort of simple calculations businesses use when deciding whether to build a factory or manufacture a new product. This change will require widespread understanding of how such analyses discount the future, are biased against environmental protection, fail to consider who would benefit and who would suffer, and make no distinction between prices and values.

We do not expect childhood education, cancer research, space exploration, foreign relations or military preparation to return the straightforward financial profits expected of a business venture. We evaluate such investments more broadly because we realize 'profit', understood purely in financial terms, is too narrow a criterion to serve as a sufficient basis for judging such activities. If we applied cost–benefit analyses to these activities, we would reject all of them, but we know better than to do that. We should use at least as sophisticated judgements for evaluating when to invest in protecting the planet's life-support potential, recognizing that, like these other expenditures, environmental initiatives represent investments, not mere costs.

Fourth, we need to respect technical environmental determinations as we respect technical determinations in more familiar fields, such as medicine and engineering. We would never expect bridge builders to compromise the safety of designs to satisfy the wishes of untrained laypersons, or survey the public regarding the appropriate dose of a medicine;[25] we should likewise reject compromises between experts and uneducated lay persons regarding critical environmental decisions. We should be as wary of claims that conflict with environmental understanding as we are of quack medical cures or miracle diets. Experts make errors and science is not perfect, but bridges are generally safe to cross, almost all flights land safely, coronavirus deaths are lower among the vaccinated than the unvaccinated and professors of climate science probably know more about that subject than a relative who wonders whether those specialists have considered the effect of clouds. Environmental science is more complex than the physics of bridges or aircraft and has a shorter track record than experimental medicine, but we should respect the value of technical expertise nevertheless. I do not mean to suggest that decisions of what to do should be handed over to technical specialists, but specialists' insights should serve as a starting point for informing societal value judgements and their resulting decisions. (Environmental experts, meanwhile, should be scrupulously careful to avoid exaggerating concerns just as an engineer or physician should not exaggerate beyond what evidence supports.[26]) When we give due consideration to environmental expertise, we will reject pure political compromise between environmental authorities and untrained lay persons just as we would reject political compromise on the amount of cement to use in a bridge or the composition of the material in a vaccine.

Fifth, employment consequences of environmental initiatives should be treated like employment consequences of other societal shifts, not more harshly. Organized efforts to shift the economy for the sake of environmental goals, such as conversion to clean, renewable energy sources, should include meaningful consideration of those who suffer from employment consequences, such as coal miners with few or no other local employment options. However, we should not object to job losses due to environmental progress more harshly than losses caused by other economic changes, such as automation or innovation, and we should credit environmental progress for its job creation. I do not wish to treat a complex issue simplistically or ignore controversies associated with consequences of automation, and I lack appropriate knowledge and experience to propose specific responses to shifts in employment opportunities, but I see no reason to treat employment consequences of environmental progress as qualitatively different from employment consequences of other societal shifts. Meanwhile, we should recognize that depletion of nonrenewable resources destroys jobs, while overexploitation of renewable resources destroys potentiallly sustainable jobs, such as in forestry and fishing.

It will take time to lower obstacles to environmental progress systematically, because society will not immediately invest more heavily in systems analysis, environmental monitoring, research, and critical thinking skills, and will not immediately overcome double standards of decision-making. In the meantime, opportunities exist to overcome obstacles as they are encountered.

Suggestions for overcoming obstacles to specific projects

A given effort may encounter any or all of the obstacles discussed in this book. Precisely which pertain, and how best to avoid or surmount them, depends on the nature and scale of a project. Most generally, an effective initiative must have potential to provide environmental benefits; achieve support of those (or a substantial number of those) who will determine whether to proceed and whose support will be necessary for success; secure necessary funding or other resources; be effectively implemented; avoid substantial undesirable consequences; and not be overwhelmed by other simultaneous or subsequent actions. The following more specific suggestions are generally intended for students undertaking their first environmental initiatives and may be useful for other novices in similar situations. (I hope one or more groups that include people with a wide range of environmental and other experience and perspectives, including specialists in project development, implementation and management will develop more general, comprehensive guidance applicable to the full range of potential efforts.)

The first step is to identify a problem and suitable goal. The goal might be, for example, to reduce contamination of a recycling system, restore a patch of an ecosystem, shift a building or organization to a cleaner energy source, divert organic waste from a landfill or create opportunities for commuting by bicycle. If you are committed, you will invest substantial time and effort, so carefully consider the precise goal at the outset. Write it down. Revise it until it is clear. Ask others to interpret what you have written so you can be sure their understanding matches yours, and clarify as necessary if it does not. Have you considered the problem from a systems perspective? Is your goal excessively broad or narrow? Is it realistic under the given circumstances? As you ponder these questions, distinguish what you hope to achieve from what you plan to do. If you plan to increase native vegetation on a campus, why? Water savings? Improved pollinator habitat? Reduced fertilizer consumption and runoff? Environmental education? Perhaps you have several related goals. Would native plantings be the best way to achieve the goal or goals?

Is there any chance that achievement of your goal could be environmentally counterproductive, either by creating backlash in the community or causing undesirable, unintended consequences that exceed benefits? Might it have other, non-environmental undesirable consequences? Challenge yourself and your collaborators to identify potential unintended, indirect effects. Also consider whether pursuit of this goal seems likely to be the best way to leverage your environmental effort?

Once you have identified a goal, creatively explore options for how to reach it. At least one approach may have already occurred to you. What others exist? This stage is analogous to a scientist's identification of alternative hypotheses. More than one option likely exists and the first one that occurs to you may not be most promising.

Consider the list of obstacles discussed in this book in the context of your specific goal. Do some of the obstacles seem likely to be important? How could they be overcome? Will you need better information before proceeding? Will you need to convince the community of the wisdom of your objective or need funds for project implementation or maintenance? Could implementation or maintenance break down? How will you respond if future authorities are indifferent or raise objections?

If you seek to reduce contaminants in a recycling stream, should you improve education about what is recyclable, develop guidelines for when custodial staff should reject the contents of bins, change the style or locations of containers, do something else or do all of these? If you decide that better education of the community will be necessary, how would you achieve that? Should you use postcards, notes left on doors, social media, bulletin boards, labels on bins, online quizzes, some sort of competition or prizes, volunteers who quiz passers-by, or some combination of these or other ideas? Should you attempt to simultaneously increase participation in the recycling programme or focus for the time being on reducing contamination?

If you wish to expand native vegetation, which types of vegetation? Where? Current flower beds? Future tree plantings? Lawns? Would it make more sense to focus on only one or a subset of options? Should you use small pilot projects to demonstrate potential and foster community support, or should your initial effort be more ambitious?

Try to remain inspired while avoiding emotional attachment to the first approach to a problem that occurs to you. Seek others' perspectives regarding different options, especially from people who will ask hard questions and offer constructive criticism. Consider whether multiple simultaneous actions might be most effective. If this is not the first attempt at such a goal, what can you learn from earlier efforts at your location or elsewhere?[27]

Once you have a list of alternatives for how to achieve your goal, critically evaluate each to identify potential problems and weaknesses. Some potential responses may not be worthwhile. For instance, it would be helpful if all recycling bins on a campus were identical and thus easily identified, but indoor and outdoor bins need different features and manufacturing and transporting replacement bins would consume substantial resources and incur financial costs. Replacing bins would make environmental sense only if there were reason to believe doing so would substantially improve recycling for an extended period. Would it? How much more recycling can you reasonably expect to achieve if you purchase new bins? Is there a less resource-intensive way to improve the recycling system?

Additional challenges may arise in determining what information is necessary and how it might be obtained. What information would you need if you sought to reduce recycling contamination? Would some types of information complement each other or would they be redundant? Ideal information may be unobtainable. If so, consider whether alternative information would be adequate. If recycling contamination is the concern, would it be necessary to know the percentage of bins contaminated, the percentage of contents represented by contaminants, the types of contaminants or whether bins in different locations receive different contaminants? How should materials be categorized when collecting and analysing data? Who will collect the data? Precisely how will it be analysed? Will you need advice or guidance for designing the data collection or analysis? Who could help?

Imagine the eventual graphs or other data displays you will need. What information and calculations will be required to achieve those? What concerns or confusion might arise during collection of the necessary data? For instance, when do workers empty bins?

If new containers will be necessary, from whom might they be obtained? At what cost? Which design or designs would be best?

As you develop, analyse and compare options, you may gain insights that require reiterating earlier steps, such as refining your goal, developing newly identified opportunities, seeking information you had not previously realized would be necessary or considering factors previously overlooked. Do not be dismayed by setbacks. Persist. Meanwhile, seek to strike a balance between planning and 'paralysis by analysis'.

Consider the community reception to any approach you consider. Who will be affected, either by the plan's benefits or by its other consequences? Who will need to approve the plan? Would anyone have a reason for opposition? How would your plan affect community members' workloads and daily experience? Could the plan be modified to eliminate one or more reasons for opposition, or could effective advocacy persuade anyone initially opposed? Might some opposition be rooted in misunderstanding?

Consult early on with those who would be involved in implementation and maintenance of the project and those who must approve or fund it. These individuals' responsibilities may require them to prioritize other concerns. How can your proposal be made compatible with competing priorities? Sometimes, other objectives provide ancillary benefits of an action, such as if improved recycling reduces the frequency of overflowing, unsightly trash bins or the cost of landfilling trash. In other cases, objectives may be in conflict, such as when one wishes to increase native plantings on a campus but native vegetation appears unsightly to the unfamiliar eye for several months of the year.

If your project involves more than a small, tightly knit community, beware of bad-faith arguments against your plan motivated by people with ulterior motives, such as protection of profit-generating, environmentally damaging activities. As Oreskes and Conway and others have explained, merchants of doubt may exaggerate scientific uncertainty or make deceptive arguments regarding jobs, freedoms or costs. Keep in mind the specious argumentation techniques described in Chapters 8 through 11 and the issue-priority dynamics described in Chapter 12, and be prepared to respond to such arguments and circumstances. Be ready to discuss freedoms from in addition to freedoms to, the biases of cost–benefit analyses, the folly of basing technical decisions on laypersons' opinions, the cost of delaying decisions, and the various double-standards in decision-making discussed earlier. Ensure that those with authority to approve your plan understand your critiques of any specious arguments. Unanimous support is not necessary for initiatives to proceed, but support of those with approval authority is necessary, as is support of those whose cooperation will be required. Ideally, such individuals will be receptive to compelling arguments.

If opponents fail to stop a new environmental initiative, they may seek to dilute plans, inject compromises that would cause failure, or interfere with implementation so that plans will later be perceived as ineffective and therefore lose community support. Keep in mind that implementation often depends on a wide range of people in different roles. If some of those people are indifferent or opposed, a plan's implementation may fail.[28] Seek insights from critical personnel early in your proposal development and repeatedly as planning and implementation proceeds. Identify opportunities to alter plans as necessary in response to concerns that arise.

As you consider alternative approaches, scrutinize each regarding what could go wrong. Keep in mind the lessons of arsenic in Bangladeshi wells, desertification in the Sahel, and even disastrous national efforts to constrain population growth. Recall how efforts to relieve resource shortages risk causing larger future shortages. What could cause your approach to fail? What undesirable, unintended consequences might occur? This is another time to seek assistance identifying potential plan weaknesses or unintended consequences. Ask 'Then what happens?' as you consider the effects of various aspects of your plans. You may find that an apparently promising idea appears otherwise upon further inspection. Such conclusions are disappointing but provide critical insight and valuable experience.

Carefully guarding against inadequate plans provides two benefits. Identification and correction of weaknesses reduces the chance of failure and increases the chance of success. Avoiding failure also obviates a source of resistance to subsequent projects. Failure of one project can cause resistance to future projects, as was the case with Austin College's failed swimming pool heater described in Chapter 15.

Having identified the most promising option, the next step is to develop detailed implementation protocols and make objective proposals to whichever authorities or community members must approve before the plan can proceed. Detailed plans should specify how to accomplish each necessary task, responsible personnel, and procedures for monitoring progress and detecting problems. The monitoring plan should specify data collection and analysis procedures. If the project will incur substantial financial costs, a detailed plan will enable development of budgets for implementation and operations, and foster identification of potential funding sources.

Once plans are finalized, they will need to be presented to those with final approval authority and others whose participation and cooperation will be critical. Such presentations should be informative and objective, explaining both benefits and drawbacks. Failure to explain drawbacks could cause subsequent backlash as those drawbacks become apparent. As we have seen, backlash to one project can cause resistance to future projects. Here again, when you identify potential drawbacks, audience members may raise helpful suggestions. Remain receptive to further plan refinements.[29]

Once plans have been approved and a budget is available, implementation may begin. Those responsible should ensure the project proceeds as intended while monitoring for necessary refinements and correcting any anticipated and unanticipated problems.

Once a programme is implemented, is effective, and has not caused other substantial problems, the developer's work is still not done. If those developers are students, they should work with more permanent staff and faculty to ensure programme continuation after their graduation. This is also a time to consider writing a report for those addressing similar concerns elsewhere or to help broader audiences understand the value of, and potential for, your project or environmental progress generally.

Even modest projects require substantial, sustained efforts, but successes are satisfying. Juliana Lobrecht Crownover did the work equivalent of one regular college course and as a result an entire small city began recycling. Nichole Knesek thought hard about where to look for *E. coli* in a reservoir, then collected key data that caused Texas state officials to correct a malfunctioning wastewater treatment plant.

Moreover, such early successes often provide experience that informs later, more ambitious efforts (and successful undergraduate projects strengthen résumés). Anthony Swift developed a system for measuring prairie recovery. Not many years later, as an attorney for the Natural Resources Defense Council, he led the group of major environmental organizations who stopped the Keystone XL tar sands pipeline. Now he is working to improve Canadian forest policy. Maegan Fitzgerald wrote a proposal for a campus to use modular carpeting rather than carpet rolls that required replacing an entire room's floor covering when one area was worn. (Modular carpet is routine today, but was not when Maegan wrote her proposal.) Before long she was advancing chimpanzee conservation in Africa.

Maegan recently spoke on campus. I had forgotten she wrote the carpet proposal, but when she glanced at the floor before beginning her presentation, she was obviously delighted to be standing on modular carpet. Modest projects like Maegan's do not merely provide incremental environmental benefits. They also serve as examples for others, help their developers evaluate potential career paths, and demonstrate abilities beyond conventional academic success (such as creativity, persistence, ability to persuade, and experience with project design, analysis, implementation and management).

Final comments

As Aldo Leopold argued, true sustainability of an industrial society will almost certainly require shifts in the ultimate, values-based obstacles that this book hardly addresses. I suspect an eventual, gradual reduction in population that results from freely made fertility decisions will also be necessary. Whether a few billion descendants of hunters and gatherers who are evolutionarily adapted to making decisions in small groups can learn to work in groups of millions or even billions, for the benefit of all people, including future generations, remains to be seen. In the meantime, any improvement in our proficiency at overcoming obstacles to environmental progress will help slow damage and accelerate recovery.

Because there is so much to be done, if you are just embarking on a career or otherwise wish to get involved, you have many options, from working to detect or better understand problems, to engaging with the political system to encourage action, to devising and implementing effective responses. If you imagine a career in environmental work, but are not sure precisely what that might mean in your case, you might consider whether working on one or more of the obstacles described here seems compelling to you. If so, identify people who already do that work and contact them. Good luck.

One final thought. When I teach introductory environmental studies, we discuss John McPhee's 1971 *Encounters with the Archdruid.* McPhee describes conversations during a backpacking trip through Glacier Peak Wilderness with conservationist David Brower and exploration geologist Charles Park. McPhee uses the essay as a vehicle for Brower and Park's respectful debate about whether to mine a rich lode of copper under Glacier Peak. Brower, as you might imagine, opposed mining, even exclaiming the copper would have to be removed over his dead body. He earned his moniker 'Archdruid' because many considered his views radical. Park, the exploration geologist, appreciated the issues involved but favoured mining the copper. At the end of our discussions, half a century later, I ask the students what they think happened to that copper. A large majority of students *always* predicts that the copper has been mined.

The copper is still in the ground.

A December 2020 Ipsos poll found that almost 90 per cent of people worldwide and 79 per cent of people in the US agreed with the following statement: 'I want the world to change significantly and become more sustainable and equitable rather than returning to how it was before the

COVID-19 crisis.' Only 4 per cent strongly disagreed.[30] Maybe it is not just that no mining company saw fit to mine Glacier Peak Wilderness even though they could have; perhaps, as Martin Luther King and Aldo Leopold anticipated, ideas like Brower's are headed for the mainstream even though they were considered radical just a few decades ago.

> This extraordinary time when we are globally aware of each other and the multiple dangers that threaten civilization has never happened, not in a thousand years, not in ten thousand years. Each of us is as complex and beautiful as all the stars in the universe. We have done great things and we have gone way off course in terms of honoring creation. You are graduating to the most amazing, stupefying challenge ever bequested to any generation. The generations before you failed … They got distracted and lost sight of the fact that life is a miracle every moment of your existence. Nature beckons you to be on her side. You couldn't ask for a better boss. The most unrealistic person in the world is the cynic, not the dreamer. Hope only makes sense when it doesn't make sense to be hopeful. This is your century. Take it and run as if your life depends on it.[31]

Notes

1   Lazarus, *The Making of Environmental Law*, 2004, 43–166; Ponting, *A New Green History of the World*, 2007, 101–15, 137–70, 199–230, 294–313 and other places.
2   Kelly et al., *American Paintings of the Nineteenth Century*, 350–4; Leopold, 'The population wilderness fallacy', 1918, 43; Winter, '"War in the woods"', 2021.
3   Ipsos, 'Around the world, people yearn for significant change', 2020.
4   Goldman Environmental Prize, 'Current recipients', 2021; Tyler Prize for Environmental Achievement, 2022.
5   Bromfeld, *Pleasant Valley*, 1943.
6   Bamberger Ranch, '50 Years of Conservation', n.d., 2:02–2:05.
7   Bamberger Ranch, 'Selah', n.d.; Greene, *Water from Stone*, 2007; LeBlanc, *My Stories, All True*, 2020.
8   J. David Bamberger, personal communication, 6 January 2022.
9   Ockels, *Illegal Dumping Enforcement*, 2022; Texas Illegal Dumping Resource Center, 'Enforcement training for Texas cities and counties', n.d.
10 Land Institute, 'Transforming agriculture, perennially', n.d.
11 UN Food and Agriculture Organization Commodities and Trade Division, 'Agricultural commodities', 2002.
12 Land Institute, 'The future of farming. The future of food', n.d.
13 Little Traverse Conservancy, 'Interactive preserve map', n.d.; Little Traverse Conservancy, 'Landowner resources', n.d.; Little Traverse Conservancy, 'Our mission', n.d.
14 Ricciardi and MacIsaac, 'Vector control reduces the rate of species invasion in the world's largest freshwater ecosystem', 2022; Hugh MacIsaac, personal communication, 21 October 2021. Ballast water is not the only possible method of species introduction. Others include the aquarium trade and aquaculture. Thus, ballast flushing alone cannot be expected to completely halt invasions.

15 Bamberger Ranch, 'Our story'. This quote has also been attributed to former American football coach Vince Lombardi, and perhaps to others as well.

16 Hundreds of examples are available on the websites of Second Nature (https://secondnature. org/), the EPA Green Power Partnership (https://www.epa.gov/greenpower), and the Association for the Advancement of Sustainability in Higher Education (https://www.aashe. org/). Many resources at the latter require membership for access. If you are affiliated with a university, it may have membership through which you can obtain access.

17 Austin College, 'Austin College sustainability plan', 2018; SIMAP, 'Austin College', n.d.

18 Hawken, *Blessed Unrest*, 2007, 2.

19 Leopold, *A Sand County Almanac*, 1949, 202.

20 Amanatidou et al., 'On concepts and methods in horizon scanning', 2012; Dietze et al., 'Iterative near-term ecological forecasting', 2017; Ecological Forecasting Initiative, 'About', n.d.; *Economist*, 'How spooks are turning to superforecasting in the Cosmic Bazaar', 2021; Elsawah et al., 'Scenario processes for socio-environmental systems analysis of futures', 2020; Horowitz et al., 'Keeping score', 2021; Jones et al., 'Iteratively forecasting biological invasions with PoPS and a little help from our friends', 2021; New England Complex Systems Institute, 'About NECSI', n.d.; Open University, 'Applied systems thinking in practice', n.d.; Sutherland et al., 'A 2021 horizon scan of emerging global biological conservation issues', 2021; Santa Fe Institute, 'About', n.d.

21 Schools routinely claim to emphasize critical thinking, but the actual skills and techniques of its application are, in my experience, rarely the explicit focus of actual courses or even class sessions. In contrast, endless sessions in subject after subject focus on material specific to the particular field. Critical thinking practice and topical coverage are not in conflict. The latter serves as grist for the former, but the former should not be an afterthought or expected to occur indirectly by some sort of educational osmosis. My colleagues and I seek to teach critical thinking methods in introductory environmental studies lab sessions. At the outset of those sessions, most students, despite having graduated from high school, are typically unable to provide much detail about what critical thinking actually means. I do not consider this their fault. It is a product of their prior education. We can usually tease out pieces of an explanation, but only in fragments, which convinces us that even the relatively fortunate youngsters with the opportunity to attend college or university would benefit from more explicit earlier practice.

22 I routinely have students in first-year college courses anonymously circle 'yes' or 'no' on a small slip of paper to indicate whether they ever cheated on academic work during high school. I consistently receive about 80 per cent 'yes' responses.

23 Beall, 'What I learned from predatory publishers', 2017; Retraction Watch, https:// retractionwatch.com/, accessed 20 December 2021.

24 Boyce, *The Case for Carbon Dividends*, 2019; Mufson, 'The fastest way to cut carbon emissions', 2020. Indeed, as many have noted, a carbon fee could be a 'no-regrets' policy because it would have the added advantage of accelerating the shift from dirty, non-renewable and thus non-sustainable energy sources to cleaner, renewable, potentially sustainable energy sources, and thus reduce both conventional air pollution and the hazard of dramatic energy price shocks if fossil fuel supplies decline without adequate replacements available. Moreover, as the Austin College example shows, the added cost of slightly more expensive energy sources can often be more than compensated for with savings from easy energy conservation opportunities (Austin College, 'Austin College sustainability plan', 2018).

25 Well, I guess the coronavirus pandemic has shown that many do obtain medical advice from unqualified sources, but that unfortunately often ends badly.

26 The issue of exaggeration represents a related double-standard. Society seems to expect absolute integrity of environmental scientists' pronouncements and have no tolerance for their exaggeration while opponents of environmental protection may exaggerate wildly with little apparent consequence. Thus, a politician opposed to climate change action can cavalierly pronounce that such action would destroy the economy with no basis for such a conclusion, but an environmental scientist cannot (and should not) make a similarly exaggerated opposing claim. This double standard puts a premium on avoiding excessively precise environmental pronouncements about the future. Thus, I cringe when I hear statements such as that we have X years to keep the sky from falling. The problem may be urgent; there may be a real risk of the sky falling, but if X years pass and the sky has not completely fallen, the next pronouncement from an environmental scientist will be treated with even more scepticism.

27 If you happen to be working on reducing some aspect of the environmental impact of a university or similar organization, consult available resources from the Association for the Advancement of Sustainability in Higher Education (https://www.aashe.org/) and Second Nature (https://secondnature.org/).

28 During the late 1990s, after Austin College student Juliana (Lobrecht) Crownover had convinced the Sherman, Texas, city council that the citizenry desired curbside recycling and the city had obtained a State of Texas grant to hire consultants who designed a programme, some members of the council suggested an initial pilot implementation in a subset of the city, to be later evaluated by city staff. John Ockels of the Texas Illegal Dumping Resource Center counseled me to argue against a pilot programme. He noted that no pilot was necessary because thousands of US cities were already operating effective curbside recycling programmes and qualified, professional consultants had developed a tailored design, so little could be learned from a small-scale implementation. He further warned that a pilot programme would create an opportunity for any resistant city staff to make a minimal effort, declare the pilot test a failure and argue that the council should abandon the city-wide implementation plans. Fortunately, the council voted to adopted a city-wide programme.

29 Undergraduates and others with limited presentation experience may benefit from basic guidance such as Schulze and Barton, 'How to give a good presentation', n.d.

30 Ipsos, 'Around the world, people yearn for significant change rather than a return to a "pre-COVID normal"', 2020.

31 Hawken, 'Paul Hawken's commencement address to the class of 2009', 2009.

Appendix: the six anti-environmental biases of cost–benefit analysis

Discounting the future

The first problem in applying cost–benefit analysis to environmental issues is the dependence of net present value calculations on discounted future values and the consequent short time frame of analysis. Discounting future values renders long-term consequences effectively irrelevant to net present value calculations, but long-term consequences are not irrelevant. This is but one of several anti-environmental biases of the procedure, but I consider it alone to be sufficient for rejecting cost–benefit analysis as a basis for informing what a society should do regarding environmental phenomena with long-term consequences.

Recall the formula used for calculating net present value.

$$NPV = \Sigma \frac{b_t - c_t}{(1 + d)^t}$$

where

    NPV = net present value (a unit of currency, such as dollars)
    b_t = anticipated benefits in year t (same currency)
    c_t = anticipated costs in year t (same currency)
    d = the discount rate (proportion per year, such as 0.1)

The higher the discount rate, the shorter the time before discounted present values of future costs and benefits approach zero. There is no firm theoretical basis for a particular discount rate. Analysts use rates that range from 2 per cent to 12 per cent or more. Lopez, to take one example, argues that the World Bank should use a discount rate of about 4 per cent for evaluating Latin American projects over a 100-year time frame.[1] At that rate, $100 of benefit that accrues 100 years from now has a net present value of less than $2. In other words, based on such an analysis, it would not be worth spending $2 today to obtain $100 of benefits in 100 years. Or, equivalently, it would make sense to harvest two fish today even if doing so meant that there would be 100 fewer fish to harvest 100 years from now. One suspects that future generations would object to such conclusions, but this approach is plausible if one makes the free-market enthusiasts' assumptions (Chapter 10) that a shortage of fish will lead markets to develop fish substitutes, and that removing fish from the ocean will be of no consequence beyond the market price of fish. The latter seems unlikely to be true for ecosystems.

When the analysis is extended to a longer time horizon, the effect of discounting increases exponentially. For example, at a four per cent discount rate, 100 kilograms of fish caught 200 years from now would have a net present value of only 40 grams of fish caught today. As recently as 1999 the World Bank published analyses that used discount rates of 10 or 12 per cent.[2] At a 12 per cent discount rate, if a project, say a dam, caused the death of 100 fish one hundred years from now that loss would be considered equivalent to less than 1/500th of one fish today. This is the equivalent of concluding that catching one more fish today would be a good idea even if it reduced the catch one hundred years from now by more than 80,000 fish. (As of 2021, the International Energy Agency's online comparison of the costs of various electricity generation methods allows users to select discount rates ranging from 3 to 10 per cent and defaults to 7 per cent.[3]) Such reasoning effectively treats distant consequences as worthless. In other words, long-term environmental damages and benefits are considered trivial because they have little if any effect on calculated net present value. (Intermediate years would be included in analyses, but that does not alter the basic lesson regarding the consequence of discounting for analysis of actions with long-term consequences.)

Future benefits of environmental protection are so heavily discounted (and the distant future is so hard to forecast) that cost–benefit analyses are often limited to a time frame of only 10 or 20 years. In these cases, more distant benefits of environmental protection, and costs of environmental damage, are literally omitted from consideration (and thus treated as equal to zero) in net present value calculations.

Back in the 1973, Colin Clark showed that when cost–benefit analysis is applied to questions regarding harvesting slow-growing renewable resources, such as whales, forests or soils, wiping out the resource and investing the money elsewhere will often be deemed more profitable than sustainably harvesting the resource forever.[4] Incredibly, the same conclusion would pertain to the destruction of entire ecosystems or even catastrophic alteration of the climate. For example, analyses conclude that combustion of all available fossil fuels would cause, over the next few hundred years, all Antarctic ice to melt, thereby raising oceans dozens of metres, submerging the world's coastal cities and plains.[5] But cost–benefit analysis, because it so drastically discounts the future, would effectively ignore these long-term, potentially catastrophic consequences of fossil fuel combustion.

It is not in the interest of future generations to wipe out essential resources, submerge the world's cities or destroy the potential of the planet to provide ecosystem services. The future is difficult to predict, but it seems safe to assume that future generations would prefer a planet whose ecosystems continue to sustain themselves and generate the ecosystem services we depend upon.[6]

Who benefits? Who pays?

Costs and benefits do not necessarily accrue to the same individuals. Thus, net present value calculations ignore environmental justice issues both within and across generations. If I am allowed to catch 2 fish this year but doing so prevents others from catching 100 fish a century from now, I benefit but they suffer. In other words, if an activity generates short-term profits but causes long-term environmental damage one group will enjoy the profits while another group suffers the consequences. (The most extreme free-market enthusiasts would argue that allowing the present generation to catch more fish now will make society wealthier, which will result in investments in innovations that will make people better off in the future. The latter obviously occurs in some instances. I just do not think it should be relied upon where there is a chance of destroying or degrading processes essential to the planet's ability to support life.)

Costs and benefits are not only unevenly borne between generations, but also among members of a given generation. If the use of a toxin is allowed, then those who profit from its sales will benefit, but those who are exposed to its toxic effects will suffer. Conversely, if a toxin is outlawed then the manufacturers of the toxin will lose income but those who would have been exposed to the toxin will benefit. Cost–benefit analysis does not distinguish among individuals and thus ignores justice considerations regarding who benefits and who pays.

Overestimation of costs of environmental protection

The third problem with cost–benefit analysis is that analysts routinely overestimate costs of compliance with new environmental regulations.[7] For example, analysts expected sulphur dioxide pollution permits to sell for $250–350 per ton, but when a permit market for sulphur dioxide emissions became established, the price fell to just over $100 per ton.[8] Permits did not reach the anticipated price until ten years after trading began and emissions had been reduced by about 40 per cent. Later, except for a brief price spike that caused heavy coal use in response to low availability of natural gas following Hurricane Katrina, the price fell even lower.[9] Even regulatory agencies often overestimate costs.[10]

It is not surprising that many costs are initially overestimated because cost estimates are often generated by the industry that may become subject to new regulations, and therefore the estimators face an incentive to overestimate costs to bolster their arguments that new regulations would not be justified. Also, when costs are estimated the industry has not yet had time or a compelling incentive to find ways to minimize them. When overestimated costs are used in cost–benefit analyses, they tend to bias net present value calculations against regulations or other actions that seek to reduce environmental damage.[11]

Contingent valuation

The next problem with using cost–benefit analysis for evaluating environmental proposals results from the challenge of specifying values for environmental damages and benefits. Since the procedure is based on tallying monetary costs and benefits, everything included must have a monetary value, but the benefits of environmental protection and costs of environmental damage generally do not have market values because they are not traded in markets. To be included, they must be assigned values. These ascribed values are called 'shadow' prices.

Shadow prices are problematic for two reasons. One is the same reason that market prices are problematic as a basis for societal decisions (see the last section of this appendix sub-headed 'Price does not equal value'). The second reason is because they are often established using a procedure called contingent valuation, and contingent valuation is often based upon surveys of uninformed or minimally informed laypersons.

How can one know an appropriate shadow price? Sometimes one can estimate shadow prices from other available information. For example, some water-quality costs of a polluted river can be estimated from the costs to purify the polluted water for domestic consumption. (But what cost should be ascribed to other damages that result from the pollution, such as harm to aquatic species?)

Costs of air pollution are sometimes estimated on the basis of lost wages of workers made ill. But lost wages are not the only consequence of illness, and children who stay home sick from school lose no wages. How shall we ascribe a price to the loss of a day of school for a child, or to the difficulty a child has sitting still in class because ozone alerts cause cancellation of recess? How to ascribe a 'correct' price gets even more difficult when momentous, irreversible consequences are possible, such as increasing the chance that a human life will be lost, a rare species will go extinct or the stratospheric ozone layer will be damaged.

Needing to ascribe shadow prices to impacts that lack market prices, analysts typically fall back upon the assumption that 'correct' prices are those the market will bear. This assumption justifies ascribing shadow prices by contingent valuation – surveying the public to ask what they would be willing to pay for an environmental amenity or willing to accept in compensation for environmental damage.[12]

Survey respondents indicate what they would be willing to pay to, say, prevent the extinction of a species or reduce the presence of a pollutant in groundwater. But survey respondents often lack relevant technical knowledge. They may have no insight into the potential consequences of an action for themselves, their society, people elsewhere or other species. Where technical issues, such as the health consequences of a pollutant in drinking water or the importance of wolves to ecosystem functioning are involved, this procedure is analogous to choosing medical treatments by surveying laypersons rather than relying on medical experts.

Another problem is that the whole process is hypothetical. Survey respondents know that no money is actually going to change hands. But because cost–benefit analyses need prices for these items, the procedure is common.

Contingent valuation surveys often attempt to overcome the problem of ignorant survey respondents by, for example, explaining the consequences of environmental damage before asking respondents their willingness to pay, but the method remains based upon minimally informed laypersons' judgement and hypothetical payments.[13] Informing respondents before surveying them is analogous to educating laypersons about the benefits and side effects of medicines, then expecting them to make prescribing decisions. I suppose this would be preferable to asking people with *no* relevant knowledge to choose medicines, but it would be a far cry from having qualified physicians select treatments.

When our health suffers, we do not survey the public to decide what to do; we seek expert advice. Likewise, when a bridge is to be built, we do not ask laypersons where to put the supports and how much cement to use. But this is effectively what happens when contingent valuation is used as a basis for choosing shadow prices for cost–benefit analyses.

Addition of shadow prices reached an almost absurd degree in Food and Drug Administration analyses of proposed new regulations regarding tobacco use and nutritional value information on restaurant menus. Those analyses included costs for foregone pleasure lost by smokers who, after quitting, no longer enjoy the pleasure of smoking, and a charge of $5.27 billion for 'lost pleasure' suffered by people expected to choose healthier food over junk food as a result of proposed nutritional information on menus.[14] By the same rationale vaccines will soon fail cost–benefit tests because of the inclusion of costs for anxiety suffered by irrational anti-vaxxers and costs of lost income of medical workers who would have been paid for treating those who would have become sick without the vaccine.

Rather than being a rigorous analytical procedure, contingent valuation is akin to the US television game show *Family Feud*, or the British show *Pointless*, in which the objective is to identify the audience's most common answer to a question, rather than making any attempt to identify a correct answer. That may be sufficient for a game show whose purpose is entertainment and whose questions are trivial, such as favourite colours, but it is a poor basis for making decisions about acceptable blood-lead concentrations, the risks of introducing a non-native species or the fate of the stratospheric ozone layer.

No measurement systems are perfect, but a measurement system with so many problems should not serve as a basis for deciding whether society should act to protect the environment upon which we all depend. Shadow price estimates can be useful for helping people understand that environmental damages have costs and they can be useful for informing policy choices when setting consumption fees designed to discourage environmental damage (such as a carbon tax, a topic beyond our scope here), but their shaky foundation should not serve as a basis for analyses intended to help society decide whether to prevent environmental damage.

Underestimation of benefits of environmental protection

Sometimes, rather than attempting to estimate shadow prices with contingent valuation surveys, cost–benefit analyses simply omit consequences that lack market prices. Moreover, analysts cannot help but omit consequences they have not imagined. Because environmental benefits, such as reduced ozone concentrations or reduced emissions of greenhouse gases, are difficult to monetize, but costs of complying with regulations (such as costs of catalytic converters or costs of foregone fish catches this year) are easier to estimate, tallies disproportionately omit the benefits but include the costs of environmental protection.[15] This creates yet another bias in net present value estimates.

Analysts routinely note some omissions and explain that decision-makers should take these omissions into consideration, but such details can get overlooked when soundbites focus on easily summarized quantitative results.[16] Professor Laurence Tribe refers to the latter tendency as the 'dwarfing of soft variables', writing:

> 'Equipped with a mathematically powerful intellectual machine, even the most sophisticated user is tempted to feed his pet the food it can most comfortably digest. Readily quantifiable factors are easier to process – and hence more likely to be recognized and then reflected in the outcome – than are factors that resist ready quantification. The result, despite what turns out to be a spurious appearance of accuracy and completeness, is likely to be significantly warped and hence highly suspect.'[17]

As noted earlier, such a result suffers from what Professor Mark Leighton calls masquerading precision – its implied precision is illusory and distracts from inaccuracy.

Consider a cost–benefit analysis of a proposed requirement for ships to avoid transferring species from one continent to another in ballast water. As we have seen, such ships appear to have been responsible for introducing dozens of species to the Great Lakes.[18] Costs to the shipping industry of proposed control mechanisms are relatively simple to estimate since appropriate flushing or treatment of water in ballast tanks could prevent transport of species. But how could one derive a monetary estimate of the benefits of such efforts? First, one would have to predict which new species would colonize in the absence of any control efforts. Then, for each expected colonizer, one would have to anticipate its particular potential impacts.

Chapter 4 discussed some of the effects of zebra and quagga mussels on the Great Lakes ecosystem. Zebra and quagga mussels are just two of numerous species introduced to the Great Lakes from ship ballasts, and waterfowl deaths due to botulism is only one of the apparent food-web impacts of the mussels. Would these costs have been included in a cost–benefit analysis?

The effect of mussels on waterfowl was unanticipated and thus would have been omitted from a tally of the benefits of ballast-water regulation, as presumably would most of the other food-web impacts of the mussels and other introduced species. Moreover, the mussels have now spread from the Great Lakes as far as Texas, where, among other things, they are impacting the water supply for the Dallas-Fort Worth metropolitan area. Had they not been transported to the Great Lakes, they would not have had a foothold in North America. Thus, a comprehensive analysis of the benefits of ballast-water regulations should include the savings of not having to contend with zebra mussels in Texas. But in practice, a cost–benefit analysis of the hypothetical, future introduction of a new species would not include such downstream effects. It would not be reasonable to expect cost–benefit analyses to identify *all* relevant consequences of a proposed action or inaction, so it also is unreasonable to treat their results as if they are accurate tallies.

Underestimation of benefits can also occur if a proposed regulation, such as sulphur dioxide control, is motivated by one particular problem, such as acidification of water, but reduces other problems, such as particulate air pollution.[19] For example, an early cost–benefit analysis intended to inform climate-change policy omitted other benefits of reduced fossil fuel use beyond greenhouse gas reduction, such as reduced conventional air pollution. The Nobel Prize-winning author wrote in the calm tone of a careful analyst that 'the calculations omit other potential market failures, such as ozone depletion, air pollution, and research and development, which might reinforce the logic behind [greenhouse gas] reduction or carbon taxes'.[20] These are major omissions.

Price does not equal value

Price is only one measure of importance, but basing societal decisions on monetary costs and benefits requires the assumption that prices are good measures of value. Allowing prices to be set by the market has all sorts of benefits, but it creates problems when those prices serve as the basis for decisions regarding how society should respond to problems, such as a pollutant in drinking water. There are two problems here; the problem of setting shadow prices that was discussed above ('contingent valuation') and the problem of market prices being affected by preferences that themselves are grounded in the capricious whims of consumers.

Prices often do not make sense because market participants are often irrational. Standard economic theory recognizes prices as manifestations of individual preferences and takes such preferences as givens.[21] The logic is that if people want to pay more for heroin than clean water, or pay a million dollars for a place to park their car, then economists have no business questioning those choices.[22] But such preferences are not rational, nor does their use achieve the value neutrality that some economists claim to seek.[23] It may be fine to ignore the question of what consumers should prefer in some limited analysis, such as whether a company stands to profit by expanding a factory, but societal decisions regarding serious matters should not depend on irrational underpinnings in market prices.

Reliance on preferences avoids the issue of what value should be placed on a particular item, but ignoring that issue does not escape the problem that some items simply should have higher values than others. For example, people should consider clean drinking water more valuable than heroin. That some people do not is hardly relevant to what should be the case.

My favourite example of market irrationality involves a dent and a dog. During 2004, my wife Helen and I paid $40 for as fine a dog as one can imagine. The dog, whose name was Sparky, did not jump up, growl at people, climb on furniture, beg for food or need a leash for a walk, and for several years functioned informally as a sort of therapy dog for restless elementary school children who patted her calmly while Helen read to their classes (Figure A.1).

Sparky died several years ago, but while she was alive someone dented two door panels on one of our cars. A body shop quoted the cost of the dent repair at $2,200, which was the approximate value of the aging car. When I declined that offer, the shop representative offered to

Figure A.1: Ben and Matt Schulze with our adopted dog Sparky in 2005. Sparky allowed small children to climb on her, did not beg for food, did not jump on furniture, and could be walked without a leash. According to the market, a nearly imperceptible dent in a car door was worth 50 dogs like Sparky. Photographer: Peter C. Schulze.

pull the dents out for $200, explaining that the repair would not, however, be perfect. I noted that the rest of the car was hardly perfect anyway and agreed to have the dent pulled. Pulling the dent worked remarkably well. Afterward, the door panels were in fact almost like new. If you looked carefully, you could see that they were not quite perfect, but a casual observer would not have noticed anything wrong.

I felt quite rational opting for the much less expensive repair, but according to market prices, after the dent was pulled for $200, the barely perceptible imperfection that remained had a market value of $2,000 – the difference between the market prices for the two repair options. So, according to the market, the remaining, almost imperceptible dent had the same value as fifty of the greatest dog I have even known. Clearly, prices do not equal values.

In summary, cost–benefit analysis is a useful tool for individuals and organizations attempting to maximize financial profits of investment decisions and for predicting the behaviour of market participants. (My colleagues and I have used it for the latter purpose.[24]) But we expect too much if we rely upon cost–benefit analysis as a basis for judging the wisdom of major societal decisions because it is invariably biased against the future, fails to distinguish who benefits from who pays, fails to recognize that price is not equal to value and depends upon many judgement calls regarding shadow prices, how severely to discount the future and what to include or exclude from analysis. Cost–benefit analyses provide precise results, but that precision is a masquerade that comes at the cost of biased inaccuracy. The considerable logic of asking the more general qualitative, complex question of whether benefits are worth their costs all too easily devolves into simplistic net present value calculations that obscure underlying biases and assumptions and seduce with simple numbers at the bottom of a spreadsheet – numbers that are indeed simple, but also routinely misleading.

Notes

1   Lopez, H. 'The social discount rate', 2008.
2   Belli et al., *Handbook on Economic Analysis of Investment Operations*, 1998, 152; Haltiwanger and Singh, 'Cross-country evidence on public sector retrenchment', 1999, 38.
3   International Energy Agency, 'Projected Costs of Generating Electricity 2020', 2020.
4   Clark, C., 'The economics of overexploitation', 1973.
5   Winkelmann et al., 'Combustion of available fossil fuel resources sufficient to eliminate the Antarctic Ice Sheet', 2015.
6   Partridge, 'Future generations', 2003, 385–8.
7   Cohen, D. 'Climate regulations a job killer?', 2011; Gleick, 'Will new climate regulations destroy the economy?', 2014; Lazarus, *The Making of Environmental Law*, 2004, 95; Krugman, 'Cutting back on carbon', 2014; McGarity et al., *Sophisticated Sabotage*, 2004, 204–7.
8   Chestnut and Mills, 'A fresh look at the benefits and costs of the US acid rain program', 2005, 255; Schmalensee et al., 'An interim evaluation of sulfur dioxide emissions trading', 1998, 62.
9   Burtraw and Keyes, 'Recognizing gravity as a strong force in atmosphere emissions markets', 2018, 203–14; Napolitano et al., 'The U. S. acid rain program', 2007, 51–2.
10 Harrington et al., 'On the accuracy of regulatory cost estimates', 2000, 298.
11 Rosenbaum, *Environmental Politics and Policy*, 2002, 160.
12 Bishop, 'Putting a value on injuries to natural assets', 2017; Hannemann, 'Valuing the environment through contingent valuation', 1994; Mendelsohn and Olmstead, 'The economic valuation of environmental amenities and disamenities', 2009, 332–4; M. Morgan et al., 'Why conventional tools for policy analysis are often inadequate for problems of global change', 1999.
13 See for instance Wilson and Tisdell, 'How knowledge affects payment to conserve an endangered bird', 2007.
14 S. Begley, 'Exclusive', 2014; Chaloupka et al., 'An evaluation of FDA's analysis of the costs and benefits of the graphic warning label regulation', 2015, 115; Tavernise, 'In new calculus on smoking, it's health gained vs. pleasure lost', 2014.
15 EPA, 'Regulatory Impact Analysis for the Final Mercury and Air Toxics Standards', 2011, ES10-3; Heinzerling et al., 'Applying cost–benefit analysis to past decisions', 2005; Shapiro and Morrall, 'The triumph of regulatory politics', 2012, 189–93.
16 Driesen, 'Is cost–benefit analysis neutral?', 2006, footnote 21.
17 Tribe, 'Trial by mathematics', 1971, 1361–2.
18 Grigorovich et al., 'Ballast-mediated animal introductions in the Laurentian Great Lakes', 2003.
19 Chestnut and Mills, 'A fresh look at the benefits and costs of the US acid rain program', 2005, 255–64.
20 Nordhaus, 'An optimal transition path for controlling greenhouse gases', 1992, 1319.

21 Tribe, 'Policy science', 1972, 85.
22 Higgins, 'Buy condo, then add parking spot for $1 million', 2014.
23 Chaloupka et al., 'An evaluation of FDA's analysis of the costs and benefits of the graphic warning label regulation', 2015, 115; Tribe, 'Ways not to think about plastic trees', 1974, 1326.
24 Schulze et al., 'Enrichment planting in selectively logged rain forest', 1994.

References

Abt, Karen L., Robert C. Abt, Christopher S. Galik and Kenneth E. Skog. 'Effects of policies on pellet production and forests in the US South', US Forest Service General Technical Report SRS - 202, December, 2014. Accessed 1 November 2021. https://www.srs.fs.usda.gov/pubs/gtr/gtr_srs202.pdf.

Aitken, Andrew. 'Measuring welfare beyond GDP', *National Institute Economic Review* 249 (2019): R3–R16. Accessed 31 May 2022. https://doi.org/10.1177/002795011924900110.

Allen, Shamarr. 'Sorry Ain't Enough No More'. YouTube, 2010. Accessed 8 November 2021. https://www.youtube.com/watch?v=ZCTn9tqU-mE.

Alschuler, Albert W. 'Limiting political contributions after *McCutcheon, Citizens United*, and *SpeechNow*', *Florida Law Review* 67 (2016): 389–508.

Altman, Douglas. 'The scandal of poor medical research', *British Medical Journal* 308 (1994): 283–4.

Alvarez, Ramón A., Daniel Zavala-Araiza, David R. Lyon, David T. Allen, Zachary R. Barkley, Adam R. Brandt, Kenneth J. Davis, Scott C. Herndon, Daniel J. Jacob, Anna Karion, Eric A. Kort, Brian K. Lamb, Thomas Lauvaux, Johannes D. Maasakkers, Anthony J. Marchese, Mark Omara, Stephen W. Pacala, Jeff Peischl, Allen L. Robinson, Paul B. Shepson, Colm Sweeney, Amy Townsend-Small, Steven C. Wofsy and Steven P. Hamburg. 'Assessment of methane emissions from the US oil and gas supply chain', *Science* 361 (2018): 186–8.

Amanatidou, Effie, Maurits Butter, Vincente Carabias, Totti Könnölä, Miriam Leis, Ozcan Saritas, Petra Schaper-Rinkel and Victor van Rij. 'On concepts and methods in horizon scanning: lessons from initiating policy dialogues on emerging issues', *Science and Public Policy* 39 (2012): 208–21.

American Association for the Advancement of Science. 'Statement of the board of directors of the American Association for the Advancement of Science regarding personal attacks on climate scientists', 29 June 2011. Accessed 15 October 2021. https://www.aaas.org/sites/default/files/s3fs-public/0629board_statement.pdf.

American Statistician. special issue, 'Statistical Inference in the 21st Century: A World beyond p < 0.05', 73/Supplement 1 (2019): 1–401. https://www.tandfonline.com/toc/utas20/73/sup1.

Amrhein, Valentin, David Trafimow and Sander Greenland. 'Inferential statistics and descriptive statistics: there is no replication crisis if we don't expect replication', *American Statistician* 73/Supplement 1 (2019): 262–70.

Amundson, R., A. A. Berhe, J. W. Hopmans, C. Olson, A. E. Sztein and D. L. Sparks. 'Soil and human security in the 21st century', *Science* 348/6235 (2015): 1261071. Accessed 31 May 2022. https://doi.org/10.1126/science.1261071.

Ando, Amy W. 'Waiting to be protected under the Endangered Species Act: the political economy of regulatory delay', *Journal of Law and Economics* 42 (1999): 29–60.

Archer, Kelby. 'Sneed prairie prescribed fire', YouTube, 21 February 2019. Accessed 9 November 2021. https://www.youtube.com/watch?v=twEbbZvMeIM.

Armstrong, Gregory L., Laura A. Conn and Robert W. Pinner. 'Trends in infectious disease mortality in the United States during the 20th century', *JAMA* 281 (1999): 61–6.

Arrhenius, Svante. 'On the influence of carbonic acid in the air upon the temperature of the ground', *London, Edinburgh, and Dublin Philosophical Magazine and Journal of Science*, Series 5, 41 (1896): 237–76.

Arrington, Linda. 'Addition of PF10 respirator to strychnine labels as required by the EPA letter dated July 19, 2019'. EPA Office of Pesticide Programs. Accessed 5 October 2021. https://www3.epa.gov/pesticides/chem_search/ppls/036029-00007-20190930.pdf.

Associated Press. 'Industry fights safety retrofit of older rail cars', *Houston Chronicle*, 29 July 2013. Accessed 2 November 2021. http://www.houstonchronicle.com/business/energy/article/Industry-fights-safety-retrofit-of-older-rail-cars-4694557.php#/0.

Atlas, Mark. 'Enforcement principles and environmental agencies: principal–agent relationships in a delegated environmental program', *Law and Society Review* 41 (2007): 939–80.

Attina, Teresa M., Russ Hauser, Sheela Sathyanarayana, Patricia A. Hunt, Jean-Pierre Bourguignon, John P. Myers, Joseph DiGangi, R. Thomas Zoeller and Leonardo Trasande. 'Exposure to endocrine-disrupting chemicals in the USA: a population-based disease burden and cost analysis', *The Lancet: Diabetes & Endocrinology* 4 (2016): 996–1003.

Austin College. 'Climate action plan and greenhouse gas reports'. n.d. Accessed 22 April 2022. https://www.austincollege.edu/academics/majors-and-minors/center-for-environmental-studies/climate-action-plan-greenhouse-gas-reports.

Austin College. 'Austin College sustainability plan'. 2018. Accessed 29 November 2021. https://www.austincollege.edu/wp-content/uploads/2018/04/Austin-College-Sustainability-Plan-April-2018.pdf.

Ayres, Edward. 'The history of a cup of coffee', *WorldWatch* 7 (1994): 20–2.

Ayres, Robert U. 'Use of materials balances to estimate aggregate waste generation in the US'. In *Measures of Environmental Performance and Ecosystem Condition*, edited by Peter C. Schulze, 96–156. Washington, DC: National Academies Press, 1999.

Ayres, Robert U. 'On the practical limits to substitution', *Ecological Economics* 61 (2007): 115–28.

Bailar, John C. 'How to distort the scientific record without actually lying: truth, and the arts of science', *European Journal of Oncology* 11 (2006): 217–24.

Baker, Kevin. 'Freedom from inspiration', *Harper's*, March 2019: 5–7. Accessed 17 October 2021. https://harpers.org/archive/2019/03/freedom-from-inspiration-norman-rockwell-museum-at-stockbridge-roosevelt/.

Baker, Monya. '1,500 scientists lift the lid on reproducibility', *Nature* 533 (2016): 452–4.

Balirwa, John S., Colin A. Chapman, Lauren J. Chapman, Ian G. Cowx, Kim Geheb, Les Kaufman, Rosemary H. Lowe-McConell, Ole Seehausen, Jan H. Wanink, Robin L. Welcomme and Frans Witte. 'Biodiversity and fisheries sustainability in the Lake Victoria basin: an unexpected marriage?', *BioScience* 53 (2003): 703–16.

Baltic Marine Environment Protection Commission. 'About us'. Accessed 3 November 2021. https://helcom.fi/about-us/.

Bamberger Ranch. 'Our story'. n.d. Accessed 4 January 2022. https://www.bambergerranch.org/our-story.

Bamberger Ranch. 'Selah'. n.d. Accessed 31 December 2021. https://www.bambergerranch.org/.

Barba, Alisa. 'IE questions: now we're "cooking with gas"', *Inside Energy News*, 26 June 2014. Accessed 1 November 2021. http://insideenergy.org/2014/06/26/ie-questions-now-were-cooking-with-gas/.

Barbier, Edward B. *Economics, Natural-Resource Scarcity and Development: Conventional and alternative views*. London: Earthscan, 1989.

Barry, John M. 'Politics won't stop the pandemic', *New York Times*, 14 July 2020. https://www.nytimes.com/2020/07/14/opinion/coronavirus-shutdown.html.

Bazelon, E. 2017. 'The new front in the gerrymandering wars: democracy vs. math', *New York Times*, 29 August. Accessed 22 March 2022. https://www.nytimes.com/2017/08/29/magazine/the-new-front-in-the-gerrymandering-wars-democracy-vs-math.html.

Bazzano, Lydia A., Tian Hu, Kristi Reynolds, Lu Yao, Calynn Bunol, Yanxi Liu, Chung-Shiuan Chen, Michael J. Klag, Paul K. Whelton and Jiang He. 'Effects of low-carbohydrate and low-fat diets', *Annals of Internal Medicine* 161 (2014): 309–18.

Beall, Jeffrey. 'What I learned from predatory publishers', *Biochemia Medica* 27 (2017): 273–8.

Bearak, Jonathan, Anna Popinchalk, Bela Ganatra, Ann-Beth Moller, Özge Tunçalp, Cynthia Beavin, Lorraine Kwok and Leontine Alkema. 'Unintended pregnancy and abortion by income, region, and the legal status of abortion: estimates from a comprehensive model for 1990–2019', *Lancet Global Health* 8 (2020): e1152–61. https://www.thelancet.com/journals/langlo/article/PIIS2214-109X(20)30315-6/fulltext.

Beatley, Timothy. *Habitat Conservation Planning: Endangered species and urban growth*. Austin: University of Texas Press, 1994.

Beder, Sharon. *Global Spin: The corporate assault on environmentalism*. White River Junction, VT: Chelsea Green, 2002.

Begley, C. Glenn and Lee M. Ellis. 'Drug development: raise standards for preclinical cancer research', *Nature* 483 (2012): 531–3.

Begley, Sharon. 'Exclusive: FDA prices "lost pleasure" of junk food into calorie count rule', *Reuters*, 8 December 2014. Accessed 8 November 2021. https://www.reuters.com/article/us-usa-health-calories-exclusive-idUSKBN0JM0DU20141208.

Begos, Kevin. 'DOE study: fracking chemicals didn't taint water', *USA Today*, 19 July 2013. Accessed 13 October 2021. http://www.usatoday.com/story/money/business/2013/07/19/doe-study-fracking-didnt-taint/2567721/.

Beitsch, Rebecca. '14 states sue EPA over rollback of Obama-era water rule', *The Hill*, 20 December 2019. Accessed 21 October 2021. https://thehill.com/policy/energy-environment/475500-14-states-sue-epa-over-rollback-of-obama-era-water-rule.

Belli, Pedro, Jock Anderson, Howard Barnum, John Dixon and Jee-Peng Tan. *Handbook on Economic Analysis of Investment Operations*. Washington, DC: World Bank Operational Core Services Network Learning and Leadership Center, 1998. Accessed 7 November 2021. https://www.climateandforests-undp.org/sites/default/files/downloads/handbookea.pdf.

Bennagen, Ponciano L. 'Tribal Filipinos'. In *Indigenous Views of Land and the Environment*, edited by Shelton H. Davis, 67–84. Washington, DC: World Bank, 1993.

Benoît, Hugues P. and Douglas P. Swain. 'Impacts of environmental change and direct and indirect harvesting effects on the dynamics of a marine fish community', *Canadian Journal of Fisheries and Aquatic Sciences* 65 (2008): 2088–104.

Benson, Lisa M. and Karen Reczek. *A Guide to United States Apparel and Household Textiles Compliance Requirements*. Gaithersburg, MD: US Department of Commerce National Institute of Standards and Technology, 2016. Accessed 10 October 2021. https://nvlpubs.nist.gov/nistpubs/ir/2016/NIST.IR.8115.pdf.

Bernard, Tara S. 'When wrinkle-free clothing also means formaldehyde fumes', *New York Times*, 10 December 2010. Accessed 10 October 2021. http://www.nytimes.com/2010/12/11/your-money/11wrinkle.html.

Bernhardt, E. S., M. A. Palmer, J. D. Allan, G. Alexander, K. Barnas, S. Brooks, J. Carr, S. Clayton, C. Dahm, J. Follstad-Shah, D. Galat, S. Gloss, P. Goodwin, D. Hart, B. Hassett, R. Jenkinson, S. Katz, G. M. Kondolf, P. S. Lake, R. Lave, J. L. Meyer, T. K. O'Donnell, L. Pagano, B. Powell and E. Sudduth. 'Synthesizing US river restoration efforts', *Science* 308 (2005): 636–7.

Berry, Wendell. *The Way of Ignorance and Other Essays*. Washington, DC: Shoemaker and Hoard, 2005.

Bill and Melinda Gates Foundation. 'Family planning'. n.d. Accessed 18 October 2021. https://www.gatesfoundation.org/our-work/programs/global-development/family-planning.

Binder, Sarah. 'The history of the filibuster', Brookings, 22 April 2010. Accessed 27 October 2021. https://www.brookings.edu/testimonies/the-history-of-the-filibuster/.

Bishop, Richard C., Kevin J. Boyle, Richard T. Carson, David Chapman, W. Michael Hanemann, Barbara Kanninen, Raymond J. Kopp, John A. Krosnick, John List, Norman Meade, Robert Paterson, Stanley Presser, V. Kerry Smith, Roger Tourangeau, Michael Welsh, Jeffrey M. Wooldridge, Matthew DeBell, Colleen Donovan, Matthew Konopka and Nora Scherer. 'Putting a value on injuries to natural assets: the BP oil spill', *Science* 356 (2017): 253–4.

Blaustein, Andrew R., Barbara A. Han, Rick A. Relyea, Pieter T. J. Johnson, Julia C. Buck, Stephanie S. Gervasi and Lee B. Kats. 'The complexity of amphibian population declines: understanding the role of cofactors in driving amphibian losses', *Annals of the New York Academy of Sciences* 1223 (2011): 108–19.

Blyskal, Jeff and Marie Blyskal. *PR: How the public relations industry writes the news*. New York: William Morrow and Company, 1985.

Bohannon, John. 'Who's afraid of peer review?', *Science* 342 (2013): 60–5.

Bohannon, John. 'I fooled millions into thinking chocolate helps weight loss: here's how', *GIZMODO*, 27 May 2015. Accessed 14 October 2021. https://gizmodo.com/i-fooled-millions-into-thinking-chocolate-helps-weight-1707251800.

Bollen, Johannes, Bob van der Zwaan, Corjan Brink and Hans Eerens. 'Local air pollution and global climate change: a combined cost–benefit analysis', *Resource and Energy Economics* 31 (2009): 161–81.

Borenstein, Seth. 'Poll: Americans favor slightly higher bills to fight warming', *Associated Press*, 14 September 2016. Accessed 20 October 2021. https://apnews.com/article/4e555a1f920548db84aeb4c83fc1a284.

Bowerman, William W., John P. Giesy, David A. Best and Vincent J. Kramer. 'A review of factors affecting productivity of bald eagles in the Great Lakes region: implications for recovery', *Environmental Health Perspectives* 103/Supplement 4 (1995): 51–9.

Boyce, James K. *The Case for Carbon Dividends*. Medford, MA: Polity Press, 2019.

Boykoff, Maxwell T. and Jules M. Boykoff. 'Balance as bias: global warming and the US prestige press', *Global Environmental Change* 14 (2004): 125–36.

Bradford, Abigail, Jonathan Sundby, Bronte Payne and Jake Taber. 'America's top colleges for renewable energy: who's leading the transition to 100% renewable energy on campus?', *Environment America*, April 2019. Accessed 3 November 2021. https://environmentamerica.org/feature/ame/americas-top-colleges-renewable-energy.

Brancaccio, David and Katie Long. 'What if we had a Secretary of the Future?', *Marketplace Morning Report*, 1 March 2016, 00:21-00:33. Accessed 10 October 2021. https://www.marketplace.org/2016/03/01/secretary-future/.

Brennan Center for Justice. 'Who draws the maps? Legislative and congressional redistricting', 30 January 2019. Accessed 23 October 2021. https://www.brennancenter.org/our-work/research-reports/who-draws-maps-legislative-and-congressional-redistricting.

Brennan Center for Justice. 'Voting laws roundup: October 2021'. 4 October 2021. Accessed 22 October 2021. https://www.brennancenter.org/our-work/research-reports/voting-laws-roundup-october-2021.

Breyer, Stephen G., Richard B. Stewart, Cass R. Sunstein, Adrian Vermeule and Michael E. Herz. *Administrative Law and Regulatory Policy: Problems, texts, and cases*. 8th edition. New York: Wolters Kluwer, 2017.

Brody, Hugh. *Living Arctic: Hunters of the Canadian North*. London: Faber and Faber, 1987.

Bromfeld, Louis. *Pleasant Valley*. New York: Harper and Brothers, 1943.

Brookings Institution. 'Vital statistics on Congress: data on the US Congress', updated February 2021'. 8 February 2021. Accessed 10 November 2021. https://www.brookings.edu/multi-chapter-report/vital-statistics-on-congress/.

Brown, Matthew. 'Feds reverse course on wolverine protections, citing climate change "uncertainty"', *US News and World Report*, 12 August 2014. Accessed 3 November 2021. http://www.usnews.com/news/science/news/articles/2014/08/12/apnewsbreak-feds-reverse-course-on-wolverines.

Brulle, Robert J. 'Institutionalizing delay: foundation funding and the creation of US climate change counter-movement organizations', *Climatic Change* 122 (2014): 681–94.

Brulle, Robert J. 'The climate lobby: a sectoral analysis of lobbying spending on climate change in the USA, 2000 to 2016', *Climatic Change* 149 (2018): 289–303.

Brulle, Robert J. and David N. Pellow. 'Environmental justice: human health and environmental inequalities', *Annual Review of Public Health* 27 (2006): 103–24.

Buck v. Bell, 274 US 200 (1927).

Bullard, Robert D., Paul Mohai, Robin Sana and Beverly Wright. 'Toxic wastes and race at twenty, 1987–2007', Cleveland, OH: United Church of Christ Justice and Witness Ministries, 2007. Accessed 22 October 2021. https://www.learningforjustice.org/sites/default/files/documents/toxic20.pdf.

Burges, Austin E. *Soil Erosion Control*. Atlanta: Turner E. Smith, 1938.

Burtraw, Dallas and Amelia Keyes. 'Recognizing gravity as a strong force in atmosphere emissions markets', *Agricultural and Resource Economics Review* 47 (2018): 201–19.

Bush v. Vera, 517 US 952 (1996).

Bush, George W. 'Executive Order 13337: Issuance of permits with respect to certain energy-related facilities and land transportation crossings on the international boundaries of the US', Executive Order 13337, *Federal Register*, 1 May 2004, 723. Accessed 1 November 2021. http://www.gpo.gov/fdsys/pkg/WCPD-2004-05-10/pdf/WCPD-2004-05-10-Pg723.pdf.

Bushnell, Philip J. 'Solvents, ethanol, car crashes and tolerance', *American Scientist* 101 (2013): 282–91.

Buzbee, William W. 'Contextual environmental federalism', *New York University Environmental Law Journal* 14 (2005): 108–29.

Cahan, Richard and Michael Williams. *The Lost Panoramas: When Chicago changed its river and the land beyond*. Chicago: CityFiles Press, 2011.

Calderón Hinojosa, Felipe. 'The restoration revolution', *The Mark News*, 20 April 2017. Accessed 19 October 2021. http://www.themarknews.com/2017/04/20 the-restoration-revolution/.

Caldwell, John C. 'Malthus and the less developed world: the pivotal role of India', *Population and Development Review* 24 (1998): 675–96.

Cama, Timothy. 'Drillers file lawsuit to challenge Obama's new fracking rules', *The Hill*, 20 March 2015. Accessed 19 October 2021. https://thehill.com/policy/energy-environment/236429-drillers-file-lawsuit-to-challenge-fracking-rules.

Cannon, Jonathan. 'Blue-green algae health hazard in Lake Texoma', *Herald Democrat* (Sherman, TX), 28 August 2011, A8.

Carroll, Lauren. '"With certainty" cap-and-trade would wreck the economy, Rubio says', *Politifact*, 23 April 2015. Accessed 19 October 2021. https://www.politifact.com/factchecks/2015/apr/23/marco-rubio/rubio-cap-and-trade-would-hurt-economy-might-not-h/.

Carson, Rachel. *Silent Spring*. Boston: Houghton-Mifflin, 1962.

Carter, Neil. *The Politics of the Environment*. Cambridge. Cambridge University Press, 2001.

Cato Institute. 'Environmental regulation'. n.d. Accessed 19 October 2021. https://www.cato.org/environmental-regulation.

CBC News. 'Funding for experimental lakes area brings stability, opportunity for research', 16 August 2016. Accessed 11 October 2021. https://www.cbc.ca/news/canada/thunder-bay/experimental-lakes-funding-brings-stability-1.3722763.

Center for Biological Diversity. 'Landmark agreement moves 757 species toward federal protection'. n.d. Accessed 3 November 2021. https://www.biologicaldiversity.org/programs/biodiversity/species_agreement/.

Center for Biological Diversity. 'Programs'. n.d. Accessed 18 October 2021. http://www.biologicaldiversity.org/programs/index.html.

Center for Biological Diversity. 'Letter to U. S. Fish and Wildlife Service'. 9 October 2014. Accessed 15 October 2021. http://www.biologicaldiversity.org/campaigns/esa/pdfs/Scientist_Sign-on_letter-Critical_Habitat_Adverse_Mod.pdf.

Center for Biological Diversity v. Salazar, 'Stipulated settlement agreement', 10-cv-0230, US District Court, District of Columbia case 1:10-mc-00377-EGS. 12 July 2011. Accessed 3 November 2021. https://www.fws.gov/endangered/improving_ESA/WILDLIFE-218963-v1-hhy_071211_exh_1_re_CBD.PDF.

Center for Media and Democracy. 'Oregon Institute of Science and Medicine', n.d. *SourceWatch*. Accessed 15 October 2021. http://www.sourcewatch.org/index.php?title=Oregon_Institute_of_Science_and_Medicine.

Center for Media and Democracy. *SourceWatch*. n.d. Accessed 9 October 2021. https://www.sourcewatch.org/index.php?title=SourceWatch.

Cereceda, Rafael. 'The Antarctic ozone hole is among the largest on record, how does it affect me?', *Euronews*, 27 September 2021. Accessed 3 October 2021. https://www.euronews.com/green/2021/09/23/the-antarctic-ozone-hole-is-among-the-largest-on-record-again-why-and-how-does-it-affect-m.

Chagnon, Stanley A. and Mary E. Harper. 'History of the Chicago diversion'. In *The Lake Michigan Diversion at Chicago and Urban Drought: Past, present and future regional impacts and responses to global climate change*, edited by Stanley A. Chagnon, 16–38. Washington, DC: National Oceanic and Atmospheric Administration, 1994.

Chaloupka, Frank J., Kenneth E. Warner, Daron Acemoğlu, Johnathan Gruber, Fritz Laux, Wendy Max, Joseph Newhouse, Thomas Schelling and Jody Sindelar. 'An evaluation of FDA's analysis of the costs and benefits of the graphic warning label regulation', *Tobacco Control* 24 (2015): 112–19.

Chamberlain, Thomas C. 'The method of multiple working hypotheses', *Science* 148 (1965): 754–9.

Charity Navigator. 'Types of nonprofits'. n.d. Accessed 26 October 2021. https://www.charitynavigator.org/index.cfm?bay=content.view&cpid=1559.

Charles E. Young Research Library. '*Los Angeles Times* Photographs Collection'. University of California at Los Angeles. Accessed 16 November 2021. http://digital2.library.ucla.edu/viewItem.do?ark=21198/zz0002qw7r. CC BY-SA 4.0 license: https://creativecommons.org/licenses/by/4.0/deed.en.

Chen, Mei, Chi-Hsuan Chang, Lin Tao, Censheng Lu. 'Residential exposure to pesticide during childhood and childhood cancers: a meta-analysis', *Pediatrics* 136 (2015): 719–29.

Chestnut, Lauraine G. and David M. Mills. 'A fresh look at the benefits and costs of the US acid rain program', *Journal of Environmental Management* 77 (2005): 252–66.

Chirif, A., P. G. Hierro and R. C. Smith. *El Indígena y su Territorio Son Uno Solo: Estrategias para la defensa de los pueblos y territorios indígenas en la cuenca Amazónica*. Lima: Oxfam América and Coordinadora de las Organizaciones Indígenas de la Cuenca Amazónica, 1991.

Chokshi, Niraj. 'That wasn't Mark Twain: how a misquotation was born', *New York Times*, 26 April 2017. Accessed 14 October 2021. https://www.nytimes.com/2017/04/26/books/famous-misquotations.html.

Chung, Jean. 'Voting rights in the era of mass incarceration: a primer', *The Sentencing Project*, 28 July 2021. Accessed 22 October 2021. https://www.sentencingproject.org/publications/felony-disenfranchisement-a-primer/.

Cillizza, Chris. 'Donald Trump buried a climate change report because "I don't believe it"', *CNN*, 27 November 2018. Accessed 3 November 2021. https://www.cnn.com/2018/11/26/politics/donald-trump-climate-change/index.html.

Clark, Colin W. 'The economics of overexploitation', *Science* 181 (1973): 630–4.

Clark, Sara. 'In the shadow of the Fourth Circuit: Ohio Valley Environmental Coalition v. United States Army Corps of Engineers', *Ecology Law Quarterly* 35 (2008): 143–9.

Clarke, Arthur C. 'The Knowledge Explosion'. Episode of TV documentary series *Horizon*, BBC, 1964, 4:33–4:37. Accessed 10 October 2021. https://www.youtube.com/watch?v=KT_8-pjuctM.

Cobb, Jelani. 'What is happening to the Republicans?', *New Yorker*, 15 March 2021. Accessed 7 October 2021. https://www.newyorker.com/magazine/2021/03/15/what-is-happening-to-the-republicans.

Cohen, Donald. 'Climate regulations a job killer? Quit crying wolf', *Common Dreams*, 12 July 2011. Accessed 4 January 2022. https://www.commondreams.org/views/2011/07/12/climate-regulations-job-killer-quit-crying-wolf.

Cohen, Patricia. 'Economic ties among nations spur peace. Or do they?', *New York Times*, 4 March 2022. Accessed 13 April 2022. https://www.nytimes.com/2022/03/04/business/economy/ukraine-russia-global-economy.html.

Cohen, Steven. *Understanding Environmental Policy*. New York: Columbia University Press, 2006.

Collier, Kiah. 'Federal judge rules against Formosa Plastics in pollution case, calling company a "serial offender"', *Texas Tribune*, 28 June 2019. Accessed 4 November 2021. https://www.texastribune.org/2019/06/28/federal-judge-rules-lawsuit-formosa-plastics-texas-pollution-case/.

Collins, James P. 'Amphibian decline and extinction: what we know and what we need to learn', *Diseases of Aquatic Organisms* 92 (2010): 93–9.

Collins, Jason, Boris Baer and Ernst J. Weber. 'Evolutionary biology in economics: a review', *Economic Record* 92 (2016): 291–312.

Colquhoun, David. 'The reproducibility of research and the misinterpretation of p-values', *Royal Society Open Science* 4 (2017). Accessed 31 May 2022. http://dx.doi.org/10.1098/rsos.171085.

Comay, Laura B., R. Eliot Crafton and Michael Ratner. 'Arctic National Wildlife Refuge (ANWR): an overview', US Congressional Research Service, RL33872, updated 9 January 2018. Accessed 1 November 2021. https://crsreports.congress.gov/product/pdf/RL/RL33872.

Comeau, Pauline. 'New endangered species plan unveiled', *Canadian Geographic*, July/August 1998: 29–30.

Condon, Bernard. 'Fear of economic blow as births drop around world', *yahoo!finance*, 7 May 2014. Accessed 18 October 2021. https://finance.yahoo.com/news/fear-economic-blow-births-drop-162123871.html.

Condorcet, Nicolas de. *Outlines of an Historical View of the Progress of the Human Mind* (translated from French). New York: M. Carey, H. and P. Rice and Company, J. Ormrod, B. F. Bache and J. Fellows, 1796.

Conney, A. H. and J. J. Burns. 'Metabolic interactions among environmental chemicals and drugs', *Science* 178 (1972): 576–86.

Cooper, John M. (ed.). *Critias* (translated by Diskin Clay), In *Plato: Complete Works*, 1292–1306. Indianapolis: Hackett, 1997.

Copeland, Claudia. 'Mountaintop removal mining: background on recent controversies', Congressional Research Service, RS21421, 13 December 2016. Accessed 4 November 2021. https://crsreports.congress.gov/product/details?prodcode=RS21421.

Copper, Carolyn, Tom Reilly, Denise Darasaw, Tina Lovingood and Barry Parker. 'Implementation, information, and statutory obstacles impede achievement of environmental results from EPA's national hardrock mining framework'. Washington, DC: EPA Office of the Inspector General report no. 2003-P-00010, 2003. Accessed 3 November 2021. https://www.epa.gov/office-inspector-general/report-implementation-information-and-statutory-obstacles-impede.

Corasaniti, Nick, Reid J. Epstein, Taylor Johnston, Rebecca Lieberman and Eden Weingart. 'How maps reshape American politics', *New York Times*, 7 November 2021. Accessed 27 November 2021. https://www.nytimes.com/interactive/2021/11/07/us/politics/redistricting-maps-explained.html.

Corasaniti, Nick, Ella Koeze and Denise Lu. 'How Texas plans to make its house districts even redder', *New York Times*, 3 October 2021. Accessed 23 October 2021. https://www.nytimes.com/interactive/2021/10/03/us/politics/texas-redistricting-map-2022.html.

Corkery, Michael. 'As costs skyrocket, more US cities stop recycling', *New York Times*, 16 March 2019. Accessed 7 October 2021. https://www.nytimes.com/2019/03/16/business/local-recycling-costs.html.

Costanza, Robert, John Cumberland, Herman Daly, Robert Goodland and Richard Norgaard. *An Introduction to Ecological Economics*. Boca Raton, FL: St. Lucie Press, 1997.

Cox, D. R. *Planning of Experiments*. New York: Wiley, 1958.

Cox, D. R. 'Interaction', *International Statistical Review* 52 (1984): 1–24.

Crutzen, Paul J. and Eugene F. Stoermer. 'The Anthropocene', *International Geosphere-Biosphere Programme Newsletter* 41 (May 2000): 17–18. Accessed 8 November 2021. http://www.igbp.net/download/18.316f18321323470177580001401/1376383088452/NL41.pdf.

Cushman, John H. Jr. 'Industrial group plans to battle climate treaty', *New York Times*, 26 April 1998. Accessed 8 November 2021. https://www.nytimes.com/1998/04/26/us/industrial-group-plans-to-battle-climate-treaty.html.

D'Agostino, Lorena M. 'How MNEs respond to environmental regulation: integrating the Porter hypothesis and the pollution haven hypothesis', *Economia Politica* 32 (2015): 245–69.

Daily, Gretchen C. and Paul R. Ehrlich. 'Population, sustainability, and Earth's carrying capacity', *BioScience* 42 (1992): 761–71.

Dale, Tom and Vernon G. Carter. *Topsoil and Civilization*. Norman: University of Oklahoma Press, 1955.

Daley, Dave. 'New poll: everybody hates gerrymandering', *FairVote,* 12 September 2017. Accessed 23 October 2021. http://www.fairvote.org/new_poll_everybody_hates_gerrymandering.

Dallas Morning News. 'BP spill, other disasters expose technological limits', 18 July 2010. Accessed 10 October 2021. https://www.dallasnews.com/business/2010/07/17/bp-spill-other-disasters-expose-technological-limits/.

Dallas Morning News. 'Energy executives question SMU-led quake study at Austin meeting', 5 June 2015. Accessed 4 November 2021. https://www.dallasnews.com/news/texas/2015/06/06/energy-executives-question-smu-led-quake-study-at-austin-meeting/.

Daly, Herman E. *Beyond Growth*. Boston: Beacon Press, 1996.

Daly, Herman E. 'Economics in a full world', *Scientific American* 293/3 (2005): 100–7.

Daly, Herman E. and John B. Cobb, Jr. *For the Common Good*. Boston: Beacon Press, 1989.

Das, Abhijit A. and Sana Contractor. 'India's latest sterilisation camp massacre', *BMJ* 349 (2014): g7282. Accessed 31 May 2022. https://doi.org/10.1136/bmj.g7282.

Dasgupta, Partha. 'Foreword'. In *Inclusive Wealth Report 2018: Measuring progress toward sustainability*, edited by Shunsuke Managi and Pushpam Kumar, xi–xxviii. London: Routledge, 2018. Accessed 30 May 2022. https://doi.org/10.4324/9781351002080.

Davenport, Coral. 'Billionaire environmentalist to spend $25 million to turn out young voters', *New York Times*, 25 April 2016. Accessed 1 November 2021. https://www.nytimes.com/2016/04/26/us/politics/thomas-steyer-nextgen-climate-change-voters.html.

Davenport, Coral. 'Obama climate plan, now in court, may hinge on error in 1990 law', *New York Times*, 25 September 2016. Accessed 3 November 2021. https://www.nytimes.com/2016/09/26/us/politics/obama-court-clean-power-plan.html.

Davenport, Coral. 'EPA official pressured scientist on Congressional testimony, emails show', *New York Times*, 26 June 2017. Accessed 3 November 2021. https://www.nytimes.com/2017/06/26/us/politics/epa-official-pressured-scientist-on-congressional-testimony-emails-show.html.

Davenport, Coral. 'Counseled by industry, not staff, EPA chief is off to a blazing start', *New York Times*, 1 July 2017. Accessed 4 November 2021. https://www.nytimes.com/2017/07/01/us/politics/trump-epa-chief-pruitt-regulations-climate-change.html.

Davenport, Coral. 'Trump Administration loosens sage grouse protections, benefitting oil companies', *New York Times*, 15 March 2019. Accessed 3 November 2021. https://www.nytimes.com/2019/03/15/climate/trump-sage-grouse.html.

Davenport, Coral and Emmarie Huetteman. 'Lawmakers reach deal to expand regulation of toxic chemicals', *New York Times*, 19 May 2016. Accessed 1 October 2021. https://www.nytimes.com/2016/05/20/us/politics/toxic-substances-chemicals-environment.html.

Davenport, Coral and Eric Lipton. 'Scott Pruitt is carrying out his EPA agenda in secret, critics say', *New York Times*, 11 August 2017. Accessed 20 October 2021. https://www.nytimes.com/2017/08/11/us/politics/scott-pruitt-epa.html.

Davenport, Coral and Ashley Southall. 'Critics say spill highlights lax West Virginia regulations', *New York Times*, 12 January 2014. Accessed 4 November 2021. https://www.nytimes.com/2014/01/13/us/critics-say-chemical-spill-highlights-lax-west-virginia-regulations.html.

David, E. E. Jr. 'Inventing the future: energy and the CO2 "greenhouse" effect'. In *Climate Processes and Climate Sensitivity*, edited by James E. Hansen and Taro Takahashi, 1–5. Washington, DC: American Geophysical Union, 1984.

Davis, Mike. *Late Victorian Holocausts: El Niño famines and the making of the third world*. London: Verso, 2001.

Dayton, Paul K. 'Reversal of the burden of proof in fisheries management', *Science* 279 (1998): 821–2.

Deardorff, Julie. 'Scientists: nanotech-based products offer great potential but unknown risks', *Chicago Tribune*, 10 July 2012. Accessed 10 October 2021. https://www.chicagotribune.com/lifestyles/health/ct-met-nanotechnology-20120710-story.html.

Deen, Thalif. 'US lifestyle is not up for negotiation', *Inter Press Service News Agency*, 1 May 2012. Accessed 2 November 2021. http://www.ipsnews.net/2012/05/us-lifestyle-is-not-up-for-negotiation/.

Defenders of Wildlife v. Jewell, CV 14-246-M-DLC, US District Court, District of Montana case 9:14-cv-00246-DLC. 4 April 2016. Accessed 3 November 2021. https://www.fws.gov/mountain-prairie/es/Library/Order_WolverineDecision_Montana_Filed2016-04-04.pdf.

De Freytas-Tamura, Kimiko. 'In Brexit debate, English fishermen eye waters free of EU', *New York Times*, 14 April 2016. Accessed 8 November 2021. http://www.nytimes.com/2016/04/15/business/international/many-in-british-fishing-port-want-eu-out-of-their-waters.html.

Democratic National Convention. '2020 Democratic Party Platform'. Accessed 17 October 2021. https://democrats.org/wp-content/uploads/sites/2/2020/08/2020-Democratic-Party-Platform.pdf.

Dennis, Brady and Juliet Eilperin. 'EPA to make it harder to tighten mercury rules in the future', *Washington Post*, 28 December 2018. Accessed 20 October 2021. https://www.washingtonpost.com/energy-environment/2018/12/28/epa-make-it-harder-tighten-mercury-rules-future/.

Dennis, Brady and Juliet Eilperin. 'States aren't waiting for the Trump Administration on environmental protections', *Washington Post*, 19 May 2019. Accessed 1 October 2021. https://www.washingtonpost.com/national/health-science/states-arent-waiting-for-the-trump-administration-on-environmental-protections/2019/05/19/5dc853fc-7722-11e9-b3f5-5673edf2d127_story.html.

Diamond, Jared. *Collapse: How societies choose to fail or succeed*. New York: Viking, 2005.

Díaz, Sandra, Josef Settele, Eduardo S. Brondízio, Hien T. Ngo, Maximillien Guèze, John Agard, Almut Arneth, Patricia Balvanera, Kate A. Brauman, Stuart H. M. Butchart, Kai M. A. Chan, Lucas A. Garibaldi, Kazuhito Ichii, Jianguo Liu, Suneetha M. Subramanian, Guy F. Midgley, Patricia Miloslavich, Zsolt Molnár, David Obura, Alexander Pfaff, Stephen Polasky, Andy Purvis, Jona Razzaque, Belinda Reyers, Rinku R. Chowdhury, Yunne-Jai Shin, Ingrid J. Visseren-Hamakers, Katherine J. Willis and Cynthia N. Zayas. *The Global Assessment Report on Biodiversity and Ecosystem Services: Summary for policymakers*. Intergovernmental Science-Policy Platform on Biodiversity and Ecosystem Services (IPBES) secretariat, 2019, Bonn, Germany. Accessed 7 October 2021. https://ipbes.net/sites/default/files/2020-02/ipbes_global_assessment_report_summary_for_policymakers_en.pdf.

Didham, Raphael K., Yves Basset, C. Matilda Collins, Simon R. Leather, Nick A. Littlewood, Myles H. M. Menz, Jörg Müller, Laurence Packer, Manu E. Saunders, Karsten Schönrogge, Alan J. A. Stewart, Stephen P. Yanoviak and Christopher Hassall. 'Interpreting insect declines: seven challenges and a way forward', *Insect Conservation and Diversity* 13 (2020): 103–14.

Dieter, Cheryl A., Molly A. Maupin, Rodney R. Caldwell, Melissa A. Harris, Tamara I. Ivahnenko, John K. Lovelace, Nancy L. Barber and Kristen S. Linsey. 'Estimated use of water in the United States in 2015', US Geological Survey, Circular 1441, 2018. Accessed 1 November 2021. https://doi.org/10.3133/cir1441.

Dietze, Michael C., Andrew Fox, Lindsay M. Beck-Johnson, Julio L. Betancourt, Mevin B. Hooten, Catherine S. Jarnevich, Timothy H. Keitt, Melissa A Kenney, Christine M. Laney, Laurel G. Larsen, Henry W. Loescher, Claire K. Lunch, Bryan C. Pijanowski, James T. Randerson, Emily K. Read, Andrew T. Tredennick, Rodrigo Vargas, Kathleen C. Weathers and Ethan P. White. 'Iterative near-term ecological forecasting: needs, opportunities, and challenges', *Proceedings of the National Academy of Sciences of the United States of America* 115 (2017): 1424–32.

Doak, Daniel F., James A. Estes, Benjamin S. Halpern, Ute Jacob, David R. Lindberg, James Lovvorn, Daniel H. Monson, M. Timothy Tinker, Terrie M. Williams, J. Timothy Wootton, Ian Carroll, Mark Emmerson, Fiorenza Micheli and Mark Novak. 'Understanding and predicting ecological dynamics: are major surprises inevitable?', *Ecology* 89 (2008): 952–61.

Donahue, Debra L. 'Western grazing: the capture of grass, ground, and government', *Environmental Law* 35 (2005): 721–806.

Doughton, Sandi. 'Gates birth-control initiative could fire up its critics', *Seattle Times*, 7 July 2012. Accessed 18 October 2021. http://www.seattletimes.com/seattle-news/gates-birth-control-initiative-could-fire-up-its-critics/.

Downs, Anthony. 'Up and down with ecology: the issue-attention cycle', *Public Interest* 28 (1972): 38–50.

Driesen, David M. 'Is cost–benefit analysis neutral?', *University of Colorado Law Review* 77 (2006): 335–404.

DrillingEdge. 'Oil and gas production in Texas'. May 2021. Accessed 8 October 2021. http://www.drillingedge.com/texas.

Drouin, Roger. 'Wood pellets: green energy or new source of CO_2 emissions?', *YaleEnvironment*[360], 22 January 2015. Accessed 1 November 2021. http://e360.yale.edu/feature/wood_pellets_green_energy_or_new_source_of_co2_emissions/2840/.

Duffin, Jacalyn and Charles R. R. Hayter. 'Baring the sole: the rise and fall of the shoe-fitting fluroroscope', *Isis* 91 (2000): 260–82.

Duhigg, Charles. 'Clean water laws are neglected, at a cost in suffering', *New York Times*, 12 September 2009. Accessed 4 November 2021. http://www.nytimes.com/2009/09/13/us/13water.html.

Dunaway-Seale, J. 2019. 'The dredge report: what's up with digging down into White Rock Lake?', *Lake Highlands Advocate*, 21 November. Accessed 22 March 2022. https://lakehighlands.advocatemag.com/2019/11/21/the-dredge-report-whats-up-with-digging-down-into-white-rock-lake/.

Duncan, David E. 'The pollution within', *National Geographic* 210/4 (2006): 116–33.

Dwan, Kerry, Douglas G. Altman, Juan A. Arnaiz, Jill Bloom, An-Wen Chan, Eugenia Cronin, Evelyne Decullier, Philippa J. Easterbrook, Erik Von Elm, Carrol Gamble, Davina Ghersi, John P. A. Ioannidis, John Simes and Paula R. Williamson. 'Systematic review of the empirical evidence of study publication bias and outcome reporting bias', *PLOS One*, 3.8 (2008): e3081.

Earthjustice. 'Three years battling the Trump Administration's attacks on our health and environment', 17 January 2020. Accessed 21 October 2021. https://earthjustice.org/features/inside-trump-administration-public-health-environment.

Ebrahim, Shanil, Sheena Bance, Abha Athale, Cindy Malachowski and John P. A. Ioannidis. 'Meta-analyses with industry involvement are massively published and report no caveats for antidepressants', *Journal of Clinical Epidemiology* 70 (2016): 155–63.

Ecological Forecasting Initiative. 'About'. n.d. Accessed 10 April 2022. https://ecoforecast.org/.

The Economist. 'How spooks are turning to superforecasting in the Cosmic Bazaar', 15 April 2021. Accessed 7 December 2021. https://www.economist.com/science-and-technology/2021/04/15/how-spooks-are-turning-to-superforecasting-in-the-cosmic-bazaar.

Economist Intelligence Unit. 'Democracy index 2020: in sickness and in health?'. 2021. Accessed 22 October 2021. https://www.eiu.com/n/campaigns/democracy-index-2020/.

Edsall, Thomas B. 'The high cost of free speech', *New York Times*, 8 April 2014. Accessed 27 October 2021. https://www.nytimes.com/2014/04/09/opinion/the-high-cost-of-free-speech.html.

Egan, Dan and Lyndon French. 'The climate crisis haunts Chicago's future: a battle between a great city and a great lake', *New York Times*, 7 July 2021. Accessed 30 December 2021. https://www.nytimes.com/interactive/2021/07/07/climate/chicago-river-lake-michigan.html.

Ehrlich, Paul R. and Anne H. Ehrlich. *Betrayal of Science and Reason*. Washington, DC: Island Press, 1996.

Eilperin, Juliet. 'Since '01 guarding species is harder', *Washington Post*, 23 March 2008. Accessed 3 November 2021. http://www.washingtonpost.com/wp-dyn/content/article/2008/03/22/AR2008032202204.html?sid=ST200803230017.

Eilperin, Juliet and Brady Dennis. 'The EPA is about to change a rule cutting mercury pollution. The industry doesn't want it', *Washington Post*, 17 February 2020. Accessed 20 October 2021. https://www.washingtonpost.com/climate-environment/the-epa-is-about-to-change-a-rule-cutting-mercury-pollution-the-industry-doesnt-want-it/2020/02/16/8ebac4e2-4470-11ea-b503-2b077c436617_story.html.

Elliott, Justin. 'Ex-regulator flacking for pro-nuke lobby', *Salon*, 17 March 2011. Accessed 4 November 2021. http://www.salon.com/2011/03/18/jeff_merrifield_nuclear_energy_institute/.

Elsawah, Sondoss, Serena H. Hamilton, Anthony J. Jakeman, Dale Rothman, Vanessa Schweizer, Evelina Trutnevyte, Henrik Carlsen, Crystal Drakes, Bob Frame, Baihua Fu, Celine Guivarch, Marjolijn Haasnoot, Eric Kemp-Benedict, Kasper Kok, Hannah Kosow, Mike Ryan and Hedwig van Delden. 'Scenario processes for socio-environmental systems analysis of futures: a review of recent efforts and a salient research agenda for supporting decision making', *Science of the Total Environment* 729 (10 August 2020). Accessed 31 May 2022. https://doi.org/10.1016/j.scitotenv.2020.138393.

Environment Texas. 'Polluters spewed 63 million pounds of unauthorized air pollution in 2017, few penalized'. 31 January 2019. Accessed 4 November 2021. https://environmenttexas.org/news/txe/polluters-spewed-63-million-pounds-unauthorized-air-pollution-2017-few-penalized.

EPA. 'About waters of the United States'. n.d. Accessed 21 October 2021. https://www.epa.gov/nwpr/about-waters-united-states.

EPA. 'AQS memos – technical note – lead data reporting to AQS'. n.d. Accessed 16 November 2021. https://www.epa.gov/aqs/aqs-memos-technical-note-lead-data-reporting-aqs.

EPA. 'Green book national area and county-level multi-pollutant information'. n.d. Accessed 2 November 2021. https://www.epa.gov/green-book/green-book-national-area-and-county-level-multi-pollutant-information.

EPA. 'Greenhouse gas inventory data explorer'. n.d. Accessed 4 October 2021. https://cfpub.epa.gov/ghgdata/inventoryexplorer/#allsectors/allsectors/select/select/all.

EPA. 'National air quality: status and trends of key air pollutants'. n.d. Accessed 9 November 2021. https://www.epa.gov/air-trends.

EPA. 'Supplemental module: monitoring and assessment'. n.d. Accessed 16 October 2021. https://www.epa.gov/wqs-tech/supplemental-module-monitoring-and-assessment.

EPA. 'Toxic release inventory program'. n.d. Accessed 27 June 2022. https://www.epa.gov/toxics-release-inventory-tri-program.

EPA. 'Whole effluent toxicity methods'. n.d. Accessed 13 October 2021. https://www.epa.gov/cwa-methods/whole-effluent-toxicity-methods.

EPA. 'Regulatory Impact Analysis for the Final Mercury and Air Toxics Standards', EPA-452/R-11-011. December 2011. Accessed 8 November 2021. https://www.epa.gov/sites/production/files/2015-11/documents/matsriafinal.pdf.

EPA. 'Our nation's air: status and trends through 2010', EPA-454/R-12-001, February 2012. Accessed 15 November 2021. https://www.epa.gov/sites/default/files/2017-11/documents/trends_brochure_2010.pdf.

EPA. 'Overview of the Clean Power Plan: cutting carbon pollution from power plants'. 2015. Accessed 3 November 2021. https://archive.epa.gov/epa/sites/production/files/2015-08/documents/fs-cpp-overview.pdf.

EPA. 'Report: EPA deviated from typical procedures in its 2018 Dicamba pesticide registration decision', Report #21-E-0146, 24 May 2021. Accessed 30 December 2021. https://www.epa. gov/office-inspector-general/report-epa-deviated-typical-procedures-its-2018-dicamba-pesticide.

Erickson, Britt E. 'How many chemicals are in use today?', *Chemical and Engineering News*, 27 February 2017. Accessed 11 October 2021. https://cen.acs.org/articles/95/i9/chemicals-use-today.html.

Ettonson, Lara. 'US clean energy jobs surpass fossil fuel employment', National Resources Defense Council, 1 February 2017. Accessed 19 October 2021. https://www.nrdc.org/experts/lara-ettenson/us-clean-energy-jobs-surpass-fossil-fuel-employment.

European Commission. 'EU Water Framework Directive'. n.d. Accessed 3 November 2021. https://ec.europa.eu/environment/water/water-framework/index_en.html.

European Parliament. 'Directive (EU) 2018/2001 of the European Parliament and of the Council of 11 December 2018', 21 December 2018. Accessed 1 November 2021. https://eur-lex. europa.eu/legal-content/EN/TXT/?uri=uriserv:OJ.L_.2018.328.01.0082.01. ENG&toc=OJ:L:2018:328:TOC.

Evans, Daniel M., Judy P. Che-Castaldo, Deborah Crouse, Frank W. Davis, Rebecca Epanchin-Niell, Curtis H. Flather, R. Kipp Frohlich, Dale D. Goble, Ya-Wei Li, Timothy D. Male, Lawrence L. Master, Matthew P. Moskwik, Maile C. Neel, Barry R. Noon, Camille Parmesan, Mark W. Schwartz, J. Michael Scott and Byron K. Williams. '*Issues in Ecology* 20 (Winter 2016). Special issue, 'Species Recovery in the US: Increasing the effectiveness of the Endangered Species Act'.

Evans, Sydney, David Andrews, Tasha Stoiber and Olga Naidenko. 'PFAS contamination of drinking water far more prevalent than previously reported', Environmental Working Group, 22 January 2020. Accessed 10 October 2021. https://www.ewg.org/research/national-pfas-testing/.

Fang, Ferric C., R. Grant Steen and Arturo Casadevall. 'Misconduct accounts for the majority of retracted scientific publications', *Proceedings of the National Academy of Sciences of the United States of America* 109 (2012): 17028–33.

FAO (Food and Agriculture Organization of the United Nations). '1.02 billion people hungry'. Rome: FAO, 19 June 2009. Accessed 10 October 2021. http://www.fao.org/news/story/en/item/20568/icode/.

FAO (Food and Agriculture Organization of the United Nations) and Intergovernmental Technical Panel on Soils. *Status of the World's Soil Resources*. Rome: FAO and Intergovernmental Technical Panel on Soils, 2015. Accessed 18 October 2021. http://www.fao.org/3/a-bc595e.pdf.

FAO (Food and Agriculture Organization of the United Nations). *The State of Food Insecurity in the World*. Rome: FAO, 2021. Accessed 18 October 2021. https://www.fao.org/3/cb4474en/cb4474en.pdf.

Farah, Niina H. 'Supreme Court will review EPA climate authority', *E&E News*, 29 October 2021. Accessed 8 January 2022. https://www.eenews.net/articles/supreme-court-will-review-epa-climate-authority/.

Farrell, Justin. 'The growth of climate change misinformation in US philanthropy: evidence from natural language processing', *Environmental Research Letters* 14 (2019). Accessed 31 May 2022. https://doi.org/10.1088/1748-9326/aaf939.

Fernández, Stacy. 'Plastic company set to pay $50 million settlement in water pollution suit brought on by Texas residents', *Texas Tribune*, 15 October 2019. Accessed 4 November 2021. https://www.texastribune.org/2019/10/15/formosa-plastics-pay-50-million-texas-clean-water-act-lawsuit/.

Fischman, Robert L. 'The divides of environmental law and the problem of harm in the Endangered Species Act', *Indiana Law Journal* 83 (2008): 661–93.

Flanagan, Sara V., Richard B. Johnston and Yan Zheng. 'Arsenic in tube well water in Bangladesh: health and economic impacts and implications for arsenic mitigation', *Bulletin of the World Health Organization* 90 (2012): 839–46.

Flatt, Victor B. 'Dirty river runs through it (the failure of enforcement in the Clean Water Act)', *Boston College Environmental Affairs Law Review* 25 (1997): 1–45.

Flatt, Victor B. and Paul M. Collins. 'Environmental enforcement in dire straits: there is no protection for nothing and no data for free', *Notre Dame Law Review* 85 (2009): 55–87.

Flegenheimer, Matt. 'Senate Republicans deploy "nuclear option" to clear path for Gorsuch', *New York Times*, 6 April 2017. Accessed 29 October 2021. https://www.nytimes.com/2017/04/06/us/politics/neil-gorsuch-supreme-court-senate.html.

Flesher, John. 'AP exclusive: thousands of wastewater spills scar land, threaten water amid drilling boom', *FOX Business*, 9 March 2015. Accessed 4 November 2021. https://www.foxbusiness.com/markets/ap-exclusive-thousands-of-wastewater-spills-scar-land-threaten-water-amid-drilling-boom.

Folke, Carl, Reinette Biggs, Albert V. Norström, Belinda Reyers and Johan Rockström. 'Social-ecological resilience and biosphere-based sustainability science', *Ecology and Society* 21 (2016): article 41 (unpaginated). Accessed 30 May 2022. http://dx.doi.org/10.5751/ES-08748-210341.

Fontaine, Joseph J. 'Improving our legacy: incorporation of adaptive management into state wildlife action plans', *Journal of Environmental Management* 92 (2011): 1403–8.

Foote, Elisha. 'Circumstances affecting the heat of the sun's rays', *American Journal of Science and Arts*, second series, 22 (1856): 382–3.

Foote, Elisha. 'On the heat in the sun's rays', *American Journal of Science and Arts*, second series, 22 (1856): 377–81.

Ford, Henry. 'Machinery: the new messiah', *The Forum*, March 1928: 359–64. Accessed 10 October 2021. https://www.unz.com/print/Forum-1928mar-00359.

Fountain, Henry. '"Junk shot" is next step for leaking Gulf of Mexico well', *New York Times*, 14 May 2010. Accessed 9 November 2021. https://www.nytimes.com/2010/05/15/us/15junk.html.

Franco, Annie, Neil Malhotra and Gabor Simonovits. 'Publication bias in the social sciences: unlocking the file drawer', *Science* 345 (2014): 1502–5.

Frank, Kenneth T., Brian Petrie, Jonathan A. D. Fisher and William C. Leggett. 'Transient dynamics of an altered large marine ecosystem', *Nature* 477 (2011): 86–89.

Franzen, Martina, Simone Rödder and Peter Weingart. 'Fraud: causes and culprits as perceived by science and the media', *EMBO Reports* 8 (2007): 3–7.

Freedman, Lynn P. and Stephen L. Isaacs. 'Human rights and reproductive choice', *Studies in Family Planning* 1 (1993): 18–30.

Freudenburg, William, Robert Gramling and Debra Davidson. 'SCAMming environmental policy', *WorldWatch* 21 (May–June 2008): 7–11.

Friedman, Lisa. 'Biden Administration to repeal Trump rule aimed at curbing EPA's power', *New York Times*, 13 May 2021. Accessed 20 October 2021. https://www.nytimes.com/2021/05/13/climate/EPA-cost-benefit-pollution.html.

Friedman, Lisa. 'Biden Administration to restore clean-water protections ended by Trump', *New York Times*, 9 June 2021. Accessed 20 October 2021. https://www.nytimes.com/2021/06/09/climate/biden-clean-water-wotus.html.

Friedman, Lisa and Coral Davenport. 'Trump Administration rolls back clean water protections', *New York Times*, 19 September 2019. Accessed 21 October 2021. https://www.nytimes.com/2019/09/12/climate/trump-administration-rolls-back-clean-water-protections.html.

Friedman, Lisa, Kendra Pierre-Louis and Livia Albeck-Ripka. 'Law that saved the bald eagle could be vastly reworked', *New York Times*, 19 July 2018. Accessed 3 November 2021. https://www.nytimes.com/2018/07/19/climate/endangered-species-act-changes.html.

Friedman, Lisa and Brad Plumer. 'EPA announces repeal of major Obama-era carbon emissions rule', *New York Times*, 9 October 2017. Accessed 3 November 2021. https://www.nytimes.com/2017/10/09/climate/clean-power-plan.html.

Friends of the Earth. 'Issues'. n.d. Accessed 18 October 2021. https://foe.org/.

Frontline. 'Climate of Doubt' episode of series *Frontline*. Public Broadcasting Service, 23 October 2012. Accessed 20 October 2021. http://www.pbs.org/wgbh/pages/frontline/climate-of-doubt/.

Fuller, Jonathan. 'The myth and fallacy of simple extrapolation in medicine', *Synthese* 198 (2021): 2919–39.

Fuller, Jonathan and Luis J. Flores. 'The risk GP model: the standard model of prediction in medicine', *Studies in History and Philosophy of Biological and Biomedical Sciences* 54 (2015): 49–61.

Gaines, Richard. 'Senate panel hearing set for Magnuson reform', *Gloucester Times*, 11 June 2012. Accessed 2 November 2021. http://www.gloucestertimes.com/local/x1318681925/Senate-panel-hearing-set-for-Magnuson-reform.

Galbraith, John K. *The Affluent Society* (Fortieth Anniversary Edition). Boston: Houghton Mifflin, 1998.

Galloway, Gloria. 'Controversial changes to fisheries act', *Globe and Mail*, 5 August 2013. Accessed 2 November 2021. http://www.theglobeandmail.com/news/politics/fisheries-act-change-guided-by-industry/article13606358/.

Gallup. 'Confidence in institutions'. n.d. Accessed 7 October 2021. http://www.gallup.com/poll/1597/confidence-institutions.aspx#1.

Gallup. 'Economy tops voters list of key election issues'. 5 October 2020. Accessed 7 October 2021. https://news.gallup.com/poll/321617/economy-tops-voters-list-key-election-issues.aspx.

Garrett-Peltier, Heidi. 'Green versus brown: comparing the employment impacts of energy efficiency, renewable energy, and fossil fuels using an input-output model', *Economic Modelling* 61 (2017): 439–47.

Ghandnoosh, Nazgol. 'Black lives matter: eliminating racial inequity in the criminal justice system', The Sentencing Project, 3 February 2015. Accessed 23 October 2021. https://www.sentencingproject.org/publications/black-lives-matter-eliminating-racial-inequity-in-the-criminal-justice-system/.

Giesy, John P. and Robert A. Hoke. 'Freshwater sediment toxicity bioassessment: rationale for species selection and test design', *Journal of Great Lakes Research* 15 (1989): 539–69.

Gillam, Carey. 'GMO labeling foes spend big on campaigns in Oregon, Colorado', *Reuters*, 17 October 2014. Accessed 1 November 2021. https://www.reuters.com/article/us-usa-gmo-labeling-idUSKCN0I621H20141017.

Gillis, Justin and John Schwartz. 'Deeper ties to corporate cash for doubtful climate researcher', *New York Times*, 21 February 2015. Accessed 16 October 2021. https://www.nytimes.com/2015/02/22/us/ties-to-corporate-cash-for-climate-change-researcher-Wei-Hock-Soon.html.

Gleick, Peter H. 'Will new climate regulations destroy the economy? (Hint: No.)', *HuffPost*, 2 June 2014. Accessed 4 January 2022. https://www.huffpost.com/entry/will-new-climate-regulati_b_5432090.

Goethel, Daniel R., Sean M. Lucey, Aaron M. Berger, Sarah K. Gaichas, Melissa A. Karp, Patrick D. Lynch, John F. Walter III, Jonathan J. Deroba, Shana Miller and Michael J. Wilberg. 'Closing the feedback loop: on stakeholder participation in management strategy evaluation', *Canadian Journal of Fisheries and Aquatic Sciences*, 76 (2019): 1895–913.

Goldman Environmental Prize. 'Current recipients'. Accessed 28 November 2021. https://www.goldmanprize.org/prize-recipients/current-recipients/.

Goldsmith, Brian. 'A wrong turn on climate change', *The Atlantic*, 29 July 2010. Accessed 29 October 2021. http://www.theatlantic.com/politics/archive/2010/07/a-wrong-turn-on-climate-change/60598/.

Golshan, Tara. 'The "Hastert Rule," the reason a DACA deal could fail in the House, explained', *Vox*, 24 January 2018. Accessed 29 October 2021. https://www.vox.com/policy-and-politics/2018/1/24/16916898/hastert-rule-daca-could-fail-house-ryan.

Good, Chris. 'Don't blame Citizens United', *The Atlantic*, 20 October 2010. Accessed 1 November 2021. https://www.theatlantic.com/politics/archive/2010/10/dont-blame-citizens-united/64906/.

Goulson, Dave. 'An overview of the environmental risks posed by neonicotinoid insecticides', *Journal of Applied Ecology* 50 (2013): 977–87.

Government of Nepal Ministry of Health and Population Department of Health Services. 'Annual Report, 2019/2020'. Accessed 18 October 2021. https://dohs.gov.np/annual-report-2076-77-2019-20/.

Gray, Paul E. 'The paradox of technological development'. In *Technology and Environment*, edited by Jesse H. Ausubel and Hedy E. Sladovich, 192–204. Washington, DC: National Academies Press, 1989.

Green, David M., Michael J. Lannoo, David Lesbarréres and Erin Muths. 'Amphibian population declines: 30 years of progress in confronting a complex problem', *Herpetologica* 76 (2020): 97–100.

Greenberg, Jon. 'Spending bill's gun research line: does it nullify Dickey amendment?', *PolitiFact*, 27 March 2018. Accessed 14 October 2021. http://www.politifact.com/truth-o-meter/article/2018/mar/27/spending-bills-gun-research-line-does-it-matter/.

Greene, Jeffrey. *Water from Stone: The story of Selah, Bamberger Ranch Preserve*. College Station: Texas A&M University Press, 2007.

Grigorovich, Igor A., Robert I. Colautti, Edward L. Mills, Kristen Holeck, Albert G. Ballert and Hugh G. MacIsaac. 'Ballast-mediated animal introductions in the Laurentian Great Lakes: retrospective and prospective analyses', *Canadian Journal of Fisheries and Aquatic Sciences* 60 (2003): 740–56.

Groom, Nichola. 'Exclusive: controversial US energy loan program has wiped out losses', *Reuters*, 13 November 2014. Accessed 1 November 2021. http://www.reuters.com/article/us-doe-loans-idUSKCN0IX0A120141113.

Gruver, Mead. 'Wyoming laws aimed at trespassing activists struck down', *Associated Press*, 30 October 2018. Accessed 11 October 2021. https://apnews.com/article/a1cdf51f075b48729d69731dcaf0c2e1.

Gwaltney-Brant, Sharon M. 'Chocolate toxicosis in animals', *Merck Veterinary Manual*, 2021. Accessed 13 October 2021. https://www.merckvetmanual.com/toxicology/food-hazards/chocolate-toxicosis-in-animals.

Gwatkin, Davidson R. 'Political will and family planning: the implications of India's emergency experience', *Population and Development Review* 5 (1979): 29–59.

Hahn, Robert W. and Cass R. Sunstein. 'A new executive order for improving federal regulation? Deeper and wider cost–benefit analysis', *University of Pennsylvania Law Review* 150 (2002): 1489–552.

Hajnal, Zoltan, Nazita Lajevardi and Lindsay Nielson. 'Voter identification laws and the suppression of minority votes', *Journal of Politics* 79 (2016): 363–79.

Haltiwanger, John and Manisha Singh. 'Cross-country evidence on public sector retrenchment', *World Bank Economic Review* 13 (1999): 23–66.

Hance, Jeremy. 'A rich person's profession? Young conservationists struggle to make it', *Mongabay*, 16 August 2017. Accessed 11 October 2021. https://news.mongabay.com/2017/08/a-rich-persons-profession-young-conservationists-struggle-to-make-it/.

Hanlon, Michael. 'The Golden Quarter', *Aeon*. n.d. Accessed 19 October 2021. https://aeon.co/essays/has-progress-in-science-and-technology-come-to-a-halt.

Hannemann, W. Michael. 'Valuing the environment through contingent valuation', *Journal of Economic Perspectives* 8 (1994): 19–43.

Harkavy, Oscar and Krishna Roy. 'Emergence of the Indian national family planning program'. In *The Global Family Planning Revolution: Three decades of population policies and programs*, edited by Warren C. Robinson and John A. Ross, 301–23. Washington, DC: World Bank, 2007.

Harrington, Winston, Richard D. Morgenstern and Peter Nelson. 'On the accuracy of regulatory cost estimates', *Journal of Policy Analysis and Management* 19 (2000): 297–322.

Hartig, John H. *Burning Rivers: Revival of four urban industrial rivers that caught on fire*. Burlington, ON: Aquatic Ecosystem Health and Management Society, 2010.

Harvard Magazine. 'An intellectual entente', 10 September 2009. Accessed 30 September 2021. http://harvardmagazine.com/breaking-news/james-watson-edward-o-wilson-intellectual-entente.

Hawken, Paul. 'Natural capitalism', *Mother Jones*, March/April 1997. Accessed 2 November 2021. https://www.motherjones.com/politics/1997/03/natural-capitalism/.

Hawken, Paul. *Blessed Unrest*. New York: Penguin, 2007.

Hawken, Paul. 'Paul Hawken's commencement address to the class of 2009', University of Portland, 3 May 2009. Accessed 9 November 2021. https://www.commondreams.org/views/2009/05/23/paul-hawkens-commencement-address-class-2009.

Hawking, Stephen. *The Illustrated a Brief History of Time, Updated and Expanded Edition*. New York: Bantam Books, 2014.

Hayek, Friedrich A. *The Road to Serfdom*. Chicago: University of Chicago Press, 1944.

Heinzerling, Lisa. 'Climate change in the Supreme Court', *Environmental Law* 38 (2008). Accessed 3 November 2021. https://scholarship.law.georgetown.edu/cgi/viewcontent.cgi?article=1450&context=facpub.

Heinzerling, Lisa, Frank Ackerman and Rachel Massey. 'Applying cost–benefit analysis to past decisions: was environmental protection ever a good idea?', *Administrative Law Review* 57 (2005): 155–92.

Hemphill, Stephanie and Elizabeth Dunbar. 'DFL lawmaker: compromise reached on frac sand regulations', *Minnesota Public Radio*, 14 May 2013. Accessed 2 November 2021. http://minnesota.publicradio.org/display/web/2013/05/14/politics/frac-sand-mining-deal.

Heneghan, Liam. 'Is there need for "The New Wild"?: the new ecological quarrels', *Los Angeles Review of Books*, 15 October 2015. Accessed 19 October 2021. https://lareviewofbooks.org/article/is-there-need-for-the-new-wild-the-new-ecological-quarrels/.

Heniff, Bill Jr. 'The budget reconciliation process: the Senate's "Byrd Rule"', Congressional Research Service report RL30862, 22 November 2016. Accessed 29 October 2021. https://crsreports.congress.gov/product/pdf/RL/RL30862/16.

Herron, Michael C. and Daniel A. Smith. 'Race, party, and the consequences of restricting early voting in Florida in the 2012 general election', *Political Research Quarterly* 67 (2014): 646–65.

Hertwich, Edgar G. and Glen P. Peters. 'Carbon footprint of nations: a global, trade-linked analysis', *Environmental Science and Technology* 43 (2009): 6414–20.

Herzig, Rebecca. 'Removing roots: "North American Hiroshima Maidens" and the X Ray', *Technology and Culture* 40 (1999): 723–45.

Hesketh, Therese, Li Lu and Zhu W. Xing. 'The effect of China's one-child family policy after 25 years', *New England Journal of Medicine* 353 (2005): 1171–6.

Hibbs, Henry H. Jr. 'The present position of infant mortality: its recent decline in the US', *Publications of the American Statistical Association* 14 (1915): 813–26.

Higgins, Michelle. 'Buy condo, then add parking spot for $1 million', *New York Times*, 9 September 2014. Accessed 8 November 2021. http://www.nytimes.com/2014/09/10/realestate/million-dollar-parking-spot.html?_r=0,.

Highton, Benjamin. 'Voter identification laws and turnout in the US', *Annual Review of Political Science* 20 (2017): 149–67.

Hirji, Zahra. '40% of Wisconsin "frac sand" producers violated environmental rules, study says', *Pittsburgh Post-Gazette*, 16 November 2014. Accessed 4 November 2021. https://www.post-gazette.com/business/powersource/2014/11/16/40-of-Wisconsin-frac-sand-producers-violated-environmental-rules-study-says/stories/201411160235.

History, Art and Archives, US House of Representatives. 'Election statistics: 1920 to present'. n.d. Accessed 25 October 2021. https://history.house.gov/Institution/Election-Statistics/.

Hmiel, Benjamin, V. V. Petrenko, M. N. Dyonisius, C. Buizert, A. M. Smith, P. F. Place, C. Harth, R. Beaudette, Q. Hua, B. Yang, I. Vimont, S. E. Michel, J. P. Severinghaus, D. Etheridge, T. Bromley, J. Schmitt, X. Fain, R. F. Weiss and E. Dlugokencky. 'Preindustrial $^{14}CH_4$ indicates greater anthropogenic fossil CH_4 emissions', *Nature* 578 (2020): 409–12.

Hoenig, John M. and Dennis M. Heisey. 'The abuse of power: the pervasive fallacy of power calculations for data analysis', *American Statistician* 55 (2001): 19–24.

Hogue, Henry B. 'Reorganization of the Minerals Management Service in the aftermath of the Deepwater Horizon oil spill', Congressional Research Service, 7-5700, R41485, 10 November 2010. Accessed 4 November 2021. http://fas.org/sgp/crs/misc/R41485.pdf.

Holistic Management International. 'Healthy land, healthy food, healthy lives'. n.d. Accessed 6 November 2021. http://holisticmanagement.org/.

Holling, C. S. *Adaptive Environmental Assessment and Management*. London: John Wiley and Sons, 1978.

Holling, C. S. 'What barriers? What bridges?'. In *Barriers and Bridges to the Renewal of Ecosystems and Institutions*, edited by Lance H. Gunderson, C. S. Holling and Stephen S. Light, 3–34. New York: Columbia University Press, 1995.

Hope, Chris and Mat Hope. 'The social cost of CO_2 in a low-growth world', *Nature Climate Change* 3 (2013): 722–4.

Horbach, Serge P. J. M. and Willem Halffman. 'The changing forms and expectations of peer review', *Research Integrity and Peer Review* 3 (2018). Accessed 31 May 2022. https://doi.org/10.1186/s41073-018-0051-5.

Hornblum, Allen M., Judith L. Newman and Gregory J. Dober. *Against Their Will: The secret history of medical experimentation on children in Cold War America*. New York: Palgrave Macmillan, 2013.

Horowitz, Michael C., Julia Ciocca, Lauren Kahn and Christian Ruhl. 'Keeping score: a new approach to geopolitical forecasting'. Perry World House White Paper, University of Pennsylvania. February 2021. Accessed 7 December 2021. https://global.upenn.edu/sites/default/files/perry-world-house/Keeping%20Score%20Forecasting%20White%20Paper.pdf.

Howe, Peter D., Matto Mildenberger, Jennifer R. Marlon and Anthony Leiserowitz. 'Geographic variation in opinions on climate change at state and local scales in the USA', *Nature Climate Change* 5 (2015): 596–603.

Hristov, Peter, Rositsa Shumkova, Nadezhda Palova and Boyko Neov. 'Factors associated with honey bee colony losses: a mini-review', *Veterinary Sciences* 7 (2020). Accessed 31 May 2022. https://doi.org/10.3390/vetsci7040166.

Huang, Priscilla. 'Anchor babies, over-breeders, and the population bomb: the reemergence of nativism and population control in anti-immigration policies', *Harvard Law and Policy Review* 2 (2008): 385–406.

Hurlbert, Stuart H. 'Pseudoreplication and the design of ecological field experiments', *Ecological Monographs* 54 (1984): 187–211.

Hurlbert, Stuart H. and Michael D. White. 'Experiments with freshwater invertebrate zooplanktivores: quality of statistical analyses', *Bulletin of Marine Science* 53 (1993): 128–53.

Ingraham, Christopher. 'Somebody just put a price tag on the 2016 election. It's a doozy', *Washington Post*, 14 April 2017. Accessed 25 October 2021. https://www.washingtonpost.com/news/wonk/wp/2017/04/14/somebody-just-put-a-price-tag-on-the-2016-election-its-a-doozy/?utm_term=.f0564c1ef668.

Insinna, Valerie. 'Inside America's dysfunctional trillion dollar fighter-jet program', *New York Times*, 21 August 2019. Accessed 11 October 2021. https://www.nytimes.com/2019/08/21/magazine/f35-joint-strike-fighter-program.html.

Inter-American Tropical Tuna Commission. 'International dolphin conservation program (IDCP)'. n.d. Accessed 6 November 2021. https://www.iattc.org/IDCPENG.htm.

Intergovernmental Panel on Climate Change. 'Summary for policymakers'. In *Climate Change 2021: The physical science basis* (Contribution of Working Group I to the Sixth Assessment Report of the Intergovernmental Panel on Climate Change), edited by Valerie Masson-Delmotte, Panmao Zhai, Anna Pirani, Sarah L. Connors, Clotilde Péan, Yang Chen, Leon Goldfarb, Melissa I. Gomis, J. B. Robin Matthews, Sophie Berger, Mengtian Huang, Ozge Yelekçi, Rong Yu, Baiquan Zhou, Elisabeth Lonnoy, Thomas K. Maycock, Tim Waterfield, Katherine Leitzell and Nada Caud. Cambridge: Cambridge University Press, 2021. Accessed 15 October 2021. https://www.ipcc.ch/report/ar6/wg1/downloads/report/IPCC_AR6_WGI_SPM_final.pdf.

International Energy Agency. *Projected Costs of Generating Electricity: 2020 edition*. Paris: International Energy Agency. Accessed 7 November 2021. https://www.iea.org/reports/projected-costs-of-generating-electricity-2020.

International Labour Organization. 'International chemical safety cards (ICSCs)'. n.d. Accessed 11 October 2021. https://www.ilo.org/dyn/icsc/showcard.listCards3.

International Union for the Conservation of Nature (IUCN). 'Conflict and conservation'. 2021. Accessed 22 April 2022. https://portals.iucn.org/library/sites/library/files/documents/NGW-001-En.pdf.

Ioannidis, John P. A. 'Why most published research findings are false', *PLOS Medicine*, 30 August 2005. Accessed 14 October 2021. https://doi.org/10.1371/journal.pmed.0020124.

Ipsos. 'Around the world, people yearn for significant change rather than a return to a "pre-COVID normal"'. 16 September 2020. Accessed 7 November 2021. https://www.ipsos.com/en-us/news-polls/global-survey-unveils-profound-desire-change-rather-return-how-life-and-world-were-covid-19.

Isidore, Chris. 'Exxon Mobil profit is just short of record', *CNN*, 1 February 2013. Accessed 11 October 2021. http://money.cnn.com/2013/02/01/news/companies/exxon-mobil-profit/.

Jamieson, Dale. *Reason in a Dark Time*. Oxford: Oxford University Press, 2014.

Jansson, Bengt-Owe and Harald Velner. 'The Baltic: the sea of surprises'. In *Barriers and Bridges to the Renewal of Ecosystems and Institutions*, edited by Lance H. Gunderson, C. S. Holling and Stephen S. Light, 292–372. New York: Columbia University Press, 1995.

Jasanoff, Shiela. 'Science, politics, and the renegotiation of expertise at the EPA', *OSIRIS*, second series, 7 (1992): 195–217.

Jerde, Christopher, W. Lindsay Chadderton, Andrew R. Mahon, Mark A. Renshaw, Joel Corush, Michelle L. Budny, Sagar Mysorekar and David M. Lodge. 'Detection of Asian carp DNA as part of a Great Lakes basin-wide surveillance program', *Canadian Journal of Fisheries and Aquatic Sciences* 70 (2013): 522–6.

Jha, Alok. 'We must learn to love uncertainty and failure, say leading thinkers', *Guardian*, 14 January 2011. Accessed 15 October 2021. http://www.guardian.co.uk/science/2011/jan/15/uncertainty-failure-edge-question.

Jha, Alok. 'No toxic effects from controversial food packet chemical, say experts', *Guardian*, 15 February 2013. Accessed 13 October 2021. http://www.theguardian.com/society/2013/feb/15/no-toxic-effects-chemical-experts.

John, Elton H. 'Circle of Life'. Burbank, CA: Walt Disney Records, 1994.

Jones, Charles O. *The Presidency in a Separated System*. Washington: Brookings Institution, 1994.

Jones, Chris M., Shannon Jones, Anna Petrasova, Vaclav Petras, Devon Gaydos, Megan M. Skrip, Yu Takeuchi, Kevin Bigsby and Ross K Meentemeyer. 'Iteratively forecasting biological invasions with PoPS and a little help from our friends', *Frontiers in Ecology and the Environment* 19 (2021): 411–18.

Kamieniecki, Sheldon. *Corporate America and Environmental Policy: How often does business get its way?* Palo Alto, CA: Stanford University Press, 2006.

Kampourakis, Kostas and Kevin McCain. *Uncertainty: How it makes science advance*. Oxford: Oxford University Press, 2020.

Karpowitz, Christopher F. and Jeremy C. Pope. 'Who caucuses? An experimental approach to institutional design and electoral participation', *British Journal of Political Science* 45 (2015): 329–51.

Katz, Eric. 'EPA admits to altering science under Trump, pledges new course', Government Executive, 25 May 2021. Accessed 30 December 2021. https://www.govexec.com/management/2021/05/epa-admits-altering-science-under-trump-pledges-new-course/174295/.

Kelly, Franklin, Nicholai Cikovsky Jr., Deborah Chotner and John Davis. *American Paintings of the Nineteenth Century: Part 1*. New York: Oxford University Press. Accessed 30 November 2021. https://www.nga.gov/content/dam/ngaweb/research/publications/pdfs/american-paintings-19th-century-part-1.pdf.

Kendall, Lewis. 'Revealed: Covid-19 outbreaks at meat-processing plants in US being kept quiet', *Guardian*, 1 July 2020. Accessed 10 October 2021. https://www.theguardian.com/environment/2020/jul/01/revealed-covid-19-outbreaks-meat-processing-plants-north-carolina.

Kennedy, Brian. 'Public support for environmental regulations varies by state', Pew Research Center, 25 February 2016. Accessed 27 October 2021. https://www.pewresearch.org/fact-tank/2016/02/25/public-support-for-environmental-regulations-varies-by-state/.

Kidd, Karen A., Paul J. Blanchfield, Kenneth H. Mills, Vince P. Palace, Robert E. Evans, James M. Lazorchak and Robert W. Flick. 'Collapse of a fish population after exposure to a synthetic estrogen', *Proceedings of the National Academy of Sciences of the United States of America* 104 (2007): 8897–901.

Kim, Soo R. 'The price of winning just got higher, especially in the Senate', *Open Secrets*, 9 November 2016. Accessed 25 October 2021. https://www.huffingtonpost.com/opensecrets-blog/the-price-of-winning-just_b_12888366.html.

King, Martin Luther, Jr. 'How long? Not long', 25 March 1965. Accessed 17 December 2021. https://voicesofdemocracy.umd.edu/dr-martin-luther-king-jr-long-not-long-speech-text/.

Kingdon, John W. *Agendas, Alternatives, and Public Policies*. 2nd edition. New York: Longman, 2003.

Kinkela, David. *DDT and the American Century*. Chapel Hill: University of North Carolina Press, 2011.

Kirsch, Scott. *Proving Grounds: Project Plowshare and the unrealized dream of nuclear earthmoving*. New Brunswick, NJ: Rutgers University Press, 2005.

Kistemann, T., T. Classen, C. Koch, F. Dangendorf, R. Fischeder, J. Gebel, V. Vacata and M. Exner. 'Microbial load of drinking water reservoir tributaries during extreme rainfall and runoff', *Applied and Environmental Microbiology* 68 (2002): 2188–97.

Klumpp, Tilman, Hugo M. Mialon and Michael A. Williams. 'The business of American democracy: *Citizens United*, independent spending, and elections', *Journal of Law and Economics* 59 (2016): 1–43.

Knesek, Nichole. '*Escherichia coli* concentrations in Lake Texoma', Undergraduate honours thesis. Sherman, TX: Austin College, 2000.

Koffarnus, Mikhail N., David P. Jarmolowicz, E. Terry Mueller and Warren K. Bickel. 'Changing delay discounting in the light of competing neurobehavioral decision systems theory: a review', *Journal of the Experimental Analysis of Behavior* 99 (2013): 32–57.

Koh, Lian P. and David S. Wilcove. 'Is oil palm agriculture really destroying tropical biodiversity?', *Conservation Letters* 1 (2008): 60–4.

Kohler, Timothy A. and Meredith H. Matthews. 'Long-term Anasazi land use and forest reduction: a case study from southwest Colorado', *American Antiquity* 53 (1988): 537–64.

Kolata, Gina. 'Many academics are eager to publish in worthless journals', *New York Times*, 30 October 2017. Accessed 14 October 2021. https://www.nytimes.com/2017/10/30/science/predatory-journals-academics.html.

Kolbert, Elizabeth. 'The scales fall: is there any hope for our overfished oceans?', *New Yorker*, 26 July 2010. Accessed 8 January 2022. https://www.newyorker.com/magazine/2010/08/02/the-scales-fall.

Kotkin, Joel. 'Overpopulation isn't the problem: it's too few babies', *Forbes*, 27 October 2011. Accessed 18 October 2021. http://www.forbes.com/sites/joelkotkin/2011/10/27/overpopulation-isnt-the-problem-its-too-few-babies/.

Kraus, Clifford. 'Halliburton to pay $1.1 billion to settle damages in Gulf of Mexico oil spill', *New York Times*, 2 September 2014. Accessed 20 October 2021. https://www.nytimes.com/2014/09/03/business/energy-environment/halliburton-to-pay-1-1-billion-to-settle-damages-in-gulf-of-mexico-oil-spill.html.

Kreager, Philip. 'Aristotle and open population thinking', *Population and Development Review* 34 (2008): 599–629.

Krimsky, Sheldon. 'Do financial conflicts of interest bias research? An inquiry into the "funding effect" hypothesis', *Science, Technology, & Human Values* 38 (2013): 566–87.

Kristof, Nicholas. 'Contaminating our bodies with everyday products', *New York Times*, 28 November 2015. Accessed 10 October 2021. http://www.nytimes.com/2015/11/29/opinion/sunday/contaminating-our-bodies-with-everyday-products.html.

Krugman, Paul. 'Crazy climate economics', *New York Times*, 11 May 2014. Accessed 19 October 2021. http://www.nytimes.com/2014/05/12/opinion/krugman-crazy-climate-economics.html?hp&rref=opinion.

Krugman, Paul. 'Cutting back on carbon', *New York Times*, 29 May 2014. Accessed 7 November 2021. http://www.nytimes.com/2014/05/30/opinion/krugman-cutting-back-on-carbon.html.

Krugman, Paul. 'Making ignorance great again', *New York Times*, 5 June 2017. Accessed 19 October 2021. https://www.nytimes.com/2017/06/05/opinion/trump-gop-paris-climate-accord.html.

Krugman, Paul. 'Trade and peace: the great illusion', *New York Times*, 11 April 2022. Accessed 13 April 2022. https://www.nytimes.com/2022/04/11/opinion/germany-russia-ukraine-trade-gas.html.

Kuhn, Thomas S. *The Structure of Scientific Revolutions*. Chicago: University of Chicago Press, 1962.

Kuk, John, Zoltan Hajnal and Nazita Lajevardi. 'A disproportionate burden: strict voter identification laws and minority turnout', *Politics, Groups, and Identities*, 4 June 2020. Accessed 23 October 2021. https://doi.org/10.1080/21565503.2020.1773280.

Kulish, Nicholas. 'Dr. John Tanton, quiet catalyst in anti-immigration drive, dies at 85', *New York Times*, 18 July 2019. Accessed 18 October 2021. https://www.nytimes.com/2019/07/18/us/john-tanton-dead.html.

Kulish, Nicholas and Mike McIntire. 'Why an heiress spent her fortune trying to keep immigrants out', *New York Times*, 14 August 2019. Accessed 18 October 2021. https://www.nytimes.com/2019/08/14/us/anti-immigration-cordelia-scaife-may.html.

Kurlansky, Mark. *Cod: A biography of the fish that changed the world*. New York: Walker and Company, 1997.

Kurzban, Robert. 'P-hacking and the replication crisis', *Edge*, Accessed 9 November 2021. https://www.edge.org/panel/robert-kurzban-p-hacking-and-the-replication-crisis-headcon-13-part-iv.

Kusnetz, Nicholas. 'US emissions dropped in 2019: here's why in 6 charts', *Inside Climate News*, 7 January 2020. Accessed 4 October 2021. https://insideclimatenews.org/news/07012020/infographic-united-states-emissions-2019-climate-change-greenhouse-gas-coal-transportation.

Kuttipurath, Jayanarayanan, Wuhu Feng, Rolf Müller, Pankaj Kumar, Sarath Raj, Gopalakrishna Pillai Gopikrishnan and Raina Roy. 'Exceptional loss in ozone in the Arctic winter/spring of 2019/2020', *Atmospheric Chemistry and Physics* 21 (2021): 14019–37.

Kuttippurath, Jayanarayanan and Prijitha J. Nair. 'The signs of Antarctic ozone hole recovery', *Nature Scientific Reports* 7 (2017). Accessed 31 May 2022. https://doi.org/10.1038/s41598-017-00722-7.

Kuttner, Robert. 'Obama's Obama: The contradictions of Cass Sunstein', *Harper's Magazine*, December 2014: 87–92.

Lakdawalla, Emily S. 'Drilling with Curiosity', *American Scientist* 106 (2018). Accessed 31 May 2022. https://doi.org/10.1511/2018.106.3.148.

Land Institute. 'The future of farming. The future of food'. n.d. Accessed 28 November 2021. https://kernza.org/.

Land Institute. 'Transforming agriculture, perennially'. n.d. Accessed 28 November 2021. http://www.landinstitute.org/.

Laumbach, Robert J. 'Outdoor air pollutants and patient health', *American Family Physician* 81 (2010): 175–80.

Laurence, William L. 'Nuclear history due to be made in Geneva parley', *New York Times*, 7 August 1955: 1 and 3. Accessed 10 October 2021. http://timesmachine.nytimes.com/timesmachine/1955/08/07/91363462.html?pageNumber=1.

Layzer, Judith A. *Open for Business: Conservatives' opposition to environmental regulation.* Cambridge, MA: MIT Press, 2012.

Lazarus, Richard J. *The Making of Environmental Law.* Chicago: University of Chicago Press, 2004.

Lazarus, Richard J. 'Environmental law after Katrina: reforming environmental law by reforming environmental lawmaking', *Tulane Law Review* 8 (2007): 1019–58.

Lazarus, Richard J. 'Super wicked problems and climate change: restraining the present to liberate the future', *Cornell Law Review* 94 (2009): 1153–233.

League of Conservation Voters. '2020 national environmental LCV scorecard'. Accessed 7 October 2021. https://scorecard.lcv.org/sites/scorecard.lcv.org/files/LCV_2020_Scorecard_Eng.pdf.

Leber, Rebecca. 'What's Rand Paul's position on climate change? It depends on the day', *New Republic*, 7 April 2015. Accessed 21 October 2021. https://newrepublic.com/article/121469/rand-paul-takes-many-positions-climate-change.

Leber, Rebecca. 'The gas industry is paying Instagram influencers to gush over gas stoves', *Mother Jones*, 17 June 2020. Accessed 1 November 2021. https://www.motherjones.com/environment/2020/06/gas-industry-influencers-stoves/.

LeBlanc, Pamela. *My Stories, All True.* College Station: Texas A&M University Press, 2020.

Lemons, John, Kristin Sharder-Frechette and Carl Cranor. 'The precautionary principle: scientific uncertainty and type I and type II errors', *Foundations of Science* 2 (1997): 207–36.

Lentz, David L., Venicia Slotten, Nicholas P. Dunning, John G. Jones, Vernon L. Scarborough, Jon-Paul McCool, Lewis A. Owen, Samantha G. Fladd, Kenneth B. Tankersley, Cory J. Perfetta, Christopher Carr, Brooke Crowley and Stephen Plog. 'Ecosystem impacts by the ancestral Puebloans of Chaco Canyon, New Mexico, USA', *PLoS ONE* 16/10 (2021). Accessed 27 October 2021. https://doi.org/10.1371/journal.pone.0258369.

Leopold, Aldo. 'The population wilderness fallacy', *Outer's Book: Recreation*, January 1918, 43–6.

Leopold, Aldo. *A Sand County Almanac.* New York: Oxford University Press, 1949.

Leopold, Aldo. *Round River.* New York: Oxford University Press, 1993.

Le Page, Michael. 'What is the Paris climate agreement', *New Scientist*, 7 November 2019. Accessed 2 November 2021. https://www.newscientist.com/article/dn28663-what-is-the-paris-climate-agreement/.

Lerner, Kira. 'States purged 16 million voters from the roles before the 2016 election', *ThinkProgress*, 20 July 2018. Accessed 22 October 2021. https://thinkprogress.org/states-purged-16-million-voters-from-the-rolls-before-the-2016-election-1c5688dcaad7/.

Levine, Hagai, Niels Jørgensen, Anderson Martino-Andrade, Jaime Mendiola, Dan Weksler-Derri, Irina Mindlis, Rachel Pinotti and Shanna H. Swan. 'Temporal trend in sperm count: a systematic review and meta-regression analysis', *Human Reproduction Update* 23 (2017): 646–59.

Levine, Michael E. and Jennifer L. Forrence. 'Regulatory capture, public interest, and the public agenda: toward a synthesis', *Journal of Law, Economics, and Organization* 6 (1990): 167–98.

Levine, Sam. 'Voter purges: are Republicans trying to rig the 2020 election?', *Guardian*, 31 December 2019. Accessed 22 October 2021. https://www.theguardian.com/us-news/2019/dec/31/voter-purges-republicans-2020-elections-trump.

Lillis, Jeffrey, Amanda Ortez and John H. Teel. 'Grayson County, Texas Health Department blue-green algae response strategy'. 2012. Accessed 9 November 2021. https://www.co.grayson.tx.us/upload/page/0206/docs/Blue-Green_Algae_Response_Strategy.pdf.

Lindbergh, Erik. 'Apres moi le deluge', *Resilience*, 7 April 2014. Accessed 2 November 2021. http://www.resilience.org/stories/2014-04-07/apres-moi-le-deluge.

Liptak, Adam and Coral Davenport. 'Supreme Court deals blow to Obama's efforts to regulate coal emissions', *New York Times*, 9 February 2016. Accessed 3 November 2021. https://www.nytimes.com/2016/02/10/us/politics/supreme-court-blocks-obama-epa-coal-emissions-regulations.html.

Lipton, Eric. 'Ties to Obama aided in access for big utility', *New York Times*, 22 August 2012. Accessed 3 November 2021. https://www.nytimes.com/2012/08/23/us/politics/ties-to-obama-aided-in-access-for-exelon-corporation.html.

Lipton, Eric. 'Energy firms in secretive alliance with attorneys general', *New York Times*, 6 December 2014. Accessed 29 December 2021. https://www.nytimes.com/2014/12/07/us/politics/energy-firms-in-secretive-alliance-with-attorneys-general.html.

Lipton, Eric. 'The chemical industry scores a big win at the EPA', *New York Times*, 7 June 2018. Accessed 1 October 2021. https://www.nytimes.com/2018/06/07/us/politics/epa-toxic-chemicals.html.

Little Traverse Conservancy. 'Interactive preserve map'. n.d. Accessed 27 November 2021. https://landtrust.org/preserves-and-reserves/.

Little Traverse Conservancy. 'Landowner resources'. n.d. Accessed 27 November 2021. https://landtrust.org/landowner-resources/.

Little Traverse Conservancy. 'Our mission'. n.d. Accessed 27 November 2021. https://landtrust.org/.

Lochgan, Gabriel. 'The Samburu of Kenya'. In *Indigenous Views of Land and the Environment*, edited by Shelton H. Davis, 45–66. Washington, DC: World Bank, 1993.

Loken, Eric and Andrew Gelman. 'Measurement error and the replication crisis', *Science* 355 (2017): 584–5.

Lombardo, Paul A. *Three Generations: No imbeciles*. Baltimore: Johns Hopkins University Press, 2008.

Lopez, Humberto. 'The social discount rate: estimates for nine Latin American countries'. Policy research working paper number 4639. Washington, DC: World Bank, 2008. Accessed 9 November 2021. http://hdl.handle.net/10986/6659.

Lott, Melissa C. 'Solyndra: illuminating energy funding flaws?', *Scientific American*, September 2011. Accessed 7 November 2021. http://blogs.scientificamerican.com/plugged-in/2011/09/27/solyndra-illuminating-energy-funding-flaws/.

Lovejoy, Thomas. 'Let science set the facts', *New York Times*, 2 October 2013. Accessed 8 October 2021. www.nytimes.cocm/2013/10/03/opinion/let-science-set-the-facts.html?src=rechp&_r=0.

Lubowski, Ruben N., Marlow Vesterby, Shawn Bucholtz, Alba Baez and Michael J. Roberts. 'Major uses of land in the US, 2002', US Department of Agriculture Economic Information Bulletin Number 14, 2002/EIB-14. Accessed 21 October 2021. https://www.ers.usda.gov/webdocs/publications/43967/13011_eib14_1_.pdf?v=42061.

Macdonald, Theodore Jr., Dominique Irvine and L. Esther Aranda. 'The Quichua of Eastern Ecuador'. In *Indigenous Views of Land and the Environment*, edited by Shelton H. Davis, 11–30. Washington, DC: World Bank, 1993.

MacDorman, Marian F. and T. J. Mathews. 'Recent trends in infant mortality in the United States', US Department of Health and Human Services Centers for Disease Control National Center for Health Statistics Data Brief, No. 9, October 2008. Accessed 7 October 2021. https://www.cdc.gov/nchs/products/databriefs/db09.htm.

MacKenzie, Debora. 'The cod that disappeared', *New Scientist*, 16 September 1995: 24–9.

Mackinder, Evan. 'Pro-environment groups outmatched, outspent in battle over climate change legislation', *Open Secrets*, 23 August 2010. Accessed 1 November 2021. http://www.opensecrets.org/news/2010/08/pro-environment-groups-were-outmatc/.

Malbin, Michael J. and Brendan Glavin. 'CFI's guide to money in federal elections: 2016 in historical context', Campaign Finance Institute, 2018. Accessed 25 October 2021. http://www.cfinst.org/pdf/federal/2016Report/CFIGuide_MoneyinFederalElections.pdf.

Malthus, Thomas R. *An Essay on the Principle of Population*. 6th edition. In: *The Works of Thomas Robert Malthus*. Volume 2. Edited by E. A. Wrigley and David Souden. London: William Pickering, 1986.

Malthus, Thomas R. *An Essay on the Principle of Population*. Abridged text of 1803 edition with changes made in the 1806, 1807, 1817 and 1826 editions. Edited by Donald Winch. Cambridge: Cambridge University Press, 1992.

Managi, Shunsuke. 'Accounting for the inclusive wealth of nations'. In *Inclusive Wealth Report 2018: Measuring progress toward sustainability*, edited by Shunsuke Managi and Pushpam Kumar, 3–52. London: Routledge, 2018. Accessed 30 May 2022. https://doi.org/10.4324/9781351002080.

Mandavilli, Apoorva. '239 experts with one big claim: the Coronavirus is airborne', *New York Times*, 4 July 2020. Accessed 12 October 2021. https://www.nytimes.com/2020/07/04/health/239-experts-with-one-big-claim-the-coronavirus-is-airborne.html.

Mann, Michael. 'If you see something, say something', *New York Times*, 17 January 2014. Accessed 15 October 2021. http://www.nytimes.com/2014/01/19/opinion/sunday/if-you-see-something-say-something.html.

Manning, Richard. *Grasslands: The history, biology, politics and promise of the American prairie*. New York: Penguin, 1995.

Marcetic, Branko. 'The other Keystone: the Alberta Clipper, the pipeline no one is talking about', *In These Times*, 14 January 2016. Accessed 9 November 2021. http://inthesetimes.com/article/18700/other_keystone_alberta_clipper_pipeline.

Marlon, Jennifer, Peter Howe, Matto Mildenberger, Anthony Leiserowitz and Xinran Wang. 'Yale Climate Opinion Maps 2020', Yale University Program on Climate Communication, 2 September 2020. Accessed 22 October 2021. https://climatecommunication.yale.edu/visualizations-data/ycom-us/.

Marsh, George P. *Man and Nature; or, Physical Geography as Modified by Human Action*. Cambridge, MA: Harvard University Press, 1965.

Martinez, Michael, Joshua Berlinger and Dana Ford. 'Oregon standoff: all occupiers surrender; Cliven Bundy arrested', *CNN*, 11 February 2016. Accessed 17 October 2021. http://www.cnn.com/2016/02/11/us/oregon-standoff/.

Martinson, Brian C., Melissa S. Anderson and Raymond de Vries. 'Scientists behaving badly', *Nature* 435 (2005): 737–8.

Matampash, Kenny. 'The Maasai of Kenya'. In *Indigenous Views of Land and the Environment*, edited by Shelton H. Davis, 31–44. Washington, DC: World Bank, 1993.

Mayer, Jane. *Dark Money*. New York: Anchor Books, 2016.

McBride, James, Andrew Chatzky and Anshy Siripurapu. 'What's next for the WTO?', Council on Foreign Relations, 14 June 2021. Accessed 6 November 2021. https://www.cfr.org/backgrounder/whats-next-wto.

McConnell, Mitch. 'The filibuster plays a crucial role in our constitutional order', *New York Times*, 22 August 2019. Accessed 29 October 2021. https://www.nytimes.com/2019/08/22/opinion/mitch-mcconnell-senate-filibuster.html.

McDiarmid, Margo. 'Budget cuts claim famed freshwater research facility', *CBC News*, 18 May 2012. Accessed 11 October 2021. https://www.cbc.ca/news/politics/budget-cuts-claim-famed-freshwater-research-facility-1.1155136.

McGarity, Thomas O., Sidney A. Shapiro and David Bollier. *Sophisticated Sabotage: The intellectual games used to subvert responsible regulation*. Washington, DC: Environmental Law Institute, 2004.

McGauran, Natalie, Beate Wieseler, Julia Kreis, Yvonne-Beatrice Schüler, Heike Kölsch and Thomas Kaiser. 'Reporting bias in medical research: a narrative review', *Trials* 11 (2010). Accessed 30 May 2022. https://doi.org/10.1186/1745-6215-11-37.

McKibben, William. *The End of Nature*. New York: Random House, 1989.

McKibben, William. 'Armed with naïvete', *TomDispatch*, 5 January 2012. Accessed 16 November 2021. https://tomdispatch.com/bill-mckibben-buying-congress-in-2012/.

McKibben, William. 'Up against Big Oil in the midterms', *New York Times*, 7 November 2018. Accessed 1 January 2022. https://www.nytimes.com/2018/11/07/opinion/climate-midterms-emissions-fossil-fuels.html.

McPhee, John. *Encounters with the Archdruid*. New York: Farrar, Straus, and Giroux, 1971.

Mencimer, Stephanie. 'The Tea Party's favorite doctors', *Mother Jones*, 18 November 2009. Accessed 15 October 2021. http://www.motherjones.com/politics/2009/11/tea-party-doctors-american-association-physicians-surgeons#comment-243833.

Mendelsohn, Robert and Sheila Olmstead. 'The economic valuation of environmental amenities and disamenities: methods and applications', *Annual Review of Environment and Resources* 34 (2009): 325–47.

Metropolitan Water Reclamation District of Greater Chicago. 'The District to the MWRD: a history of protecting our water environment'. Accessed 2 November 2021. https://mwrd.org/history.

Michaels, David, Celeste Monforton and Peter Lurie. 'Selected science: an industry campaign to undermine an OSHA hexavalent chromium standard', *Environmental Health* 5/5 (2006). Accessed 14 October 2021. https://doi.org/10.1186/1476-069X-5-5.

Midgley, Thomas Jr. and Albert L. Henne. 'Organic fluorides as refrigerants', *Industrial and Engineering Chemistry* 22 (1930): 542–5.

Migliozzi, Blacki and Hiroko Tabuchi. 'After Hurricane Ida, oil infrastructure springs dozens of leaks', *New York Times*, 26 September 2021. Accessed 10 October 2021. https://www.nytimes.com/interactive/2021/09/26/climate/ida-oil-spills.html.

Miles, Tom. 'Mexico loses 10-year WTO battle over US tuna labeling', *Reuters*, 14 December 2018. Accessed 6 November 2021. https://www.reuters.com/article/us-usa-mexico-wto-idUSKBN1OD233.

Millennium Ecosystem Assessment. *Living Beyond Our Means: Natural assets and human well being.* 2005. Accessed 11 November 2021. http://www.millenniumassessment.org/documents/document.429.aspx.pdf.

Millennium Ecosystem Assessment. *Ecosystems and Human Well-being: Synthesis.* 2005. Accessed 19 October 2021. https://www.millenniumassessment.org/documents/document.356.aspx.pdf.

Miller, Donald L. *City of the Century: The epic of Chicago and the making of America.* New York: Simon and Schuster, 1996.

Miller, G. Tyler. *Energetics, Kinetics, and Life: An ecological approach.* Belmont, CA: Wadsworth, 1971.

Miller, Greg. 'In central California, coho salmon are on the brink', *Science* 327 (2010): 512–13.

Miller, Norman. *Cases in Environmental Politics: Stakeholders, interests, and policymaking.* New York: Routledge, 2009.

Miller, Norman. *Environmental Politics: Stakeholders, interests, and policymaking.* 2nd edition. New York: Routledge, 2009.

Mills, Alex. 'Regulators say injection wells did not cause earthquakes', *Rigzone*, 6 November 2015. Accessed 13 October 2021. http://www.rigzone.com/news/oil_gas/a/141496/Regulators_Say_Injection_Wells_Did_Not_Cause_Earthquakes.

Milman, Oliver. 'Climate scientists face harassment, threats and fears of "McCarthyist attacks"', *Guardian*, 22 February 2017. Accessed 15 October 2021. https://www.theguardian.com/environment/2017/feb/22/climate-change-science-attacks-threats-trump.

Milman, Oliver. 'Fact check: Trump's Paris climate speech claims analyzed', *Guardian*, 1 June 2017. Accessed 19 October 2021. https://www.theguardian.com/environment/ng-interactive/2017/jun/02/presidents-paris-climate-speech-annotated-trumps-claims-analysed.

M. N. 'On improvement of lands in the central region of Virginia', *Farmers' Register* 1 (1834): 585–9. Accessed 9 October 2021. Reproduced at Biodiversity Heritage Library website. http://www.biodiversitylibrary.org/item/69021#page/607/mode/1up.

Mohai, Paul, David Pellow and J. Timmons Roberts. 'Environmental justice', *Annual Review of Environment and Resources* 34 (2009): 405–30.

Mohr, Holbrook, Justin Pritchard and Tamara Lush. 'BP's gulf oil spill response plan lists the walrus as a local species', *Christian Science Monitor*, 9 July 2010. Accessed 4 November 2021. http://www.csmonitor.com/From-the-news-wires/2010/0609/BP-s-gulf-oil-spill-response-plan-lists-the-walrus-as-a-local-species.-Louisiana-Gov.-Bobby-Jindal-is-furious.

Molina, Mario J. and F. Sherwood Rowland. 'Stratospheric sink for chlorofluoromethanes: chlorine atom-catalysed destruction of ozone', *Nature* 249 (1974): 810–12.

Montgomery, David R. 'Soil erosion and agricultural sustainability', *Proceedings of the National Academy of Sciences of the United States of America* 104 (2007): 13268–72.

Mooney, Chris. 'Beware "sound science." It's doublespeak for trouble', *Washington Post*, 29 February 2004. Accessed 3 November 2021. https://www.washingtonpost.com/archive/opinions/2004/02/29/beware-sound-science-its-doublespeak-for-trouble/8e4aaeed-f918-4cc1-8508-3e38b3cfb613/.

Moore, Jack. 'When Denver rejected the Olympics in favour of the environment and economics', *Guardian*, 7 April 2015. Accessed 5 November 2021. https://www.theguardian.com/sport/blog/2015/apr/07/when-denver-rejected-the-olympics-in-favour-of-the-environment-and-economics.

Moore, Marianne V. and Robert W. Winner. 'Relative sensitivity of *Ceriodaphnia dubia* laboratory tests and pond communities of zooplankton and benthos to chronic copper stress', *Aquatic Toxicology* 15 (1989): 311–30.

Mora, Camilo. 'Revisiting the environmental and socioeconomic effects of population growth: a fundamental but fading issue in modern scientific, public, and political circles', *Ecology and Society* 19 (2014): 38–47.

Morgan, Edmund S. (ed.). *Not Your Usual Founding Father: Selected readings from Benjamin Franklin*. New Haven: Yale University Press, 2006.

Morgan, M. Granger, Max Henrion and Mitchell Small. *Uncertainty: A guide to dealing with uncertainty in quantitative risk and policy analysis*. Cambridge: Cambridge University Press, 1990.

Morgan, M. Granger, Milind Kandlikar, James Risbey and Hadi Dowlatabadi. 'Why conventional tools for policy analysis are often inadequate for problems of global change', *Climatic Change* 41 (1999): 271–81.

Moskowitz, Daniel B. 'SCOTUS 101: closing down covenants', *HistoryNet*, June 2018. Accessed 1 November 2021. https://www.historynet.com/scotus-101-closing-down-covenants.htm.

Mufson, Steven. 'The fastest way to cut carbon emissions is a "fee" and a dividend, top leaders say', *Washington Post*, 13 February 2020. Accessed 31 December 2021. https://www.washingtonpost.com/climate-environment/the-fastest-way-to-cut-carbon-emissions-is-a-fee-and-a-rebate-top-leaders-say/2020/02/13/b63b766c-4cfc-11ea-bf44-f5043eb3918a_story.html.

Muir, John. *A Thousand Mile Walk to the Gulf*. Boston: Houghton Mifflin, 1916. Excerpted in *American Earth: Environmental writing since Thoreau*, edited by Bill McKibben, 85–9. New York: Penguin, 2008.

Mukunda, Gautam. 'Long crisis ahead: aftermath of the election will reverberate for years', *Nasdaq*, 5 November 2020. Accessed 28 October 2021. https://www.nasdaq.com/articles/long-crisis-ahead%3A-aftermath-of-the-election-will-reverberate-for-years-2020-11-05.

Murray, Iain. 'Obama's climate plan: it's for the kidz', *National Review*, 25 June 2013. Accessed 19 October 2021. http://www.nationalreview.com/corner/351946/obamas-climate-plan-its-kidz-iain-murray.

Mwaikambo, Lisa, Ilene S. Speizer, Anna Schurmann, Gwen Morgan and Fariyal Fikree. 'What works in family planning interventions: a systematic review', *Studies in Family Planning* 42 (2011): 67–82.

Myers, Ransom A. and Boris Worm. 'Rapid worldwide depletion of predatory fish communities', *Nature* 423 (2003): 280–3.

Myers, Scott M., Robert G. Voigt, Robert C. Colligan, Amy L. Weaver, Curtis B. Storlie, Rueth E. Stoeckel, John D. Port and Slavica K. Katusic. 'Autism spectrum disorder: incidence and time trends over two decades in a population-based birth cohort', *Journal of Autism and Developmental Disorders* 49 (2019):1455–74.

Nagourney, Adam. 'A defiant rancher savors the audience that rallied to his side', *New York Times*, 23 April 2014. Accessed 17 October 2021. http://www.nytimes.com/2014/04/24/us/politics/rancher-proudly-breaks-the-law-becoming-a-hero-in-the-west.html.

Nalder, Eric. 'Big oil spends cash by the barrel to keep double bottoms from becoming a rule', *Seattle Times*, 14 November 1989. Accessed 2 November 2021. https://special.seattletimes.com/o/news/local/exxon/series/03_congress.html.

Napolitano, Sam, Jeremy Schreifels, Gabrielle Stevens, Maggie Witt, Melanie LaCount, Reynaldo Forte and Kenon Smith. 'The U. S. acid rain program: key insights from the design, operation, and assessment of a cap-and-trade program', *Electricity Journal* 20 (2007): 47–58.

NASA Earth Observatory. 'Serendipity and stratospheric ozone'. n.d. Accessed 14 October 2021. https://earthobservatory.nasa.gov/features/RemoteSensingAtmosphere/remote_sensing5.php.

NASA Science. 'Mars Polar Lander/Deep Space 2', MARS Exploration Program, n.d. Accessed 14 October 2021. http://mars.jpl.nasa.gov/msp98/news/mco990930.html.

National Conference of State Legislatures. 'Voting outside the polling place: absentee, all-mail and other voting at home options', 24 September 2020. Accessed 22 October 2021. https://www.ncsl.org/research/elections-and-campaigns/absentee-and-early-voting.aspx.

National Conference of State Legislatures. 'Redistricting and the Supreme Court: the most significant cases', 14 September 2021. Accessed 25 October 2021. https://www.ncsl.org/research/redistricting/redistricting-and-the-supreme-court-the-most-significant-cases.aspx.

National Pesticide Information Center. 'DDT fact sheet'. 1999. Accessed 7 October 2021. http://npic.orst.edu/factsheets/ddtgen.pdf.

Natter, Ari. 'States move to roll back environmental rules in Trump's wake', *Bloomberg*, 5 May 2019. Accessed 10 October 2021. https://www.bloomberg.com/news/articles/2017-05-05/states-move-to-roll-back-environmental-rules-in-trump-s-wake.

Natural Resources Conservation Service. '2007 National Resources Inventory', US Department of Agriculture, April 2010. Accessed 21 October 2021. https://www.nrcs.usda.gov/Internet/FSE_DOCUMENTS/nrcs143_012269.pdf.

Natural Resources Defense Council. 'Our work'. n.d. Accessed 18 October 2021. https://www.nrdc.org/.

Nature. 'Challenges in irreproducible research', 18 October 2018. Accessed 9 November 2021. https://www.nature.com/collections/prbfkwmwvz/.

Nellis, Ashely. 'The color of justice: racial and ethnic disparity in state prisons', The Sentencing Project, 13 October 2021. Accessed 22 October 2021. https://www.sentencingproject.org/publications/color-of-justice-racial-and-ethnic-disparity-in-state-prisons/.

Newbold, Heather (ed.). *Life Stories: World-renowned scientists reflect on their lives and the future of life on earth*. Berkeley: University of California Press, 2000.

New England Complex Systems Institute. 'About NECSI'. n.d. Accessed 7 December 2021. https://necsi.edu/about/.

New York Times. 'Water in Chicago River', 14 January 1900, 14. Accessed 2 November 2021. https://timesmachine.nytimes.com/timesmachine/1900/01/14/101045067.html?pageNumber=14.

New York Times. 'Chicago poisons St. Louis', 21 September 1903, 1. Accessed 2 November 2021. https://timesmachine.nytimes.com/timesmachine/1903/09/21/102022930.html?pageNumber=1.

New York Times. 'Abundant power from atom seen', 17 September 1954, 5. Accessed 10 October 2021. https://www.nytimes.com/1954/09/17/archives/abundant-power-from-atom-seen-it-will-be-too-cheap-for-our-children.html.

Nikiforuk, Andrew. *Tar Sands: Dirty oil and the future of a continent*. Vancouver: Greystone, 2010.

Nobel Prize. 'Paul Müller: facts', Nobel Prize in Physiology or Medicine 1948. Accessed 7 October 2021. https://www.nobelprize.org/prizes/medicine/1948/muller/facts/.

Nobles, Ryan, Ted Barrett, Manu Raju and Alex Rogers. 'Senate Republicans block January 6 commission', *CNN Politics*, 28 May 2021. Accessed 1 January 2022. https://www.cnn.com/2021/05/28/politics/january-6-commission-vote-senate/index.html.

Nordhaus, William D. 'An optimal transition path for controlling greenhouse gases', *Science* 258 (1992): 1315–20.

Nosek, Brian A., Charles R. Ebersole, Alexander C. DeHaven and David T. Mellor. 'The preregistration revolution', *Proceedings of the National Academy of Sciences of the United States of America*. 115 (2018): 2600–6.

No-To-Bac advertisement, 'Coffin Nails', *Harper's Weekly*, 11 April 1896: 368. Accessed 9 November 2021 . https://tobacco.harpweek.com/asp/ViewArticleText.asp.

Oak Ridge Associated Universities Museum of Radiation and Radioactivity. 'Vita Radium Suppositories'. n.d. Accessed 9 November 2021. https://www.orau.org/health-physics-museum/collection/index.html.

Obama, Barack H. 'President Barack Obama's inaugural address', *The White House,* 21 January 2009. Accessed 2 November 2021. https://obamawhitehouse.archives.gov/blog/2009/01/21/president-barack-obamas-inaugural-address.

Obama, Barack. 'President Obama's Oval Office address on the BP oil spill: "A faith in the future that sustains us as a people"', 16 June 2010. Accessed 4 November 2021. https://obamawhitehouse.archives.gov/blog/2010/06/16/president-obamas-oval-office-address-bp-oil-spill-a-faith-future-sustains-us-a-peopl.

Ockels, John H. *Illegal Dumping Enforcement*. Sherman, TX: John Ockels, 2022. http://tidrc.com/2022BookOrder.html.

O'Connor, Anahad. 'Is there an optimal diet for humans?', *New York Times*, 18 December 2018. Accessed 11 October 2021. https://www.nytimes.com/2018/12/18/well/eat/is-there-an-optimal-diet-for-humans.html.

Okonjo-Iweala, Ngozi. 'Launch event of ministerial statements on trade, environment and sustainable development', WTO, 15 December 2021. Accessed 4 January 2022. https://www.wto.org/english/news_e/spno_e/spno20_e.htm.

Olson, Mancur. *The Logic of Collective Action*. Cambridge, MA: Harvard University Press, 1965.

Open Secrets. 'Dark money basics'. n.d. Accessed 26 October 2021. https://www.opensecrets.org/dark-money/basics.

Open Secrets. 'Outside spending'. n.d. Accessed 27 October 2021. https://www.opensecrets.org/outsidespending/.

Open University. 'Applied systems thinking in practice'. n.d. Accessed 7 December 2021. https://www.open.ac.uk/stem/engineering-and-innovation/research/applied-systems-thinking-practice.

Oregon Institute of Science and Medicine. 'Global warming petition project'. Accessed 10 November 2021. http://www.petitionproject.org/index.php.

Oreskes, Naomi. 'The scientific consensus on climate change', *Science* 306 (2004): 1686.

Oreskes, Naomi. 'Playing dumb on climate change', *New York Times*, 4 January 2015. Accessed 13 October 2021. https://www.nytimes.com/2015/01/04/opinion/sunday/playing-dumb-on-climate-change.html.

Oreskes, Naomi and Erik M. Conway. *Merchants of Doubt*. New York: Bloomsbury, 2010.

Orr, David. 'Four challenges of sustainability', *Conservation Biology* 16 (2002): 1457–60.

Orr, David. 'Systems thinking and the future of cities', *Resilience*, 30 May 2014. Accessed 5 November 2021. https://www.resilience.org/stories/2014-05-30/systems-thinking-and-the-future-of-cities/.

O'Shaughnessy, Patrick T. 'Parachuting cats and crushed eggs: the controversy over the use of DDT to control malaria', *American Journal of Public Health* 98 (2008): 1940–8.

O'Sullivan, Jim. 'Two utilities opt out of Cape Wind', *Boston Globe*, 6 January 2015. Accessed 17 October 2021. https://www.bostonglobe.com/metro/2015/01/06/major-setback-for-cape-wind-project/kggnYeAXRj03PyfIUn2iIM/story.html.

Overdevest, Christine, Cailin H. Orr and Kristine Stepenuck. 'Volunteer stream monitoring and local participation in natural resource issues', *Human Ecology Review* 11 (2004): 177–85.

Palmer, M. A., E. S. Bernhardt, W. H. Schlesinger, K. N. Eshleman, E. Foufoula-Georgiou, M. S. Hendryx, A. D. Lemly, G. E. Likens, O. L. Loucks, M. E. Power, P. S. White and P. R. Wilcock. 'Mountaintop mining consequences', *Science* 327 (2010): 148–9.

Parker, Carol M. 'The pipeline industry meets grief unimaginable: Congress reacts with the Pipeline Safety Improvement Act of 2002', *Natural Resources Journal* 44 (2004): 243–82.

Parker, Theodore. *Ten Sermons of Religion*. Boston: Crosby, Nichols, 1853.

Parrish, Will. 'Revealed: legislator's pro-pipeline letters ghostwritten by fossil fuel company', *Guardian*, 2 July 2020. Accessed 1 November 2021. https://www.theguardian.com/us-news/2020/jul/02/us-legislators-pro-pipeline-letters-ghostwritten.

Partridge, Ernest. 'Future generations'. In *Companion to Environmental Philosophy*, edited by Dale Jamieson, 377–89. Malden, MA: Blackwell, 2003.

Patel, Manvendra, Rahul Kumar, Kamal Kishor, Todd Mlsna, Charles U. Pittman Jr. and Dinesh Mohan. 'Pharmaceuticals of emerging concern in aquatic systems: chemistry, occurrence, effects, and removal methods', *Chemical Reviews* 119 (2019): 3510–673.

Peterson, Thomas C., William M. Connolley and John Fleck. 'The myth of the 1970s global cooling scientific consensus', *Bulletin of the American Meteorological Association* 89 (2008): 1325–37.

Pew Research Center. 'Public and scientists' views on science and society'. 29 January 2015. Accessed 15 October 2021. https://www.pewresearch.org/science/2015/01/29/public-and-scientists-views-on-science-and-society/.

Phillips, Ari. 'Preparing for the next storm: learning from the man-made environmental disasters that followed Hurricane Harvey', Environmental Integrity Project, 16 August 2018. Accessed 11 October 2021. http://www.environmentalintegrity.org/wp-content/uploads/2018/08/Hurricane-Harvey-Report-Final.pdf.

Pidot, Justin. 'Forbidden data: Wyoming just criminalized citizen science', *Slate*, 11 May 2015. Accessed 11 October 2021. https://slate.com/technology/2015/05/wyoming-law-against-data-collection-protecting-ranchers-by-ignoring-the-environment.html.

Pimm, S. L., C. N. Jenkins, R. Abell, T. M. Brooks, J. L. Gittleman, L. N. Joppa, P. H. Raven, C. M. Roberts and J. O. Sexton. 'The biodiversity of species and their rate of extinction, distribution, and protection', *Science* 344/6187 (2014): 987–98.

Pinchot, Gifford. 'Prosperity', excerpted in *American Earth: Environmental writing since Thoreau*, edited by Bill McKibben, 173–80. New York: Penguin, 2008.

Plato. *The Fables of Phaedrus*, Book IV, Fable II, 'The Weasel and the Mice'. (Henry Thomas Riley, translator). London: George Bell and Sons, 1887. Accessed 29 December 2021. http://www.gutenberg.org/files/25512/25512-h/25512-h.htm.

Platt, John R. 'Strong inference', *Science* 146 (1964): 347–53.

Plumer, Brad. 'Trump put a low cost on carbon emissions. Here's why it matters', *New York Times*, 23 August 2018. Accessed 3 November 2021. https://www.nytimes.com/2018/08/23/climate/social-cost-carbon.html.

Polsby, Daniel D. 'Buckley v. Valeo: the special nature of political speech', *Supreme Court Review* 1976 (1976): 1–43.

Ponting, Clive. *A New Green History of the World*. New York: Penguin, 2007.

Popovich, Nadja. 'Where Americans (mostly) agree on climate change policies, in five maps', *New York Times*, 1 November 2018. Accessed 4 October 2021. https://www.nytimes.com/interactive/2018/11/01/climate/climate-policy-maps.html.

Popovich, Nadja, Livia Albeck-Ripka and Kendra Peirre-Louis. 'The Trump Administration is reversing 100 environmental rules. Here is the full list', *New York Times*, 20 May 2020. Accessed 3 November 2021. https://www.nytimes.com/interactive/2020/climate/trump-environment-rollbacks.html.

Popular Science. 'Hints from the model garage', January 1963: 166. Accessed 16 November 2021. https://books.google.com/books?id=wzsEAAAAMBAJ&source=gbs_navlinks_s.

Population Connection. 'Why population?'. n.d. Accessed 18 October 2021. https://populationconnection.org/why-population/.

Price, Huw. 'Cambridge, cabs and Copenhagen: my route to existential risk', *New York Times Opinionator*, 27 January 2013. Accessed 29 December 2021. https://opinionator.blogs.nytimes.com/2013/01/27/cambridge-cabs-and-copenhagen-my-route-to-existential-risk/.

Princeton University. 'The OTA legacy', Princeton University, Office of Technology Assessment Legacy website. Accessed 10 October 2021. https://www.princeton.edu/~ota/.

Puit, Glenn. 'Survey finds little support for new roads: Petoskey more interested in bike paths, sidewalks, transit', *Great Lakes Bulletin News Service*, 31 July 2007. Accessed 5 November 2021. http://www.mlui.org/mlui/news-views/articles-from-1995-to-2012.html?archive_id=807#.YYVH51NOm0s.

Puit, Glenn. 'Existing roads, tight zoning, bike paths, transit could solve problem', *Great Lakes Bulletin News Service*, 7 December 2007. Accessed 5 November 2021. http://www.mlui.org/mlui/archives.html?archive_id=834#.YYVIiFNOm0s.

Quinn, Daniel. *Ishmael*. New York: Bantam/Turner, 1992.

Qureshi, Zaina P., Enrique Seoane-Vazquez, Rosa Rodriguez-Monguio, Kurt B. Stevenson and Sheryl L. Szeinbach. 'Market withdrawal of new molecular entities approved in the United States from 1980 to 2009', *Pharmacoepidemiology and Drug Safety* 20 (2011): 772–7.

Rabin, Roni C. 'The drug-dose gender gap', *New York Times*, 28 January 2013. Accessed 9 November 2021. https://well.blogs.nytimes.com/2013/01/28/the-drug-dose-gender-gap/.

Rahman, Mahmuder. 'An interview with Mahmuder Rahman: Bangladesh's arsenic agony', *Bulletin of the World Health Organization* 86 (2008): 11–12.

Rampell, Catherine. 'No one in their right mind would design a government that works like ours', *Washington Post*, 9 December 2021. Accessed 1 January 2022. https://www.washingtonpost.com/opinions/2021/12/09/no-one-their-right-mind-would-design-government-that-works-like-ours/.

Reclamation Era. 'Pollution control agency welcomed to Interior', 52 (August 1966): 58–61.

Red River Authority of Texas. 'Water quality monitoring programs'. n.d. Accessed 3 November 2021. http://www.rra.texas.gov/.

Reichenbach, Hans. *The Rise of Scientific Philosophy*. Berkeley: University of California Press, 1951.

Reilly, Mollie. 'Berkeley may put climate change warnings on gas pumps', *Huffington Post*, 18 June 2014. Accessed 8 October 2021. https://www.huffpost.com/entry/berkeley-gas-pumps_n5507844?ec_carp=3103398823819379469.

Reilly, Philip R. 'Involuntary sterilization in the US: a surgical solution', *Quarterly Review of Biology* 62 (1987): 153–70.

Reinhart, Alex. *Statistics Done Wrong*. San Francisco: No Starch Press, 2015.

Reis, S., P. Greenfelt, Z. Klimont, M. Amann, H. ApSimon, J.-P. Hettelingh, M. Holland, A.-C. LeGall, R. Maas, M. Posch, T. Spranger, M. A. Sutton and M. Williams. 'From acid rain to climate change', *Science* 338 (2012): 1153–4.

Renfrew, Daniel and Thomas W. Pearson. 'The social life of the "forever chemical"', *Environment and Society* 12 (2021): 146–63.

Republican National Committee. 'Republican Platform 2020'. Accessed 17 October 2021. https://prod-cdn-static.gop.com/docs/Resolution_Platform_2020.pdf.

Retraction Watch. [blog]. n.d. Accessed 20 December 2021. https://retractionwatch.com/.

Reuben, Susan H. 'Reducing environmental cancer risk: what we can do now', President's Cancer Panel 2008–9 Annual Report. Washington, DC: US Department of Health and Human Services, National Institutes of Health, National Cancer Institute. April 2010. Accessed 13 October 2021. http://deainfo.nci.nih.gov/advisory/pcp/annualReports/pcp08-09rpt/PCP_Report_08-09_508.pdf.

Reusser, Lucas, Paul Bierman and Dylan Rood. 'Quantifying human impacts on rates of erosion and sediment transport at a landscape scale', *Geology* 43 (2015): 171–4.

Reuters. 'Enbridge plans Alberta Clipper pipeline boost despite US delays', 21 August 2014. Accessed 1 November 2021. https://www.reuters.com/article/enbridge-inc-albertaclipper-idUSL2N0QR2HD20140821.

Reuters and Andrea Shalal. 'USTR Tai calls for bold action to put climate at center of trade policy', 15 April 2021. Accessed 4 January 2022. https://www.reuters.com/business/environment/us-trade-chief-tai-says-climate-key-priority-trade-policy-2021-04-15/.

Revkin, Andrew C. and Katharine Q. Seelye. 'Report by EPA leaves out data on climate change', *New York Times*, 19 June 2003. Accessed 3 November 2021. https://www.nytimes.com/2003/06/19/us/report-by-epa-leaves-out-data-on-climate-change.html.

Reynolds, Molly E. 'Republicans in Congress got a "seats bonus" this election (again)', Brookings Institution, 22 November 2016. Accessed 25 October 2021. https://www.brookings.edu/blog/fixgov/2016/11/22/gop-seats-bonus-in-congress/.

Reznik, Gayle L., Dave Shoffner and David A. Weaver. 'Coping with the demographic challenge: fewer children and living longer', US Social Security Administration Office of Policy, *Social Security Bulletin* 66 (2005/2006). Accessed 18 October 2021. http://www.ssa.gov/policy/docs/ssb/v66n4/v66n4p37.html.

Ricciardi, Anthony and Hugh J. MacIsaac. 'Impacts of biological invasions on freshwater ecosystems'. In *Fifty Years of Invasion Ecology: The legacy of Charles Elton*, edited by David M. Richardson, 211–24. Oxford: Wiley-Blackwell, 2011.

Ricciardi, Anthony and Hugh J. MacIsaac. 'Vector control reduces the rate of species invasion in the world's largest freshwater ecosystem', *Conservation Letters* (2022). Accessed 30 May 2022. https://doi.org/10.1111/conl.12866.

Richardson, Jessica. 'Pottsboro is fined by TCEQ', *Herald Democrat* (Sherman, Texas), 8 November 2007.

Ricketts, Sue, Greta Klinger and Renee Schwalberg. 'Game change in Colorado: widespread use of long-acting reversible contraceptives and rapid decline in births among young, low-income women', *Perspectives on Sexual and Reproductive Health* 46 (2014): 125–32.

Rigby, M., S. Park, T. Saito, L. M. Western, A. L. Redington and X. Fang. 'Increase in CFC-11 emissions from eastern China based on atmospheric observations', *Nature* 569 (2019): 546–50.

Risky Business Project. 'The economic risks of climate change in the US', June 2014. Accessed 20 October 2021. https://riskybusiness.org/report/national/.

Roberts, Andrea L., Kristen Lyall, Jaime E. Hart, Francine Laden, Allan C. Just, Jennifer F. Bobb, Karestan C. Koenen, Alberto Ascherio and Marc G. Weisskopf. 'Perinatal air pollutant exposures and autism spectrum disorder in the children of Nurses' Health Study II participants', *Environmental Health Perspectives* 121 (2013). Accessed 30 May 2022. http://dx.doi.org/10.1289/ehp.1206187.

Robertson, Grant and Jacquie McNish. 'Inside the oil-shipping free-for-all that brought disaster to Lac-Mégantic', *Globe and Mail*, 17 June 2014. Accessed 17 October 2021. https://www.theglobeandmail.com/report-on-business/industry-news/energy-and-resources/a-pipeline-on-wheels-how-a-changing-industry-brought-disaster-to-lac-megantic/article15711624/.

Rockström, Johan, Will Steffen, Kevin Noone, Åsa Persson, F. Stuart Chapin III, Eric Lambin, Timothy M. Lenton, Marten Scheffer, Carl Folke, Hans J. Schellnhuber, Björn Nykvist, Cynthia A. De Wit, Terry Hughes, Sander van der Leeuw, Henning Rodhe, Sverker Sörlin, Peter K. Snyder, Robert Costanza, Uno Svedin, Malin Falkenmark, Louise Karlberg, Robert W. Corell, Victoria J. Fabry, James Hansen, Brian Walker, Diana Liverman, Katherine Richardson, Paul Crutzen and Jonathan Foley. 'Planetary boundaries: exploring the safe operating space for humanity', *Ecology and Society* 14 (2009): article 32. Accessed 21 October 2021. http://www.ecologyandsociety.org/vol14/iss2/art32/.

Rogers, Alan R. 'Evolution of time preference by natural selection', *American Economic Review* 84 (1994): 460–81.

Rogich, Don, Amy Cassara, Iddo Wernick and Marta Miranda. *Materials Flows in the US: A physical accounting of the US industrial economy*. Washington, DC: World Resources Institute, 2008.

Rosenbaum, Walter A. *Environmental Politics and Policy*. 5th edition. Thousand Oaks, CA: CQ Press, 2002.

Rosner, David and Gerald Markowitz. 'Why it took decades of blaming parents before we banned lead paint', *Atlantic*, 22 April 2013. Accessed 5 October 2021. https://www.theatlantic.com/health/archive/2013/04/why-it-took-decades-of-blaming-parents-before-we-banned-lead-paint/275169/.

Rovelli, Carlo. 'Science is not about certainty', *New Republic*, 11 July 2014. Accessed 17 December 2021. https://newrepublic.com/article/118655/theoretical-phyisicist-explains-why-science-not-about-certainty.

Royal Government of Bhutan. 'Draft national population policy'. 2018. Accessed 18 October 2021. https://www.gnhc.gov.bt/en/wp-content/uploads/2019/06/Draft-NPP-final-14-Jan-2019.pdf.

Rulli, Maria C., Stefano Casirati, Jampel Dell'Angelo, Kyle F. Davis, Corrado Passera and Paolo D'Odorico. 'Interdependencies and telecoupling of oil palm expansion at the expense of Indonesian rainforest', *Renewable and Sustainable Energy Reviews* 105 (2019): 499–512.

Rust, Susanne and Louis Sahagún. 'Must reads: post-Hurricane Harvey, NASA tried to fly a pollution-spotting plane over Houston. The EPA said no', *Los Angeles Times*, 5 March 2019. Accessed 11 October 2021. https://www.latimes.com/local/california/la-me-nasa-jet-epa-hurricane-harvey-20190305-story.html.

Saad, Lydia. 'Americans as concerned as ever about global warming', *Gallup*, 25 March 2019. Accessed 7 October 2021. https://news.gallup.com/poll/248027/americans-concerned-ever-global-warming.aspx.

Salzman, James and Barton H. Thompson Jr. *Environmental Law and Policy*. 4th edition. New York: Foundation Press, 2014.

Sampaio, Gilvan, Carlos Nobre, Marcos H. Costa, Prakki Satyamurty, Britaldo S. Soares-Filho and Manoel Cardoso. 'Regional climate change over eastern Amazonia caused by pasture and soybean cropland expansion', *Geophysical Research Letters* 34 (2007): L17709. Accessed 30 May 2022. https://agupubs.onlinelibrary.wiley.com/doi/full/10.1029/2007GL030612.

Sample, Ian. 'Total recall … of unsuccessful attempts to land on Mars', *Guardian*, 20 October 2016. Accessed 14 October 2021. https://www.theguardian.com/science/2016/oct/20/total-recall-of-unsuccessful-mars-lander-schiaparelli-exomars.

Sánchez-Bayo, Francisco and Kris A. G. Wyckhuys. 'Worldwide decline of the entomofauna: a review of its drivers', *Biological Conservation* 232 (2019): 8–27.

Santa Fe Institute. 'About'. n.d. Accessed 10 October 2021. https://www.santafe.edu/about/overview.

Savory, Allan. *Holistic Management: A new framework for decision making*. Washington, DC: Island Press, 1988.

Savory Institute. 'Our mission'. n.d. Accessed 6 November 2021. https://savory.global/our-mission/.

Sawyer, Kathy. 'Mystery of orbiter crash solved', *Washington Post,* 1 October 1999. Accessed 14 October 2021. https://www.washingtonpost.com/wp-srv/national/longterm/space/stories/orbiter100199.htm.

Schattschneider, Elmer E. *Politics, Pressures, and the Tariff.* New York: Prentice-Hall, 1935.

Scheffer, Marten, Steve Carpenter, Jonathan A. Foley, Carl Folke and Brian Walker. 'Catastrophic shifts in ecosystems', *Nature* 413 (2001): 592–6.

Schindler, David W., K. H. Mills, D. F. Malley, D. L. Findlay, J. A. Shearer, I. J. Davies, M. A. Turner, G. A. Lindsey and D. R. Cruikshank. 'Long-term ecosystem stress: the effects of years of experimental acidification on a small lake', *Science* 228 (1985): 1395–401.

Schlanger, Zoë and Elijah Wolfson. 'How to defuse the population bomb: the earth's too crowded, so better family planning may be humanity's last hope to save us from ourselves', *Newsweek,* 26 December 2014. Accessed 18 October 2021. https://www.newsweek.com/2014/12/26/fixing-crowded-earth-293024.html.

Schlefer, Jonathan. 'Today's most mischievous misquotation', *Atlantic,* March (1998): 16–19.

Schmalensee, Richard, Paul L. Toskow, A. Denny Ellerman, Juan Pablo Montero and Elizabeth M. Bailey. 'An interim evaluation of sulfur dioxide emissions trading', *Journal of Economic Perspectives* 12 (1998): 53–68.

Schneider, Judy. 'House and Senate rules of procedure: a comparison', Congressional Research Service Report for Congress RL30945, 16 April 2008. Accessed 29 October 2021. https://crsreports.congress.gov/product/pdf/RL/RL30945.

Schulenberg, Thomas S. 'Obituary: Theodore Parker III', *Independent,* 11 August 1993. Accessed 11 October 2021. http://www.independent.co.uk/news/people/obituary-theodore-parker-iii-1460656.html.

Schultz, Kai. 'In Bhutan, happiness index as gauge for social ills', *New York Times,* 17 January 2017. Accessed 5 November 2021. https://www.nytimes.com/2017/01/17/world/asia/bhutan-gross-national-happiness-indicator-.html.

Schulze, Peter C. 'I = PBAT', *Ecological Economics* 40 (2002): 149–50.

Schulze, Peter C. 'Evidence that fish structure the zooplankton communities of turbid lakes and reservoirs', *Freshwater Biology* 56 (2011): 352–65.

Schulze, Peter C. and Lance F. Barton. 'How to give a good presentation', Council on Undergraduate Research. Accessed 13 December 2021. https://www.cur.org/assets/1/7/How_to_Give_a_Good_Presentation__CUR.pdf.

Schulze, Peter C. and Arthur S. Brooks. 'The possibility of predator avoidance by Lake Michigan zooplankton', *Hydrobiologia* 146 (1987): 47–56.

Schulze, Peter C., J. Hayley Gillespie, J. Russell Womble and Alexandra F. Silen. 'The effect of suspended sediments on Lake Texoma *Daphnia*: field distributions and in situ incubations', *Freshwater Biology* 51 (2006): 1447–57.

Schulze, Peter C., Mark Leighton and David R. Peart. 'Enrichment planting in selectively logged rain forest: a combined ecological and economic analysis', *Ecological Applications* 4 (1994): 581–92.

Schulze, Peter C., Kellie J. Wilcox, Anthony Swift and Janet L. Beckert. 'Fast, easy measurements for assessing vital signs of tall grassland', *Ecological Indicators* 9 (2009): 445–54.

Schwartz, John. 'Ban on microbeads proves easy to pass through pipeline', *New York Times,* 22 December 2015. Accessed 1 October 2021. https://www.nytimes.com/2015/12/23/science/ban-on-microbeads-proves-easy-to-pass-through-pipeline.html.

Schwartz, Mark W. 'The performance of the Endangered Species Act', *Annual Review of Ecology and Systematics* 39 (2008): 279–99.

Science History Institute. 'Digital collections'. Accessed 16 November 2021. https://digital.sciencehistory.org/.

Searchinger, Timothy D., Tim Beringer, Bjart Holtsmark, Daniel M. Kammen, Eric F. Lambin, Wolfgang Lucht, Peter Raven and Jean-Pascal van Ypersele. 'Europe's renewable energy directive poised to harm global forests', *Nature Communications* 9 (2018): 3741. Accessed 28 March 2022. https://doi.org/10.1038/s41467-018-06175-4.

Selin, Henrik and Stacy D. VanDeveer. 'Global climate change: beyond Kyoto'. In *Environmental Policy: New directions for the 21st century,* edited by Norman J. Vig and Michael E. Kraft, 278–98. 8th edition. Thousand Oaks, CA: CQ Press, 2013.

Sellye, Katharine Q. 'Koch brother wages 12-year fight over wind farm', *New York Times,* 22 October 2013. Accessed 17 October 2021. https://www.nytimes.com/2013/10/23/us/koch-brother-wages-12-year-fight-over-wind-farm.html.

Sguotti, Camilla, Saskia A. Otto, Romain Frelat, Tom J. Langbehn, Marie Plambech Ryberg, Martin Lindegren, Joël M. Durant, Nils Christian Stenseth and Christian Möllmann. 'Catastrophic dynamics limit Atlantic cod recovery', *Proceedings of the Royal Society B* 286 (2019): 20182877. Accessed 30 May 2022. http://dx.doi.org/10.1098/rspb.2018.2877.

Shabecoff, Philip. 'Scientist says budget office altered his testimony', *New York Times*, 7 May 1989. Accessed 3 November 2021. https://timesmachine.nytimes.com/timesmachine/1989/05/08/issue.html.

Shapiro, Stuart and John F. Morrall III. 'The triumph of regulatory politics: benefit–cost analysis and political salience', *Regulation and Governance* 6 (2012): 189–206.

Shelton, Janie F., Estella M. Geraghty, Daniel J. Tancredi, Lora D. Delwiche, Rebecca J. Schmidt, Beate Ritz, Robin L. Hansen and Irva Hertz-Picciotto. 'Neurodevelopmental disorders and prenatal residential proximity to agricultural pesticides: the CHARGE study', *Environmental Health Perspectives* 122 (2014): 1103–9.

Sheppard, Kate. 'Perry officials censored climate change report', *Mother Jones*, 12 October 2011. Accessed 3 November 2021. https://www.motherjones.com/politics/2011/10/perry-officials-censored-climate-report/.

Sierra Club. 'Explore issues'. n.d. Accessed 18 October 2021. https://www.sierraclub.org/about-sierra-club.

SIMAP. 'Austin College'. n.d. University of New Hampshire Sustainability Institute. Accessed 22 April 2022. https://unhsimap.org/public/institution/648.

Simmons, Joseph P., Leif D. Nelson and Uri Simonsohn. 'False-positive psychology: undisclosed flexibility in data collection and analysis allows presenting anything as significant', *Psychological Science* 22 (2011): 1359–366.

Simon, Julian. *The Ultimate Resource.* Princeton: Princeton University Press, 1996.

Simon Does. 'Population Connection brand identity'. n.d. Accessed 18 October 2021. http://simondoes.com/our-work/identity/population-connection-brand-identity/.

Sinclair, A. R. E. and Andrea E. Byrom. 'Understanding ecosystem dynamics for conservation of biota', *Journal of Animal Ecology* 75 (2006): 64–79.

Sinclair, A. R. E. and J. M. Fryxell. 'The Sahel of Africa: ecology of a disaster', *Canadian Journal of Zoology* 63 (1985): 987–94.

Sinclair, Barbara. *Unorthodox Lawmaking: New legislative processes in the US Congress.* 5th edition. Thousand Oaks, CA: CQ Press, 2017.

Sinclair, Upton. *I, Candidate for Governor: And how I got licked.* Berkeley: University of California Press, 1994.

Siviter, Harry, Emily J. Bailes, Callum D. Martin, Thomas R. Oliver, Julia Koricheva, Ellouise Leadbeater and Mark J. F. Brown. 'Agrochemicals interact synergistically to increase bee mortality', *Nature* 596 (2021): 389–92.

Skeptical Science. 'The escalator'. n.d. Accessed 17 November 2021. https://skepticalscience.com/escalator.

Smith, Adam. *The Wealth of Nations.* New York: Modern Library, 2000.

Smith, Allan H., Elena O. Lingas and Mahfuzar Rahman. 'Contamination of drinking-water by arsenic in Bangladesh: a public health emergency', *Bulletin of the World Health Organization* 78 (2000): 1093–103.

Smith, Daniel E. 'Voter suppression policies in the 2016 campaign cycle'. In *The Roads to Congress 2016*, edited by Sean D. Foreman and Marcia L. Godwin, 27–42. Cham: Palgrave Macmillan, 2018.

Smith, Zachary. *The Environmental Policy Paradox.* 4th edition. Upper Saddle River, NJ: Prentice-Hall, 2004.

Soffen, Kim. 'Independently drawn districts have proved to be more competitive', *New York Times*, 1 July 2015. Accessed 25 October 2021. https://www.nytimes.com/2015/07/02/upshot/independently-drawn-districts-have-proved-to-be-more-competitive.html.

Sorokowski, Piotr, Emanuel Kulczycki, Agnieska Sorokowska and Katarzyna Pisanski. 'Predatory journals recruit fake editor', *Nature* 543 (2017): 481–3.

Stauber, John and Sheldon Rampton. *Toxic Sludge is Good for You! Lies, damn lies, and the public relations industry.* Monroe, ME: Common Courage Press, 1995.

Stern, Alexandra M. 'Sterilized in the name of public health: race, immigration, and reproductive control in modern California', *American Journal of Public Health* 95 (2005): 1128–38.

Strahan, Susan E. and Anne R. Douglass. 'Decline in Antarctic ozone depletion and lower stratospheric chlorine determined from aura microwave limb sounder observations', *Geophysical Research Letters* 45 (2018): 382–90.

Stuart, Colin. 'Are nanotextiles making fabric laws wear thin?', *Guardian*, 4 October 2011. Accessed 10 October 2021. https://www.theguardian.com/nanotechnology-world/nanotextiles-fabric-laws-science-nanotechnology.

Stuart, Tessa. 'Big oil's best-kept secret', *Audubon*, March–April 2015. Accessed 16 October 2021. https://www.audubon.org/magazine/march-april-2015/big-oils-best-kept-secret.

Sullivan, John V. 'How our laws are made', House of Representatives Document 110–49. July 2007. Accessed 29 October 2021. https://www.congress.gov/help/learn-about-the-legislative-process/how-our-laws-are-made.

Sullivan, Sean. 'What is a 501(c)4, anyway?', *Washington Post*, 13 May 2013. Accessed 26 October 2021. https://www.washingtonpost.com/news/the-fix/wp/2013/05/13/what-is-a-501c4-anyway/?utm_term=.b4cf9a36290c.

Sunstein, Cass. R. 'Biden chooses a pragmatic path for regulation', *Bloomberg*, 22 January 2021. Accessed 20 October 2021. https://www.bloomberg.com/opinion/articles/2021-01-22/regulation-under-biden-cost-benefit-analysis-with-a-new-twist.

Suryanarayanan, Sainath and Daniel L. Kleinman. 'Be(e)coming experts: the controversy over insecticides in honey bee Colony Collapse Disorder', *Social Studies of Science* 43/2 (2013): 215–40. Accessed 30 May 2022. https://doi.org/10.1177/0306312712466186.

Sutherland, William J., Philip W. Atkinson, Steven Broad, Sam Brown, Mick Clout, Maria P. Dias, Lynn V. Dicks, Helen Doran, Erica Fleishman, Elizabeth L. Garratt, Kevin J. Gaston, Alice C. Hughes, Xavier Le Roux, Fiona A. Lickorish, Luke Maggs, James E. Palardy, Lloyd S. Peck, Nathalie Pettorelli, Jules Pretty, Mark D. Spalding, Femke H. Tonneijck, Matt Walpole, James E. M. Watson, Jonathan Wentworth and Ann Thornton. 'A 2021 horizon scan of emerging global biological conservation issues', *Trends in Ecology and Evolution* 36 (January 2021). Accessed 30 May 2022. https://doi.org/10.1016/j.tree.2020.10.014.

Swasey, Benjamin. 'Map: mail-in voting rules by state – and the deadlines you need', *National Public Radio*, 14 October 2020. Accessed 22 October 2021. https://www.npr.org/2020/09/14/909338758/map-mail-in-voting-rules-by-state.

Tarlo, Emma. *Unsettling Memories: Narratives of the emergency in Delhi*. Berkeley: University of California Press, 2003.

Tate, Curtis. 'Rail industry pushes feds to drop crude-oil reporting rule', *Sacramento Bee*, 6 October 2014. Accessed 17 October 2021. https://www.sacbee.com/news/business/article2622114.html.

Tavernise, Sabrina. 'In new calculus on smoking, it's health gained vs. pleasure lost', *New York Times*, 6 August 2014. Accessed 8 November 2021. http://www.nytimes.com/2014/08/07/health/pleasure-factor-may-override-new-tobacco-rules.html.

Taylor, Adam. 'A timeline of Trump's complicated relationship with the TPP', *Washington Post*, 13 April 2018. Accessed 7 November 2021. https://www.washingtonpost.com/news/worldviews/wp/2018/04/13/a-timeline-of-trumps-complicated-relationship-with-the-tpp/?utm_term=.315483203eb1.

Temple, James. 'What is geoengineering – and why should you care?', *MIT Technology Review*, 9 August 2019. Accessed 1 November 2021. https://www.technologyreview.com/2019/08/09/615/what-is-geoengineering-and-why-should-you-care-climate-change-harvard/.

Terrio, Paul J. 'Relations of changes in wastewater-treatment practices to changes in stream-water quality during 1978–88 in the Chicago area, Illinois, and implications for regional and national water-quality assessments'. Washington, DC: US Geological Survey Water-Resources Investigations Report 93-4188, 1994. Accessed 11 November 2021. https://pubs.usgs.gov/wri/1993/4188/report.pdf.

Texas Commission on Environmental Quality. 'Texas SIP revisions'. Accessed 2 November 2021. https://www.tceq.texas.gov/airquality/sip/sipplans.html/#sips.

Texas Illegal Dumping Resource Center. 'Enforcement training for Texas cities and counties'. Accessed 27 November 2021. http://tidrc.com/.

Texas Parks and Wildlife Department. 'Mission and philosophy'. n.d. Accessed 3 November 2021. https://tpwd.texas.gov/business/about/mission/.

Texas Water Development Board. '2022 state water plan'. n.d. Accessed 1 November 2021. http://www.twdb.texas.gov/waterplanning/swp/2022/index.asp.

Thomas, Cal. 'The pope, the globe and the facts', *Washington Times*, 24 June 2015. Accessed 14 October 2021. http://www.washingtontimes.com/news/2015/jun/24/cal-thomas-the-pope-the-globe-and-the-facts-on-glo/.

Thompson, Steve and Anna Kuchment. 'Seismic denial? Why Texas won't admit fracking wastewater is causing earthquakes', *Dallas Morning News*, 17 November 2016. Accessed 4 November 2021. http://interactives.dallasnews.com/2016/seismic-denial/.

Thomson, Ryan, Johanna Espin and Tameka Samuels-Jones. 'Green crime havens: a spatial cluster analysis of environmental crime', *Social Science Quarterly* 101 (2020): 503–13.

Thoreau, Henry D. *The Portable Thoreau*, edited by Carl Bode. New York: Penguin, 1977.

Tian, Zhenyu, Haoqi Zhao, Katherine T. Peter, Melissa Gonzalez, Jill Wetzel, Christopher Wu, Ximin Hu, Jasmine Prat, Emma Mudrock, Rachel Hettinger, Allan E. Cortina, Rajshree Ghosh Biswas, Flávio Vinicius Crizóstomo Kock, Ronald Soong, Amy Jenne, Bowen Du, Fan Hou, Huan He, Rachel Lundeen, Alicia Gilbreath, Rebecca Sutton, Nathaniel L. Scholz, Jay W. Davis, Michael C. Dodd, Andre Simpson, Jenifer K. McIntyre and Edward P. Kolodziej. 'A ubiquitous tire rubber-derived chemical induces acute mortality in coho salmon', *Science* 371 (2020): 185–9.

Tilman, David, Peter B. Reich and Johannes M. H. Knops. 'Biodiversity and ecosystem stability in a decade-long grassland experiment', *Nature* 441 (2006): 629–32.

Todd, G. Daniel, Carolyn Harper, Paula Burgess, David Wohlers, Michael H. Lumpkin, Christina Coley and Courtney M. Hard. 'Toxicological Profile for Diazinon'. Washington, DC: US Department of Health and Human Services Public Health Service Agency for Toxic Substances and Disease Registry. September 2008. Accessed 11 October 2021. http://www.atsdr.cdc.gov/ToxProfiles/tp86.pdf.

Tresaugue, Matthew. 'Court overturns EPA's cross-state pollution rule', *Houston Chronicle*, 21 August 2012. Accessed 4 November 2021. https://www.chron.com/news/houston-texas/article/Court-overturns-EPA-s-cross-state-pollution-rule-3805282.php.

Tribe, Laurence H. 'Trial by mathematics: precision and ritual in the legal process', *Harvard Law Review* 84 (1971): 1329–93.

Tribe, Laurence H. 'Policy science: analysis or ideology', *Philosophy and Public Affairs* 2 (1972): 66–110.

Tribe, Laurence H. 'Ways not to think about plastic trees: new foundations for environmental law', *Yale Law Journal* 83 (1974): 1315–48.

Truskey, Mark. 'Climate change is just "weather"', *Dallas Morning News*, 27 January 2016.

Tsang, Ruth, Lindsey Colley and Larry D. Lynd. 'Inadequate statistical power to detect clinically significant differences in adverse event rates in randomized controlled trials', *Journal of Clinical Epidemiology* 62 (2009): 609–16.

Tschinkel, Walter R. *The Fire Ants*. Cambridge, MA: Harvard University Press, 2006.

Tucker, Todd. 'TransCanada is suing the US over Obama's rejection of the Keystone KL pipeline. The US might lose', *Washington Post*, 8 January 2016. Accessed 9 November 2021. https://www.washingtonpost.com/news/monkey-cage/wp/2016/01/08/transcanada-is-suing-the-u-s-over-obamas-rejection-of-the-keystone-xl-pipeline-the-u-s-might-lose/.

Tucker, Todd. 'There's a big new headache for the Green New Deal', *Washington Post*, 28 June 2019. Accessed 6 November 2021. https://www.washingtonpost.com/politics/2019/06/28/theres-big-new-headache-green-new-deal/.

Tyler Prize for Environmental Achievement. Accessed 31 May 2022. https://tylerprize.org/.

Udall, Stuart L. *The Quiet Crisis*. New York: Avon Books, 1963.

Ulrich, Lawrence. 'With gas prices less of a worry, buyers pass hybrid cars by', *New York Times*, 14 May 2015. Accessed 2 November 2021. http://www.nytimes.com/2015/05/15/automobiles/wheels/with-gas-prices-less-of-a-worry-buyers-pass-hybrids-cars-by.html.

UN Environment Program Global Marine Oil Pollution Information Gateway. 'Helsinki Convention'. n.d. Accessed 3 November 2021. http://oils.gpa.unep.org/framework/region-2-next.htm.

UN Food and Agriculture Organization Commodities and Trade Division. 'Agricultural commodities: profiles and relevant WTO negotiating issues'. Rome: FAO. March 2002. Accessed 29 November 2021. https://www.fao.org/3/y4343e/y4343e00.htm#Contents.

UN Framework Convention on Climate Change. 'The Paris Agreement'. n.d. Accessed 3 November 2021. https://unfccc.int/process-and-meetings/the-paris-agreement/the-paris-agreement.

US Army Corps of Engineers. 'Mission overview'. n.d. Accessed 3 November 2021. http://www.usace.army.mil/Missions.aspx.

US Army Corps of Engineers. 'Welcome to Lake Texoma'. n.d. Accessed 11 October 2021. https://www.swt.usace.army.mil/Locations/Tulsa-District-Lakes/Oklahoma/Lake-Texoma/.

US Capitol Visitors Center. 'Committees'. n.d. Accessed 29 October 2021. https://www.visitthecapitol.gov/sites/default/files/documents/resources-and-activities/CVC_HS_ActivitySheets_Committees.pdf.

US Census Bureau. 'Wealth, asset ownership, and debt of households detailed tables: 2018'. 2018. Accessed 22 October 2021. https://www.census.gov/data/tables/2018/demo/wealth/wealth-asset-ownership.html.

US Census Bureau. 'National population totals: 2010–2020'. July 2021. Accessed 27 October 2021. https://www.census.gov/programs-surveys/popest/technical-documentation/research/evaluation-estimates/2020-evaluation-estimates/2010s-totals-national.html.

US Centers for Disease Control, Agency for Toxic Substances and Disease Registry. 'Interaction Profiles for Toxic Substances'. n.d. Accessed 12 October 2021. https://www.atsdr.cdc.gov/interactionprofiles/index.html.

US Central Intelligence Agency. 'China: people and society', *World Factbook*, n.d. Accessed 18 October 2021. https://www.cia.gov/the-world-factbook/countries/china/#people-and-society.

US Central Intelligence Agency. 'Guide to country comparisons', *World Factbook*, n.d. Accessed 16 November 2021. https://www.cia.gov/the-world-factbook/references/guide-to-country-comparisons/.

US Central Intelligence Agency. 'India: people and society', *World Factbook*, n.d. Accessed 18 October 2021. https://www.cia.gov/library/publications/the-world-factbook/fields/2018.html.

US Congress. 'Public Law 88-609', 88th Congress, S. 2701, September 22, 1964. Accessed 7 October 2021. https://www.govtrack.us/congress/bills/88/s2701/text.

US Congress, Office of Technology Assessment. *Preparing for an Uncertain Climate, Volume I.* OTA-0-567. 1 October 1993. Washington, DC: US Government Printing Office. Accessed 29 December 2021. https://ota.fas.org/reports/9338.pdf.

US Department of Energy. 'US Energy and Employment Report', January 2017. Accessed 19 October 2021. https://www.energy.gov/sites/prod/files/2017/01/f34/2017%20US%20Energy%20and%20Jobs%20Report_0.pdf.

US Department of Health and Human Services, Centers for Disease Control and Prevention. 'Achievements in public health, 1900–1999: improvements in workplace safety – US, 1900–1999', *Morbidity and Mortality Weekly Report* 48 (1999): 461–9. Accessed 7 October 2021. https://www.cdc.gov/mmwr/preview/mmwrhtml/mm4822a1.htm.

US Department of the Interior Bureau of Ocean Energy Management. 'Lease sale 257'. Accessed 7 October 2021. https://www.boem.gov/Sale-257.

US Department of the Interior Office of Surface Mining Reclamation and Enforcement. 'Stream protection rule'. n.d. Accessed 4 November 2021. https://www.osmre.gov/programs/rcm/StreamProtectionRule.shtm.

US Department of the Treasury. 'Spending explorer'. 2022. Accessed 8 April 2022. https://www.usaspending.gov/explorer/agency.

US Department of Transportation Pipeline and Hazardous Materials Safety Administration. 'Advancing the safe transportation of energy and hazardous materials'. n.d. Accessed 3 November 2021. https://www.phmsa.dot.gov/.

US Department of Transportation Pipeline and Hazardous Materials Safety Administration. 'PHMSA and pipelines FAQs'. n.d. Accessed 3 November 2021. https://www.phmsa.dot.gov/faqs/phmsa-and-pipelines-faqs#QA_1.

US Federal Election Commission. 'Election and voting information'. n.d. Accessed 29 October 2021. https://www.fec.gov/introduction-campaign-finance/election-and-voting-information/.

US Fish and Wildlife Service. 'FWS authoritative geospatial data'. n.d. Accessed 11 November 2021. https://fws.maps.arcgis.com/home/index.html.

US Fish and Wildlife Service. 'US federal endangered and threatened species by calendar year'. n.d. Accessed 16 November 2021. https://ecos.fws.gov/ecp/report/species-listings-by-year-totals.

US Fish and Wildlife Service and US National Marine Fisheries Service. 'Policy for evaluation of conservation efforts when making listing decisions', *Federal Register* 68 (2003): 15100–15. Accessed 3 November 2021. https://www.govinfo.gov/content/pkg/FR-2003-03-28/pdf/03-7364.pdf.

US Fish and Wildlife Service and US National Oceanic and Atmospheric Administration. 'Endangered and threatened wildlife and plants: revision of the regulations for listing species and designating critical habitat', *Federal Register* 83 (2018): 35193–201. Accessed 3 November 2021. https://www.govinfo.gov/content/pkg/FR-2018-07-25/pdf/2018-15810.pdf.

US Fish and Wildlife Service. 'Endangered and threatened wildlife and plants: revised designation of critical habitat for the northern spotted owl', *Federal Register* 86 (2021): 62606–66. Accessed 28 June 2022. https://www.govinfo.gov/content/pkg/FR-2021-11-10/pdf/2021-24365.pdf#page=1

US Fish and Wildlife Service. 'Listed species summary (boxscore)'. 31 May 2022. Accessed 31 May 2022. https://ecos.fws.gov/ecp/report/boxscore.

US Geological Survey. 'About us'. n.d. Accessed 3 November 2021. http://www.usgs.gov/aboutusgs/.

US Geological Survey. 'National Water Information System: site inventory for Texas'. Accessed 11 October 2021. http://waterdata.usgs.gov/tx/nwis/inventory.

US Government Accountability Office. 'Technology assessments'. n.d. Accessed 10 October 2021. https://www.gao.gov/science-technology.

US Government Accountability Office. 'Endangered species: spotted owl petition beset by problems', GAO/RCED-89-89, 21 February 1989. Accessed 3 November 2021. http://www.gao.gov/products/137989.

US Government Accountability Office. 'Uranium mining: opportunities exist to improve oversight of financial assurances', May 2012. GAO-12-544. Accessed 9 November 2021. http://www.gao.gov/assets/600/590929.pdf.

US Internal Revenue Service. 'Public disclosure and availability of exempt organizations returns and applications: documents subject to public disclosure'. 7 September 2021. Accessed 26 October 2021. https://www.irs.gov/charities-non-profits/public-disclosure-and-availability-of-exempt-organizations-returns-and-applications-documents-subject-to-public-disclosure.

US National Institutes of Health. 'Total NIH budget authority: FY 2019 operating plan'. Accessed 10 November 2021. https://report.nih.gov/nihdatabook/report/5.

US National Institutes of Health. 'Estimates of funding for various research, condition, and disease categories (RCDC)'. 25 June 2021. Accessed 10 November 2021. https://report.nih.gov/funding/categorical-spending#/.

US National Oceanic and Atmospheric Administration. 'The NOAA annual greenhouse gas index (AGGI)', Spring 2021 update. Accessed 4 October 2021. https://gml.noaa.gov/aggi/aggi.html.

US National Science Foundation. 'NSF & Congress: final action completed on appropriations for FY19'. n.d. Accessed 10 November 2021. https://www.nsf.gov/about/congress/116/highlights/cu19_0222.jsp.

US National Science Foundation. 'FY 2022 budget request to Congress'. n.d. Accessed 10 November 2022. https://www.nsf.gov/about/budget/fy2022/index.jsp.

US National Science Foundation. 'Federal R&D funding, by budget function: fiscal years 2018–20'. 4 December 2019. Accessed 9 November 2021. https://ncses.nsf.gov/pubs/nsf20305/#data-tables.

US National Science Foundation Long Term Ecological Network. 'Cedar Creek Ecosystem Science Reserve'. Accessed 16 November 2021. https://lternet.edu/site/cedar-creek-ecosystem-science-reserve/. CC BY-SA 4.0, https://creativecommons.org/licenses/by/4.0/deed.en.

US President's Science Advisory Committee, Environmental Pollution Panel. *Restoring the Quality of Our Environment: Report of the Environmental Pollution Panel of the President's Science Advisory Committee*, November 1965.

Valek, Erika R. 'Challenges of Utilizing Municipal Compost as an Amendment in Boreal Forest Reclamation Subsoil Material'. Unpublished master's thesis. Edmonton: University of Alberta, 2018. Accessed 1 November 2021. https://era.library.ualberta.ca/items/bb624b65-606a-4212-9708-30bb7b98dca8/view/3ef02161-4c99-46ec-8d8d-eb42b1feff27/Valek_Erika_R_201808_MSc.pdf.

Van der Linden, Sander and Breanne Chryst. 'Why the "new statistics" isn't new', *The Psychologist* 28 (2015): 610.

Vergara, Walter and Sebastian M. Scholz (eds). 'Assessment of the risk of Amazon dieback', Washington, DC: World Bank, 2011. Accessed 2 November 2021. https://openknowledge.worldbank.org/handle/10986/2531.

Vitousek, Peter M., Paul R. Ehrlich, Anne H. Ehrlich and Pamela A. Matson. 'Human appropriation of the products of photosynthesis', *BioScience* 36 (1986): 368–73.

Vogel, Kenneth P., Jim Rutenberg and Lisa Lerer. 'The quiet hand of conservative groups in the anti-lockdown protests', *New York Times*, 21 April 2020. Accessed 1 November 2021. https://www.nytimes.com/2020/04/21/us/politics/coronavirus-protests-trump.html.

Vose, Clement E. *Caucasians Only: The Supreme Court, the NAACP, and the restrictive covenant cases*. Berkeley: University of California Press, 1959.

Vucetich, John A. and Michael P. Nelson. 'Conservation, or curation?', *New York Times*, 20 August 2014. Accessed 3 November 2021. https://www.nytimes.com/2014/08/21/opinion/conservation-or-curation.html.

Wagner, David L., Eliza M. Grames, Matthew L. Forister, May R. Berenbaum and David Stopak. 'Insect decline in the Anthropocene: death by a thousand cuts', *Proceedings of the National Academy of Sciences of the United States of America* 118 (2021): e2023989118. Accessed 30 May 2022. https://doi.org/10.1073/pnas.2023989118.

Walford, Cornelius. *The Famines of the World, Past and Present*. London: Edward Stanford, 1879.

Wall Street Journal Editorial Board. 'Trump bids Paris adieu: growth and innovation are better forms of climate insurance', *Wall Street Journal*, 1 June 2017. Accessed 9 November 2021. https://www.wsj.com/articles/trump-bids-paris-adieu-1496358860.

Wang, Marian. 'Uncoordinated coordination: six reasons limits on super PACs are barely limits at all', *ProPublica*, 21 November 2011. Accessed 26 October 2021. https://www.propublica.org/article/coordination-six-reasons-limits-on-super-pacs-are-barely-limits-at-all.

Wang, Y. Claire. 'The dangerous silence of academic researchers', *Chronicle of Higher Education*, 24 February 2015. Accessed 15 October 2021. http://chronicle.com/article/The-Dangerous-Silence-of/190251/?cid=at&utm_source=at&utm_medium=en.

Warren, Elizabeth. 'The Trans-Pacific Partnership clause everyone should oppose', *Washington Post*, 25 February 2015. Accessed 7 November 2021. https://www.warren.senate.gov/newsroom/op-eds/2015/02/25/washington-post-op-ed-the-trans-pacific-partnership-clause-everyone-should-oppose-1.

Washington Post. 'Annotated transcript: the Aug. 6 GOP debate', 6 August 2015. Accessed 5 November 2021. https://www.washingtonpost.com/news/post-politics/wp/2015/08/06/annotated-transcript-the-aug-6-gop-debate/?utm_term=.08ca9992bfcf.

Washington Public Disclosure Commission. 'Follow the money'. n.d. Accessed 1 November 2021. https://www.pdc.wa.gov/.

Wasserstein, Ronald L. and Nicole A. Lazar. 'The ASA's statement on p-values: context, process, and purpose', *American Statistician* 70 (2016): 129–33.

Weale, Albert. *The New Politics of Pollution*. Manchester: Manchester University Press, 1992.

Weigel, Brian M. and Jeffrey J. Dimick. 'Development, validation, and application of a macroinvertebrate-based Index of Biotic Integrity for nonwadeable rivers of Wisconsin', *Journal of the North American Benthological Society* 30 (2011): 665–79.

Weinzettel, Jan, Edgar G. Hertwich, Glen P. Peters, Kjartan Steen-Olsen and Alessandro Galli. 'Affluence drives the global displacement of land use', *Global Environmental Change* 23 (2013): 433–8.

Wernick, Iddo K. and Jesse H. Ausubel. 'National material metrics for industrial ecology'. In *Measures of Environmental Performance and Ecosystem Condition*, edited by Peter C. Schulze, 157–73. Washington, DC: National Academies Press, 1999.

Whitehouse, Sheldon. 'The fossil fuel industry's campaign to mislead the American people', *Washington Post*, 29 May 2015. Accessed 15 October 2021. http://www.washingtonpost.com/opinions/the-fossil-fuel-industrys-campaign-to-mislead-the-american-people/2015/05/29/04a2c448-0574-11e5-8bda-c7b4e9a8f7ac_story.html.

Whitley, Heather P. and Wesley Lindsey. 'Sex-based differences in drug activity', *American Family Physician* 80 (2009): 1254–8.

Whitney, Gordon G. 'An ecological history of the Great Lakes forest of Michigan', *Journal of Ecology* 75 (1987): 667–84.

Wilco Distributors. 'Rodent baits, rodent traps, rodent solutions'. n.d. Accessed 5 October 2021. https://wilcodistributors.com/.

Wilson, Clevo and Clem Tisdell. 'How knowledge affects payment to conserve an endangered bird', *Contemporary Economic Policy* 25 (2007): 226–37.

Wilson, Edward O. 'The global solution to extinction', *New York Times*, 12 March 2016. Accessed 11 October 2021. https://www.nytimes.com/2016/03/13/opinion/sunday/the-global-solution-to-extinction.html.

Wilson, Reid. 'Initiative spending booms past $1 billion as corporations sponsor their own proposals', *Washington Post*, 8 November 2013. Accessed 1 November 2021. http://www.washingtonpost.com/blogs/govbeat/wp/2013/11/08/initiative-spending-booms-past-1-billion-as-corporations-sponsor-their-own-proposals/.

Wines, Michael. 'Endangered or not, but at least no longer waiting', *New York Times*, 6 March 2013. Accessed 3 November 2021. http://www.nytimes.com/2013/03/07/science/earth/long-delayed-rulings-on-endangered-species-are-coming.html?pagewanted=all.

Wines, Michael. 'In Alaska, a battle to keep trees, or an industry, standing', *New York Times*, 27 September 2014. Accessed 19 October 2021. https://www.nytimes.com/2014/09/28/us/a-battle-to-keep-trees-or-an-industry-standing.html?_r=0.

Winkelmann, Ricarda, Anders Levermann, Andy Ridgwell and Ken Caldeira. 'Combustion of available fossil fuel resources sufficient to eliminate the Antarctic Ice Sheet', *ScienceAdvances* 1 (2015): e1500589. Accessed 7 November 2021. https://doi.org/10.1126/sciadv.1500589.

Winter, Jesse. '"War in the woods": hundreds of anti-logging protesters arrested in Canada', *Guardian*, 24 June 2021. Accessed 9 January 2022. https://www.theguardian.com/environment/2021/jun/24/british-columbia-logging-ancient-growth-protests.

Wolf, Nicky. '"America is not a planet": Republicans resist climate change action at debate', *Guardian*, 17 September 2015. Accessed 3 November 2021. https://www.theguardian.com/us-news/2015/sep/17/marco-rubio-chris-christie-climate-change-republican-debate.

Wootton, David. '"Origin Story" review: the view from above', *Wall Street Journal*, 18 May 2018. Accessed 9 November 2021. https://www.wsj.com/articles/origin-story-review-the-view-from-above-1526592346.

World Bank. 'Arable land (hectares per person)'. n.d. Accessed 16 November 2021. https://data.worldbank.org/indicator/AG.LND.ARBL.HA.PC.

World Bank. 'CO2 emissions (kt)' and 'CO2 emissions (kg per 2015 US$ of GDP)'. n.d. Accessed 3 February 2022. https://data.worldbank.org/indicator/EN.ATM.CO2E.KT and https://data.worldbank.org/indicator/EN.ATM.CO2E.KD.GD.

World Wildlife Fund. 'Baltic Sea scorecard'. Accessed 3 November 2021. http://wwf.fi/mediabank/1077.pdf.

WTO. 'Mexico etc. versus US: "tuna-dolphin"'. n.d. Accessed 6 November 2021. https://www.wto.org/english/tratop_e/envir_e/edis04_e.htm.

WTO. 'DS384: United States: certain country of origin labelling (COOL) requirements'. n.d. Accessed 6 November 2021. http://www.wto.org/english/tratop_e/dispu_e/cases_e/ds384_e.htm.

WTO. 'US – restrictions on imports of tuna: report of the panel', (DS29/R), 16 June 1994. Accessed 6 November 2021. https://www.wto.org/english/tratop_e/dispu_e/gatt_e/92tuna.pdf.

WTO. 'DS26: European communities: measures concerning meat and meat products (hormones)'. 2009. Accessed 6 November 2021. http://www.wto.org/english/tratop_e/dispu_e/cases_e/ds26_e.htm.

WTO Committee on Trade and the Environment. 'Communication on trade and environmental sustainability', WTO, 22 December 2021. Accessed 4 January 2022. https://docs.wto.org/dol2fe/Pages/SS/directdoc.aspx?filename=q:/WT/CTE/W249R3.pdf&Open=True.

Wu, H. X., C. L. Evreux-Gros and J. Descotes. 'Influence of cimetidine on the toxicity and toxicokinetics of Diazinon in the rat', *Human and Experimental Toxicology* 15 (1996): 391–5.

Wu, Tim. 'The oppression of the supermajority', *New York Times*, 5 March 2019. Accessed 22 October 2021. https://www.nytimes.com/2019/03/05/opinion/oppression-majority.html.

Wyoming Senate. 'Enrolled act no. 61, Senate', 2015. Accessed 9 November 2021. http://legisweb.state.wy.us/2015/Enroll/SF0012.pdf.

Yale Program on Climate Change Communication. 'Yale climate opinion maps 2020'. Accessed 11 November 2021. https://climatecommunication.yale.edu/visualizations-data/ycom-us/.

Yang, Raymond S. H. 'Introduction to the toxicology of chemical mixtures'. In *Toxicology of Chemical Mixtures*, edited by Raymond S. H. Yang, 1–10. San Diego: Academic Press, 1994.

Yardley, Jim and Laurie Goodstein. 'Pope Francis, in sweeping encyclical, calls for swift action on climate change', *New York Times*, 18 June 2015. Accessed 15 October 2021. https://www.nytimes.com/2015/06/19/world/europe/pope-francis-in-sweeping-encyclical-calls-for-swift-action-on-climate-change.html.

Yeakel, Justin D. and Jennifer A. Dunne. 'Modern lessons from ancient food webs', *American Scientist* 103 (2015): 188–95.

Yeoman, Barry. 'The inside story of Shell's Arctic assault', *Audubon*, January–February 2016. Accessed 4 November 2021. https://www.audubon.org/magazine/january-february-2016/the-inside-story-shells-arctic-assault.

Yetisen, Ali K., Hang Qu, Amir Manbachi, Haider Butt, Mehmet R. Dokmeci, Juan P. Hinestroza, Maksim Skorobogatiy, Ali Khademhosseini and Seok H. Yun. 'Nanotechnology in textiles', *ACS Nano* 10 (2016): 3042–68.

Zacks Equity Research. 'TC Energy (TRP) files $15B suit against U.S. over Keystone XL', *yahoo!finance*, 29 November 2021. Accessed 4 January 2022. https://finance.yahoo.com/news/tc-energy-trp-files-15b-123412925.html.

Zeebe, Richard E. and James C. Zachos. 'Long-term legacy of massive carbon input to the Earth system: Anthropocene versus Eocene', *Philosophical Transactions of the Royal Society A* 371 (2013): 20120006. Accessed 30 May 2022. http://dx.doi.org/10.1098/rsta.2012.0006.

Zhu, John, Yujuin Yang, Holly Holmquist and Nathan Leber. 'Projected reservoir rating curves based on sedimentation surveys and its application in water planning in Texas', *World Environmental and Water Resources Congress 2018*. Accessed 1 November 2021. https://doi.org/10.1061/9780784481417.035.

Zwann, Rolf A., Alexander Etz, Richard E. Lucas and M. Brent Donnellan. 'Making replication mainstream', *Behavioral and Brain Sciences* 41 (2017): e120. Accessed 31 May 2022. https://doi.org/10.1017/S0140525X17001972.

Index

European Union (EU) 211, 262
eutrophication 102
evolutionary tendencies 8, 77
exacerbation of problems 213–16
exemptions 209–10, 220–1
expenses of running for office 177
experiments 47–52, 54–8
expert opinion
    caution of 106
    consensus in 268
    diversity of 106–8
    policy aversion of 108–11
    purported 115
    reliance on 105
    shortage of 38–9
exposure to dosage, *high* and *low* 79
extinction of species 5, 9, 167
extrapolation 77–80
extreme values 84
ExxonMobil 48

factors in independent variables 51
false positives 87–8
    and false negatives 66–7, 70–1
Farb, Peter 29
Federal Elections Commission 179
federal government power 10–13, 172
felon voting 174–5
Ferguson (Missouri) 174–5
fertility rates 130–1
fertilizer 132
filibusters 183, 187
financing of political campaigns 177–82,
    192–4
fisheries 57–8, 132, 208, 211, 222, 228–9
Fitzgerald, Maegan 289
Food and Agriculture Organization 29, 78, 132
food production 144
Foote, Elisha 13, 26
Ford, Gerald, administration of 243
Ford, Henry, 146, 148
forestry 132, 134
Formosa Plastics 245
fracking 28, 70–1, 137, 248
Franklin, Benjamin 13, 103
fraud 83, 88–9
free-market enthusiasts 268
free markets 137–47, 160, 259–64
free speech 179–82
freedom
    to destroy environments 134
    of earlier generations 133–4
    four types of 122
    freedom to and *from* 122–3
    from rules 131, 160
    political and *economic* 121
    restrictions on 121–2
Freudenburg, William 118
Friends of the Earth 123
'front groups' 194–5
Frost, Robert 163
Fukushima meltdown (2011) 19
future generations xxi, 132, 151
Galbraith, John Kenneth 30
Galton, Francis 127
Gandhi, Indira 126

Gandhi, Mahatma 13
Garnett, Hugh 37
gasoline 203
General Motors 194
genetically modified foods 193
'geoengineering' 212
gerrymandering 171, 175–7, 185
Gessell, Gerhard 128
Glacier Peak Wilderness 291
global warming 13, 108, 222
goal-setting 284–5
Goodall, Jane 270
Gore, Al 184
government branches, rules of 165–6
Gramling, Robert 118
Grand Banks 132
grapefruit 52
grassland 7
gravity, law of 77
greenhouse gas emissions 5, 13, 26, 35,
    107, 141, 193, 213, 232–5, 240–1,
    256–7, 260–1

Haileybury College 126
Hansen, James 109
harm 47, 71
    uncertainty of 118
Hastert rule 188
Hawken, Paul 275–6, 291
hazards 10, 19–21, 25–6, 67–71
    intrinsic nature of (statistical) 62
    new 240–1
Heneghan, Liam 141
Henne, Albert 20
Henry, Patrick 5
Hirata, Kimiko 270
history and historical perspective 1–2,
    10, 35–6
holding variables constant 52, 78
Holling, C.S. 217
Holmes, Oliver Wendell 128
Honeycutt, Michael 42
Hope, Chris and Mat 152
hourly workers 173
Houston 29, 42
Hoyt, Kenneth 245
hunger 29, 124–6
Hurricane Harvey 42
hypotheses 73–7, 83, 86–89
    multiple 89
    testing of 45, 51, 54, 58

immediate improvement 163–4
impact, environmental xix, 141, 163, 219,
    256, 259
implementation (policy) 202, 217–20, 234–50
inaction as a choice 117
incentives 193
    perverse 205–6
incompetence 85–8
India 126–7
indigenous peoples and cultures 134, 269
Indonesia 211
inductive reasoning 73–7, 80
    limitations of 74
industry capture 248–50

infant mortality 13, 211–12
inferential reasoning 73, 76–7
influence on policy 171–3
    of states 174, 182–5
information needs 286
Inhofe, James 113–14
initial expenditures 149
injustice, environmental 172
Inness, George 269–70
innovation 137–8, 141
insects 35, 38–9
Instagram 196
interaction (statistical) 52–4
interest groups 164, 192
international trade 259–64
'invisible hand' 139
Iowa 184

*Journal of American Physicians and
    Surgeons* 115
Jackson, Rob 70
Jackson, Wes 273–4
Jamieson, Dale xix–xx
Jaws (film) 42
Jefferson, Thomas 187
John, Elton 162
Johnson, Lyndon B. 13
Jones, Charles 186
jurisdictional overlaps 230–2

Keystone XL pipeline 210
King, Martin Luther Jr. xxi, 276, 291
Knesek, Nichole 41, 231, 289
knowledge and understanding
    incompleteness of 208–9
    limits to 6–9, 30
Kraft, Robert 182
Krugman, Paul 144
Kuhn, Thomas 89
Kuttner, Robert 134
Kyoto Protocol 260–1

Lac-Mégantic 19, 123
Lake Texoma 41–2, 230
land ethics 160
Land Institute (Kansas) 273–4
land-use 122
Laughlin, Harry 127
Lavigne, Sharon 270
laws, environmental 165, 238, 261
Layzer, Judith A. xix
Lazarus, Richard 189, 208
lead 4, 13, 22–3, 203
legislation, environmental see laws
Lehigh University 24
Leighton, Mark 155, 300
Leopold, Aldo xxi, 3–6, 158, 160, 269–70,
    276, 290–1
Lespets, Léo 23
Likens, Gene 270
Little Traverse Conservancy 274
livelihoods at stake 192

Lombardo, Paul 127
Los Angeles 2, 3, 134

Maathai, Wangari 270
McConnell, Mitch 182, 187
McCutcheon case 177, 179
MacIsaac, Hugh 57, 207, 274
McKibben, Bill 20, 179, 181
McPhee, John 290
Madison, James 187
Malheur Refuge 123
malpractice, scientific 88
Malthus, Thomas 5, 29, 124–6
Mann, Michael 109
market fundamentalism 138
marketing and marketing decisions 30, 48,
    256, 276
markets 141, 144–5
Marsh, George Perkins 5
'masquerading precision' 155
measurement 57, 86–7
medical insurance 25
medical systems 40
Mencimer, Stephanie 115
'merchants of doubt' 111–19
methodological details 85
Middlebury College 182
Midgley, Thomas 20–3
military conflict 133
Miller, Norman 248
Miller, Tyler 223
Minerals Management Service 248–9
minority views 171–2
mismatch, geographical 226–32
Molina, Mario 20–1
monitoring 39–43, 57, 217
    of beaches 230–1
Monteverde Reserve 38–9
Montreal Protocol (1987) 21
mortality 130
Muir, John 5
Muller, Paul 21
multiple-comparison tests 87
mussels 54–7

narrative accounts xix
National Academy of Engineers xxii
National Aeronautics & Space Administration
    (NASA) 42
National Council of State Legislatures 173–4
National Economic Research Associates 140
natural capital, depletion of 132–3
natural equilibria 212
Natural Resources Defense Council 123
natural sciences xxii
natural selection 8
Nehru, Jawaharlal 126
Nepal 130–1
net present value 152–5, 160
    calculation of 294–6
New Hampshire 184
new technology 44
Newsweek 108
Nile Perch 211
Nixon, Richard, administration of 243
Nobel Prizes 21

nomadic pastoralism 212
'nuclear option' 187
nuclear power 146, 148
null hypotheses 51, 63, 73

Obama, Barack 224, 248
    administration of 110, 154, 166, 187, 207,
        219, 239–41, 245, 249–50, 263
objectives 162
objectivity 108
obstacles to environmentalism xix, xxii, 6–9,
        19–20, 38, 50, 64, 102, 108, 112, 144,
        151, 163, 166–7, 175, 184–6, 202,
        267–8
    categories and subsets of 6, 9, 18
    conceptual 9–10
    overcoming of 278–84
    practical 9
Ockels, John 247, 272–3
Office of Technology Assessment 27, 30
oil prices 137
oil spills 13, 28
one-child policy 127
one-sided stories 116
Operation Plowshares 24
opponents of environmentalism xix, 11 105,
        111, 121, 134, 140, 146, 155, 160, 164,
        171, 182, 188, 193–4, 197–8, 202, 219
Oregon 115
Oreskes, Naomi xix, 111–12
Orr, David xxi–xxii
overestimation of costs 156–7
overharvesting 149–50
ozone depletion 2, 20–1, 54, 84–5, 102, 104,
        119, 220

'packing' 175
Paris Accord 140, 232
Park, Charles 290
Parker, Theodore xxi, 38–9
partial knowledge 208–9
particulates 208
peer review 83, 86, 113–16
pest resistance 77
'Petition Project' 114–15
petitions, electronic 195
Petoskey (Michigan) 255–6
p-hacking 88
photographic identification of voters 174
photosynthesis 213
Pidot, Justin 40
Pinchot, Gifford 5
Pipeline and Hazardous Material Safety
        Administration 237
Plato 5–6, 150, 168
Platt, John R. 89
policy issues 164
political action committees (PACs) 178–80
political climate 10–12
pollution and pollution monitoring 2–5, 26,
        36–7, 40, 131, 134, 138, 141, 152, 166,
        172–3, 207–9, 216, 221
Pont Julien 158–9
Poor Laws 125–6
population change 1, 8, 29, 123–6, 130,
        214, 216

in relation to immigration 129–30
Population Connection 123
positive feedback 29–30, 125, 129–30, 167,
        213, 216
post hoc or *a posteriori observations* 87–8
Poudenas, Roxanne 23
practicability 146
precautionary principle 24–6, 281–2
prediction 30, 77, 80, 105, 108
pregnancy, unintended 128–9
presidents of universities and colleges 162
press releases 196–7
pride in being correct 84
primaries, presidential 184
prior studies 67
priorities 162
private and public groups 193
probability theory 61
problems, environmental 1, 7, 11, 13, 24, 44,
        60, 102, 198, 217, 224–32
    anticipated 33, 40–1
    gradualness of 163–4
    inconspicuous, undetected or *unrecognized*
        18–20
    incremental nature of 35, 167
    long-term and *short-term* 216
    persistence of 5, 141
    present & future 150–1
    repeatedly-deferral action on 166–9
    transboundary 229
profiling of voters 174
progress, environmental xix, 4, 10–13, 160,
        185, 203, 207, 250, 259
    barriers to 217
    impeding of 31
    public demand for 104
proponents of environmentalism 122, 140,
        155, 197
protection, environmental 182–6, 192, 196,
        206, 216–17
    barriers to 188–9
    costs and benefits of 149–52, 155 197–8
    unwarranted 152, 160
Pruitt, Scott 153, 248
public confidence in scientific conclusions 88
public opinion xix, 104–7, 111, 163–4,
        167, 194–5
public relations 194– 6
publication of scientific findings 83
purged electoral rolls 174
p-values 63–71, 86–8

quantitative relationships 7
Quebec 19, 123
Quinn, Daniel 30

racial discrimination 172– 4
racism 129, 172
radium 23
Reagan, Ronald 152, 244
recapitulation 267–9
recycling 204–6, 235, 286
'red' states 183
redistricting committees 177
redlining 172
regression, appropriateness of 86

Department of Agriculture 211
Department of Energy 70
farmland in 133
Fish and Wildlife Service 220
Forest Service 118
Geological Survey 41, 230
Government Accountability Office 231
Supreme Court 128, 177, 179, 181, 240–1
see also under National
urgency, perceived lack of 162

value as distinct from price 158, 302–4
vested interests 111
vetoed bills 188
Virginia 127–8
Vonnegut, Kurt 30
voting, impediments to 171–5

water supply 214, 236
Walford, Cornelius 125
Wall Street Journal 115, 138
Wallace, Robert 38
Wang, Claire 109
water quality 42
waters, territorial 208, 228
wealth transfers 254
wealthy individuals and organizations 171–2,
    178–81
West Virginia 246
Western States Petroleum Association 123
wetlands
    artificial 197–8
    preservation of 154
Whitehouse, Sheldon 112
wilderness concept 145
wildlife 3
women, exclusion of 78–9
Women's Day (magazine) 22
Wootton, David 137
work, unpaid 50
workplace accidents 13, 26
World Bank 295
World Health Organization (WHO) 65, 211
World Trade Organization (WTO) 260–3
World Wildlife Fund 229
Wurth, Al 24
Wyoming 40

X-ray pedoscopes 23

Yale Project 116

zoning 172

Printed in the USA
CPSIA information can be obtained
at www.ICGtesting.com
LVHW070756141023
760420LV00011B/30